Storage Networks:
The Complete Reference

About the Author

Robert Spalding, a technology consultant, leveraged his 30 years of advanced technology experiences to develop *Storage Networks: The Complete Reference* for McGraw-Hill/Osborne. Being at the computer technology forefront, he was one of the first to use dyadic processing within the mainframe environment, setting the foundations for high-end symmetrical processing. His open systems management research and study led the way in developing the first management tools for massive parallel processing configurations that are still used today. As a research analyst covering the storage industry, he identified and published the early research that evolved into complex storage network technologies of today.

Robert is currently working on advanced storage strategies for imaging technologies and distribution as well as archival technologies for unstructured data products such as audio and video. *Storage Networks: The Complete Reference* is the latest in a string of more than 50 publications that include research papers, technical articles, and music compositions. He can be reached through his independent consultancy at RobertSpalding@kentrow.com

About the Contributing Writers

Ian Spalding has worked as a technical writer and editor for several start-up companies. He is currently at work on his first novel.

Himanshu Dwivedi is a Managing Security Architect at @stake, Inc., where he leads the Storage Center of Excellence (CoE), which focuses research and training around storage technology, including Network Attached Storage (NAS) and Storage Area Networks (SAN). At @stake, Himanshu forms part of the San Francisco-based Professional Services Organization (PSO) providing clients with network architecture assessments, attack and penetration services, secure network design, and secure server analysis. He is also part of the @stake Academy, where he is a lead instructor in several security classes.

Himanshu is considered an industry expert in the area of SAN security, specifically Fibre Channel Security. He has given numerous presentations and workshops regarding the security in SANs, including the SNIA Security Summit, Storage Networking World, TechTarget, the Fibre Channel Conference, SAN-West, and SAN-East. He holds a wide spectrum of well-diversified security experiences, specializing in the telecommunications industry. Additionally, Himanshu has worked with major organizations in the United States, Europe, South America, and Asia, including some of the major software, manufacturing, and financial-based entities.

About the Technical Editor

Giota Vavasis Then (Patty) started her professional career in 1982 as an applications programmer. In 1986, Patty began using her programming skills in the data center to write utilities for data-center automation as an MVS Systems Programmer while supporting 24/7 Enterprise Data Center operations. While in this capacity, Patty developed expertise in areas of Data Center Security, Storage Management, Capacity Planning, Performance Measurement and Modeling, Business Continuance, and Disaster Recovery, to name a few. In 1992, Patty moved from working in the data center to working as a vendor. Past companies she has represented include Hitachi Data Systems, EMC Corp, StorageTek, and, most recently, XIOtech/Seagate Technologies.

Patty has held various positions over the last 21 years in the IT industry, such as Systems Support Engineer, Sales and Consulting Engineer, National Accounts Manager, Customer Service District Manager, Product Marketing Manager, and Sales and Education Consultant.

Awarded numerous honors over the years for her outstanding contributions, Patty currently heads the "Consortium Technologies Group," a consulting and education practice based in the Tampa Bay Area, that brings together a team of world-renowned experts with real-world customer-focused experience.

Storage Networks:
The Complete Reference

Robert Spalding

McGraw-Hill/Osborne

New York Chicago San Francisco
Lisbon London Madrid Mexico City
Milan New Delhi San Juan
Seoul Singapore Sydney Toronto

McGraw-Hill/Osborne
2600 Tenth Street
Berkeley, California 94710
U.S.A.

To arrange bulk purchase discounts for sales promotions, premiums, or fund-raisers, please contact **McGraw-Hill**/Osborne at the preceding address. For information on translations or book distributors outside the U.S.A., please see the International Contact Information page immediately following the index of this book.

Storage Networks: The Complete Reference

1234567890 CUS CUS 019876543

ISBN 0-07-222476-2

Publisher
  Brandon A. Nordin

Vice President & Associate Publisher
  Scott Rogers

Acquisitions Editor
  Franny Kelly

Project Editor
  Jody McKenzie

Technical Editor
  Giota Vavasis Then (Patty)

Copy Editors
  Mike McGee
  Lisa Theobald

Proofreader
  Susie Elkind

Indexer
  Karin Arrigoni

Computer Designers
  Lucie Ericksen
  John Patrus

Illustrators
  Lyssa Wald
  Michael Mueller
  Alex Putney

Series Design
  Peter F. Hancik

This book was composed with Corel VENTURA™ Publisher.

Contents at a Glance

Contents

Part I

Concepts of Storage Networking

Part II

Storage Fundamentals

Part V

Application—Putting It Together

Part VI

Management—Keeping It Running

Part VII
Appendixes

Foreword

Sean Derrington
Senior Program Director
Infrastructure Strategies
META Group, Inc.

IT organizations (ITOs) increasingly view storage as a strategic differentiator for existing and new applications. Many ITOs recognize the critical role information plays in the business, and leveraging that information requires an unassailable storage infrastructure foundation. I believe forward-looking ITOs have to continue to decouple storage and server selection. This aids in ensuring storage solutions are viewed as much more than an afterthought for new applications. For most organizations, I believe this is a best practice, and the trend will continue as the storage market matures in technical capabilities and more IT professionals become well versed in the arts and values of storage. Even though current capital expenditures are under extreme scrutiny (and will continue to be through 2003), leading ITOs are acquiring storage solutions on a tactical basis—yet, they are planning and selecting the vendors on a strategic basis.

Overall, storage is moving to a services model, comparable to that of IP networking and (future) application infrastructure. Storage services will be tiered in function, price, and complexity, and delivered to applications and lines of business. For ITOs to deliver on this direction, storage (all aspects of it—disk, tape, disaster recovery, capacity planning, and so on) must be perceived and treated as an infrastructure component. Infrastructure components are common and reusable across as many consumers (for example, applications and servers) as possible; storage should be no different. Consequently, this requires a storage infrastructure to be an initial consideration (not an afterthought) to drive business priorities. Moreover, infrastructure design and planning teams must have seats at the business project table and translate technology into business value.

Typically, IT architects create architectural principles and guidelines addressing three- to five-year planning cycles, while infrastructure teams design and plan component technologies (vendor- and product-specific), targeting current through 36-month requirements. The challenge going forward will be how ITOs handle the transition from storage infrastructure planning and design to storage operations. This is a critical success factor for ITOs in general, but especially for storage management, because capabilities are rapidly maturing and vendors are rapidly innovating. I believe that, through 2004, storage infrastructure and storage operations may be organizationally in the same group—but in the longer term (2005/06), I believe these responsibilities will diverge and become distinct groups, mirroring current systems, network, and application infrastructure and operations teams. The objective of infrastructure planning is *"to determine the scope, scale, and design of infrastructure necessary to provide application service levels required by the business in the short, medium, and long term."* Furthermore, *"the primary design goal for information systems must be to enable rapid change in business processes and in the applications and technical infrastructure that enable them!"*

The implementation of automated networked storage (Storage Area Network [SAN] or Network Attached Storage [NAS]), which rationalizes (reduces the number of variants in) storage management applications and optimally integrates these functions, will need to leverage tiered storage software, hardware, and professional services to be able to measure (both internally and for the business) a successful storage infrastructure. Automated networked storage will provide businesses with agility, dramatically increase productivity, and enable ITOs to manage terabytes and petabytes successfully and cost-effectively. This book will address, in detail, the various architectural considerations, the components that satisfy each storage architecture, and various connectivity options for a networked storage environment.

Storage and Application Service-Level Agreements (SLAs)

Because all applications and servers are not created equal (as determined by business requirements), prioritization for storage services (from premium enterprise-class to internal workgroup storage) must be evaluated. By 2004/05, more than 60 percent of the servers in the data center will be connected to networked storage, and I expect more than 70 percent of storage capacity to be networked in this time frame. Although there can be modest increases in procurement costs to network storage, the resulting benefits in management productivity, increased utilization, agility, infrastructure and operations personnel savings, and scalability are substantial.

Servers sharing external storage resources can also aid in holistic capacity planning and increase overall capacity utilization (such as in GB/TB, Fibre Channel [FC] fabrics, and external subsystems—impacting data-center floor space, and so on). For applications that are more volatile, storage can be reassigned to the servers as the capacity threshold (60–80 percent utilization) is reached. This is an area where enterprise storage procurement and capacity planning are important (compared to internal storage). I generally recommend a six- to nine-month buying cycle for enterprise storage and a competitive storage environment. Overall, ITOs can plan on an approximate 35 percent per year decrease in hardware prices (8–10 percent per quarter) and, given the state of the current global economy, should proceed cautiously on long-term acquisitions (12+ months).

Storage Management

Enterprise storage management will likely surface as the most significant contributor to ITO operational savings, because human resources remain the highest data-center cost. These costs will be increasingly important as more servers participate in networked storage (the disk and tape SAN). ITOs must continue to remove the dependencies and "stove piped" thinking of operating systems and storage management. Many operational economies of scale and flexibility will be gained by employing such an approach (for example, capacity managed per administrator). Certainly, storage management will still need to interface with the other operational disciplines (such as systems management, network management, database administration), but a center of storage management excellence is the design objective.

The goal is to streamline and automate many of the daily tasks that consume staff resources. For example, during the past 24 months, FC fabric management has moved to a core function under the purview of many enterprise storage vendors. And I believe additional tasks, such as storage provisioning/allocating (reducing the number of individuals involved and the time required from hours or days to minutes), resource management (which users/applications are using particular capacities), and topology mapping (which resources—physical or logical—are allocated to applications) will be among the first tasks within multivendor storage administration.

The key is to examine how and which operational tasks can be automated and leveraged (across server operating systems and multivendor storage hardware), enabling storage capacity to increase while storage infrastructure and storage operations staff remain constant—or, hopefully, decrease over time.

For automation efficiencies, storage operations should identify solutions that are seamlessly integrated—that is, a single application that can incorporate various functions (possibly multivendor) and not a loosely coupled launching pad (or iconic launch) for disassociated islands of automation. Solutions leveraging a central repository (persistent database) serving as the "storage management data warehouse" would enable ITO efficiencies gained through the function of individual "management components." Moreover, harnessing this repository and "feeding" (analogous to the real-time data warehousing feedback loop) information to other management elements or ISV applications (such as for chargeback/billing) will be of significant value. Without this next level of integration/consolidation, users will duplicate efforts, not achieve the ability to scale (performance, capacity, and so on) their environments, nor control storage staff costs.

I believe storage provisioning/allocation will be one of the initial fully automated areas, yet this will require organizational (at minimum, functional) changes, because currently this task typically transcends individual and possibly departmental responsibilities (for example, server, database, storage). Simplifying storage allocation, which requires a multitude of individual tasks, is not a simple problem to solve. It typically involves the following:

- Assigning/configuring the appropriate LUNs from the physical storage subsystem

- Identifying and allocating the number and location of host interconnects on the array

- Masking the LUNs to the particular server(s)

- Zoning the FC switched fabric

- Incorporating and modifying any necessary FC security policies (if available)

- Ensuring the volume manager/file system and the application and/or database on the host(s) are updated, and incorporating the desired changes

- Ensuring other storage management applications (for instance, backup/recovery, remote replication services) comprehend the changes and the implications of such changes in storage policies

Center-of-excellence (COE) best practices dictate investigating the benefits/returns of consolidation and integration tasks, the most significant of which are those that have the greatest, most immediate impact on the costs that govern operations. Those gains will be seen as an annuity to the business, versus one-time savings. This annuity could be significant not just in dollars, but also in business agility and infrastructure flexibility.

Application Recoverability

Application/DBMS recoverability is one of the most compelling reasons for networked storage (predominately SAN-based storage) participation. Based on the mean time to recovery (the time it takes from the recognition of a failure to the time the application begins accepting transactions again—not simply restoring information from tape to server) discussed with the business, numerous technology options can assist in meeting those requirements. Snapshot or volume-based replication (either local or remote) can dramatically reduce the recovery times to minutes, preventing the need for a tape restore (but not eliminating the need for tape backup/recovery).

Although restoration is a significant and necessary capability, the "state" of the information/data can be much more important than the existence of the information. Recovering data in an inconsistent state—or data from one database that reflects a point in time that is significantly different from another reliant database—is often useless. Consistently managing replication and recovery options (possibly from multiple vendors) will prove to be operationally beneficial, as will rationalizing backup/recovery software and hardware across as many platforms as possible (often excluding the mainframe). Consistently managing various storage vendors' snapshot/volume replication can provide further operational savings, striving for policy-based automation. Moreover, just as all applications are not created equal, storage replication software is no different. Integration with operating systems, clustering software, applications, and databases, as well as quiescent time (the time required for a consistent view of the application), will often differentiate offerings, given that replication software has become much more prominent during the past 36 months.

Data and Media Center of Excellence

There are three high-level layers of the data and media COE: conceptual (policy), physical (infrastructure), and operations (operational). Each of these three is a superset comprised of multiple functional and subfunctional elements. Each of the functions within each category and associated job titles (suggested) are detailed as follows and serve as a guideline for functional and organizational structure.

It is also important to note that, although many of these functional categories exist in the mainframe environment, simply having mainframe personnel responsible for all systems is not necessarily appropriate. There must be a balance of people, processes, and technology to create an effective COE, and the technologies are often quite different between mainframe and non-mainframe environments. Nonetheless, COEs should be viewed holistically and include the following.

Policy

Policies offer the highest-level view of storage management, dictate the required infrastructure to meet policy mandates, and should be governed by a storage policy director (SPD). These policies, which are interdependent and should be viewed holistically, include the following:

- **Service portfolios and service-level agreements**   SPDs should determine what service packages they will offer to business units, as well as the associated cost/service tradeoffs, based on the needs of the business units.

- **Data protection strategies**   Not all data is created equal, and the data protection mechanisms should be aligned with the service portfolio.

- **Vendor selection strategies**   ITOs should determine, as a matter of policy, whether to pursue a best-of-breed multivendor strategy (albeit rationalized and not a vendor "du jour" strategy), or a "one throat to choke" single-vendor strategy. This will vary from one category to another, but should be done with an eye toward strategic objectives, which are not always mutually exclusive. Either way, rigorous interoperability mandates should be a prerequisite for consideration to enable maximum deployment flexibility.

Infrastructure

After the overall storage policies have been determined, a storage infrastructure architect should be responsible for designing and implementing the components needed to achieve the service goals. This will include device and network management (at the functional level) as well as a multitude of subfunctions, including the following:

- **Physical topology design**   In most organizations, it will be necessary to use and integrate SAN, NAS, and direct-attached storage either for optimum performance or for security requirements and data protection. The ability of vendors to not only function/coexist, but also support (via customer and professional services expertise) these advanced heterogeneous environments (multiprotocol, multivendor, multifunction, cross-organizational, and cross-regional) will determine the most appropriate platforms (both hardware and software) on which to base infrastructure for the flexibility to adapt, as subelements of technology evolve over time.

- **Performance modeling and monitoring**   The storage infrastructure architect should be responsible for not only designing sufficient resources, but also for ensuring that service levels are met. This includes storage components (for example, disk arrays) as well as storage networks (such as FC fabrics) and working with IP networking personnel, in the case of NAS.

- **Security**   Security is an underaddressed area in storage management, due mostly to the current lack of capability, but should be made the responsibility of the storage infrastructure architect working in conjunction with the enterprise security architect.

Other subfunctional tasks may include physical subsystem and tape library design, fault and performance management, virtualization, SAN management, and enterprise planning/design/procurement.

Operations

Operational procedures will not vary greatly from current practices, but should be managed by dedicated storage administrators. Functionally, traditional systems management should remain within the systems management group, and the key is to begin separating the storage operations from systems, database, and application management. To what degree will certainly be dependent on each organization, but the three main functional disciplines are:

- **Performance management**   This consists of performance modeling and management (including FC-based networks), asset management, chargeback, and billing by application of business unit.

■ **Resource management**   This involves resource allocation or provisioning—the actual assignment of storage (for example, LUNs, data zones, volumes) according to architectural/application requirements, as well as quota management, usage management (for instance, by application or individual user), metering, and capacity planning.

■ **Availability management**   This deals with backup/recovery operations. Backup/recovery should be included with storage management, not systems management. This includes backup/recovery scheduling, media management, and problem resolution. High-availability server clustering management (in conjunction with systems management), hierarchical storage management (where applicable), and replication (for example, remote replication for business continuity) are also of consideration.

Similar to balancing the handoffs with enterprise architects, infrastructure, operations, and lines of business, the data and media COE is no different. As can be seen, some of the functions and subfunctions transcend the policy, infrastructure, and operations categories. Communication among groups is a key element for a successful storage infrastructure that is adaptable to change and is measurable.

Actionable Items

ITOs should undertake the following initiatives:

■ **Rationalizing storage hardware and storage software**   This should encompass all aspects of storage across the server and application portfolio. Certainly, storage life cycles must be considered, yet a rationalization strategy (reducing variations—both vendor and configuration) will provide significant strategic value, even in tactical times.

■ **Creating a storage infrastructure**   ITOs should begin networking storage resources (SAN, NAS, and backup/recovery architectures), leverage tiered storage offerings (for example, internal storage, midrange, enterprise) and functional software (say, replication, server cluster integration, and backup/recovery), and look to common components (such as FC switches, host bus adapters, and so on) where possible. They should also seek new elements that adhere to intensive interoperability standards and procedures to ensure maximum configuration flexibility.

■ **Optimizing storage operations**   This includes rationalizing and consolidating management tools and personnel responsibilities; consistent storage management of multivendor environments is beginning to emerge and is a significant strategic directive.

■ **Creating a data and media center of excellence**   ITOs should employ a center of excellence using the guidelines outlined in the previous section.

Outsourcing

From 2003 through 2006, as ITOs adopt a storage service delivery model resembling that of traditional outsourcers, accurately measuring storage services and metrics will be a critical success factor in ITOs not only gaining credibility, but also in justifying (and making an informed decision about) whether a storage and storage management sourcing strategy should be employed. ITOs can use three categories when determining measurable metrics. The initial set comprises alternatives to the traditional ROI/total cost of ownership senior management mandate and is primarily an internal benchmark of (current and future) capabilities that quantify how the strategy is providing value. The second and third sets, technical and operational, are more strategic because some of these measurements are not possible with some storage vendors. However, ITOs should keep the measurements simple, limiting the metrics to those that are the most important to the business. Often, using network-based SLAs (for example, web hosting) as a framework and mapping them to storage services provides a good starting point. The three categories available to ITOs are:

- **Internal benchmarking** This includes storage managed per administrator, percentage of storage utilization, days storage in inventory, data life-cycle multiplier, data availability, and mean time to recovery.

- **Technical measures** These include storage availability, storage latency, data migration/exit clause, diagnostic, capacity utilization, performance, resource utilization, and mean time and maximum time to recover/resolve.

- **Operational measures** These include maximum time to notify, moves/adds/changes, project-specific SLAs, and vendor responsiveness.

Conclusions

ITOs are increasingly realizing the importance of storage, particularly among midsize companies that have historically not had requirements for enterprise storage capabilities. Through 2005/06, most organizations will have organized around, and created, a storage infrastructure and operations team (the data and media center of excellence). Consequently, it is imperative that ITOs begin to view storage in regards to the strategic importance it will have—even in difficult economic environments that often, and many times incorrectly, result in solely tactical decisions. ITOs should undertake a strategic evaluation examining how daily functions can be leveraged across (and automated by) multivendor capabilities, and how tasks currently consuming significant resources can be dramatically reduced (for example, recovery, provisioning, and procurement).

Moreover, as storage technologies continue to mature and more servers participate in networked storage (SAN and NAS), ITOs will be forced into measuring delivered capabilities as storage becomes a service that is delivered to the business in business speak (such as performance, availability, flexibility to change), and associated cost tradeoffs based on their selection of tiered services is clearly understood.

Robert Spalding has been a respected authority on storage and storage management for the past 20 years. Having worked with Robert in the past, he was the first person to begin describing the need, and preparations necessary, for an adaptive storage infrastructure. In doing so in 1995, Bob began speaking about the need for a Chief Storage Officer.

Much of this thought leadership has manifested itself in Robert's published works, and specifically in this book, *Storage Networks: The Complete Reference*. As an industry analyst covering the entire storage and storage management market, it has been my experience that simple yet technical reference books are extremely useful. I'm sure storage professionals will benefit greatly by having this as a staple manual on their desk. Enjoy.

Sean Derrington is a leading authority on storage and storage management infrastructures. He specializes in storage subsystems, Fibre Channel, Storage Area Networks, Network Attached Storage, backup/recovery, and disaster recovery architectures, with a concentration on e-business, transactional, and analytic storage infrastructures. Sean joined META Group in July, 1995. He has a B.S. degree in Material Science and Engineering as well as a B.S. degree in Engineering and Public Policy, both from Carnegie Mellon University. Sean can be reached at sean.derrington@metagroup.com.

Acknowledgments

Writing a technical book is very much like building a house. It springs from inspiration, necessity, aesthetics, multiple talents, and hard work. Nothing would get published if the myriad of small tasks were not completed to meet deadlines from a project plan. My appreciation goes to all of those talented people who worked and contributed to this book.

If there is any dedication of this book it is to Donn Thornton for his inspiration. Donn was instrumental in teaching me the value of understanding, listening, and more importantly thinking, not only outside the box, but outside the universe. This book moved forward with the help of Kevin Ansell, whose experiences and discussions helped me through many difficult times. My thanks and appreciation goes out to Kevin for his sense of humor and encouragement.

Franny Kelly, acquisition editor at McGraw-Hill/Osborne, championed keeping this project alive and on schedule. My thanks to Franny for trusting me with the completion of this large project. Regarding the tremendous task of assembling all the writing into a real-live book, I'd like to convey my sincere thanks to my project editor, Jody McKenzie. Jody (along with her talented copyeditors) was critical to my technical dissertations becoming a coherent set of text and artwork and, subsequently, a completed manuscript.

I admit it; technically, I had help. Patty Then, storage consultant extraordinaire proved a much-needed sounding board in the review and validation of a wide set of technical concepts and specifications that make up this book. Patty's knowledge of systems, storage infrastructures, and data centers was a key resource in illustrating the technical aspects of the SAN. She is one of those rare individuals versed in performance, capacity planning, and operational experiences that span both mainframe and open systems. I also need to thank Himanshu Dwivedi for his work in Chapter 25 on the increasing interests and concerns regarding security in storage infrastructures.

My thanks and appreciation also go to Ian Spalding, technical and creative writer, for his last-minute assistance in writing some of the key chapters from my encrypted notes. In addition, Ian was enlisted again to assist in proofing the book before final publication. We all wish you the best of success on your first novel.

Finally, all of this work would not have been possible without the support, assistance, inspiration, and help from my partner and wife, Artie. Her help in moving this book toward completion was more than anyone could ask. Thank you.

Robert Spalding
February, 2003

Introduction

Storage networking represents a fundamental paradigm shift in how data is stored and accessed within computer systems. Consistent with any major technological change, storage networking brings with it the challenge to understand new models of storage architectures and, more importantly, the realities of integrating new solutions into the data center. *Storage Networks: The Complete Reference* was researched, designed, and developed to be a general, yet pragmatic, reference for those in the IT community who are already entrenched (or plan to be involved) in this fast moving, and at times, difficult-to-understand storage foundation for the future.

I believe storage networks to be the first major enhancement in computer architecture since the client/server revolution began in the late 1980s. Since that time, the need to store greater amounts of data has never ceased. The success of the client/server phenomenon pushed the processing power of the server component technologies to new levels that in turn exceeded the limits of storage devices and their related connectivity components. This situation drove systems and storage vendors to develop an ever-increasing, yet short-lived, set of disk and tape products that reflected the exponential appetite of end users for increasing capacities of online data. Within the search for higher capacity devices with faster access to data, the combined interests of the vendor and user communities lead to the development and formation of two influential standards, the Peripheral Component Interface (PCI) and the Small Computer Systems Interconnect (SCSI). These standards formed the initial foundations that focused attention on the I/O challenges within the client/server architectures and enabled, more than ever before, peripheral components to be connected to servers allowing additional devices to operate using those connections.

However, even these innovations could not effectively manage the torrent of storage demands that increased exponentially during the 1990s. The storage industry and data centers of the time searched for new ways that this overwhelming capacity of storage could be installed and accessed. This provided much of the emphasis to shift the storage connectivity paradigm from a direct connect model to a network model. With storage networking concepts emerging as a viable storage solution, this enabled two things. First, it uncovered an existing model of storage networking from the shadows of a specialized UNIX orientation, the Network Attached Storage (NAS) device. Secondly, it encouraged and spawned the integration of existing technologies to proliferate storage on its own network, thus developing into the Storage Area Network (SAN) model.

Storage networking products both in the SAN and NAS industries proliferated during the late 1990s when the technology investments were at their peak. The disparate innovation and technology du jour development this often produced has leveled into an established industry with both established and entrepreneurial players. Storage networking has crossed the product chasm and continues to evolve rapidly, although with more emphasis on data-center value and integration. Advancements are moving forward with storage initiatives such as iSCSI and connectivity through related advancements like InfiniBand and RapidIO.

Unfortunately, the value that storage networking brings to the IT community remains so diverse that it can easily become compromised by the complexities of installation and management. The most important aspect to storage networking is leveraging the value of a diverse set of solutions. I believe this will be the critical motivator in the evolution of storage networking both now and in the foreseeable future. Establishing an understanding of storage networking and identifying components of a storage networking solution and their application within the data center became key design goals for this book.

Storage Networks: The Complete Reference was designed to be a general reference for the IT community. The book was developed to address the pragmatic issues that relate to learning a new technology, understanding it, and applying it from an IT perspective. As with all reference material, it can be used in a number of ways. First, as a reference in understanding the concepts behind storage networks. Secondly, as a tool to help plan and target applications of the technology. Finally, the book is meant as an extended reference in helping your activities move beyond installation and into maintenance and management. However, it can also be used as a curriculum for classroom studies, whether employing the complete book or its parts in a formal or informal educational setting. Usage of the book depends on your existing knowledge of computers and, specifically, storage systems.

The book is intended for IT professionals who have a need to understand storage networking and its related issues from a data-center perspective. The examples in the book are composites of real-life situations and are intended to reflect major points in planning, installing, and managing storage networking in the data center.

I believe storage networking will continue to evolve into its own infrastructure, and storage networking will form the cornerstone of this migration and evolution, subsequently changing the landscape of data centers of the future.

The
Complete
Reference

Storage
Networks

Part I

Concepts of Storage Networking

The
Complete
Reference

Chapter 1

The Data Storage and Data Access Problem

Computer storage, the ubiquitous component that has invaded both our personal and working space, has taken on a life of its own with the new technology of storage networking. Like it or not, we've become a global society with a currency of information that's exchanged within today's computer networks. Nearly every aspect of our world, including the places where we live and work, are accessible through the Internet—the data from which is stored on enormous online informational databases.

Our lives revolve around computer technology. Although we don't always realize it, accessing information on a daily basis the way we do means there must be computers out there that store the data we need, making certain it's available when we need it, and ensuring the data's both accurate and up-to-date. Rapid changes within the computer networking industry have had a dynamic effect on our ability to retrieve information, and networking innovations have provided powerful tools that allow us to access data on a personal and global scale.

Both the proliferation of data and the dynamics of storing it have given way to changes in how computer storage is used and accessed. The networking innovations have driven global, local, and personal computing to greater levels of sophistication in storage technology. Because of this, we're now faced with the problems of what data to keep, how to keep it, and where to keep it. And if I do keep it, just where do I put it? We store information everywhere these days. We keep diskettes and CDs stuffed in our desks at home, collect disk and tape files at work, while countries as a whole continuously add to the mountains of archived computer tapes kept at cavernous hiding places over fear of nuclear fallout.

With so much data to store and with such global access to it, the collision between networking technology and storage innovations was inevitable. The gridlock of too much data coupled with too many requests for access has long challenged IT professionals. To storage and networking vendors, as well as computer researchers, the problem is not new. And as long as personal computing devices and corporate data centers demand greater storage capacity to offset our increasing appetite for access, the challenge will be with us. Chapter 1 will explore the data access challenges, driven by networking innovation, against data storage, exponentially increasing with innovation in media, capacity, and deployment.

The Challenge of Designing Applications

Storing and accessing data starts with the requirements of a business application. What many application designers fail to recognize are the multiple dependent data access points within an application design where data storage strategies can be key. Recognizing the function of application design in today's component-driven world is a challenging task, requiring understanding, analysis, and experience. These functions are necessary to facilitate user data within applications. The most fundamental and dependent to the application is the data storage strategy used. Be it a file orientation or relational model, this becomes a major factor in the success of the application. (See Figure 1-1.)

In all fairness to the application designers and product developers, the choice of database is really very limited. Most designs just note the type of database or databases required, be it relational or non-relational. This decision in many cases is made from economic and existing infrastructure factors. For example, how many times does an application come online using a database purely because that's the existing database of choice for the enterprise? In other cases, applications may be implemented using file systems, when they were actually designed to leverage the relational operations of an RDBMS.

Whether intelligently chosen or selected by default, the database choice leads directly to the overall interaction the application will have with storage. The application utilizes, and is dependent upon, major subsystems, such as memory management (RAM and system cache), file systems, and relational and non-relational database systems. Each of these factors affects the storage environment in different ways. An application with no regard for these factors results in application functionality that doesn't account for the availability, limitations/advantages, and growth of storage resources. Most business applications simply don't take into consideration the complexity of storage performance factors in their design activities. Consequently, a non-linear performance-scaling factor is inherent in business applications, regardless of whether the application is an expensive packaged product or an internally developed IT utility program. (See Figure 1-2.)

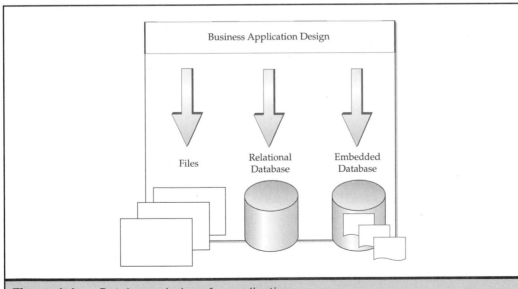

Figure 1-1.   *Database choices for applications*

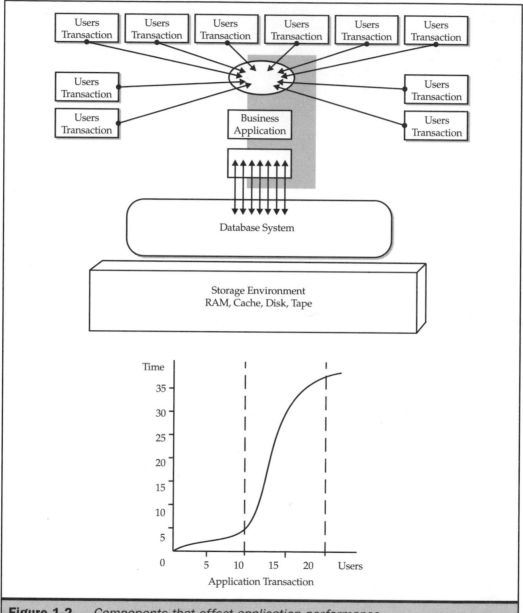

Figure 1-2. *Components that effect application performance*

Non-Linear Performance in Applications

The major factors influencing non-linear performance are twofold. First is the availability of sufficient online storage capacity for application data coupled with adequate temporary storage resources, including RAM and cache storage for processing application transactions. Second is the number of users who will interact with the application and thus access the online storage for application data retrieval and storage of new data. With this condition is the utilization of the temporary online storage resources (over and above the RAM and system cache required), used by the application to process the number of planned transactions in a timely manner. We'll examine each of these factors in detail.

First, let's look at the availability of online storage. Certainly, if users are going to interact with an application, the information associated with the application needs to be accessible in real time. Online storage is the mechanism that allows this to happen. As seen in Figure 1-3, the amount of online storage required needs to account for sufficient space for existing user data, data the application requires, and unused space for expanding the user data with minimal disruption to the application's operation.

However, as users of the application submit transactions, there must be locations where the application can temporarily store information prior to the complete execution of the transactions—successful or otherwise. Given that online storage is the permanent record for the application, the use of RAM (the computer's memory resource) and system or disk cache (a temporary memory resource associated with the CPU component or online storage component, also depicted in Figure 1-3) is used. Because of disk cache's

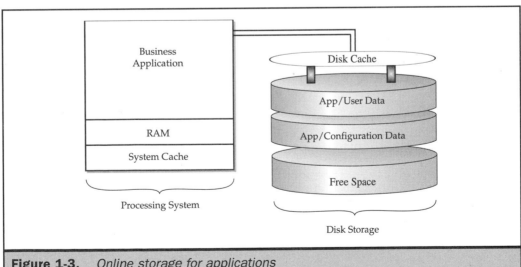

Figure 1-3. *Online storage for applications*

high speed and capability to place significant amounts of application data temporarily until the complete execution of the transaction, this storage strategy not only provides the fast execution of data, but also the necessary recovery information in case of system outage, error, or early termination of the application transaction.

Second, among the factors influencing non-linear performance, is the number of users accessing the application or planning data access. Indicated in Figure 1-4, the number of

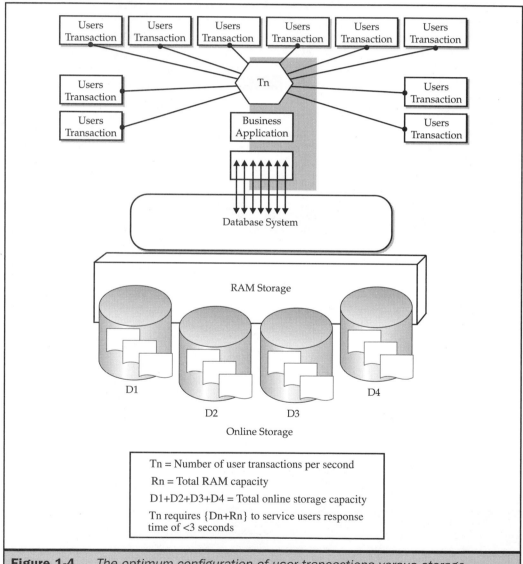

Figure 1-4.   *The optimum configuration of user transactions versus storage resources*

user transactions accessing storage resources will correspond linearly to the amount of time each transaction takes to complete (provided optimum resources are configured). Therefore, configurations can be developed so a fixed number of users will be serviced within an acceptable response-time window (given optimum storage resources). Although these optimum configurations depend on server computing capacity and adequate network resources, the transactional demands of the application rely on the storage infrastructure. (See Figure 1-5.)

It's unlikely that application designers will ever fully develop systems that take into account the necessary optimum storage configurations. The use of pre-existing components for database and file access will continue, further removing the application from the storage infrastructure. These tendencies have placed additional demands on storage strategies in order that the balance between application and storage resources can be maintained. To address the data storage/data access problem, designers have been forced to think outside of the box.

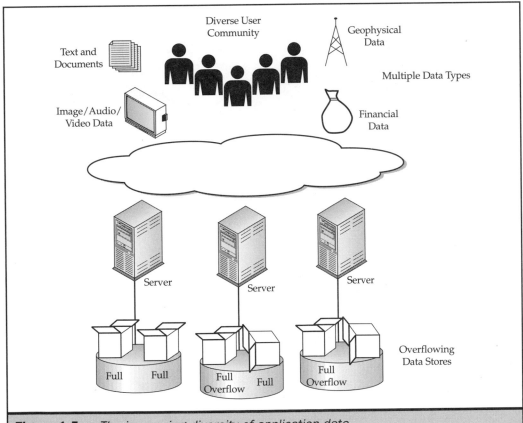

Figure 1-5.   *The increasing diversity of application data*

The Client/Server Storage Model

Our storage configurations today reflect the characteristics of the client/server model of distributed computing. Evolving out of the centralized mainframe era, the first elementary configurations of networking computers required a central computer for logging in to the network. This demanded that one computer within a network be designated, and that the necessary information be stored and processed on that computer in order for other users to access the network. Thus, the network server became the location where (on its hard drive) network information was stored. When users logged in from their client computers, they first accessed the information on the network server. Figure 1-6 shows the structure most storage configurations use today: the client/server storage model.

The client/server storage model provides data storage capabilities for the server component as well as storage for the network clients. Coupled with online storage, the servers became larger machines with increased RAM and cache to handle the multiple requests for network access demanded by users. The online storage devices also became more robust. With larger capacities, its own caching mechanisms, and greater external connectivity for expansion, it enabled faster data access. However, servers quickly

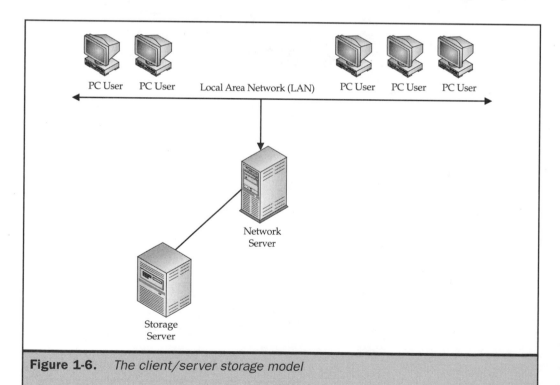

Figure 1-6.   *The client/server storage model*

reached their maximum performance capacities as the client user community demand grew faster than server capabilities. After a while, the optimum storage configuration became almost impossible to achieve given server performance limitations.

Along with the demand for client network connectivity, sharing information on the server increased the need for capacity, requiring networks to use multiple servers. This was not due so much to server capacity but that online storage needed to be large enough to handle the growing amount of information. So, as demand for online information increased so did the need for storage resources, which meant the number of servers had to increase as well.

This quickly grew into the world of server specialization. The network servers had to handle just the amount of work necessary to log clients into and out of the network, keep their profiles, and manage network resources. Client profiles and shared information were now being kept on their own file servers. The demand for online storage space and multiple access by clients required that multiple servers be deployed to handle the load. Finally, as the sophistication of the centralized mainframe computers was downsized, the capability to house larger and larger databases demanded the deployment of the database server.

The database server continues to be one of the main drivers that push the client/server storage model into new and expanded storage solutions. Why? Initially, this was due to size. The amount of information stored within the databases, driven by user demands, quickly surpassed the capacities of the largest online storage providers. In addition, the architecture of the relational model of databases (from products like Oracle, Sybase, IBM's DB2) had a tremendous amount of overhead to provide the extremely attractive functionality. Consequently, the user data only utilized half of the space needed, with the database occupying the remaining half.

As the relational database model became pervasive, the amount of databases within the network grew exponentially. This required that many databases become derivatives of other databases, and be replicated to other database servers within the enterprise. These activities began to drive the storage growth rates to extremely high levels—on average, 75 percent, but greater than 100 percent occurred in some cases.

The database server model also required that servers become more robust and powerful. Servers supporting databases evolved into multiple CPUs, larger amounts of RAM, levels of system cache, and the capability to have several paths to the external storage resources. Essentially, these became configured exclusively as storage servers, with RAM size, cache, and disk storage capacities being key configuration elements. However, it also required system and storage planners to provide additional network paths to online storage resources in order to keep up with user demand. Figure 1-7 depicts the level of sophistication required as database servers became the dominant storage consumers.

As data grows, storage solutions with the client/server storage model continue to be problematic. Even the multiple CPU servers and multigigabyte storage capacities could not ensure the server's capability to provide optimum client access. Limits

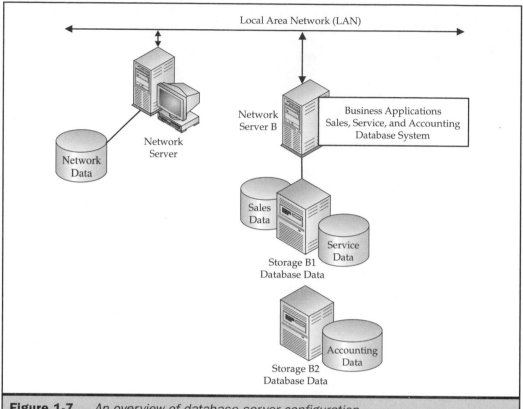

Figure 1-7.   *An overview of database server configuration*

to the size of database systems, increasing content of database transactions, and the advent of new datacentric applications required more sophistication within the storage systems. However, it also demanded that more servers be used to provide access to application information. As a result, growth rates began to show a varied and asymmetrical growth trend: some servers were deployed with more storage than required, wasting space; while other servers continued to be split because their capacity was exceeded, causing application outages due to space shortages.

An example is the exponential growth factors for storage supporting the data warehouse and data mart application segments. Typical of this is a target marketing application that ensures customers with good credit are selected and matched with offerings for financial investments. These matches are then stored and targeted for mailings in which responses are tracked. Figure 1-8 illustrates the operational complexities of storage exploitation with these environments.

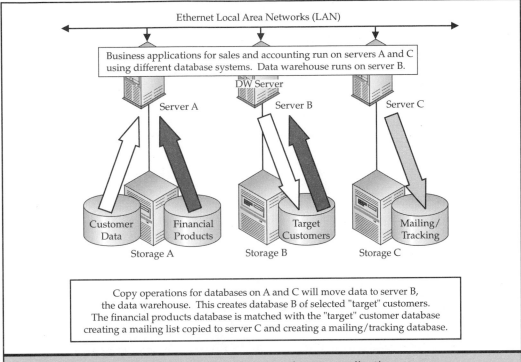

Figure 1-8. *Data moving through a data warehouse application*

The actual data traverses from online storage "A" on server A, where the customer activity and tracking database resides, to populate the data warehouse server online storage "B" on server DW. This selection of good customers from server A populates the database on server DW's online storage "B" where it is matched with financial investment product offerings also stored on server A. Subsequently, the aggregate data on C is developed from combining good customers on server B to form a mailing and tracking list stored on server DW's online storage "C."

As we have described in our example, data moves from server to server in the client/server storage model. The capability to store multiple types of data throughout the network provides the foundation for selecting, comparing, and utilizing this data for business purposes throughout the enterprise. However, this comes at a price since databases are costly in terms of large external storage and server resources, which they require to both process data and communicate with the network. Moreover, the capability to maintain these environments—database systems, more sophisticated hardware, and storage infrastructure—requires additional technicians and programmers.

As data grows, so does user access. The problem of access has to do with understanding the challenges of the client/server storage model—the biggest challenge being the Internet. The amount of data stored from the Internet has stressed the most comprehensive systems and pushed centralized mainframes back into the limelight purely on their strength in supporting thousands of online users. However, largely due to the economics of client/server systems, Internet infrastructures continue to be based on the client/server storage model.

As web servers began to grow due to the ease of deploying web pages, not to mention the capability to connect to an existing networking structure (the Internet, for instance), the amount of users able to connect to a web server became limited only by addressing and linking facilities. Given the client/server connectivity, servers on the Internet essentially had no limitations to access, other than their popularity and linking capability. Because of this, an even more aggressive move was required to populate multiple servers and specialize their uses. The example shown in Figure 1-9 shows how web servers specialize in user access, user profiles and accounts, web pages,

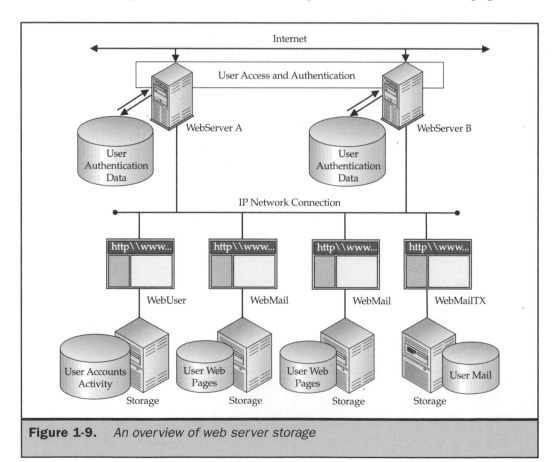

Figure 1-9.   *An overview of web server storage*

and mail. Web servers are also replicated to balance the demands of users accessing particular sites.

If we examine the performance and growth factors for storage supporting the web server applications, we find data moving in a fairly predictable way. A typical example is the infrastructure of an Internet service provider (ISP). Although they support multiple web-based applications, their main service is to provide personal users with access to the Internet. Therefore, they store two fundamental items, user profiles and mail, as well as links to other servers on the Internet. Figure 1-9 illustrates the operational simplicity of storage exploitation within these environments.

The actual data traverses from online storage on web server A, where the customer authentication and access takes place, then moves to online storage on WebUser servers where profiles, activity tracking, and home pages are stored. Essentially, the user waits here after logging in, until they issue a request. If the request is to check e-mail, the WebUser transfers the request to the WebMail server where the request is placed in an index and transferred to the location of the user's mail. In this example, we're using WebMail TX.

However, if the user issues a request to access another URL in order to browse an outside web page, the WebUser server will send the request to web server A or B. Either of these servers will transmit the request through the Internet, locate the outside server, bring back the web page or pages, and notify the WebUser server who in turn will transmit the web page(s) to the customer's client PC.

Although Figure 1-6 is a simple example of an ISP's web server configuration, the process becomes convoluted upon much interaction with the ISPs storage infrastructure. We can estimate the scope of this infrastructure by multiplying the number of customers by one million. If each customer stores 8MB of data within their profiles, e-mail, and activity tracking, this becomes 8 terabytes, or 8 million MBs, of necessary online data storage. In estimating the scope of interaction (or data access), each customer issues, on average, 20 requests for data with most being outside the ISP infrastructure. Each request requiring, on average, 500KB of data to be transferred, therefore becomes 10MB of data transferred. Multiplying this by one million customers equals 10 terabytes of data transferred through the ISP storage infrastructure every half hour.

The capability to maintain these environments, like the database server environments with database systems, multiple servers, and exponentially expanding storage infrastructure, requires an ever-increasing number of skilled technicians and programmers.

Reaching the Client/Server Storage Limitations

The preceding examples of datacentric applications, data warehouses, and ISPs demonstrate the increasing limitations of the client/server storage model. As the demand for data and online storage continues, capacities and functionality must grow to meet these challenges. Although disk drives, are becoming physically smaller and are holding increased amounts of data, and temporary storage devices such as caching have advanced, they cannot overcome the I/O limitations of the client/server architecture.

We are left asking ourselves: Is it necessary to go through the server just to get to the data? Why can't we maximize all the online storage we have? The amount of servers we have has far exceeded our capability to manage the attached storage. Isn't there a way to share data among servers rather than duplicate it throughout a company?

In addition, for every byte stored on disk there is the possibility that someone will access it. More and more users are coming online through Internet-based capabilities. Increased functionality and access to a diversity of data has created an informational workplace. Our own individual demands to store more and more data are pushing the limits of computer networks. It will be an increasing challenge to accommodate a global online community with client/server storage configurations.

The Boot Disk of Innovation

Data flow challenges have historically been the "boot disk" of innovation. The data storage/data access problems have prompted the industry to bootstrap itself with creative solutions to respond to the limitations of the client/server storage model. In 1995, in what began as efforts to decouple the storage component from the computing and connectivity elements within a computer system, became a specialized architecture that supported a significantly dense storage element (size, for example) with faster connectivity to the outside world. Combining elements from the storage world with innovation from networking technologies provided the first glimpse into how the industry would address the data storage/data access phenomenon. The collaborative evolution of these two distinct entities, storage and networking, formed the genesis of what we know today as storage networking.

As with most "out of the box" innovations, storage networking combines aspects of previous ideas, technologies, and solutions and applies them in a totally different manner. In the case of storage networking, it changes the traditional storage paradigm by moving storage from a "direct" connection to the server to a "Network" connection. This design places storage directly on the network. This dynamic change to the I/O capabilities of servers by decoupling the storage connectivity provides a basis for dealing with the non-linear performance factors of applications. It also sets the foundations for highly scalable storage infrastructures that can handle larger data access tasks, share data across servers, and facilitate the management of larger online storage capacities. All of which are foundations for building a new storage infrastructure and provisioning a comprehensive data storage/data access strategy.

However, this architectural change comes with costs. It requires rethinking how applications are deployed and how the existing client/server storage model should evolve, and, how to develop new storage infrastructures. This will require a revised view of IT storage infrastructure strategies. Characterized by struggles over size and access, IT professionals and storage vendors have moved to the front lines of the battle.

The Complete Reference

Storage
Networks

Chapter 2

The Battle for Size and Access

Chapter 2 will begin to define the general concepts of the storage networking model and the differences between it and the client/server storage model. We'll explore the details of how application design and system implementation influences storage infrastructures. With these discoveries, we'll begin to demonstrate the benefits of storage networking and how it meets the challenges posed by traditional client/server storage implementations as discussed in Chapter 1. By understanding the characteristics of business and support applications, the inherent value in putting storage on the network begins to take shape. Using standard IT planning activities and the upfront knowledge of application-oriented issues, integrating storage networking design benefits prior to system implementations will greatly increase an IT organization's ability to develop a successful storage infrastructure.

Client/server storage continues to use an I/O bus connectivity standard to communicate with storage devices, both from an internal and external perspective to the server. The I/O bus standard has evolved from original ISA bus configurations (standard to early PC servers) to today's Peripheral Component Interconnect or PCI. The server uses the I/O bus to connect with a storage device; however, it then communicates with the device through a device-specific language or protocol.

These range from ATA and ASA device protocol standards to SCSI, the Small Computer Storage Interface protocol. SCSI is the most popular among device vendors and customers for use with externally connected storage devices because of their capability to support multiple devices and more sophisticated data protection strategies such as RAID (Redundant Array of Inexpensive Disks). It is important to distinguish between the bus and device communications standards and methods because device communication protocols, like SCSI, and data protection architectures, like RAID, will continue to be used within storage networking solutions. However, as we'll discover, the I/O bus connectivity model will give way to network connectivity architecture. (More detailed information on the I/O bus, bus standards, and device protocols can be found in Chapters 6 and 7.)

As indicated in Figure 2-1, the storage devices were directly connected to the server, regardless of the type of protocol. This required all communications with the data stored on the storage devices to be handled by the server. As we have seen from examples of data warehousing and web site data movement, this places a tremendous amount of overhead on the server. Rendering it, as we have seen, to further specialization just to handle the overhead of dealing with application data.

Storage networks changed this entire model by creating unique network-based storage architectures that enhance existing client/server computing topologies. By allowing storage devices to be connected directly to an existing network, or through its own (storage) network, creates two important changes to traditional storage configurations:

■ By providing more direct access paths between storage devices, servers, and the clients, the user transactions can go more directly to the data, bypassing much of the overhead of I/O operations and unnecessary access to and through the server.

■ Storage networking grants business applications greater access to data with increased efficiency. In other words, storage networking makes it easier for applications to share data, providing servers the capability to connect to larger amounts of data.

Storage networking technologies have evolved into two distinct models—Network Attached Storage, commonly referred to as NAS, and Storage Area Networks, referred to as SAN. NAS allows storage to be placed onto an existing client/server network based upon Ethernet standards utilizing the standard TCP/IP network protocols. SANs, on the other hand, create a unique network just for storage and are based on a protocol called Fibre Channel. (More information can be found in Chapter 16.)

Both NAS and SAN are depicted in Figures 2-2 and 2-3, respectively, showing enhancements to the client/server computing model.

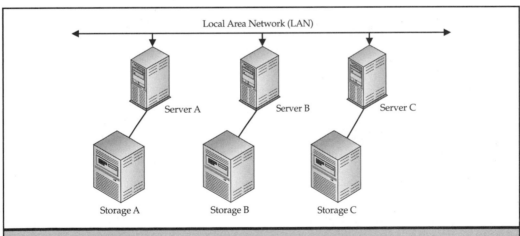

Figure 2-1. *Directly connected storage in traditional client/server environments*

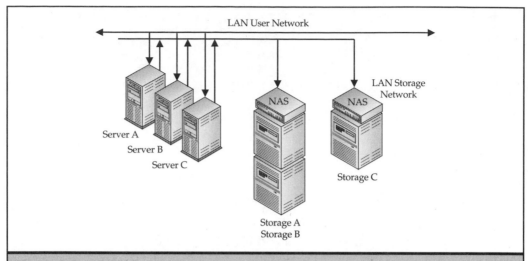

Figure 2-2. *NAS example showing enhancements to data access*

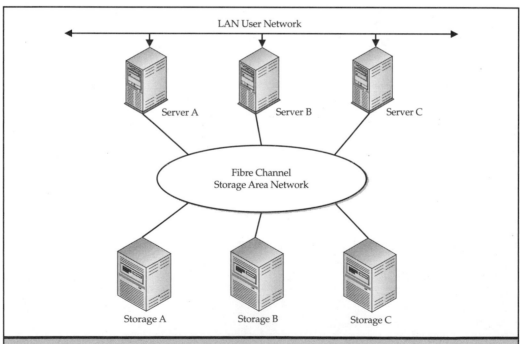

Figure 2-3. *SAN example showing enhancement to data size*

Metro Data Areas—A Look to the Future of Storage Infrastructures

In the future, distributed computer systems will increasingly take on characteristics of our urban and transportation infrastructures. Our data is stored in large server farms that produce circumstances and problems similar to those in a large metropolitan area, managing traffic flow in and out, policing and monitoring performance and security, and handling overcrowding and sprawl and the occasional accident.

Fueled by powerful servers connected to larger and larger storage systems, the Internet will continue to evolve into a complex array of data highways that literally crisscross the globe. This complex network of highways allows users to access data regardless of location, application logic, or specific storage system. These conditions will accelerate the growth of concentrated data areas that serve both public and private data highways (e.g., Internet and intranet networks).

Metro Data Areas will be located in corporate data centers, Internet service provider infrastructures, government and public institutions, and small business computer configurations. Research indicates that Metro Data Area evolution is being driven by an almost 100 percent annual growth in online storage. The Metro Data Area will be driven into the next generation of storage technology in an attempt to deal with this congestion and scalability dilemma and to construct a data transportation system that will handle the tremendous amount of data moving in and out of these areas.

Be prepared for the rush hour commute. How long will it eventually take to get your data?

Why Storage Networking Makes Sense

Many IT support organizations comment on their applications, saying, "We have bigger data, more sources, and need a single distribution strategy." In the eyes of IT, this translates as:

- **Bigger data** The data stored online and transferred between storage and server has increased in size, and the amount of data transmitted between server and client PC is much larger, driven by structured data (text and numeric data) combined with unstructured data (images, audio, and video).

- **More sources** The application must work on several sources of data to satisfy the client transaction. This means there are several online storage units that the server must connect to process the application.

- **Single distribution strategy** The results of the application need to be placed in a central location for access. Generally, this means one thing: Internet accessibility.

The Problem: Size

IT organizations also discuss ways in which they will address these problems. A typical snippet of conversation might sound like this: "We must have wider bandwidth for data transfers from storage. The problem is size. The databases we work with are exceeding the limitations of the server's storage connectivity." This translates as:

- *Wider bandwidth is needed*. The connection between the server and storage unit requires a faster data transfer rate. The client/server storage model uses bus technology to connect and a device protocol to communicate, limiting the data transfer to about 10MB per second (maybe 40MB per second, tops).

- *The problem is size*. The database and supporting online storage currently installed has exceeded its limitations, resulting in lagging requests for data and subsequent unresponsive applications. You may be able to physically store 500GB on the storage devices; however, it's unlikely the single server will provide sufficient connectivity to service application requests for data in a timely fashion—thereby bringing on the non-linear performance window quite rapidly.

Solution   Storage networking enables faster data transfers, as well as the capability for servers to access larger data stores through applications and systems that share storage devices and data.

The Problem: Access

Others in IT may argue the point, saying, "Actually, the real problem is access. We don't have sufficient resources to access the application server. This will only get worse if we go to a single distribution strategy." This translates as:

- *The problem is access*. There are too many users for the supported configuration. The network cannot deliver the user transactions into the server nor respond in a timely manner. Given the server cannot handle the number of transactions submitted, the storage and server components are grid locked in attempting to satisfy requests for data to be read or written to storage.

- *The single distribution strategy needs revisiting*. A single distribution strategy can create an information bottleneck at the disembarkation point. We will explore this later in Parts III and IV of this book where application of SAN and NAS solutions are discussed. It's important to note, however, that a single distribution strategy is only a logical term for placing user data where it is most effectively accessed. It doesn't necessarily mean they are placed in a single physical location.

Solution   With storage networking, user transactions can access data more directly, bypassing the overhead of I/O operations and unnecessary data movement operations to and through the server.

As we have demonstrated, albeit at a very high level, storage networking strategies can address each of these issues and make application strategies like single distribution a successful reality. However, this book's definition of storage infrastructures encompasses the entire IT experience, including both business and overhead applications. To understand storage networking technology and its benefits, it's important we define a few terms, especially those regarding applications that have evolved to drive the storage configurations.

Business Applications Defined for Storage

Business applications, or, more specifically, *enterprise* business applications, will be most effected by and find value in storage networking. In order to completely understand this phenomenon, we must first define an enterprise business application, as well as differentiate it from maintenance applications and support programs processed within IT organizations.

Microsoft defines enterprise business applications as complex, scalable, distributed, component-based, and mission-critical applications that may be deployed on a variety of platforms across corporate networks, intranets, or the Internet.[1] Enterprise business applications are datacentric and user friendly, but must meet stringent requirements for security, administration, and maintenance. Beyond these common qualities, Microsoft further characterizes enterprise business applications by highlighting three specific attributes, which include:

- **Large**   A long-lived, multiuser, multideveloper, multimachine, multicomponent application that can manipulate massive data and utilize extensive parallel processing, network distributed resources, and complex logic, as well as be deployed across multiple platforms and interoperate with many other applications.

- **Business oriented**   To meet specific business requirements, the application encodes business policies, processes, rules, and entities, is developed in a business organization, and is deployed in a manner responsive to business needs.

- **Mission critical**   An enterprise business application must be robust enough to sustain continuous operations, be extremely flexible for scalability and deployment, and allow for efficient maintenance, monitoring, and administration.

Further noted is the difference in scope between enterprise applications—for example, multiuser, interactive, highly available architectures, and personal applications intended for single-user interactions. Although many PC applications function as the client in client/server architectures, and active code is commonly distributed to our client through Java or Java-like applications, they lack the distributed nature and high availability requirements previously stated.

---

[1]   Reference Microsoft Publication, Visual Studio - Developing for the Enterprise, Document No. DTX03-55298-0598

Maintenance and Support Applications

Supporting large, highly available business applications and their infrastructures are numerous maintenance and support applications. These are implemented within support infrastructure areas. IT management must use these applications, often called tools and utilities, to maintain the mission-critical characteristics of enterprise applications. (More information on management practices and processes can be found in Chapter 21.)

It is important to differentiate between these two distinct types of applications, especially given the often confusing and misleading global use of the term *application* among software and hardware vendors. This difference is important due to IT organizational boundaries that focus IT specialties between the programming and design personnel, the people who develop and implement the business applications, and systems support and administration personnel—the people who support the infrastructure.

The maintenance and support applications have evolved to demonstrate the same non-linear performance that business applications do (see Chapter 1 for a refresher on this). Therefore, they can perform just as poorly and be just as degrading to the operations of the data center as their business counterparts. The support applications have the following distinct attributes:

- Their results are focused upon supporting and maintaining server platforms and components that create a continuous operational infrastructure.

- They enhance IT's abilities to maintain levels of reliability, availability, and serviceability for the data center and evolving Metro Data Areas.

- The usage of support applications provides necessary information to maintain a scalable and manageable data center and Metro Data Area infrastructure.

The tools and products within these areas defined as storage management applications can be some of the most datacentric within the data center. They are defined by the following broad categories:

- **Archive/Backup/Recovery**   Provides IT with the tools to initiate data protection policies that copy data, provide recovery mechanisms, and move data to offline storage media.

- **Storage Resource Management**   Enhances the usage of resources that make up the storage infrastructure. These include utilities such as monitoring the activity of stored data, mechanisms, and the enforcement of online storage space quotas, as well as the collection of historical I/O system information and status.

- ■ **Storage Data Management** Complements the storage infrastructure with enhancements to file/systems, volume management strategies, fault tolerant mechanisms, and utilities such as online space data maintenance activities, defragmentation, optimization, and compression.

- ■ **Storage Security** A new category that has extended into the storage area from network user authentication and resource access technologies.

Although storage management applications are necessary in providing an organized and manageable environment, they are not business applications. The characteristics and base purposes of both are very different. While business applications automate and ultimately provide the process whereby the business runs (as well as directly impact overall business performance), storage management applications are considered "necessary evils" and "maintenance overhead" to business application processing and availability. Make no mistake, the "evils" of support tools and practices are a necessary cost of doing business, and when not managed effectively, they will impact business performance.

Building the Business Application

In trying to bring more and more data into play, application designers typically place things closest to the user. However, as we learned in Chapter 1, if this is done without regard for storage or data infrastructures, the application can be quickly compromised once in production. The application design process (as shown in Figure 2-4) will then give way to the realities of system implementation (as shown in Figure 2-5).

The application designers concentrate on the business requirements and produce a requirements document. This determines what will be provided to end users at the completion of the development process. The document, once finished and signed off by management, will also be used as a basis for an external design document. This is generally comprised of an external view of end-user functions, access points, and outputs. It's possible that sources, types, and quantities of data will be factored into external design discussions. This is followed by internal design activities where the application programmers determine the logic and identify external software development components to be used in building the application system.

It is during the internal design process that application designers and programmers work with database administrators to provide a logical design for the application data. Unfortunately, in many cases the physical attributes of the database requirements remain unaddressed. These design activities are followed by an iterative process of actually building (for example, coding) the application by a team of application programmers.

As components are completed, they are tested on their own—something known as unit testing—and then integrated with other components to form a major function

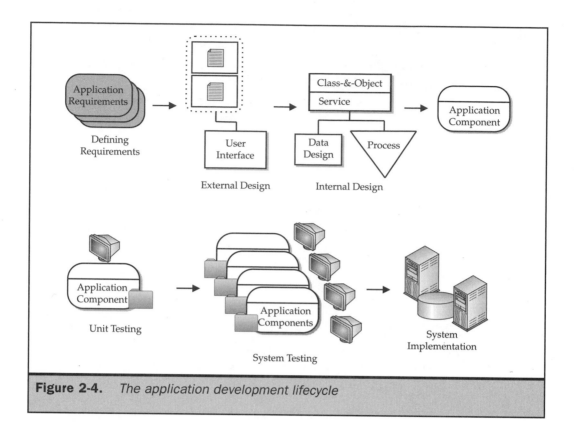

Figure 2-4.   *The application development lifecycle*

of the application system. These functions or combined sets of components are integrated and tested in what evolves into a larger process of system testing. As all the components come together, user testing and acceptance begins, where actual end users test the system for accuracy and functionality. The components are modified in an iterative process as functionality errors are encountered. Once the system is completely tested by a segment of end users and signed off by management, the system moves into production mode. This is where the application first encounters the storage infrastructure.

Moving into production mode is a tricky business. In large systems, other activities come into play such as user education, migrating users from older systems into new systems, and ensuring that the application's business data stays in sync from one system to the next.

However, as the new business applications progress to this point, implementation will produce some interesting challenges, especially in the absence of storage infrastructure information and planning. Now it's a matter of how the application works with an

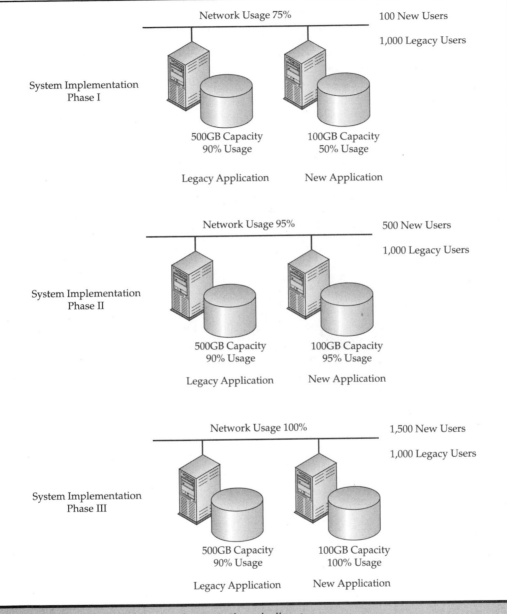

Figure 2-5.   *Application implementation challenges*

unknown server and storage infrastructure. If the storage infrastructure has not been taken into account, the window of application non-linear performance (see Chapter 1) becomes very thin and quickly results in an unresponsive application as soon as users and data are applied in production mode. (See Figure 2-6.)

A third process in the application development cycle, albeit unplanned, is a post-implementation analysis and understanding of the real storage and data access requirements of the application system. This generally results in quickly provisioning additional resources into the storage configurations to handle the production processing. Due to the immediacy of this action, the resources are provisioned at a macro level without accounting for growth or scalability.

Obviously, the third process should be integrated into the application's development process, probably somewhere between the external and internal design activities. However, this requires two major pieces of information. First is the availability of storage solutions to offer to the application designers. Secondly, a more detailed understanding of input and output processes is needed to enhance the application's design through I/O processing and storage requirements beforehand. (More information on this can be found in Chapters 6, 7, and 8.)

It is important to note that enterprise storage infrastructures deal with multiple applications and should be seen in context of an enterprise view rather than addressed piecemeal for each application system. This becomes problematic, however, during an implementation frenzy when the new applications are being deployed online. This points out another level of difficulty: developing an effective storage strategy that works with the traditional client/server storage model. The ability to look at the requirements from a cumulative perspective, noting the data size, characteristics, and access requirements on an enterprise scale, requires storage configurations that support multiple applications in a scalable manner. The application design-development-implementation process will not change, it will only get faster and less resource-aware. Accounting for it through an enterprise storage infrastructure strategy helps, but this must be integrated with storage solutions that mediate the challenge. (This forms a whole topic outside the scope of this book. Additional information can be found later in Chapter 17.)

The Benefits of Storage Networks on Business Applications

As stated previously, storage networking technology is being implemented to deal with extreme congestion and scalability issues within enterprise data centers. (See the Metro Data Areas sidebar earlier in this chapter.) IT management can expect the following benefits with the design and implementation of storage networking configurations and solutions.

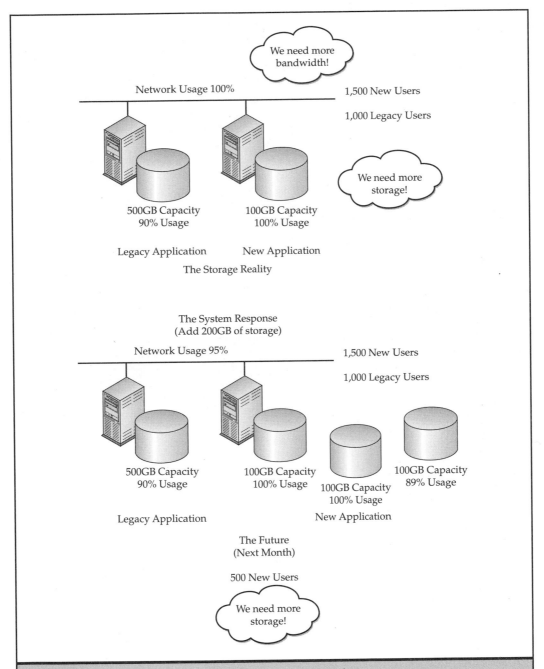

Figure 2-6.   *The realities of application implementation*

Scalability of Access to Business Application Data

Figure 2-7 demonstrates the shift from centralized data access to networked data access for both SAN and NAS configurations, respectively. The platform benefits are clear, more servers can connect and utilize storage devices concurrently, thereby eliminating congested access to single servers, as well as the complexities and overhead involved in maintaining multiple copies of data for each server. From the business application perspective, this allows the application logic to be distributed throughout the servers, maintains centralized access to the data associated with the application, and eliminates a single point of failure for the application.

Note *One associated attribute of this configuration could be a storage protection strategy of data mirroring or RAID functionality to reduce the single point of failure for data availability.*

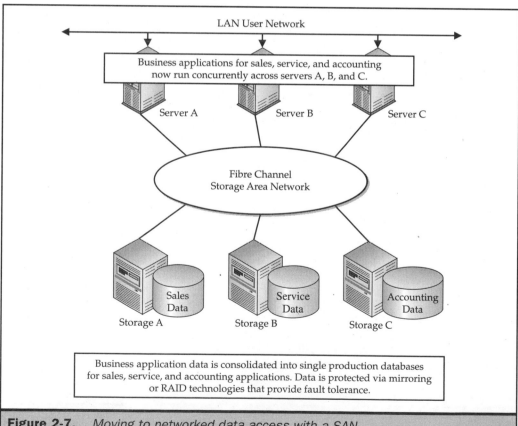

Figure 2-7. *Moving to networked data access with a SAN*

Consolidation of Business Application Data

Since maintaining multiple, synchronized copies of data is no longer necessary, storage devices previously connected directly to servers can now be used more efficiently by serving multiple servers with multiple sets of data. Eliminating the copying/synchronization process increases business application availability and reliability by decreasing data maintenance down times (copying/synchronization) and enhancing data integrity by eliminating state/timing differences from multiple copies of application data.

Faster Access to Data Through Improved Bandwidth and Centralized Configurations

The increased bandwidth associated with moving to storage network configurations has clear advantages in the amount of data transferred. Data now moves up to two times faster using Fibre Channel protocols than directly connected storage devices using SCSI protocol. Within SAN environments, this requires a new network using Fibre Channel (FC) protocol. NAS configurations offer even higher levels of Ethernet speed when configured on dedicated subnetworks that do not conflict with client network traffic. Both technologies allow for configurations that can sustain an increased number of business application transactions while setting a foundation for maintaining consistent and reliable response times.

Note   *NAS boxes are used as thin servers with large storage capacities that remain dedicated to processing I/O requests through a distributed file system identified to subscribing application servers. As a result, NAS configurations become dedicated I/O extensions to multiple servers. Usage will continue to increase capability to run popular relational databases in scope as NAS becomes a reality.*

Increased Business Application Availability Through Efficiencies in Storage Management

As noted previously, there are multiple maintenance/support applications necessary to maintain platform environments. Figure 2-8 demonstrates the capability of devices within a SAN configuration to communicate with each other, thereby allowing many of the sever-based, datacentric maintenance/support applications to be optimized. Support applications can now be offloaded from the initiating server, which means data is copied from storage network device to storage network device (for example, disk-to-disk, disk-to-optical, disk-to-tape, and so on). Most business applications suffer during this maintenance process because data is unavailable during the time it is being copied. Although necessary for maintaining storage backup procedures and policies, this type of operation (in other words, copying data directly from device to device) can

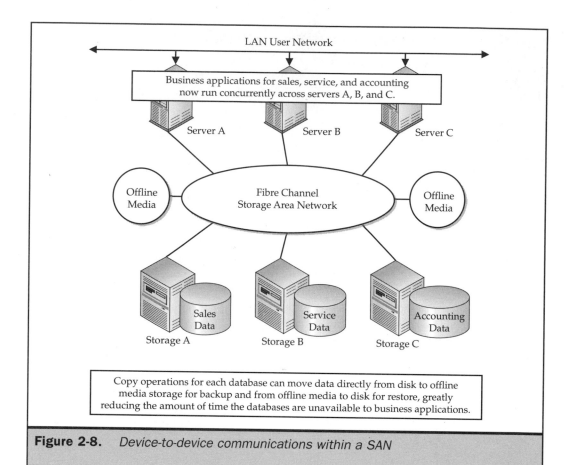

Figure 2-8.   *Device-to-device communications within a SAN*

greatly improve the availability of business applications by reducing the time data is
unavailable. Unfortunately, NAS suffers from its server-based architecture (albeit a
thin server) and attachment to an Ethernet network. Backup and recovery operations
are generally handled by a dedicated sever within the subnetwork. Presently, NAS
configurations do not allow for optimization strategies such as device-to-device
communication, as done in SAN configurations.

The Effects of Storage Networks on IT Organizations

A quote for your consideration: "Storage networking? Why yes, storage has always been networked. I know every morning when I come in and log in to the network, I access the sales tracking files positioned on the server. I also know that when the server goes down, I can't get to those files shared by the sales territory managers. Networked storage being new? It's always been in the computer systems I've used. Yep, couldn't live without it."

This manager of computer applications is obviously commenting on the new concept of networking storage. In his mind, storage has always been networked and is certainly not a new concept to him. In fact, as you've probably deduced, he's developed his professional activities to be dependent on storage shared on a network, across departments, and accessible to both headquarters and remote personnel. What he's talking about is the concept of the client/server storage model that has existed for many years and is now taken for granted in most global 2000 companies within the world.

And now, another quote from another IT professional: "Storage networking? No, we haven't gone in that direction yet. We're still waiting for the technology to become more mature and stable. However, we have plans to implement a SAN within the next year's planning cycle. We're still relying on our direct attached storage systems to get us through these next budget cycles. Now, to be fair, I'm not sure what the web guys are doing. They may have some other configuration they're working with."

What this IT manager of technical services is commenting on is the company's direction in implementing storage networking in the form of a SAN. Same company, same network, as described by his peer in the applications area, although in his mind, storage networking is a completely different animal than the traditional client/server storage model of storage networking.

If we next talk to the Internet/intranet infrastructure manager, we may yet find another story.

"Storage networking? Well, not really. We have Network Attached Storage that supports our web servers. That's really different from storage networks, isn't it? I'm not sure. In any event, our NAS storage boxes serve us well in allowing multiple storage locations that the web servers can go to for web pages, storing customer transaction data, customer files, and profiles. Of course, much of the transactional data gets downloaded to the application servers for processing accounts and updating the real financial records. So, I guess, yes we have networked storage across our enterprise. I think the server guys are looking at SANs though, so you may want to talk with them."

The point is that storage networking can and will be implemented across a broad range of services within the data center. Although it is increasingly available through two distinct architectural models, SAN and NAS, it is not readily recognized or understood within the data center. In order to utilize this new technology effectively, you must understand what's driving the storage infrastructures (which we have done in Chapters 1 and 2), as well as the details of each storage networking model, which will allow you to design and implement effective solutions.

Most managers responsible for application design and development think of storage as a necessary systems infrastructure—one that should always be there—so we must proceed with the knowledge that some things can be changed, while others can only be influenced. Part I of this book was designed not only as an introduction to storage networking but as an initial discussion regarding storage networks within the data center. If your job involves the technical services of your data center, you may want your peers in application development to read Part I (or perhaps purchase their own copy). It may spark an ongoing dialogue that finds each of you moving toward activities that drive and build a storage networking infrastructure unique to your environment.

Storage
Networks

Chapter 3

Decoupling the Storage Component: Putting Storage on the Network

In Chapter 2, we found the increasing size of online data to be a driving factor in pushing the limitations of the traditional client/server storage model. The processes that surround the design and development of business applications, and which fuel data growth, are not equipped to supplement the planning and design of storage infrastructures, no matter how critical storage becomes. Once applications reach production stage, the realities regarding actual users and the limitations of current storage environments are quickly quantified in application performance. The addition of support applications, generally addressed as an after thought, will further increase demands on new or current storage devices. As the likelihood of major renovations to existing storage infrastructures increases, post-implementation enhancements become very active, while the impact on business driven by the risk to successful application implementation becomes an even greater concern.

A solution to these problems is the design and implementation of more scalable and responsive storage infrastructures based upon storage networking concepts. As we discussed in Chapter 2, storage networking requires separating the traditional storage components from their server counterparts. This is a major shift from tightly coupled architectures of the traditional client/server era. However, once implemented, users can greatly benefit from increased scalability in both size and access and lower the risk of application implementation and maintenance failures.

This chapter will explore the concepts surrounding one of the current and increasingly popular models of storage networking: Network Attached Storage or NAS. NAS facilitates the decoupling of storage from the server by allowing storage to be directly connected to existing client/server networks. It provides a method of addressing the data access and storage challenges, while creating a scalable storage infrastructure that will support multiple applications. In addition, this model can compensate for the lack of planning that generally arises in the implementation frenzy of application development, not to mention the ad hoc need to provide ongoing storage capacity for business demands.

The NAS Idea

Prior to the days of Windows networking, Java downloads, and the commercialization of the ARPANET, early users of computer networks worked within the UNIX operating system environments. ARPANET, incidentally, was the global Internet's progenitor; it stood for Advanced Research Projects Agency Network, an agency of the U.S. Department of Defense. As their networks and applications grew, they found the problem of storage an increasing frustration. Providing storage on one's own workstation that was shared within the network could be hazardous to your work as well as to the users that shared that data. Accessing storage on someone else's workstation was just as frustrating, especially if they had left and turned off their computer for the night (see Figure 3-1).

Then an idea occurred to them. If users are going to share files, why not simply dedicate a computer to house large and shared files? For example, a computer connected to an existing network could have storage space shared with users throughout the

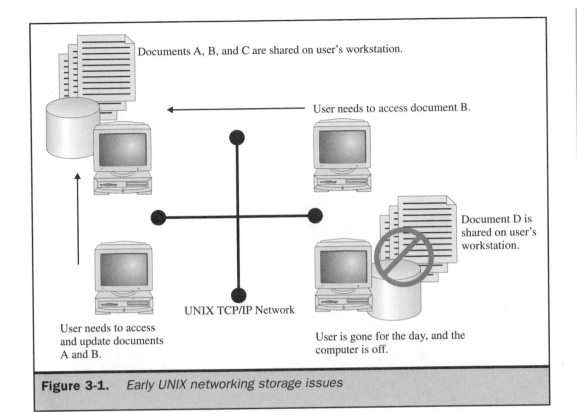

Documents A, B, and C are shared on user's workstation.

User needs to access document B.

Document D is shared on user's workstation.

UNIX TCP/IP Network

User needs to access and update documents A and B.

User is gone for the day, and the computer is off.

Figure 3-1.   *Early UNIX networking storage issues*

network. That's exactly how early networked UNIX environments evolved to share data and depend on a file "Server," as depicted in Figure 3-2.

Given that working environment, the next logical step was the innovation of a server optimized for file I/O. The reasoning was that additional overhead for the operating system wasn't needed; the server should have the capacity for larger disk storage space, and be reliable most of the time. Any additional functionality that a user might require, like running other applications, or displaying and using graphic functions, wouldn't be needed.

Thus, it's necessary that a computer used in this fashion incorporate a large amount of disk storage to be integrated with a "thin" OS that only does I/O, and that it can be attached to existing networks. In addition, it should allow users to access their files on this special server as if the files were on their own workstation, essentially allowing the files to be shared with other users throughout the network. As UNIX environments became the platform for innovation—due to its unrestricted code base, use with academic communities, and virtually free price tag—the setting for the development of an optimized network file server was put in motion.

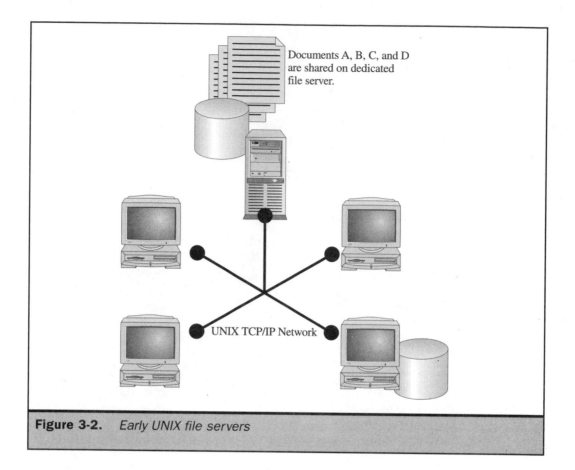

Documents A, B, C, and D are shared on dedicated file server.

UNIX TCP/IP Network

Figure 3-2.   *Early UNIX file servers*

NAS Evolution and Development

The built-in networking functionality of UNIX prompted the development of a system that not only allowed users to share files across the network but which provided a method of organizing data that allowed the server to share its files with users within the network. Thus, the importance of the UNIX file system became apparent. The file system, as shown in Figure 3-3, forms the foundation for data sharing.

The file system is a method by which data is organized and accessed within a computer system. Generally a component of the operating system, it's employed by users and the OS itself. On behalf of application programs and interactive users, the system organizes data into logically defined instances, where the operating system can find information it needs to collect data on their behalf, and perform an I/O function to satisfy their request. The OS and the users form logical associations between the segments of data—which are referred to as files—through a naming convention as defined by the operating system.

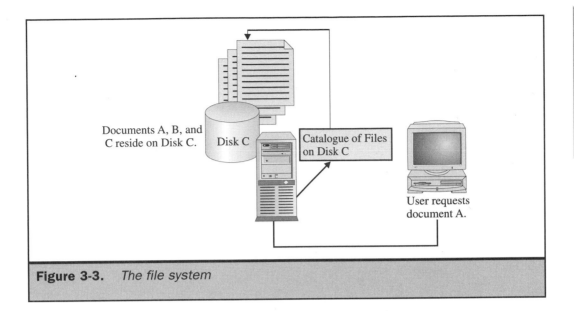

Figure 3-3.   *The file system*

Emergence of the Network File System (NFS) drove the innovation behind the development of a special computer—whose only job was to do I/O. Two pioneering innovators, Auspex and Network Appliance, became the first to offer a downsized UNIX OS with larger amounts of disk storage and the capability to connect to a TCP/IP network. It leveraged an NFS file system organization that allowed users and their client computers to connect to their data, as shown in Figure 3-4. The result was the emergence of the first Network Attached Storage product.

The early NAS storage devices were UNIX-based and used largely in areas of academic research, scientific applications, and computer science development. The early deployment provided a method of storing large amounts of data used in research areas, such as simulating meteorological conditions, geological conditions, and nuclear testing—in other words, it aided any project that involved massive amounts of data which couldn't be easily stored on individual workstations or file servers. Early NAS products also proved to be quite productive in code development areas, where computer code had to be shared between developers and development teams. Figures 3-5a and 3-5b depict these types, respectively.

The emergence of networking required the file system to become shared throughout the computers on the network. Consequently, the network file system allows a computer to make available its file system to other users within the network. Other systems and users within the network can attach to the file system and access the data. The remote files from the shared computer are thus seen as local files by the local operating system, thereby providing a virtual set of files which don't actually exist on the local computer. Instead, their location is *Virtual*, or *Virtualized*.

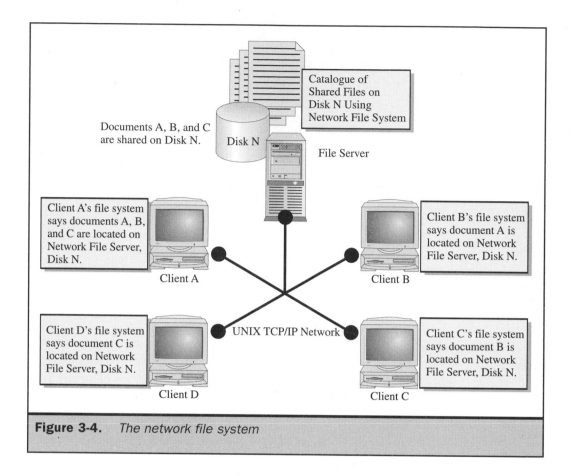

Figure 3-4.   *The network file system*

The next evolution was the integration into the traditional client/server environments supporting Windows operating systems. This initially provided a much more hybrid approach, given the capacities of early windows networks, proprietary protocols, and usage of database servers running UNIX. The first stage of Windows networking was the formation of a type of network file server, still in use today, using proprietary networking systems. Figure 3-6 depicts these early configurations that functioned as "File Servers," not necessarily network attached storage, but which served in a similar capacity to the early UNIX servers mentioned previously.

However, Windows did have the capability to perform Remote Procedure Calls (RPCs) and through this function it was able to participate within a networked file system. The capability to provide and link to network drives became the Windows NFS compatible architecture, with the capability to participate within TCP/IP networks as well as proprietary networks based on Novell and Banyan proprietary packet-switched architectures. (More detailed information on file systems, network drives, and virtualization can be found in Part II of this book.)

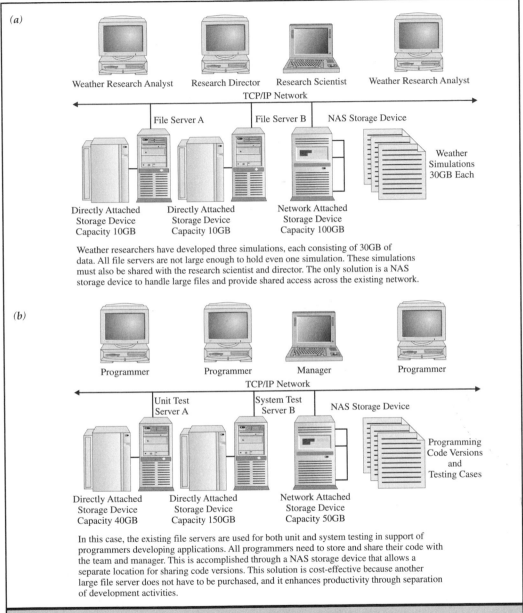

Figure 3-5.   (a) Early NAS scientific applications; (b) Early NAS code development applications

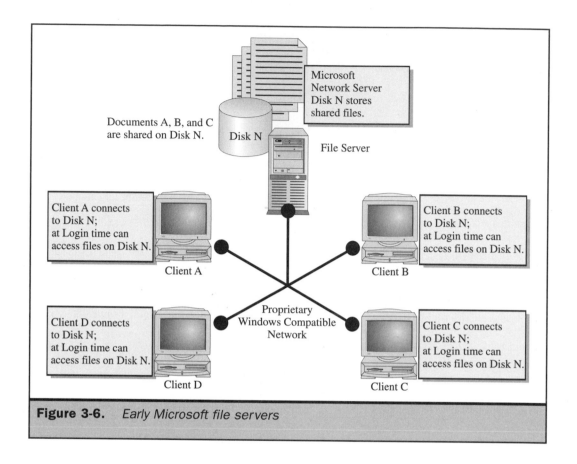

Figure 3-6. *Early Microsoft file servers*

These networking architectures gave way to the networking protocol standards of TCP/IP, based upon the standard OSI model. (Open Systems Interconnection is a standard description or "reference model" for how messages should be transmitted between any two points in a telecommunication network.) Although largely driven by everyone's attempt to integrate with the Internet and growing web application infrastructure, this was something that the early UNIX users had long been doing—for example, already connecting to ARPANET.

These activities caused the development of a file system for use within the prolific web server software. Although Internet servers evolved and consisted largely of UNIX-based servers, the web application software phenomenon was founded on Windows systems. This formed the basis of the Common Internet File System (CIFS), a file system that was compatible with Windows web Internet environments and which could participate within a standard TCP/IP networked environment—and thus within UNIX-based environments.

Therefore those NAS vendors who already supported TCP/IP networks and network file systems, moved quickly to support multiple operating environments and file systems. Today's NAS devices come in a wide variety of flavors. However, most industry leaders support both UNIX-based environments based upon an NFS file system architecture with support for Windows through CIFS file systems. As indicated in Figure 3-7 these offerings often allow both systems access to a NAS device.

As we discussed previously, early NAS devices supported UNIX environments only. These file-oriented servers were used in academic, government, and computer science applications in which data requirements surpassed standard internal and external storage devices where no other device could be used. These environments furthered the "black box" characteristics of NAS as a storage device. The reason being that users could not configure NAS servers to run other applications or even access the OS itself. The OS in the NAS box is what is called a Real-Time Operating System (RTOS), a clever name for a specialized UNIX OS with a special set of functions for a specific assignment. In the NAS case, this was file I/O—for example, the capability to optimize the execution of file access to the connected storage, and leverage the NFS system as a shared catalogue for network users.

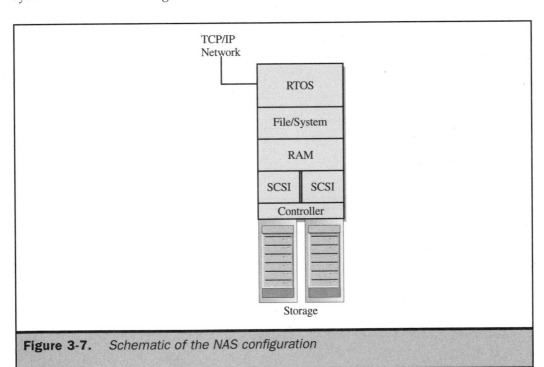

Figure 3-7.   *Schematic of the NAS configuration*

An Operational Overview of NAS

NAS boxes remain thin servers with large storage capacities that function as dedicated I/O file servers. Requests from clients are routed to the NAS server through network file systems that are installed on subscribing application servers. As a result, NAS configurations become dedicated I/O extensions to multiple servers. Usage has given way to popular relational databases (for example, Microsoft SQL/Server and Oracle's relational database products), although these remain problematic given their file orientation (see the section titled "NAS Caveats" later in this chapter).

NAS servers work today in a number of different environments and settings, the most diverse being in storage networking. However, their value continues to focus on data access issues within high-growth environments, as well as how they address particular size challenges found in today's diversity of data types.

Leveraging NAS for Data Access

The inherent value of NAS continues to be its capability to provide storage quickly and cost effectively by using the resources that already exist in the data center. Today's solutions offer compatibility in both UNIX and Windows environments and connect easily into users' TCP/IP networks.

A typical solution for handling a large number of users who need access to data is depicted in Figure 3-8. Here, an end-user constituency of 1500 is represented. In the

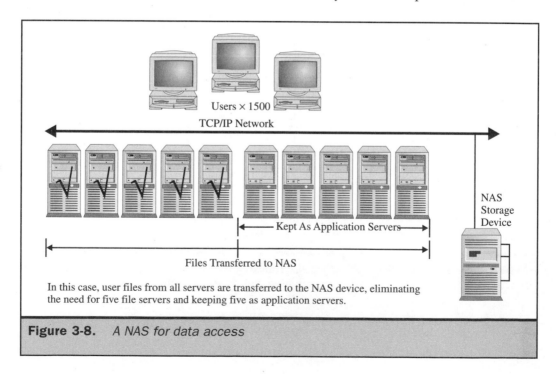

In this case, user files from all servers are transferred to the NAS device, eliminating the need for five file servers and keeping five as application servers.

Figure 3-8.   *A NAS for data access*

scenario, the users access data files under 100KB in size for read-only purposes that are stored across a number of servers. If the user base increases by another thousand over the next year, the workload could be handled by upgrading current servers as well as adding new servers with larger storage sizes to support this increase in data and traffic. This solution, however, would be costly and difficult to manage.

However, as Figure 3-8 shows, the NAS solution is used to combine the data spread across the current ten servers, placing it on the NAS storage device. Users' requests for data now come to one of the five application servers attached to the network and are then redirected to the NAS box where their request for data from a particular file is executed. Upon completion of the requested I/O operation within the NAS box, the data request is redirected to the requesting user. Because the NAS devices are optimized to handle I/O, their capacity for I/O operations exceeds typical general-purpose servers. The increased I/O capacity accounts for the collapsing of servers from ten to five. Moreover, they can scale higher in storage capacity. As the users and their respective data grows, increasing the NAS devices provides a more scalable solution for handling increased data access requirements within the scenario.

This solution does two major things for the data center. First, it provides a much larger window in which the applications can operate before they reach the non-linear performance curves. Given that both users and storage resources can increase on a linear basis, this adds to the value and stability of the enterprise storage infrastructure and can support multiple applications of this type through these configurations.

Secondly, it provides a cost-effective solution by applying optimized resources to the problem. By utilizing resources that existed within the data center—for example, existing server file systems and the TCP/IP network—it eliminated the need for additional general-purpose servers and associated network hardware and software. More importantly, it reduced the need for additional personnel to manage these systems.

Leveraging NAS for Data Size

The ability of a single server to handle large amounts of data is becoming a common problem. As Figure 3-5 illustrates, a configuration supporting storage of geophysical data can be tremendously large but with relatively few users and less-sensitive availability requirements. However, storing gigabyte-sized files is a problem for general-purpose servers. Not only is it difficult to access the data, but it's also very costly to copy the source data consisting of external storage devices such as tape to the processing servers.

By adding a NAS solution to this scenario (see Figure 3-9), the data, as in our first example, is consolidated on the NAS devices and optimized for I/O access through the network. Although the sizes of the files accessed are much larger, the number of users are low and the resulting user requests for data can be handled by the existing network. Therefore, the current resources are effectively utilized within the required service levels of the sophisticated applications.

In this case, the user requests for data are similarly received by the server and redirected to the NAS devices on the existing network. The NAS completes the requested I/O, albeit one that is much larger in this case, achieving levels of 300 to 500MB per file, and is then redirected by the server back to the requesting user. However, an additional

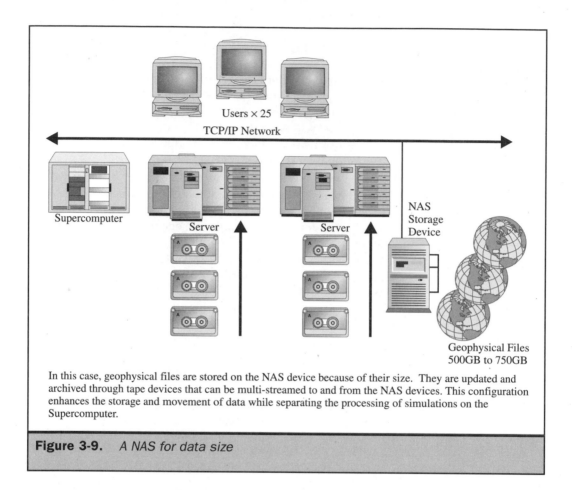

In this case, geophysical files are stored on the NAS device because of their size. They are updated and archived through tape devices that can be multi-streamed to and from the NAS devices. This configuration enhances the storage and movement of data while separating the processing of simulations on the Supercomputer.

Figure 3-9.   *A NAS for data size*

anomaly to this example is the sourcing of the data through tapes that are sent to the data center. The tapes are read from the server and copied directly to the NAS devices. Conversely, data from the NAS is archived back to tape as new simulations are developed. Given that multiple servers can reach the NAS devices, multiple input streams can be processing simultaneously in order to perform I/O to and from the offline media, which in this case are the tape units.

This solution, although different in perspective from our first example, provides the same benefits. The larger window of operation for the application itself demonstrates that appropriate storage resources balanced with data size and the number of users will stabilize the linear performance of the application. It also shows that NAS provides a more cost-effective solution by consolidating the data within an optimized set of devices (for instance, the NAS devices) and utilizing the existing resources of the data center which in this case were the server and associated file systems and network resources.

NAS Caveats

The caveats for NAS are twofold. The architecture employed by NAS products does not lend itself to applications that are dependent on sophisticated manipulation of the storage media—meaning any application that either has its own embedded file system to map and store data to the online storage directly, or that works with data management products, such as relational databases, which do the same. Secondly, applications that deal with highly volatile data do not perform well—in other words, data that is subject to constant and continuous updating by a large user base.

Writing to disk directly is a characteristic of many applications first developed within the UNIX operating environment. Relational databases commonly have this architecture. The problem manifests itself in performance as these systems have developed their own ways of manipulating data and in a sense have their own internal file system. Having these run under an additional file system penalizes the application by forcing it to do certain things twice.

However, any application that contains a database designed in a monolithic fashion will have performance problems when operating within NAS storage environments. For example, e-mail applications have embedded databases that are not scalable. The monolithic nature of their databases can therefore force all traffic into a single path or device creating a performance bottleneck and recovery problem if the storage device or path is encumbered in any way.

On the other hand, NAS provides the most cost-effective solution for applications that are file-oriented, contain read-only files, or which have large user bases. The architecture behind NAS within these application environments provides a scalable way for large numbers of users to obtain information quickly without encumbering the servers. This also provides an effective way to upgrade storage quickly through existing networking resources. This has proven itself within the ISP data centers where NAS storage devices are the solution of choice given their capability to handle large amounts of data through the storage of web pages, and users who require random read-only access.

We have discussed both the NAS architecture and issues in summary fashion. More detailed discussions of the components that make up the NAS solution, how they operate, and how to apply the NAS solution in data center settings will be discussed in Part V of this book.

Storage
Networks

Chapter 4

Decoupling the Storage Component: Creating a Network for Storage

C hapter 3 summarized the architecture, configurations, and benefits as well as caveats of putting storage on an existing network using NAS storage devices. NAS can use existing network resources and excels in addressing large-scale data access read-only applications. However, it is limited by its file-oriented I/O architecture that limits this storage networking solution when addressing heavy online transactional processing (OLTP) applications.

An alternative to NAS is the other cornerstone of storage networking, the Storage Area Network (SAN). SANs, like their counterparts in NAS, allow storage to be connected to a network and provide access to multiple clients and servers. The fundamental differences are the methods in which they accomplish this. SANs require their own network to operate, which provides a significant increase to throughput. SANs also provide direct I/O access from the devices connected to the network, thus providing yet another fundamental shift in distributing the I/O workload among applications.

This chapter will discuss the fundamental concepts of the Storage Area Network as well as providing an insight into the evolution of distributing I/O operations within and throughout processing configurations. Because SANs fundamentally shift the I/O architecture of processing configurations by moving direct storage operations to a network, it's important to understand a holistic picture of how these complex technologies developed. Within this chapter is a brief discussion of the evolutionary ancestors of the SAN, most of which have not been rendered obsolete or extinct. Many of the solutions may be configurations installed within your data center.

The Data-centric World

We live in a data-centric world that consumes information at an amazingly fast pace. The information we process as individuals all starts out as data stored somewhere and, more importantly, is a requirement driven by an application that generates the information that we are presented with. Where did all these applications come from and why do they require such vast amounts of data? Certainly these are questions that are beyond the scope of this book; however, they remain the fundamental driving force behind the innovation and advancement of I/O processing.

The support of the increasing data-centric nature of OLTP and data analysis application systems evolved through experiences in large database applications using centralized mainframe configurations. Even as some high-end processor configurations became distributed by connecting systems within a tightly coupled network, the ability to handle high I/O transactional rates and large-scale databases exceeded their limitations. The advancement and proliferation of relational database solutions exacerbated the problem with its exponential storage resource appetite when compared to traditional processing of the time. As this relational database phenomenon filtered into the client/server processing configurations, this increased not only the number of server configurations, but their complexities and challenges as well. It also provided another target to support the ever increasing population of data-centric applications.

Many of today's applications rely on some form of relational database products that, as discussed in Chapter 3, were designed to work directly with disk storage devices. In addition to this evolution of processing, combining large user populations with Very Large Data Bases (VLDB) requires a greater sophistication of I/O and storage functionality than what is available on traditional, albeit large-scale, mainframe, client/server storage systems, or NAS.

The effects of the high end OLTP and data-centric data warehouse applications accelerated the advancement of I/O architectures within high-end server systems and mainframes. These also spawned the development of increasingly complex distributed processing configurations to support the growth of I/O operations driven by business requirements that called for increasing amounts of data to be available online. These advancements have taken the form of Symmetric Multiprocessing Systems (SMP) and Massive Parallel Processing (MPP) systems. These architectures advanced the I/O capabilities and functionality of traditional computer systems, and as a lasting effect set a foundation for the development of storage area networking.

Distributing Computer Processing

The enhancement to traditional systems architectures by computer designers in meeting the requirements of data-centric applications was to distribute the I/O processing. The efforts in research and design moved I/O further away from the computer elements, (CPU, RAM, and bus connectivity components), which in turn provided an opportunity to increase the number of I/O paths to storage devices.

Symmetric Multiprocessing Systems (SMP)

Symmetric Multiprocessing Systems (SMP) became one of the first alternative designs to offer the use of more than one CPU component, as indicated in Figure 4-1. This first became available with IBM mainframes to increase the throughput scalability and

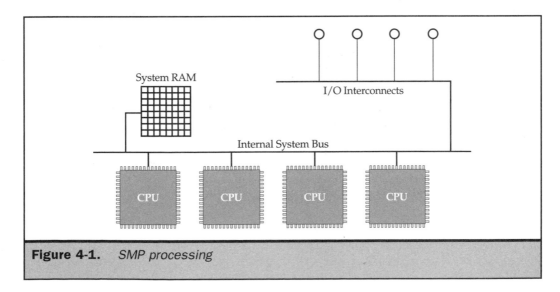

Figure 4-1.   *SMP processing*

processing capabilities by providing additional CPU components. The machines that tightly integrated these features with the operating system (MVS) were known by their design terms of dyadic, triadic, and quadratic, depending on the number of CPUs available on the machine. This further enhanced the processing of IBM mainframe configurations with their available loosely clustered systems of MVS-JES2 and little-known tightly coupled clustered systems of MVS_JES3 (see the Note in this section).

This type of architecture has become widely available through all major system vendors as the SMP designs provided an entry into increased processing power necessary to handle larger applications. However, as with IBM mainframe configurations that are integrated with MVS features and functions, all SMP systems are closely integrated with operating systems features. This is necessary to handle the additional activities of processing with more than a single CPU, sharing memory resources and spaces, and coordination within a shared I/O bus. Although they provide additional processing capacities for large-scale applications, they also bring their own limitations. Two are very apparent in Figure 4-1: the sharing of system RAM and the scalability of the I/O system.

Note   *Multiple Virtual Systems (MVS) is a proprietary operating system offered by IBM and used exclusively with its mainframe computer systems. Available since the middle 1970s, MVS's longevity can partly be attributed to its modular architecture. This allows software subsystems to specialize in particular areas of operation. MVS was early in its move to separate I/O functions into a separate subsystem. In addition, it offers proprietary subsystems of Job Entry Subsystems (providing two alternatives, JES2 and JES3) that provide, among many other functions, the inter-systems communications necessary for a cluster of mainframes to share processing workloads. IBM installations are moving to zOS, an enhanced version of MVS that supports POSIX compliance and open systems standard functionality such as TCP/IP access and web software services.*

Massive Parallel Processing Systems (MPP)

Another advancement from the traditional client/server model was the innovation of Massively Parallel Processing Systems (MPP). These systems enabled multiple computer systems, each specializing in a particular aspect of an application process communicating through a high-speed link. The ability to apply parallel tasks to complex applications provided the processing throughput necessary to complete what was once considered impossible. The MPP architecture evolved into two categories of machines: one for process intensive applications and one for database intensive applications. Each machine category was differentiated by its high-speed link architecture, its integrated database functionality, and configuration flexibility.

The links could be network or switched based (or in some cases a hybrid of both). This link provided a communications network that enabled each node to work on individual processing tasks, while controlling its own systems resources, as illustrated in Figure 4-2. This delineates the node structure within the MPP system whereby each computing node does not share computer resources such as CPU, RAM, or local I/O, thus acquiring the name "Shared Nothing" configurations.

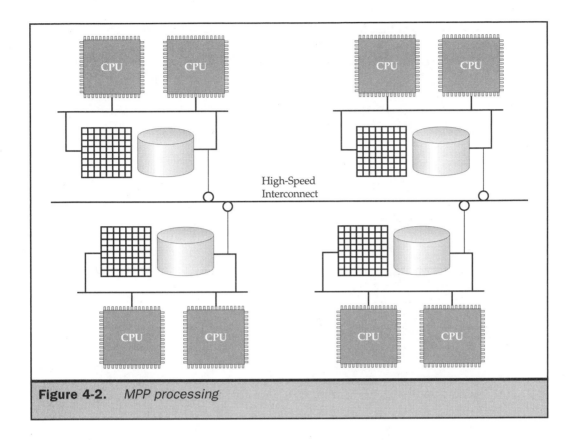

Figure 4-2.   *MPP processing*

Even with the potential that MPP architectures demonstrated, the complexities have proved far greater and limited the proliferation of these machines as general-purpose servers. The complicated enhancements to operating systems communications to enable the coordination of multiple single-image operating systems has proved to be problematic and costly. In addition, the overhead required as increased computing nodes are added increases in a non-linear fashion and consequently limits the effectiveness and throughput. The size, operational complexities, and management challenges of MPP configurations have limited their usage to specialized applications.

Distributing I/O Processing

As advancements were being made in SMP and MPP architectures, storage technologies remained tightly coupled with their computer counterparts. They continued to lag behind processing advancements and followed an I/O execution model of direct attachment to the server regardless of whether it was connected to SMP configurations or MPP processing nodes. However, some advancement was made with shared I/O as evidenced in particular MPP configurations. Sometimes considered the predecessor to the SAN, the "shared nothing" model can be viewed as a logical extension to the MPP parallel environments.

(Additional discussions of the SMP and MPP models of processing and I/O systems can be found in Part II.)

The processing advancements driven by SMP and MPP technologies began to set the foundation for advanced storage architectures. Storage provided the focal point to integrate several innovations such as an enhanced I/O channel protocol, a high-speed interconnection, and "shared nothing" architecture to support the ever increasing need for data access resulting from exponential increases in data size.

An Enhanced I/O Protocol—Fibre Channel

Fibre Channel is a layered connectivity standard, as illustrated in Figure 4-3. It demonstrates the channel characteristics of an I/O bus, the flexibility of a network, and the scalability potential of MIMD computer architectures.

> **Note**   *MIMD stands for Multi-Instruction Multi-Data. It defines a computer design taxonomy in which multiple instructions can be executed against multiple data sources. Although synonymous with MPP computer configurations, the MIMD operations can also be supported by SMP configurations where application tasks are processing in parallel by multiple CPUs operating on multiple data sources. Because MPP configurations are made up of discrete computers, their I/O scalability is much greater than SMP configurations that must share I/O operations across a single bus configuration.*

In implementation, fibre channel uses a serial connectivity scheme that allows for the highest-level bandwidth of any connectivity solution available today, 10gigbit. This architecture allows for implementations to reach as high as 200MB/sec burst rate for I/O operations, with aggregate rates depending on workload and network latency considerations. Regardless of the latency issues, this is a tremendous enhancement to throughput over traditional bus connectivity.

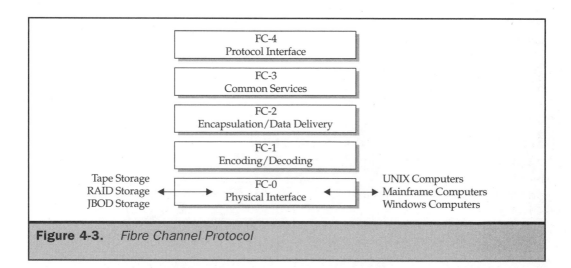

Figure 4-3.   *Fibre Channel Protocol*

A High-Speed Interconnect—Switched Fabric Network

FC operates on a serial link design and uses a packet type of approach for encapsulation of the user data. FC transmits and receives these data packets through the node participants within the fabric. Figure 4-4 shows a simplified view of the FC fabric transmission from server node to storage node. The packets shipped by FC are called frames and are made up of header information, including addresses, the user data at an incredible 2,048 bytes, 2k bytes per frame, and ERC information.

"Shared Nothing" Architecture

As we discussed earlier in Chapter 2, these systems form the foundation for Massively Parallel Processing (MPP) systems. Each node is connected to a high-speed interconnect and communicates with all nodes within the system (see Figure 4-5). These self-contained computer nodes work together, or in parallel, on a particular workload. These systems generally have nodes that specialize in particular operations, such as database query parsing and preprocessing for input services. Other nodes share the search for data within a database that is distributed among nodes specializing in data access and ownership. The sophistication of these machines sometimes outweighs their effectiveness, given that they require a multi-image operating system, for example an OS on each node, sophisticated database, and storage functions to partition the data throughout the configuration, and finally, the speed, latency, and throughput of the interconnect. In these systems, both workload input processing and data acquisition can be performed in parallel, providing significant throughput increases.

Each of these seemingly disparate technologies evolved separately: fabrics coming from developments in the network industry, Fibre Channel resulting from work on scientific device interconnects, and "shared nothing" architectures arising from parallel processing advancements and developments in the VLDB technologies. Directing these technologies toward storage formed an entirely new network that provides all the benefits of a fabric, the enhanced performance of frame-level protocols within Fibre

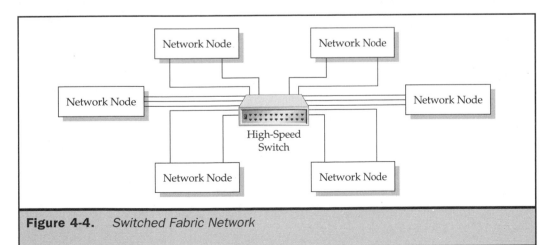

Figure 4-4.   *Switched Fabric Network*

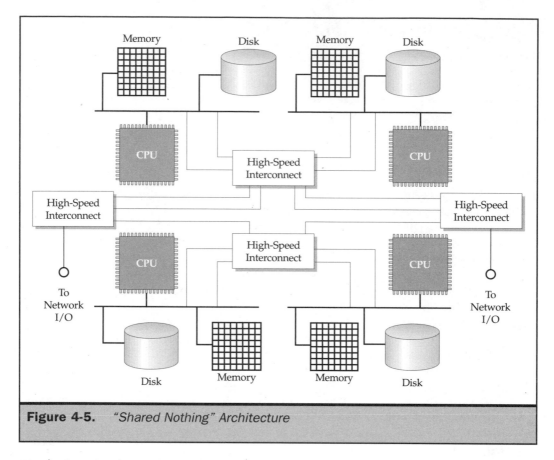

Figure 4-5.   *"Shared Nothing" Architecture*

Channel, and the capability for multiple application and storage processing nodes to communicate and share resources.

The SAN Idea

Direct connect storage in the client/server storage model proved to have limitations in bandwidth, the maximum number of devices available on a bus, and concurrency of traffic. Attaching application servers and Fibre Channel storage devices to a central location creates a network of server and storage devices. This configuration allows the application servers to access the storage devices in a network fashion. In other words, the devices, both servers and storage, must have an address on the network, have the capability to log in, and have methods available to communicate with other devices within the network.

As depicted in Figure 4-6, servers and storage devices participate in the network. All devices log in to the network, or fabric OS, which is done by sending messages through Fibre Channel protocol frames.

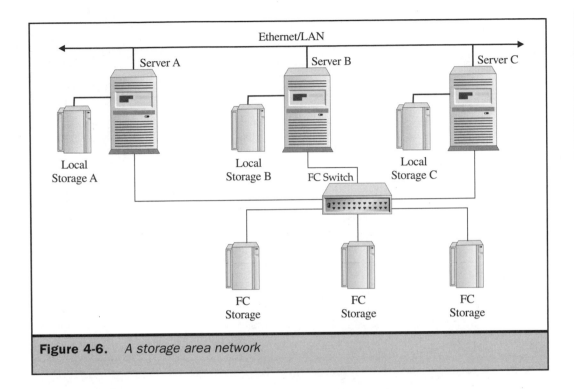

Figure 4-6.   *A storage area network*

SAN Evolution and Development

The first stage of SAN evolution was the development of Fibre Channel (FC)-based storage devices used with direct connections, or a point-to-point configuration. These storage devices used FC addressing to process requests to and from the connected devices, presumably a storage array attached to a server. Although this enhanced the bandwidth of transferred data, FC devices had the capacity to handle 100 MBps, and were limited to the two devices within the point-to-point configuration. Although this worked well and used the existing device communications of SCSI commands, it proved restrictive in regards to the growth of large storage infrastructures.

As shown in Figure 4-7, the second stage employed arbitrated loop architectures, letting more devices participate through the use of FC Hubs. This allowed storage devices to continue operating within an arbitration scheme to share bandwidth, but allowed additional devices to participate within a network fashion. Although this worked better than point-to-point solutions, the overhead necessary to mediate the Hub, adding additional devices within the loops required sharing the bandwidth and thus sacrificed much of the high-speed efficiencies gained with FC devices.

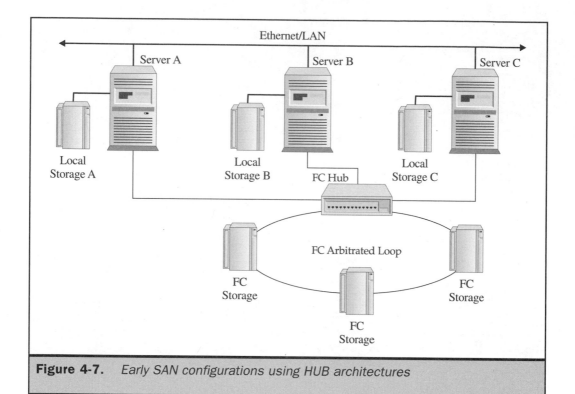

Figure 4-7.   *Early SAN configurations using HUB architectures*

The most current state of SAN configuration is the switched fabric network, as shown in Figure 4-8. This configuration allows "any-to-any" device communications to take place within the network. Each device participating within the network gets full use of 100 MBps bandwidth without sacrificing its performance as other devices are added. Minimal overhead to moving FC frames through the network is accomplished through an FC network switch.

Switched Network allowed a significant increase in the number of devices connected with the network. This allowed for servers and storage devices to be connected in a network fashion and communicate bidirectionally in an "any-to-any" manner.

An Operational Overview of SAN

SANs are constructed with many new components from the storage network. The foundation is the FC switch, which provides the physical connection that allows "any-to-any" communications within the fabric. SAN switches provide the hardware and software foundations needed to facilitate the network—the hardware itself being composed of ports that permit the connection of FC-based devices, such as storage arrays and servers.

To participate in the storage network servers requires a special host adapter, similar to a network adapter known as an FC Host Bus Adapter (HBA). The HBAs supply the

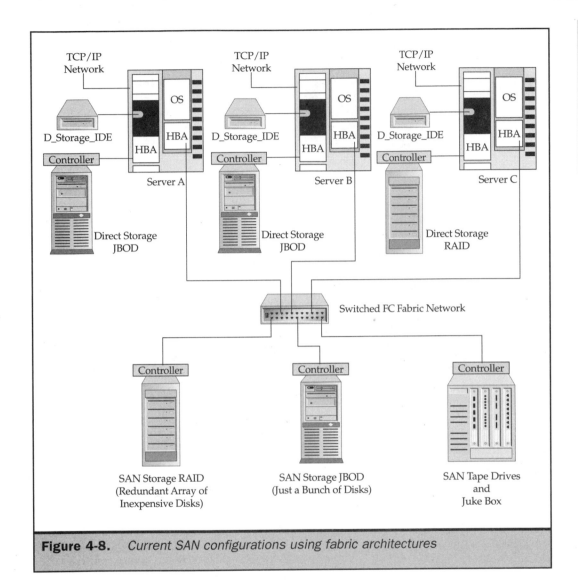

Figure 4-8.   *Current SAN configurations using fabric architectures*

storage network drivers that allow the server to communicate with the switch and
ultimately log in and communicate with storage devices.

Finally, storage devices used with the fabric must be FC-compliant devices (that is,
they must speak FC to communicate with the network). As with Ethernet networks,
early users of SANs required the use of bridges and routers to allow traditional storage
devices (such as tape drives) to participate within the fabric. These devices translated
FC protocols to SCSI bus level protocols, basically breaking frames down into bus
segments so a SCSI-level device (such as a tape drive) could be connected to the FC
fabric network.

SANs for Data Access

As more paths to data become available, so does the theoretical limit of users accessing that data. SANs have the capability to increase the number of paths to the data by way of the number of actual I/O paths, or through the actual transfer of data to the application and, subsequently, the user. If we add up the FC's capability to operate at gigabit speeds, the SANs' capacity to support a large user base becomes apparent. An example is depicted in Figure 4-9.

SANs for Data Size

The best example for dealing with size is data warehouses. As described in Chapter 1, these datacentric applications have extreme data storage requirements in terms of the number of bytes of online storage. What makes these applications particularly difficult to configure is the complexity involved in processing the data and the movement of large subsets of data to source and process complex transactions. Figure 4-10 shows the use of SANs to enhance a particular data warehouse application in terms of the size of databases involved. This also pertains to SANs data movement activities, which are accomplished while maintaining a service level.

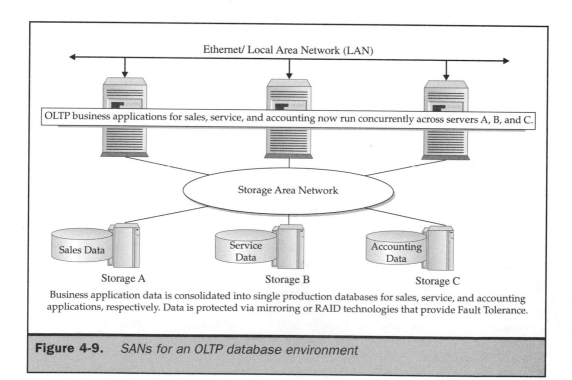

Figure 4-9.   *SANs for an OLTP database environment*

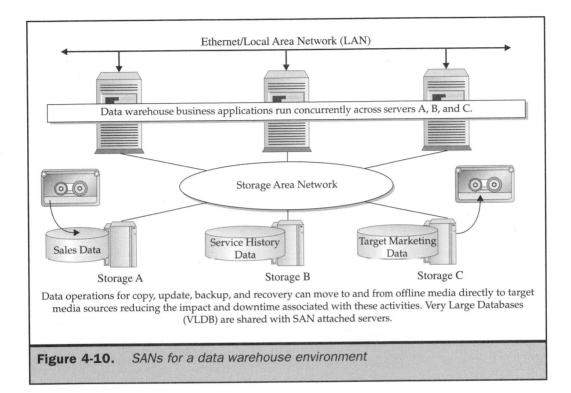

Figure 4-10. *SANs for a data warehouse environment*

The Caveats for SAN

The caveats for SAN are several. The main issues of complexity and cost center around the heterogeneous nature of the SAN itself. Because SANs are configured with several discrete components (see Figure 4-5), the complexity of configuration and implementation becomes a challenge.

Cost becomes an issue as the SAN devices remain fairly new to storage infrastructure markets and therefore have not reached commodity-pricing status. It's also important to note the rapid change due to the relative immaturity of the products, and the reliance on other areas of technologies such as Operating Systems, storage devices, and management software. The associated cost in terms of user knowledge and training in new technologies that make up the SAN—such as switches, fabrics, Fibre Channel, and HBAs—contribute to this caveat.

However, an often-overlooked challenge is the esoteric nature of the logical extensions of a server's software that deals with storage. File systems, volume managers, and physical I/O operations all play necessary roles in performing storage operations. Within the SAN, these operations become more logical and have to coexist with other servers that share the fabric network and devices connected. I/O functions must extend into the fabric itself and operate through Fibre Channel software, storage software, and device micro-code, all being remote to the server. These new software functions encapsulated within the FC fabric (some of them user accessible and some micro-code enabled) drive the next logical caveat: management.

Management of the SAN remains problematic even though new products and solutions continue to appear. However, this scenario of rapid change, due to the newness of the technology, largely renders only management solutions, which in the end will be merely transient given that SANs will continue to outgrow their simple configurations, add significant new functions from software vendors, and become integrated with other network and server technologies.

On the other hand, SANs provides the next generation of scalable solutions for large-scale enterprise applications. The SAN architecture supports environments that require scalable solutions for large user populations that access datacentric (that is, database-driven) information that has read/write volatility. This has proven itself within the enterprise data centers where SANs are the solution of choice given their capability to handle large amounts of data, using applications such as OLTP and Data Warehousing. In addition, customers who are dealing with large volumes of unstructured data (such as audio, video, and static images) are migrating to SANs to support these applications.

In discussing both the NAS and SAN architectures in summary fashion, a more thorough picture of the components that make them up will come to light. How these technologies operate, as well as how to apply their value to solutions within data center settings, will be discussed in greater detail in Parts V and VI.

The
Complete
Reference

Storage
Networks

Part II

Storage Fundamentals

Chapter 5

Storage Architectures

In Part II, we will review the basic elements and devices that make up computer storage. Although the level of information will be summary in detail, these are the components you are likely to encounter in dealing with changes to storage infrastructures brought on by storage networking. In many instances, it will be these devices, their performance, and logical configurations that are overlooked as they extend beyond the bounds of typical storage systems. As such, they are critical factors when addressing issues affecting storage performance. More importantly are the effects these elements, devices, and components will have when integrating storage networking into your infrastructure.

In Part I, the decoupling of storage devices caused us to reevaluate the necessary functions to develop an optimum data highway to the server. This quickly becomes a complex task as some storage devices become remotely connected, such as disks and disk controllers. With the introduction of networking and switching technologies, their capabilities and functionality begins to change and their operation with other components that transport data to and from the CPU can become compromised. However, understanding how data travels in traditional direct connect configurations can be complex in and of itself. It is imperative that these situations are understood both in context with data center practices and storage device principles of operations, prior to an in-depth discussion of storage networking.

Storage Elements

Storage can be defined as the components and locations where data is staged before and after it is accessed by the computer's central processing unit (CPU). The components that make up specific storage devices in today's computers are multifold, however they still have one main objective. They move data in the most efficient manner in and out of the CPU to process application program instructions.

The storage locations are multifunctional in usage and multidimensional in capacity. Figure 5-1 depicts the locations where data is stored for action by the CPU. Although you wouldn't expect to classify some of these locations as storage, their purpose is to provide a location for data, albeit temporary in many cases, before or after operation by the CPU. A parochial view of hard disk or archival storage does not take into account all the components involved in transporting data to and from processing objectives. By gaining a complete understanding of all storage locations, we systemically address all the elements that affect the supply of data to the CPU and therefore the system's potential, improving application program performance and storage device optimization.

Storage locations are characterized by their volatility and temporary nature. This is demonstrated through their effect on the data stored within each storage component. Data stored on hard magnetic disk, tape, or optical is considered non-volatile and therefore stores data permanently in context with its logical form—for example, a customer file, binary program, or an image. In contrast to these devices, there are the components such as system level cache, controller cache, memory buffers, and disk read/write

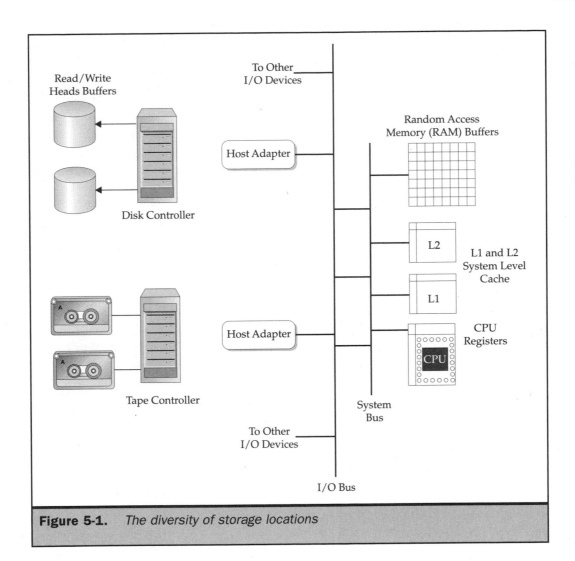

Figure 5-1. *The diversity of storage locations*

cache-buffers that are highly volatile. These components are used for only temporary locations and are staged in physical locations in increasing proximity to the CPU. The nearest component to the CPU is the fastest, and thus it is more volatile with the data it transports.

Component speed and CPU proximity drive the balance between slower and faster elements that make up this store and forward like architecture. As we saw in Figure 5-1, many of the faster components are necessary to account for the slower performance of others. Moving data into position to be accessible by the CPU requires staging areas such as system level cache so that CPU processing does not have to wait for a slow mechanical device such as a disk drive to transport a copy of its data to the CPU. The same can be said for the reverse operations; once the CPU has completed its instructions, it can use a staging area such as system level cache so it does not have to wait for the write operation to be complete out to the slower disk drive or be forced to wait the time it takes to flush and rewrite the buffer space in memory.

The corollary, or trade-off to this condition, is the economics of speed and capacity to price. Consequently, the faster the component, the higher the price for parking data. An example of the dynamics of price difference can be found in the comparison of solid-state disks (SSD) versus magnetic disks. Each can perform similar functions, however the SSD made up of logic circuits from silicon wafers in the form of a chip is much more expensive than its counterpart, the magnetic disk, which operates using mechanical devices and electronics on magnetic media. Although each stores data, the SSD device, operating electronically within a chip, is exponentially faster than the mechanical operation of the magnetic disk. Although there are many examples within the storage hierarchy, the point is the following: it becomes economically prohibitive to store large capacities on higher performing components.

Although it's possible to load small databases into the main memory of large machines, you still have the problem of keeping the permanent copy up to date in case of hardware or software error or system termination. Therefore, we find the additional corollary to speed and capacity is reliability. As system outages occur, the temporary storage locations are flushed or cleared, at which point the potential for data loss is imminent, and for most users, unacceptable. Therefore, recovery of the data that was contained within these storage locations has to be taken into account. This becomes especially challenging as we discover that some storage components are accessed remotely as networks are introduced into the connectivity scheme. As a result, many components (such as controller caches) become shared. We will examine in more detail the capability to recover various storage elements within these conditions later in Part IV, and how they will become critical design factors in Part III, regarding both NAS and SANs.

Data Storage Hierarchy

The benefits of understanding all the elements of storage is that it begins to form a foundation for working with data volatility and the effective use of the multifunctional components that data must traverse to satisfy the application. As previously stated, the effect these components have on system and application performance, such as controller cache and a disk's average access response time performance can be the difference between effective utilization strategies and overcompensation for device inefficiencies. With this knowledge, the traditional data storage hierarchy (as shown in Figure 5-2) takes on new and challenging characteristics.

The data storage hierarchy extends from the CPU to the storage media. The following highlights some of the major components that make up this data highway:

■ **CPU Registers**   The component of the central processing unit that stores program instructions and intermediate, prestage, and post operations data.

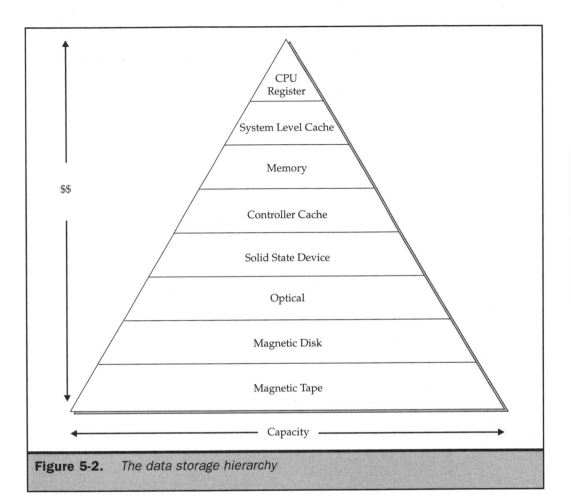

Figure 5-2.   *The data storage hierarchy*

- ■ **First Level L1 Cache**   The component that provides a data staging area closest to the central processing unit; employed for prestaging and post-staging data used by the CPU instructions.

- ■ **Second Level L2 Cache**   The component that provides additional data staging areas to the CPU, but which are further away and which act as supplements to the L1 cache component.

- ■ **Memory Buffers**   Locations within the memory where data is staged for pre and post-processing by CPU instructions.

- ■ **Direct Memory Access (DMA)**   A component that allows peripherals to transfer data directly into and out of computer memory, bypassing processor activities.

- **Host Adapter Cache/Buffer**   The component within a device adapter that provides staging for data that is being read or written to disk storage components.

- **Hard Disk Controller Cache/Buffer**   An additional component that provides another staging area for read data that is waiting to move into the memory or L2 or L1 cache, or waiting to be written into locations within the disk storage media.

- **Hard Disk**   The component that provides a permanent location for system and application data slated to be stored for access by system and applications programs.

- **Archival Storage**   The locations where data is stored for later use. This may be for archiving historical data no longer needed for business or systems applications, or for copies of business or systems data needed for recovery operations in the event of system outages or other computer disasters.

Storage Systems

Storage systems have been evolving to logical stand-alone extensions to the client/server processing architecture (refer to Chapters 1 and 2). Consequently, we have storage systems that are larger, in terms of floor space, than the servers they connect to, and costlier, in terms of dollars with software and IT administration. Storage infrastructure costs make up nearly 75 percent of the cost of a client/server configuration. Why? Because we require more and more data to be available online—in other words, to be available to the end users through some form of interactive application. The result is more disks being attached to the client/server model. With the increase in the number of devices, the resulting complexity in meeting these demands is enabled through the Data Storage Hierarchy.

So, what makes up storage systems for the data center? There are multiple components that make up the storage infrastructure that has evolved into a highway for moving data. As discussed previously, the objective for these components has not changed— that is, they are used to stage data as close to the central processing units as possible, and as we have demonstrated, extend the storage highway into the servers themselves. This can drive the boundaries of the traditional views of storage into new perspectives and extend the discussion of what makes up storage systems for the data center. For our discussion, we have simplified our taxonomy to encompass the major functional configurations in which storage systems are deployed. To accomplish this, we have included in our examples the components that continued to be housed in the server. By way of definition and illustration, we have also added a new definition to our discussion, the workload. Consider Figure 5-3 when viewing our examples.

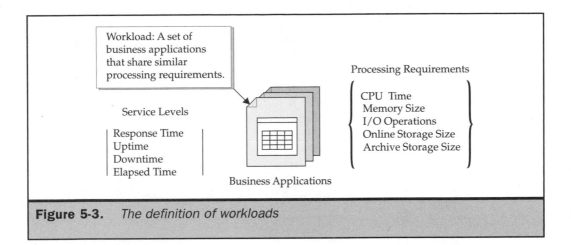

Figure 5-3.   *The definition of workloads*

Typical Storage System Configurations

Online storage systems define a variety of configurations used to support applications that require immediate access to business and systems data, as shown in Figure 5-4. These configurations form the basis for support of many of the additional workloads required to operate the data center.

OLTP Workload and Typical Configurations

Online Transaction Processing (OLTP) storage systems are configured with high-performance storage hardware and software components to support business applications in processing transactions in a real-time setting. These environments employ a predefined end-user response time that has a prescribed set of business data operating within several conditional states.

Application performance is expressed as service levels within the data center. Service levels are guarantees or targets defined between end-user and data center management. These generally consist of elements of application availability (up time) and performance (response time). Additional information and discussion can be found in Part VI.

Batch Workload and Typical Configurations

Batch processing storage systems are configured to support applications that are processed in a background fashion and which don't support end-user access, but that nonetheless require immediate access to business and systems data to meet a predefined elapsed time interval for processing. These environments are often highly integrated with OLTP

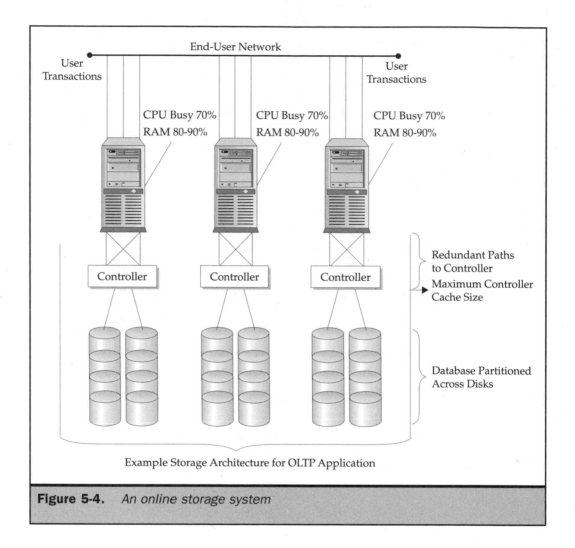

Figure 5-4.   *An online storage system*

environments and process data captured as a result of the OLTP system, as shown in Figure 5-5. However, unlike OLTP systems, they are usually optimized toward high throughput without regard to transactional service levels or response times. Additional discussions in Part VI will address the interaction between batch and OLTP workloads and the impact they can have on their respective service levels.

Archival Storage

Archival storage depicts a system used to support applications that archive business and systems data no longer needed for online applications, or the copies of business and

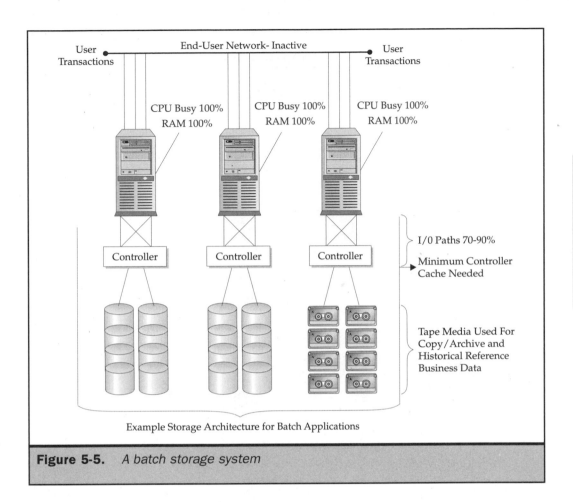

Example Storage Architecture for Batch Applications

Figure 5-5.   *A batch storage system*

systems data needed for recovery operations in the event of system outages, data corruption, or disaster planning.

Data Protection Configurations

Data protection storage systems are configured to support maintenance applications that copy data in both logical and segmented forms for later reconstruction. Most are processed in a background fashion and therefore don't support end-user access, but nonetheless require immediate access to business and systems data to meet predefined elapsed time intervals for processing. These environments are often highly integrated with both OLTP and batch environments and provide recovery of business and systems data in the event of various system outages. These systems are usually optimized toward high throughput without regard to transactional service levels or response times, as shown in Figure 5-6.

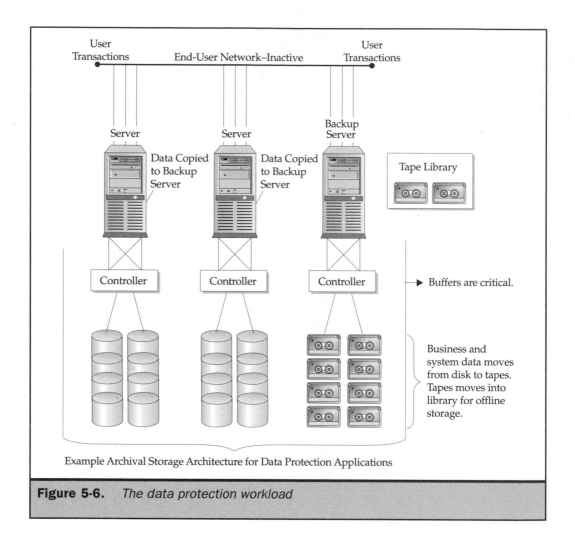

Example Archival Storage Architecture for Data Protection Applications

Figure 5-6. *The data protection workload*

Near-Line Storage Configurations

Hierarchical Storage Management (HSM) storage systems (illustrated in Figure 5-7) typically support OLTP applications but are configured with lower performance, and higher capacity, storage hardware, and software components. These systems support a business application's capability to process transactions in a near-real time setting, meaning that some user transactions are asynchronous and can take longer to complete as compared to real-time OLTP response times. However, these environments run with a predefined end-user response time, that although longer, runs with a prescribed set of business data that operates within several conditional states.

STORAGE FUNDAMENTALS

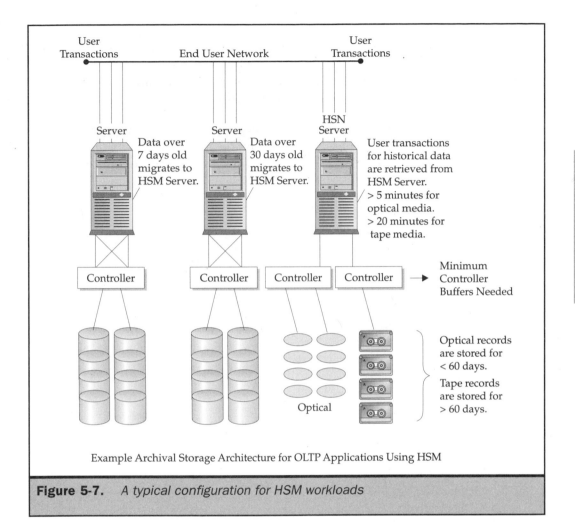

Example Archival Storage Architecture for OLTP Applications Using HSM

Figure 5-7.   *A typical configuration for HSM workloads*

In all fairness to the complexities of large data centers, these systems, in practice, are integrated within the existing production configurations. For example, in most cases the online storage configuration that supports the OLTP application is the same one that supports the batch cycle during an off-shift cycle. Whether this is the most effective for batch workloads is a discussion of our first corollary: speed and capacity versus price. The archive system is often integrated into systems that support some level of HSM or near-line system. Again, whether it interferes with backup jobs run at night is a discussion of our second corollary: speed and capacity versus reliability.

Consequently, when evaluating storage systems, one must take into account the multifunction requirements placed upon it. The likelihood that the most end-user sensitive configurations, such as OLTP- and HSM-like workloads, will take precedence in resources and administration is quite high. These are the systems that generally provide support for the end user's day-to-day business operations and which bring visibility to its customers.

With our global definitions and typical workloads, the online storage (OLTP) configurations will form the primary foundation for the storage infrastructure. This will be enhanced and augmented with other, albeit less time-sensitive applications, such as HSM supported applications, the application batch cycle, and last but not least, the archival of data, backup, and recovery jobs necessary for data protection, disaster planning, and legal purposes.

The Complete Reference

Storage Networks

Chapter 6

Device Overviews

Magnetic disks form the foundation of online storage systems. These devices are augmented in storage architectures with magnetic tape, enabling an economical and enduring media for storing historical information. Additional storage technologies such as solid-state disks and optical devices play both specialized and enabling roles that support these two fundamental storage devices. Although the concepts in this chapter may seem elementary in nature, the mastery of these storage principles are an integral part of understanding how to apply these basic storage components optimally when designing and implementing a storage network.

Storage architectures must support various, and at times, disparate business applications. These applications demonstrate various I/O requirements that place a demand on the storage devices. The specific I/O requirements for the application are referred to as an I/O workload (more information about I/O workloads can be found in Chapter 17). The understanding of storage at the device level will contribute to developing an entire storage system that forms the critical basis for all application performance.

Application systems designed with the supporting storage devices in context with workloads begin to develop into responsive infrastructures. Without device knowledge and consideration, storage systems often form monolithic storage farms that dictate a one size fits all approach. Such conditions set the stage for unresponsive and costly application performance. With today's Plug and Play implementation frenzy, the thought and analysis given aligning compatible storage devices with storage workloads is generally an afterthought (more information regarding workload planning for storage networks are contained in Part V and Chapters 21 and 22).

Peripheral Connectivity Components and Concepts

Peripheral devices are conceptually defined as those computer elements that are not part of the computer's motherboard but must attach to the periphery of this self-contained system. Storage peripheral devices are connected using two distinct functions, the host adapter and the controller. Although at times they are integrated into one device, the distinctions between the two, though often fuzzy, are required for all storage attachment. These devices are depicted in Figure 6-1, which illustrates their proximity to the main computer system. The basic functionality of the host adapter allows peripheral devices to connect to a server's internal bus system. The controller's basic function, although it has many, allows multiple devices to communicate through one adapter path. Together they form the connectivity structure of a server's I/O system.

This encompasses all devices that process I/O from the server to include storage, but also printers, plotters, graphic displays, keyboards, and other devices that interact and are directly connected to the system. For our discussion, we will focus on storage devices. However, we will devote a portion of our discussion to network connectivity adapters given their integration and importance in developing storage networks.

A short discussion about network connectivity can provide an important set of principles that encompass the functions of direct device connectivity and how networks interface with the server. As shown in Figure 6-2, the Network Interface Card (NIC)

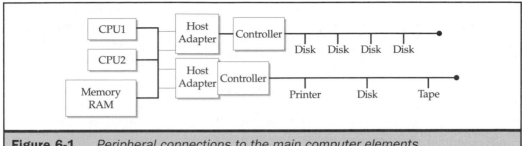

Figure 6-1. *Peripheral connections to the main computer elements*

connects the system bus to the external network, be it a local area network (LAN) or a wide area network (WAN). The components are the same as with any host adapter; it consists of an electronics card that connects to the server motherboard or a backplane.

This is supported by a set of related software that interacts with the low-level hardware protocols and the operating system, sometimes referred to as firmware or microcode. Firmware refers to software instructions that interact directly with microprocessor components. These instructions are specific to the type of microprocessor being used and generally not accessible to users.

Note *A backplane is a type of connector circuit board where the board has no other circuitry than to connect together bus slots or connectors. Thus, an entire computer system can reside on a motherboard that can connect into a backplane for common I/O attachment. Refer to blade computing, high-end SMP, and shared I/O configurations in Chapter 7 and Appendix D.*

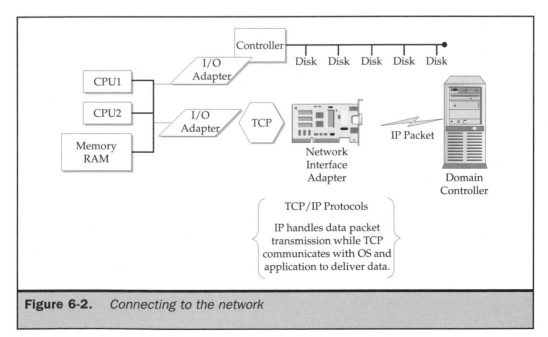

Figure 6-2. *Connecting to the network*

The functions of the Network Interface Card (NIC) are to transmit the identity of the server to the network, receive messages addressed to the server, and translate the network protocols to pass on to the operating system components. The user or application data and instructions encapsulated within the networking protocols can now be used by the server's applications.

On the out-bound side, the reverse takes place. The application turns over its data and target location to the operating system, which works with the NIC software drivers to encapsulate the data and ensure it's transmitted in the correct way to the network.

The network software that enables this communicates and works with the NIC in TCP (Transmission Control Protocol) or IP (Internet Protocol). Together they form what is called the TCP/IP software layers, or stacks—the open systems standard used by all computer manufacturers to communicate within networks. As previously illustrated, we can view TCP/IP simply as the message format and envelope, where TCP allows the application and operating system to encapsulate the user data while the IP portion contains the envelope that transports the data to its network target locations.

As discussed previously, all peripheral devices have a host adapter and controller component. This concept, although viewed somewhat more abstractly in networks, is the same. However, to place this in its proper perspective we must view the other devices in the network as being externally connected, be they servers or clients. That means the controller functionality in networks consists of switches and routers that interconnect the multiple devices—in this case, other computers that are attached to the network.

Figure 6-3 extends the network diagram into the area of controllers, with switches, routers, telephone exchange equipment, and other WAN-related communication devices.

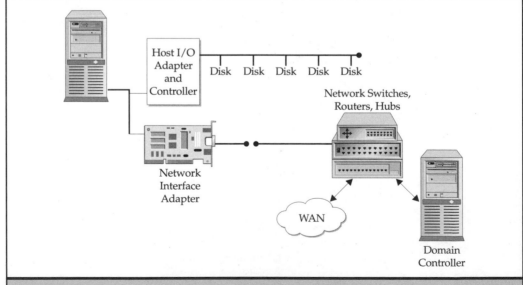

Figure 6-3.   *Overview of connectivity inside the network*

As indicated in this illustration, the equipment and software that make up the network are numerous; however, none of it needs to be known by the server or client, other than the network address. We have seen the high-level benefits and configurations when this concept is extended into storage components. Unlike traditional transient network traffic, storage I/O operations require a more defined protocol using the same host adapter and controller concepts.

The Host Adapter

The host adapter connects the computer's system bus to the external pathway where various devices are attached. In many cases, this is another bus technology, one that specializes in communicating with specific device types and which requires unique commands to perform I/O operations with the server. Host adapters consist of two main components. First is a hardware component, generally in the form of electronic cards that attach to the server motherboard or backplane (more about bus connectivity in Chapter 7). Just as important is the related software component that allows the specific devices to drive the underlying hardware bus protocols, the operating system, and, ultimately, the application.

The combined components, as shown in Figure 6-4, consist of microcode that functions within the electronic card circuitry, microcode of the basic input/output (BIOS) that exists on the computer's motherboard, and high-level software that executes on the computer. The high-level software (commonly called drivers) works with the hardware microcode to provide the device command set (native I/O calls), services for the device, the operating system interface, and error recovery and checking routines. All of these functions communicate with the operating system through the BIOS microcode embedded in the computer's motherboard. Any device utility software running on the computer will use the same native software.

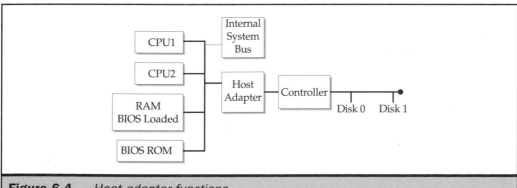

Figure 6-4.   *Host adapter functions*

Host adapters are provided as bundled solutions from storage vendors, or piecemeal through a host of hardware vendors. This requires the configuration activities to be both challenging and creative. Regardless of how the solution is acquired, the configurations are pretty standard, albeit limited. First, there are only so many host adapters you can attach to a server. This is a function of the server itself and, more specifically, the bus technology within the server. Second is the effect of multiple software drivers that can operate within a single server system—which means that having multiple vendor software drivers can become risky, given the different implementation that occurs within the division between the hardware (for example, the microcode) and the high-level software driver executing within the server.

This requires a homogeneous approach to implementation—in other words, a common vendor solution to host adapters running on a single server. In addition, the number of adapters available for an individual server—more specifically, the server's bus—defines the high end of paths that can be physically configured for directly connected I/O peripherals. This presents a theoretical limiting factor in storage sizes given the type of workload.

The number of paths, as depicted by Figure 6-5, shows the limitations of single path configurations when dealing with even medium-sized databases. Other components within the storage hierarchy will also be affected.

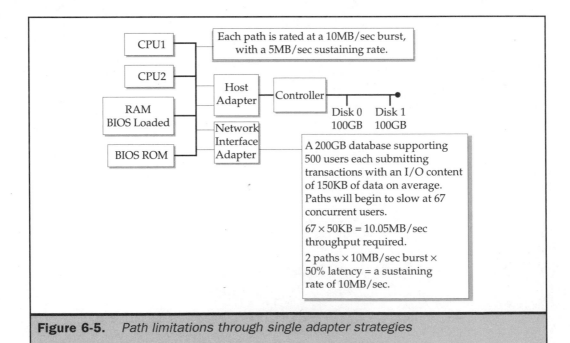

Figure 6-5. *Path limitations through single adapter strategies*

The Controller

The controller allows multiple devices to be connected to the adapter. As the adapter forms the primary path to and from the server, the controller provides the connectivity to the actual devices that communicate with the server. As indicated in Figure 6-6, the controller functions can be manifold but primarily control the flow of data to and from the devices. In doing so, it provides an addressing scheme for the devices, shields the server from the operational complexities of the device, and provides another temporary location for data (prior to it being written or cached) for faster access.

Like adapters, controllers consist of both hardware and software components. However, their primary functionality is driven by hardware microcode, as indicated in Figure 6-6.

By keeping track of a disk's position and being the initiator of the drive's read/write electronics (see the next section for more details on magnetic head disk assemblies, referred to as *HDA* mechanisms), the controller provides data buffering between the disk and the host interface or adapter with its error detection, correction, retry, and recovery functions. Both of these functions are susceptible to changes in connectivity due to their communications with the operating system.

The controller also offers the system's attached disks as an acceptable storage location even though the actual physical mapping may be very different. This allows the controller to translate I/O system requests into actual physical commands that can be executed on the real disk drive. Typical in most systems, the controllers and operating system view the disk drive locations as a linear pool of logical locations. This level of abstraction translation, though having existed in I/O configurations for many years, is necessary to translate logical blocks of data into physical addresses on the storage media.

This is a key concept within the controller functionality. It demonstrates how the operating system communicates within a logical set of storage locations that are considered virtual to the controller, which translates those locations into the physical realities the controller must manage. Figure 6-7 represents an overview of how logical views are mapped into physical views.

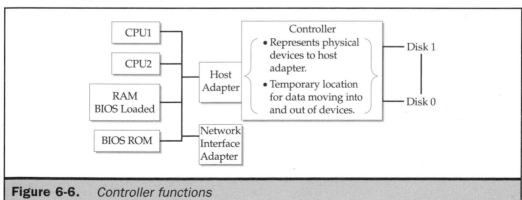

Figure 6-6. *Controller functions*

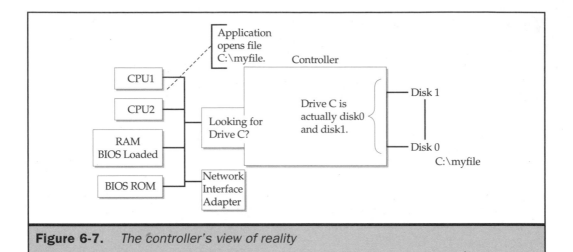

Figure 6-7.   *The controller's view of reality*

Magnetic Disk Storage

Magnetic disk storage is the packaging of magnetic media disks, packaged read/write head electronics on a spinning electro-mechanical device. Disks are made up of round platters coated with a magnetic material that can be written and read electronically through the encoding of the magnetic media with binary data.

Figure 6-8 shows the platters that make up the magnetic media and the read/write electronics that surround the disks, all of which resembles old analogue record players. The read/write electronics are recording heads that both read and write data. As discussed previously, the head assembly can house data buffers that compensate for delays in reading or writing data.

The platters are organized into tracks, concentric rings that form the writable surface of the platter. These are further divided into sectors which form the smallest readable/writable units on the disk. As the disk rotates, portions of the sectors become visible as the read/write heads are positioned to that track.

Drives are made up of more than one disk, with each storing data on both sides. Each surface must have its own read/write head and a set of tracks which can be accessed through a single position (for instance, when vertically aligned). This is called a cylinder. Given this organization, every sector on the drive can be uniquely addressed by its cylinder, head, and sector numbers.

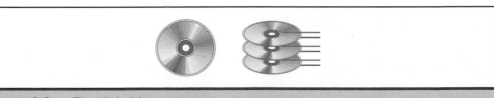

Figure 6-8.   *The disk drive anatomy*

Sectors are important because they are the fundamental metric that determines the size of data stored within the disk. The number of bytes in a sector corresponds to the disk's formatted capacity. As indicated in Figure 6-8, the sector must contain information about addresses and synchronizing HDA error corrections in the header fields. Given that the header and associated synchronization gaps are not usable for data, the formatted capacity is always less. Formatting a drive writes the header information and arbitrary data pattern to verify correct error checking. Although entire drives are normally formatted at one time, a technique called *soft sectoring* allows a single track or hard sector to be formatted.

Technical specifications that surround disks include the capacity, transfer rate, and average access time. Each metric is important when considering the given workload supported. While capacity may be an issue, the number of transactions necessary to read data from the disk may compromise seek time. On the other hand, large transfers of data (like that used by datacentric applications in data warehousing) may push capacity and transfer rates to their optimum while sacrificing average seek time.

Capacity, as mentioned previously, comes in two forms: formatted and unformatted. As you've probably guessed, the larger the disk, the greater the amount of addressing and error correction code (ECC) overhead, thereby reducing space for actual user data.

Transfer rate and throughput refers to the speed at which the HDA processes read and write operations. Throughput is the amount of data the drive can deliver or accept at the interface on a sustained basis. This is important because the term "interface" can have many connotations and implementations.

Average access time is the time needed to position the HDA to a specific cylinder, as well as and the time it takes for the requested sector to rotate under the heads. Thus, disk rotation speeds are related to capacity.

Disk Systems

By integrating controllers into the disk assemblies, we begin to have complete storage systems. These come in an amazing amount of configurations and offerings, but the basic model is the attached controller that uses multiple disks drives within the enclosure.

As disk drives are linked together, they form an array. This is used for basic capacity and performance enhancements. Disks configured in this manner can be used individually as Disk1 through Disk4, as shown in Figure 6-9, or they can be used in an integrated fashion by combing the capacities of the array and using them as one large disk. For example, in Figure 6-9, Disk1 through 4 can be combined to form a virtual disk *V* which can use the entire capacity of the array. In this scenario, the application I/O sees disk *V* as one large disk drive even though it's only a virtual representation of the four physical drives. The application and the operating system understands that data can be stored on disk drive *V* and lets the controller take care of where the data is actually written using the pool of disks 1 through 4.

This forms the basis for advanced functionality in storage systems such as Redundant Arrays of Independent Disks (RAID) and the concept of storage virtualization. The functionality of RAID provides disk redundancy, fault tolerant configurations, and data

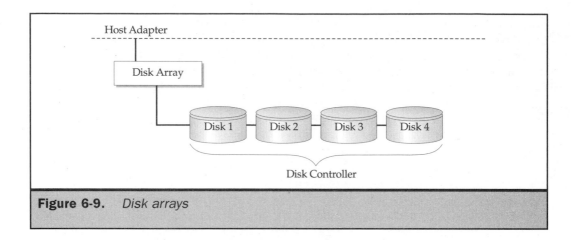

Figure 6-9.   *Disk arrays*

protection resiliency. All this is facilitated through the controller mechanisms discussed previously and illustrated in Figure 6-6. The RAID decoupling of the physical drives from the application software I/O requests has driven the usage and advancement of storage virtualization technologies and products.

Letting the server's operating system believe it has a pool of storage capacity frees up the I/O manager services, allowing it to perform other tasks, and facilitates the development of applications without the low-level coding of specific I/O calls. Remember, there is no such thing as a free lunch and the translation of calls to the virtual pool of data has to be processed either in the storage controller or in the third-party storage software running on the server. It may even be a combination of both. Either way, the overhead continues to exist, although it may be offloaded and rely on RAID processed within the controller.

Disk Arrays

The first level of storage array configuration is JBOD (Just a Bunch Of Disks), depicted in Figure 6-9. JBOD links a set of disk drives together to form an array where each drive becomes an addressable unit. These provide additional capacity; however, they do not provide any fault resiliency in the event of an inoperable drive. Partitioning data throughout the disks and providing a layer of virtualization services can be done through software, which is generally part of the I/O management of the operating system. These functions are also available through third-party software applications.

Although these functions offer a level of data redundancy (depending on the sophistication of the software), they do not provide any method of fault tolerance for continuous operations in the event of a lost disk drive. Consequently, while these guarantee some data loss protection, they do not guarantee that the data remains available even if disk drives become inoperable within the array. Functions that provide continuous operations and fault resiliency are provided by RAID.

RAID Storage Arrays

RAID is, as its name implies, a redundant array of independent disks that becomes an addressable unit made up of separate and independent disk drives (shown in Figure 6-10). The main difference from JBOD arrays is that RAID partitions data throughout the array and recovery functions. The recovery functions are developed using disk parity information that is calculated to reassemble missing data from a failed drive to the remaining drives within the array. The data is distributed throughout the array in a manner most effective to the recovery and protection strategy. RAID has several levels in which these recovery and protection strategies can be implemented.

The various RAID levels of implementation provide recovery and data protection that is appropriate to the application's and user's continuity requirements. This allows for performance, data protection, and automatic recovery from drive failures within the array. RAID has become the de facto standard for disk hardware fault tolerance functions. As an accepted standard, all storage manufacturers offer it; however, all storage vendors have also evolved into a diversity of proprietary functions that define the type of fault tolerant protection offered. These are encapsulated within the storage firmware run on the controller and are referred to as both RAID software functions and RAID firmware.

To make things more confusing, some RAID functions can be provided through software that runs on the server. This differentiation becomes distinct as we look at the standard RAID levels as defined throughout the industry. As such, RAID functionality can be selected either through hardware or software components, or a combination of both.

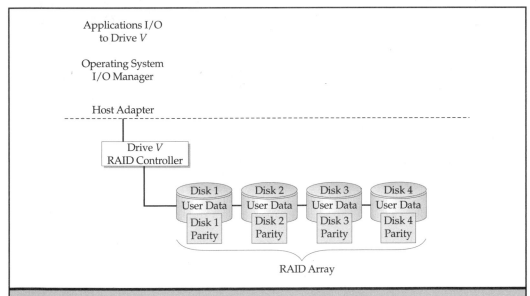

Figure 6-10.   *The basic RAID architecture for a storage array*

RAID configuration levels range from numbers 0 through 5 for basic RAID services; however, extended RAID levels, although proprietary to vendor implementations, have gone beyond basic configurations. Given the numerous options for partitioning data and the diversity of ways that parity information can be calculated and partitioned, the options for RAID can be numerous. Through the evolution of real experiences and exposure to typical applications and I/O workloads, two of the five have proven the most valuable, and therefore are the most popular. These are RAID levels 1 and 5. RAID levels 1 and 5 will most likely be the ones implemented within the data center. However, we will pay particular attention to RAID level 4 as an example of how a vendor can use a proprietary and bundled level.

RAID level 0 simply uses the storage array for partitioning of data without any disk parity information. This provides for data protection without a recovery mechanism should any of the data become unavailable from a failed drive. Many software-only data protection mechanisms use a RAID level 0 configuration, where the data is written to primary and secondary files. Similar to RAID level 1 (mirroring) without any disk recovery mechanism, this is sometimes called software mirroring. In other cases, the data is striped across the disk array for performance reasons. This allows the disk write process to take advantage of several head and disk assembly mechanisms for multiple files with high disk write requirements.

RAID level 1 offers the ability to provide a primary and secondary set of data. As one file is updated, its secondary is also updated, keeping a safe copy for data protection just like RAID level 0. The major difference is the calculation of parity information, as shown in Figure 6-11. This is used in the event a disk drive fails within the RAID array. In that case, the available mirrored copy of the data continues processing. When the drive failure is corrected, the unavailable copy of the mirror is reassembled through the parity information contained within the RAID controller. Theoretically, the data is never unavailable and remains online for the application use.

RAID level 5 is a partitioning of the data across the RAID array for performance purposes. This is depicted in Figure 6-12 along with the complement of disk parity information also striped across the array. In the event of a disk failure, the missing data is reassembled through the parity information processed by the RAID controller. Once the failed disk drive is corrected, the data is reassembled back onto the failed drive and the entire array is back in full operation. Theoretically, the data is never unavailable as in RAID level 1.

RAID levels 2 and 3 are derivatives of mirroring and level 5, and use different strategies for storing the parity information. Although RAID level 4 is also a derivative of level 5, it provides striping across the array of user data, and reserves a disk within the array for processing of parity data (shown in Figure 6-13). This is used in some NAS solutions where the storage is bundled and the RAID array processing is hardcoded within the package—in other words, you don't have the option to move to other RAID levels.

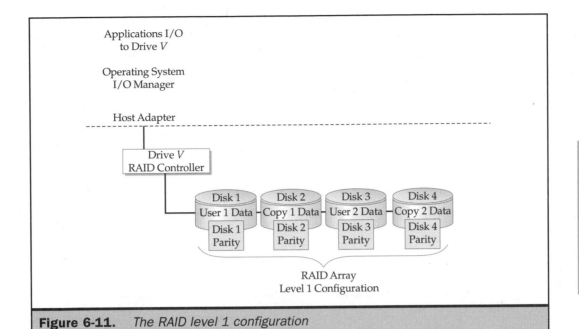

Figure 6-11.   *The RAID level 1 configuration*

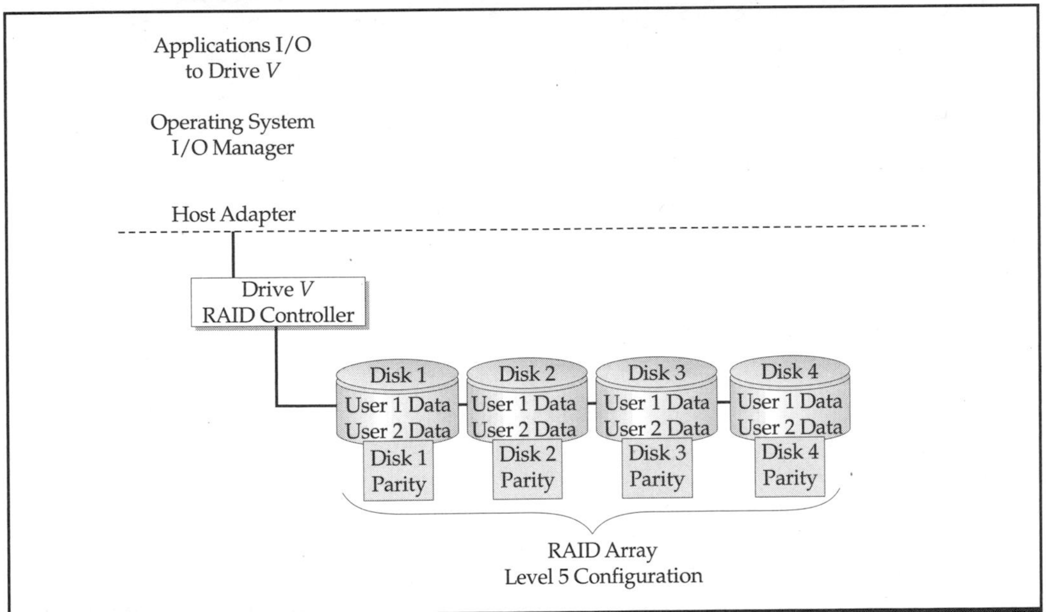

Figure 6-12.   *The RAID level 5 configuration*

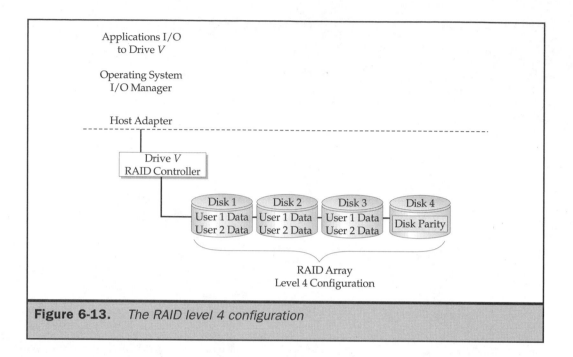

Figure 6-13.   *The RAID level 4 configuration*

Magnetic Tape Storage

Tape is the most ubiquitous form of storage today, with more data being stored on tape than any other media. Although tape storage started as the earliest form of mass storage, it survives today due to its cost resiliency and continued capability to store large amounts of systems and application data for safekeeping.

Tape Drives

The most important aspect of tape systems is their sequential nature. Even though a good deal of innovation has been applied to tape technology, write mechanisms, and optimization, the information remains sequentially bound. This is important because of throughput of write processes and speed of access. The ability to find a specific location with tape media requires the transport system to sequentially move throughout the tape to a specific sector.

Once the location is found, it can read the information and reposition itself for additional operations. Within the writing operation, the tape must be positioned in the proper location and written sequentially. Although this has been enhanced through software utilities that provide tape catalogue information that speeds location search for data that has been written to tape, the random nature of access that is inherent with magnetic disks does not exist within tape.

Another important operational note that should not be overlooked is the effect of tape controller functionality. The tape controller, as shown in Figure 6-14, is necessary

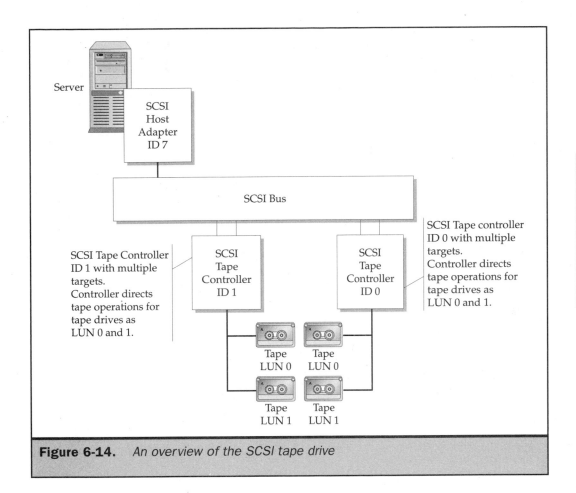

Figure 6-14.   *An overview of the SCSI tape drive*

for many control functions. Among the most important is the capability to address multiple drives within the tape system. Just as with disk controllers, tape controllers provide a level of transparency to the operating system and applications. In addition, and most importantly, the majority of controllers will have some form of error recovery and correction when dealing with data as it comes from the system bus, generally from the RAM buffers. If the tape system has error recovery code (ERC) in its controller, the system RAM will dump its contents to the tape controller buffers and refresh its buffer locations for another load. If not, there is a long wait as the RAM buffers slowly transfer their locations to the read/write head and wait for confirmation.

The effects of tape devices and operations within a storage network environment cannot be overlooked. We will discuss tape systems associated with SAN and NAS in Parts III, IV, and V. However, it's important to point out that fast system resources, such as RAM, become further decoupled from slower devices like tape media through the separation of network devices. As a result, the timing and throughput differences can become magnified and problematic.

Formats

Like disks, a distinguishing characteristic of tape drives is the format used to write and read data to and from the media. Popular formats in today's data center environments range from Digital Linear Tape (DLT), the most popular for commercial enterprises, to new formats such as Linear Tape Open (LTO). The general format specifies the type of media and the technique the tape heads use to write the data, most of which are supported by an open standard so that multiple vendors can provide an approximation of an interoperable solution.

The tape media is divided into parallel tracks. The number of tracks, the configuration of the read/write heads, and the mechanisms surrounding tape transport all make up the uniqueness of each format. Regardless of format, the tape media is formatted into blocks. As discussed, the format of the tape depends on the geometry of the media, the layout of the drive heads, and the transport control mechanisms, which all go together to define the size of the block in bytes that can be written. Blocks make up segments that can be referenced within the location of the media for faster access. Each segment has certain blocks that contain error correction codes and space for directories used by software utilities reserved within track 0 or a special directory track.

Read/Write Mechanisms

The read/write head mechanisms determine not only the format of the tape (tracks, parity, density, and so on), but more importantly the throughput and density of the write process and the speed of the read process. In most cases, today's tape drives contain read/write heads that perform dual roles. Surrounded by a read head, a write can take place as the read function verifies the operation, and vice versa as the tape transport changes direction. As mentioned earlier in our discussion of controllers, today's tape systems support increased levels of data buffering and, in some cases, caching, file systems, and fault-tolerant configurations similar to RAID technologies with disk systems.

Tape Systems

The utilization of tape systems predates all other mass storage strategies used for commercial and scientific computing. The importance of tape in data centers, both present and future, cannot be overlooked. In understanding this legacy form of storage, there are two important points to consider. First is the natural extension to tape systems (which is unlike online disk media): the Tape Library. As data centers create sets of information for recovery, archival, and legal purposes, the tapes must be stored in environments that are secure, environmentally protected, and accessible through some form of catalogue structure. Second, is the level of sophistication vendors have developed to support the offline, nearline, and online strategies that encompass tape usage.

The Tape Library

Let's first examine the tape library. Tape libraries provide both logical and physical archival processes to support the data center. The most important aspect of the library is rapid access to archived information. This requires some type of index, catalogue, and structure whereby the tape hardware working with the catalogue and archival software can locate a tape, mount in a drive, verify (yes, it's very important to verify it's the right tape), and read.

Provisioning and preparation follows this to support all the direct copying that is done. Generally performed during an off-shift, production information is written to tapes for a multitude of purposes. Although in many cases this will be the backup/recovery process, the sophistication of application jobs will utilize several levels of backup to ensure user data integrity is maintained. Also important is the type and form of copying that is performed in moving data to and from an online media. This means that some processes copy all data from the disk, regardless of the application, while others copy data to tape using specific file information, and yet others provide sophisticated update processes to archived data only changed if the online data has changed. Some of the more sophisticated processes take periodic "snapshots" of production data and copy these to other online or offline media.

Auto-loader libraries are highly sophisticated mechanical hardware that automate much of the provisioning and preparation in administrating tape media. Auto-loader development was driven largely by the need to provide a cost-effective way to eliminate the mundane and manual job of mounting tapes. Another major value is the ability to provide a larger number of pre-stage tapes for tasks like nightly backup and archival processing. Auto-loader libraries are integrated with tape drives and controller mechanisms and provide various additional levels of functionality in terms of buffering, error recovery, compression, and catalogue structure. Enterprise-level media libraries use mega-libraries, called *silos,* to provide an almost fully automated set of tape activities.

As you would suspect, many enterprise-level tape library systems are integrated into storage area networks. These SANs enable tape library systems to translate the SCSI-based tape drive operations with the Fibre Channel–based SAN network. NAS, on the other hand, has only recently integrated tape systems into its solutions. These can become more problematic given the direct attached internal storage characteristics of the NAS device.

How these processes and resources are managed requires a good deal of planning and execution within a generally tight time schedule. In order for this to happen, the correct amount of blank media should be available, formatted, and mounted in a timely fashion, the scheduling and processing of jobs needs to proceed according to a predefined schedule, and any exceptions must be handled in a timely manner.

Optical Storage

Optical storage serves as a media where laser light technologies write information in a fashion similar to disk architectures. Although logically they share similar characteristics, such as random access of the stored data and have head disk assemblies (HDAs) to read the media, these similarities disappear with the media used and operation of the read/write assembly. Optical storage compact discs (CD-ROMs) and DVDs (digital video disks) are driven by laser technology. As we all know, CDs and DVDs are removable storage with much higher densities than traditional diskette technology. As such, they have become a very successful product distribution media, replacing tapes.

Optical has achieved notoriety as a new distribution format in the fields of software, entertainment, and education. However, only recently have they been able to function as a reusable media with digital read/write capabilities. Unfortunately, their speed and throughput have not met requirements for use within the data center for commercial backup/recovery, or other archival media.

CDs and DVD optical media have never been favored as a replacement for magnetic disks or tapes in larger enterprise data centers. However, they has been slowly gaining a niche in the support of special applications that deal with unstructured data, the distribution of data, and delivery of information. Examples are datacentric objects like videos, integrated audio/video application data, and entertainment and educational integrated video, image, audio, and text information. The basic configurations for optical media are very much like tape drives and libraries. In commercial applications, they are supported through optical libraries which include multiple drives and auto-loader slots for selecting media.

The major difference between magnetic disks and tape is the use of lasers to write information on the optical media. This requires modifying a type of plastic media through the use of the laser beam, either by bleaching it, distorting it, or creating a bubble. The data is written in tracks but uses a different geometry that employs a spiraling technique to format the tracks from the center of the disk to its outer areas. Regardless of how it forms the modification, this is the method of writing data to the optical disk. When accessed for read operations, the optical device turns at a variable rate so that access throughout the disk is close to linear.

However, even with optical attributes and increased data capacities, the optical media has yet to achieve the throughput necessary for online transactional multiuser systems, or the necessary controller sophistication for data protection and recovery operations. Consequently, optical libraries will not proliferate within storage network installations even though they are heavily used in applications that favor imaging, videos, and audio. Systems that are SCSI-based can participate with SANs through a bridge/router device (see Chapter 14) and are available as NAS devices using a NAS microkernel front end with optical drives and autoloader hardware attached.

The
Complete
Reference

Storage
Networks

Chapter 7

Connectivity Options

In previous chapters, we discussed how effective storage systems are developed from the integration of multiple storage devices. Understanding the structure of these devices can help effectively utilize these technologies to support a single complex workload or a combination of disparate workloads. Underlying these concepts of storage architecture, device operation, and anatomy are the connectivity strategies that complete the data highway system. All these elements will begin to come together in this chapter as we discuss the connectivity options available to transport and deliver data from the storage system components to the computer.

Traditional system connectivity strategies have long been based upon bus architectures. A computer bus is defined as the lines and controls that connect the diverse components of a computer, ultimately making it a complete system. As we discussed in Chapter 5, this connectivity is required for the internal server components, CPU, RAM, and cache. Obviously, we know that external I/O components, such as storage devices, disks and tapes, and other peripherals like displays, keyboards, and mouse devices also require this connectivity, but in a different manner. This chapter will begin to explain the components and operation of typical bus- and network-oriented technologies, and the creative uses of various buses and network connectivity components that form the foundation for large multiple user systems.

The ability to connect storage systems through networks has greatly impacted the storage I/O industry. All of it surrounds the connectivity strategy, and the movement of storage systems from discrete bus technologies to network-oriented architectures. Understanding the bus is paramount to leveraging the movement of storage I/O into this new network model.

Another important reason to cover traditional bus technologies contrasted against the new network interconnects is that existing buses do not go away. They remain, and will remain, fundamental to getting data to and from the CPU (refer to Chapter 5 for more information). Moving data from the storage device through the storage system and on to the server within a network infrastructure still requires the effective operation of an internal bus. In order to be effective, traditional bus components must be optimized since they become parts of a new storage connectivity infrastructure. Otherwise, the most advanced and feature-rich storage network falls short at the server.

Connections: Getting on the Bus

Internal traffic within a computer's motherboard is handled through a set of fast connections etched into the circuitry, enabling transfer of data to and from the CPU and internal temporary data locations—for example, RAM, cache, and CPU registers. The connectivity for external (external to the motherboard) hardware is handled through the edge (of the board) as an expansion to the board. Take a look at Figure 7-1, which shows a universal computer bus.

These connections to the outside world (external to the motherboard) are referred to as expansion buses and I/O channels. They provide hardware attachment mechanisms

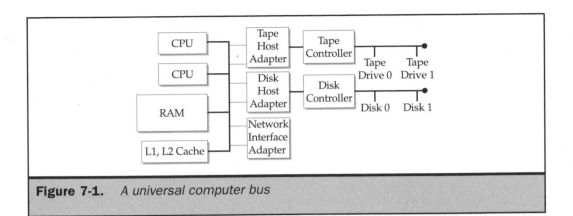

Figure 7-1. *A universal computer bus*

that extend the system capabilities beyond what is on the motherboards. This is where I/O devices are connected and, as we discussed earlier, where the host adapter components are attached. It is here where we require our first transfer ticket provided by the host adapters, to get from one bus to the other. As the internal components require a bus to connect to each other, the I/O devices also have that same need. As Figure 7-1 illustrates, the internal bus, I-bus, is adapted to the I/O bus, each transferring and controlling data for the connected components. Each bus controls devices with different mechanisms, different timings, and capacities.

The buses provide the following fundamental functions. As we can see, these are largely electronic mechanisms that do their work internally through a host of components. As we will explore later, the bus mechanisms must be able to work with particular devices that speak their language and have common electronic traits to move data.

Underlying all these sophisticated and complex electronics are several fundamental elements that make up the characteristics of the I/O bus, as shown in Figure 7-2. These include: throughput (commonly referred to as bandwidth), address space (how wide the bus is), interrupt processing (or can I react to external events and change processing modes?), and electro-mechanical attributes, such as how long can I be before my signal is degraded, and am I a circuit board or a backplane—in other words, will I connect to the motherboard or will the motherboards connect to me.

Bandwidth

Bandwidth is the amount of information the bus can transport during a given time. This is usually measured in MB per second. This is a derivative of clock speed and data width. In other words, a bus using a 5MHz clock speed and a 4 byte data width has a throughput, or bandwidth, of $5 \times 4 = 20$MB per second. Keep in mind this is what is called aggregate throughput; it is reduced by protocol overhead. We will discuss real speeds in more detail later in the chapter.

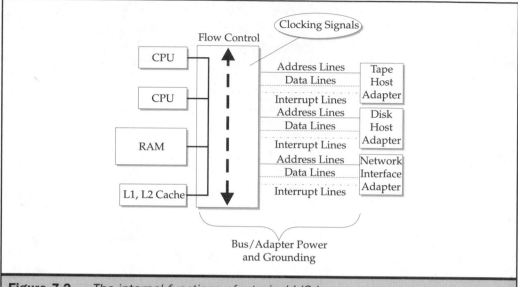

Figure 7-2.   *The internal functions of a typical I/O bus*

Addressing

The address space provides the capability to determine unique identities for source and destination of communications within the bus itself. This is determined by the width of the address component; the larger the address space, the more device operations can be supported. Generally, most buses operate today with 32-bit addressing architectures, providing an address space of 4GB. (This is important if you are working with older bus technology or an advanced technology such as InfiniBand or Fibre Channel; see Part V.)

Interrupt Functions

An external event may occur at any time and the bus must be able to take action in order to continue processing. This interrupt processing is the fundamental concept behind the interactive system's processing that must occur with multiuser, multitasking workloads. The I/O bus must be capable of interruption of a data transfer from disk to tape for an event with a higher priority. Be it an error processing routine or a call to read a block of data from an application, without this capability the bus could not be used for interactive applications, instead it could only be used for a single device.

Electro-Mechanical

Internal buses on the motherboard may only be inches long; external I/O connections must extend several feet or meters. These connections are generally some type of shielded cable and will be placed into areas of electromagnetic interference. I/O buses must have attributes that protect the signal's integrity while providing an adequate physical extensibility. The cable for an I/O bus is defined with regard to its maximum length, resistance, whether shielded or unshielded.

The motherboard of a computer will have a number of connections or slots that are nothing more than bus connections. Host adapters are connected at these edge points. The other type of connectivity is the backplane (refer to Chapter 6). The backplane can have no other electronics or circuitry than to provide connection points for host adapters. However, a backplane can also be used to connect complete motherboard systems together along a shared bus. These will be used in tightly coupled SMP and MPP systems. They are also becoming popular for use with integrating thin computing nodes (for example, a system-on-board or a motherboard with no peripherals), which entails sharing a common external bus that may be a network or another type of system interconnect—used explicitly in something referred to as blade computing. (Refer to Chapter 20 regarding future protocols such as InfiniBand, an external example, and Rapid IO, an internal example.)

Bus Evolution

The importance of bus evolution is visible in terms of the clocking signal increases, numbers of data lines, interrupt sharing, and something called bus mastering. Bus mastering allowed additional processors and devices (for example, IDE and SCSI adapters) to contend for bus processing. By contrast, previous architectures where the system processor had complete control of the bus and scalability became problematic.

The decoupling of the bus through bus mastering from a single point of control came with IBM's Micro Channel Architecture (MCA); however, it was enhanced with EISA to include auto and software configuration functions. This first laid the groundwork for plug 'n play functionality, while the second aided in reconfiguring the bus (changing device priorities, addressing, and so on).

Note   *This standard bus architecture (Extended Industry Standard Architecture or EISA) extends the ISA standard from a 16-bit to a 32-bit interface.*

The physical decoupling and enhanced scalability of the bus was achieved with the Peripheral Component Interconnect Standard (PCI) and the resulting PCI mezzanine bus architecture. This was the first bus implementation not tightly coupled with the system processor. This allowed the PCI bus to expand its connectivity by using a re-configurable structure and bridging, as necessary, to add additional hardware devices.

Bus Operations

Buses operate by requesting the use of paths to transfer data from a source element to a target element. In its simplest form, a controller cache, defined as a source, transfers data to a disk, defined as a target. The controller signals the bus processor that he needs the bus. When processing, control is given to the controller cache operation. It owns the bus for that operation and no one else connected to the bus can use it. However, as indicated earlier, the bus processor can interrupt the process for a higher priority process and give control to that device.

This is called a bus arbitration scheme, as shown in Figure 7-3. The devices connected to the bus arbitrate for bus control based on a predefined set of commands and priorities. The devices can be both source and target for data transfers. This type of internal communication makes up the bus protocol and must be available to all sources and targets—for example, connected devices that participate within the I/O bus.

Parallel vs. Serial

Bus operations will perform data transfer operations using parallel or serial physical connections. These two connections perform the same task, but have distinct architectures, each with their own pros and cons. It's likely you'll be confronted with each as storage systems begin to integrate both for their strengths. Over and above this option is the secondary choice of the type used within each category, such as point-to-point and differential for parallel SCSI and various serial implementations. It's important to understand the limitations, as well as the strengths, when applying these to particular application requirements.

Parallel connections for storage utilize multiple lines to transport data simultaneously. This requires a complex set of wires making parallel cables quite large and thus

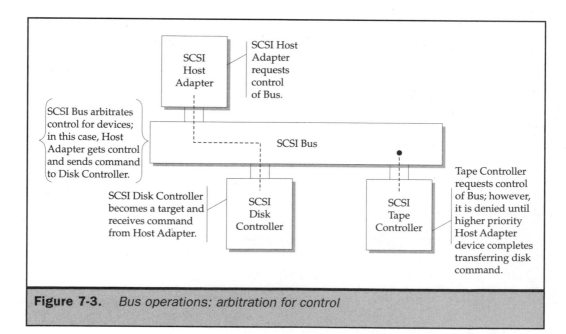

Figure 7-3. *Bus operations: arbitration for control*

subjecting them to an increased overhead of ERC (error, recovery, and correction), length limitations, and sensitivity to external noise. Of the parallel connections, there are two types: the single ended bus and the differential bus. The single ended bus is just what it describes, a connection point where devices are chained together with a termination point at the end. On the other hand, a differential bus is configured more like a circuit where each signal has a corresponding signal. This allows for increased distances and decreasing sensitivity to external noise and interference among the multiple wires that make up the cable. Of these two parallel connections, differential will be the more effective for high-end storage systems; however, they are also more costly given the increases in function and reliability.

Serial connections are much simpler, consisting basically of two wires. Although they pass data in serial fashion, they can do this more efficiently with longer distances, and with increased reliability. High-speed network communications transmission media such as ATM and fiber optics already use serial connections. Wide buses that use parallel connections have the potential for cross-talk interference problems, resulting in intermittent signaling problems, which ultimately show up in reliability and performance issues for storage operation. The use of two wires allows substantially improved shielding. Although it may seem counter-intuitive, serial connections can provide greater bandwidth than wide parallel connections. The simpler characteristics of a serial connection's physical make-up allow a clock frequency to be increased 50 to 100 times, improving the throughput by a multiple of 200.

Differences in Bus and Network Architectures

Computer networks connect various devices of individual characteristics so they may communicate with one another. Some networks are peer-oriented, where all the devices are deemed equal and vie for network transport resources, transmission, and reception. Other networks (the majority of networks in use today) are hierarchical, where some devices have control and authority over other devices regarding who and how they can communicate, when they can transmit, and when and what they can receive. However, both architectures all share similar functions in that they transmit and receive data according to some type of predefined standard.

This demonstrates two distinct differences from bus architectures. First, networks have a defined transmit and receive function. This allows networks to continually pass data into the network path and receive data without regard for control and operation of the connection. This is different than a bus where strict flow control and arbitration takes place with devices assuming control over the path. Second, networks enable data transmissions over a long distance. Networks provide computers a method of transmitting and receiving data over great distances without regard to the underlying communications infrastructure. This requires network architectures to encapsulate the data to be sent over various types of media and transmission circuitry.

For the majority of networks today this is accomplished through a defined standard called TCP/IP. As we mentioned previously, this is a layered approach to communication functions that address all the requirements of transferring data from one device to another while making the communications transparent to the computer's application. Figure 7-4 shows the standard layers of TCP/IP. However, underlying the complexities of these functions is the simple concept of encapsulation and transmission. TCP provides the functions for taking the data from the application and OS and wrapping them in a form that will fit into the IP envelope. IP then acts as the envelope by putting the TCP wrapper into the IP packet (nee envelope) and sending it into the network with the appropriate addressing information.

The reverse happens on the receiving end. The IP functions receive packets addressed to its host device and pass these to TCP. TCP unwraps the data and presents it to the receiving application.

IP communications take place via multiple types of physical media. The media affects the integrity of the communications, the speed of the transmission, and the distances supported. Regardless of the media, the electronic standard that guides transmissions at the wire level is Ethernet. Working from packet encapsulation architecture, data packets once they hit the network vie for transmission time, resources, and priority. Obviously, the most prominent performance characteristic is the size of the packet. Packet size is determined by the implementation of Ethernet standards. These standards, as they are implemented in vendor network devices, such as NICs, switches, and routers, support this physical level of interface to the network. Capacities differ from standard Ethernet connections to the multi-gigabit capacity for Gigabit Ethernet (Gbe).

Most application transactions that access the network (this includes the application data, overhead of TCP/IP, and network error, recovery, and correction) will exceed the packet size, even for Gbe networks. So, moving data from a server to a client or from a server to a backup device can utilize larger and larger quantities of network bandwidth. Given this condition, nearly all remote application transactions will be accomplished through multiple packet transmissions.

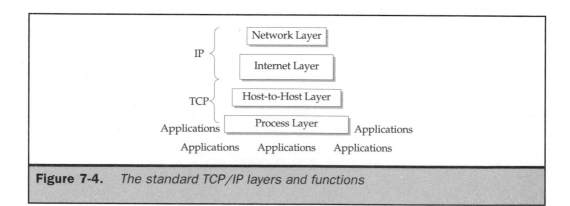

Figure 7-4.   *The standard TCP/IP layers and functions*

Similar in fashion to the bus, its bandwidth, addressing, and interrupt functions also drive the network. However, major differences show up in interrupt functions (in other words, how do I get access to the network and utilize its resources?). Additional differences show up in the capacities of bandwidth, given the diversity of physical media that networks have to traverse. Physical addressing, an integral part of a network's topology, also becomes diverse, driven by the particular implementation of the networking standard a vendor's devices are supporting (for example, fast Ethernet and gigabit Ethernet).

The PCI Bus

As mentioned previously, today's standard for connecting peripherals into the motherboard is the Peripheral Component Interconnect (PCI). The operation is straightforward with the PCI bus. PCI determines, through the use of the PCI controller, the destination of the data. The destination could be local or to an expansion slot. If it is destined to an expansion slot address, the host adapter takes over and translates the protocol from PCI to host adapter protocol. This could be IDE, SCSI, USB, or Firewire.

The importance of the PCI bus is that it decouples control of the data path to the PCI bus itself. Therefore, it puts more performance responsibility on the PCI bus components, and relies on its bandwidth and speed characteristics. Most PCI buses today have a 32-bit bandwidth with various clock speeds ranging from 33MHz to 1GHz. The other importance of the PCI bus is its mezzanine architecture, whereby expansion of the bus itself can take place, extending the scalability of the number of peripherals connected.

The SCSI Bus

The most popular storage bus in use today is the SCSI bus. The Small Computer System Interface (SCSI) is a standard that allows the connection of various devices through a parallel interface. Although the standard calls for support of multiple devices, general usage has been to externally connect disk and tape systems to the server. Given the bandwidth, addressability, and speed, it has become the defacto standard for the external connection of storage devices into open computing systems encompassing both UNIX and Windows.

The SCSI bus allows connections from eight to sixteen devices in a single bus. The operation is through initiator and target architecture. Only two devices can use the bus at one time. The initiator gains control of the bus and transfers the command to a device on the bus. The receiving device is the target and processes the command. It then sends a response back to the initiator. SCSI devices connected to the bus are identified by their SCSI ID, which also serves as its address. The ID identifies the device's priority for arbitration—0 being lowest and 7 or 15 being the highest.

It is possible for one server to have multiple host SCSI adapters with access to multiple SCSI buses. Although these, by convention, will have different SCSI IDs, they are completely separate as they communicate through the host adapter to the PCI bus. As previously discussed, the software drivers assign the SCSI ID's. However, the SCSI controller provides the actual access to the physical device. The controller does this by assigning each device a Logical Unit Number (LUN). This, in effect, virtualizes the devices that are connected behind the controller.

Figure 7-5 depicts the most common SCSI configurations where servers with a single initiator support multiple targets (such as controllers). In this configuration, controllers support multiple LUNs or disks attached. Figure 7-6 also depicts a configuration with multiple servers supporting multiple targets. Although each target or controller is unique, multiple LUNs are addressed with similar LUN addresses. This works because the controllers own and direct each of their LUNs.

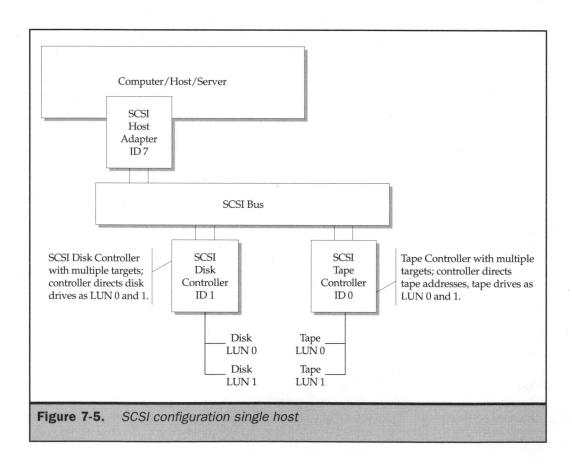

Figure 7-5.   *SCSI configuration single host*

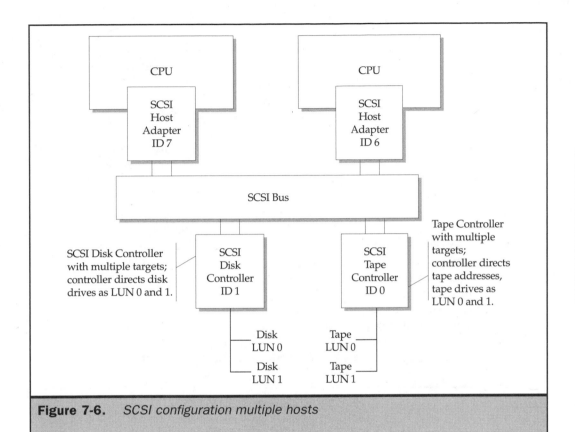

Figure 7-6. *SCSI configuration multiple hosts*

Fibre Channel

It's a network... it's a bus... no, it's Fibre Channel. Fibre Channel is a layered connectivity standard that has the characteristics of a bus, the flexibility of a network, and the scalability potential of MIMD (multi-instruction multidata) configurations. In implementation, it uses a serial connectivity scheme that allows for the highest level bandwidth of any connectivity solution available today. This architecture allows for implementations to reach a burst rate as high as 200 MBps for I/O operations, with aggregate rates depending on workload and network latency considerations. Regardless of the latency issues, this is a tremendous enhancement to throughput over traditional bus connectivity.

STORAGE FUNDAMENTALS

Note *Multi-instruction multidata computer taxonomy (known as MIMD) occurs where multiple instructions are executed with operations on multiple data sources. This has become synonymous with MPP computer configurations where parallel processing at the CPU level and I/O levels exemplify this theoretical term.*

To say that Fibre Channel is a network architecture or that Fibre Channel is a serial bus connectivity standard is an exercise for the esoteric debating society. Discussion here will result in nothing more than a last word at the science club meeting. In all fairness to the innovations surrounding Fibre Channel (FC), it was designed incorporating the characteristics of both to meet the growing scalability requirements of computer connections. It has accomplished this task in particular with storage systems.

The FC standard is implemented using a layered protocol consisting of five levels. As depicted in Figure 7-7, the first three levels deal with the physical attributes. As shown here, these are FC-0 through FC-2. These layers control the lowest level operations, from media types supported, to signal encoding for transmission, to the encapsulation and transmission control functions. FC-3 through FC-4 provide attributes for common services and mapping to other protocols. The most popular so far being the SCSI and IP mappings that support storage system operation and remote linking to IP networks.

FC can be implemented through three different topologies, as indicated in Figures 7-8, 7-9, and 7-10. These range from the most simple, point-to-point configurations, to the more complex, albeit more powerful, fabric implementation. The Fibre Channel Arbitrated Loop

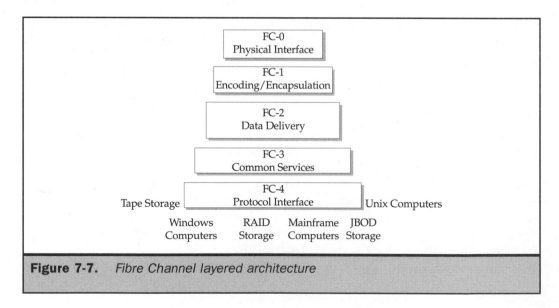

Figure 7-7.   *Fibre Channel layered architecture*

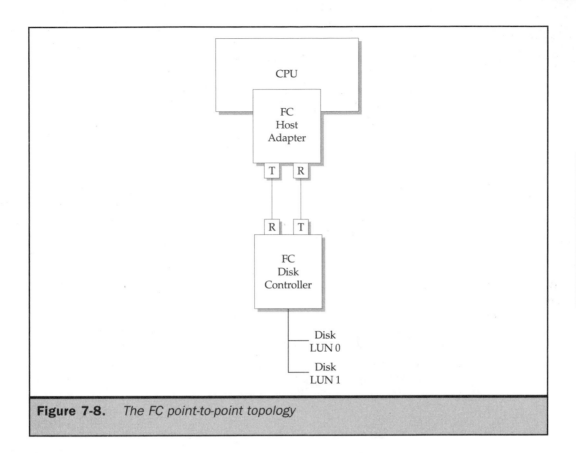

Figure 7-8. *The FC point-to-point topology*

(FC-AL) topologies have served as a transitional move as FC storage systems moved from FC Hub configurations, where the FC-AL provided access to the bandwidth benefits of the protocol; however, the loop arbitration overhead sacrificed most of these enhancements.

Fibre Channel Operation

FC operates on a serial link design and uses a packet type of approach for encapsulation of the user data. FC transmits and receives these data packets through the node participants within the fabric. Figure 7-11 shows a simplified view of the FC fabric transmission from server node to storage node. The packets shipped by FC are called frames and are made up of header information that include addresses, user data (encapsulating an incredible 2,192 bytes per frame), and error recovery code (ERC) information.

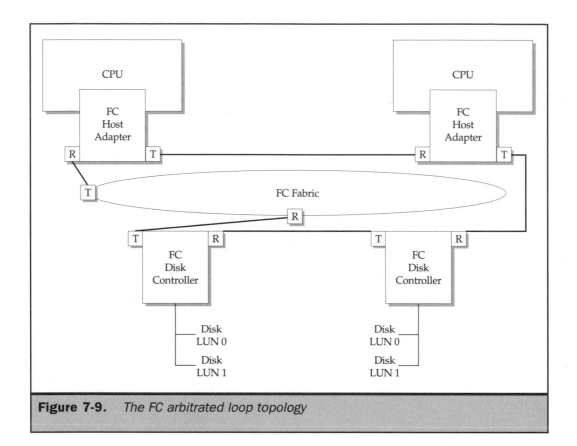

Figure 7-9.   *The FC arbitrated loop topology*

Each device that uses the FC Fabric is a node. FC provides both flow control and addressing for nodes when they contact and log in to the fabric, as illustrated in Figure 7-11 where Node 01 is assigned the port address of N01-fabric1. This is the N-Port address for the external device, in this case a Host Adapter for a server. This is connected to Fabric port F-01 of the switch's fabric (in other words, the fabric switch with an address of F01-fabric1 is shown as a fabric port). The storage system is connected using the same pattern.

The devices are controlled using calculations of available buffer space within each device as well as knowledge of time sequences, thereby keeping frame overflows to a minimum. Finally, the fabric itself executes under a predefined and supported class of service. Of these classes, only two are appropriate for typical storage systems: Class 2 and Class 3. These define a network connectionless service this way: acknowledgement of transmission is designated as Class 2; no notification of transmission is displayed as Class 3.

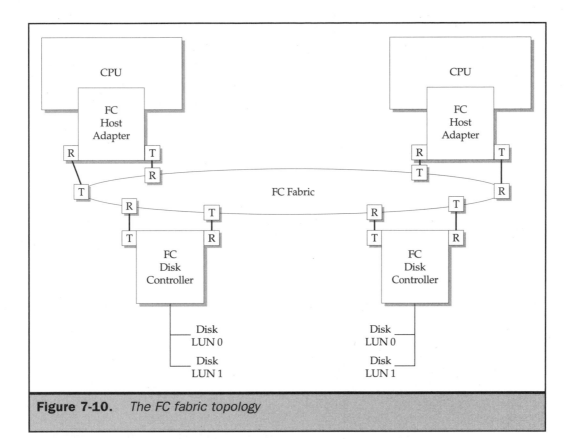

Figure 7-10. *The FC fabric topology*

Other I/O Buses

As peripheral devices increased in both number and diversity, the need to connect these to the computer system quickly and efficiently also grew. With devices such as digital cameras, larger external and removable storage devices, scanners, printers, and network options, the diversity and flexibility of the traditional computer bus was expanded to include support for all these devices. The systems and storage industry responded with innovative solutions that enhanced and implemented the traditional computer bus with serial technologies and higher speed protocols such as Firewire. In this section, we discuss two of the most popular bus evolutions: the Universal Serial Bus (USB) and Firewire. USB and Firewire have been successful solutions in the workstation and PC industry. Other evolutions to the traditional bus architecture are evident in the opposite side of the spectrum in the super computer and parallel processing industries. These technologies, driven by complex computational problems, have resulted in creative architecture that bind multiple computers together applying their combined power. These architectures are characterized by their creative bus implementation in

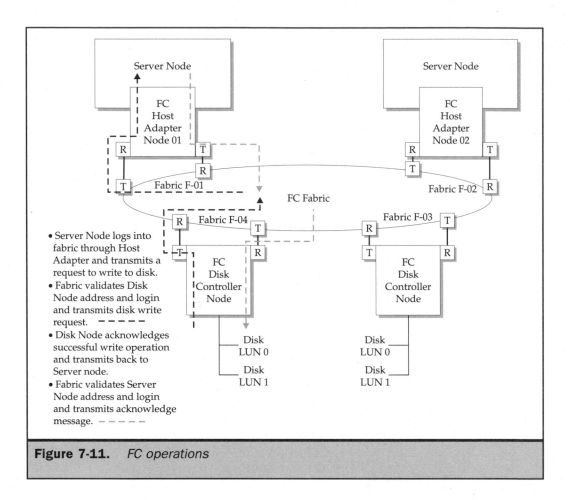

Figure 7-11. FC operations

connecting hundreds of processors and peripheral devices together. We summarize some general configurations in our discussion of these creative bus strategies.

USB and Firewire

Like the SCSI standard, the Universal Serial Bus (USB) and IEEE1394 standard, Firewire, was developed into a product to serve the multiple and diverse types of external devices that can interface with a single PC or workstation user. Used almost entirely for single user systems, the bus concept is similar to SCSI in terms of a host adapter translating PCI communications to USB or Firewire adapters whose protocols communicate within serial bus architectures. One of the differences is the support for the diverse and often disparate number of peripheral devices requiring connection to single user systems. These devices range from mice to joysticks to optical scanning equipment. With the exception of CDs, storage has come late to this area and remains lacking in providing levels of functionality needed for server level implementation.

Both of these solutions are ways of expanding the I/O capability of computers; however, the use of USB or Firewire disks for large-scale commercial use has not taken hold. Although this came about for many reasons, it is primarily due to the direction the USB standard took to support asynchronous and isochronous data transfers within a half duplex architecture. This limited performance for any bandwidth gains provided by a serial connection. In addition, disk manufacturers have not supported the serial interface and command structure used with disk drive functions. Finally, the limiting number of devices that can be addressed and the inability to deal with advanced storage features such as controller/LUN functions and RAID partitioning will continue to orient USB toward the single-user PC market.

Creative Connection Strategies

There are many ways of connecting peripherals to the server. Using the bus, network, and hybrid technologies that we discussed earlier, these strategies/implementations have evolved from the exotic innovations of supercomputing, alternatives to symmetrical multiprocessing (SMP), and developments within distributed computing architectures. All of these provide some type of high-speed interconnect between computing nodes that enable increased parallel computing tasks, allow support for larger workloads and increased data sizes, and which give way to increased overall performance scalability. These interconnects can be characterized as implementations of various bus and network technologies that produce non-standard configurations. Generally, these implementations demonstrate characteristics of a network with sophisticated data distribution functions that leverage specific CPU architectures (for example, IBM RISC-based systems, SUN Sparc systems, and Intel CISC systems).

There are three general types of high-speed interconnect topologies that have been commercialized. These are the shared nothing, shared I/O, and shared memory models. These models supplement the basic components of computer systems (for instance, RAM, CPU, and internal Bus), and provide an extension to a tightly coupled or loosely coupled set of distributed computer systems.

Shared Nothing

Figure 7-12 illustrates the configuration of a shared nothing system. These systems form the foundation for Massively Parallel Processing (MPP) systems, where each computer node is connected to a high-speed interconnect and communicates with nodes within the system to work together (or in parallel) on a workload. These systems generally have nodes that specialize in particular functions, such as database query parsing and preprocessing for input services. Other nodes share the search for data within a database by distributing it among nodes that specialize in data access and ownership. The sophistication of these machines sometimes outweighs their effectiveness, given that it requires a multi-image operating system (for instance,

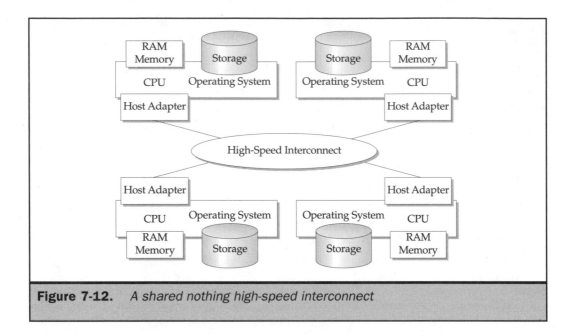

Figure 7-12.   *A shared nothing high-speed interconnect*

an OS on each node), sophisticated database and storage functions to partition the data throughout the configuration, and the speed, latency, and throughput of the interconnect. In these systems, both workload input processing and data acquisition can be performed in parallel, providing significant throughput increases.

Shared I/O

Figure 7-13 indicates the configuration of a system that has shared I/O. Although more common than the MPP machines, the shared I/O requires the computer systems to share a common I/O bus and therefore extend the capability to provide additional access to larger amounts of data. Operation of these machines requires that a single image operating system control the operation of I/O and application processing across the computing nodes and shared I/O. These systems offer enhanced access to large amounts of data where I/O content can be large and multiple computing nodes must operate in parallel to process the workload.

Shared Memory

Figure 7-14 shows the most common of alternative interconnects: the shared memory model. This makes up most of the high-end SMP machines where multiple CPUs share a large RAM, allowing CPUs to process workloads in parallel with enhanced performance from a common RAM address space that's both physical and virtual. Also operating under a single image operating system, these systems enhance the capability to process workloads that are high-end OLTP with small I/O content.

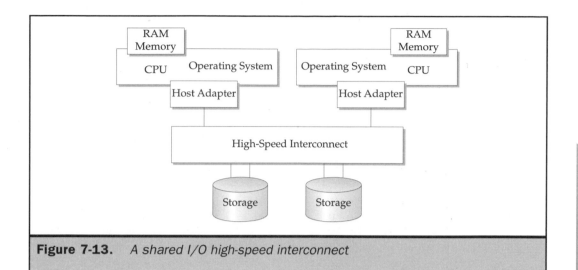

Figure 7-13.   *A shared I/O high-speed interconnect*

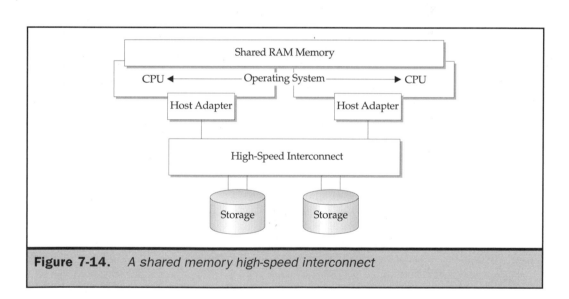

Figure 7-14.   *A shared memory high-speed interconnect*

Chapter 8

Data Organizational Methods

Without the ability to view, manipulate, and update data stored on the computer, the most sophisticated storage infrastructure is meaningless. Our last storage fundamental covers the methods and types of organizational models used to facilitate the productive use of stored data. Data organizational models and methods are part of the entire storage infrastructure. Their proximity to other elements within the infrastructure indicates that structures, such as file systems and databases, are the critical connectivity between application and end user. Data is stored for many different reasons and accessed in as many ways to support a rapidly changing business environment. The knowledge, awareness, and insight to the diversity of data organizational models is as important and critical as that of storage systems and connectivity options.

Organizing Data

Data in computer systems is organized by creating databases. Databases are defined as a collection of interrelated material stored in an environment that is both convenient and efficient to use in retrieving information. This is done through a combination of file systems, database management systems (DBMS), and applications. Combined with an effective storage system, the database can offer an environment where data can not only be stored and updated on a reliable basis but also be accessed in multiple ways.

Underlying the DBMS is the file system that works as a component of the operating system. The file system functions as the operating system's ability to organize and retrieve the physical data that exists on attached storage media and within memory devices. File systems deal with the physical aspects of storage media, the data locations, as they are stored within the media segments, and the status of the data within. They also provide the first level of transparency to the user or owner of the data.

Database management systems (DBMS) provide methods for defining the data, enhanced access to data generally through some type of enhanced indexing system, and functions for maintaining the data structures as well as the data itself. Defining and accessing the data through a DBMS, users can additionally perform calculations and logical functions on the stored data, and present the data in enhanced views (usually tabular reports that include graphics and charts).

Business applications take advantage of the file system and DBMS functions by using their transparent data retrieval and dealing directly with the data without having to understand or know the underlying operations of the DBMS or a native file system. As we indicated in Chapter 1, most application designers and programmers can use these high-level functions without regard to the underlying hardware and software infrastructure. Others can be locked into specific DBMSs and file systems that have become standardized within their data centers.

Interrelationships of Performance

File systems, database systems, and storage systems are interrelated and dictate levels of performance for the storage infrastructure. File systems, for their part, form the basis for efficient and effective access to an application's data. Problems occur, however, when the file system is doing its job with unoptimized disks, insufficient disk space, or bandwidth constraints in the bus. As application performance becomes problematic, the file system attributes should be considered for better alignment with the available storage infrastructure.

Many relational databases don't use an operating system's file system at all. Given that's the case in many database instances, then what substitutes the functionality of the file system within the database? Actually, many database systems interact closely with installed storage systems through the use of their own file system and virtual I/O manager.

Finally, many applications rely on the interaction of files that are networked. This provides yet another dimension to the interrelationship of the file system to storage and the challenges to the integrity and reliability of the data stored within a network.

Virtualization Times Three

Data organizational methods begin the first slide into the confusion of virtualization. This is because File Systems provide a layer of abstraction to the physical location of data, the location of disks, and the storage media itself. Database systems further abstract the physical data, physical location, and the actual data. Finally, the application using both organizational methods will further hide (for example, virtualize) the complexities of finding and managing the data. In many cases, we are left with the question of where the actual data is.

The operating system component that encompasses the allocation of space, data structures, and which keeps track of these organizational storage criteria is the File System. File Systems operate within the I/O manager component of the OS. In most operating systems, such as UNIX and Windows, the file system operates as a driver or an additional service that will interact with the OS's I/O management component. This allows multiple file systems to simultaneously operate on a single server.

Requirements for Enterprise-Class File Systems

Enterprise-class file systems need far more than convenience and efficiency to be considered adequate support for enterprise OLTP, data warehouse, Internet, and complex batch operations. The following are some of the global requirements that should be addressed by any enterprise-class file system and the issues they raise:

- **Security** Limiting user access to files and exercising control over sensitive physical resources—such as volumes and system files—continue to be the two major requirements for security within file systems. This has become cumbersome as multiple and often duplicate security functions are offered by both file and database systems. From the storage perspective, there exists a lack of effective and integrated resource security and control functions that are available within the storage infrastructure components.

■ **Data Recovery** Disasters, both large and small, are going to occur. The ability to recover in a timely fashion has long been a requirement, as databases become systems of record for both large and small enterprises. This, however, becomes more sophisticated and complex as recovery functions for databases differ from recovery functions for file systems which, in turn, differ from the recovery system of an entire application.

■ **Fault Resiliency/Tolerance** This is the "timely" part of the recovery requirement. Most notably, the requirement that says you have to be up for 24/7. Although a noble thought, the reality of keeping an enterprise system available in this manner does not exist yet. Having said that, however, the functionality to repair and recover from most hardware failures without disrupting the application can be accomplished at various levels. The problem continues to be that enterprise application systems are likened to living entities that consume resources, and many of these are just temporary and need to be refreshed from time to time. Secondly, the ability to design and place card-holders (for lack of a better term) in the processing time frames has failed to mature with the sophisticated hardware/recovery systems available today.

Note *24/7 systems have existed for some time in mainframe configurations, with full redundancy at various levels. However, as data centers migrate their operations from the mainframe to open systems using commodity-based platforms, additional levels of maturity must evolve before open system hardware and software provide the same levels of desired fault tolerance.*

■ **Support for Advanced Storage Systems and Application Requirements** Last, but certainly not least, is the support for future enhancements to disk drives, disk formats, tape, and so on. There's no question that this is an important factor given that databases and file systems are closely tied to their storage relatives and must keep up. The typical IT oversight in this requirement concerns the effects that support of back level software (for instance, file systems and databases) has on hardware manufacturers. Although it looks altruistic on the outside, inefficiencies develop when this continues for any length of time.

File Systems

From the most academic definition, the file system is a logical sequence of blocks on a storage media. Files are a basic construct of the operating system. With the exception of certain data (refer to relational databases further in this chapter), all data is kept in some type of file format. As such, it requires a system to maintain and manage the relationship with storage on behalf of the operating system. These file system functions are shown in Figure 8-1 and can be categorized in the following manner: allocation, management, and operations. These functions are described as follows:

- **Allocation**   File systems provide the capability to organize I/O devices into functioning units of storage.
- **Management**   File systems provide the activities necessary to track, protect, and manipulate data stored within the I/O devices.
- **Operations**   File systems locate logical sequences of data (for instance, a file) through various search methods depending on data recoverability and the sophistication of the system.

Allocation

The file system allocates the two most important elements of the storage media, the volume, which defines the physical device, and its related attributes. Secondly, the files, which are collections of data, are accessible through some type of naming convention to the operating system and, subsequently, the applications are stored physically on the storage media. In today's environments, multiple products can

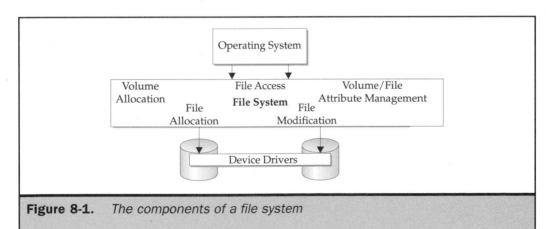

Figure 8-1.   *The components of a file system*

make up these components. Accessible as add-ons to the basic components of the operating system, these products support two distinct but interrelated functions: file management and volume management. These products are available as recoverable, journal, or high-performance file systems and as enhanced or extended volume managers.

Volume Definition

Allocation of space within storage, especially in disks, begins with the initialization or formatting of the physical device itself. This is done by creating a volume that corresponds to a logical partition of space on a disk. Given the esoteric nature of volume initialization, volumes can be assigned to part of a disk or can span physical disks.

The activity of formatting defines the smallest unit of addressable space within the device and the creation of special files that will act as directories or catalogues for file allocation and access. In Microsoft operating systems, these are referred to as clusters and are mapped to the physical sectors of the physical disk. In UNIX, this is generally defined, given there are multiple UNIX variants, as a *super block*. Consequently, there exists a relationship between the file system allocation and the actual physical attributes of the disk, such as capacity and density. Both file system units—clusters and blocks— have an integral number of physical sectors. Therefore, large physical disks storing small files can become very inefficient when the lowest unit of storage is a cluster that utilizes multiple large sectors.

In addition, the overhead necessary to put the disk into activity (for instance, its formatting) explains the difference between formatted capacities of a drive versus unformatted capacity.

File Allocation

Once a volume is initialized, it is ready to store a file or logical sets of blocks. Files are allocated according to the attributes set with volume formatting. Given that, a file is allocated space through its smallest unit of measurement, which is the cluster or block. Files are tracked through special files that have been created with volume allocation. These master file tables (MFT), as they exist in Microsoft OSs (or inodes, as they're referred to in UNIX systems), contain data about the volume, space attributes, and files stored within the volume.

Access to files starts here with the master file table or inode. Within these special files are indexing information, security access lists, file attribute lists, and any extended attributes that the file may have. Once the file has been created, these attributes are managed from these locations stored on the volume.

Management

The MFT, file allocation table, or super block-inode structures are increasingly being referred to as metadata. Metadata simply means information about data. As we discussed previously, the operating system requires a function to store and access data. One of these is the fundamental boot structure needed by the OS to initialize itself during a power up or restart sequence. In addition to the metadata files allocation during formatting, the process identifies and creates a boot file that becomes instrumental in locating the special system information needed during the OS boot processes.

Another important allocation during this process is the creation of a log file, thereby providing a recoverable file system, one that is required for enterprise-level operations. A recoverable file system ensures volume consistency by using logging functions similar to transaction processing models. If the system crashes, the file system restores the volume by executing a recovery procedure that utilized activity information stored within the log file.

In file systems, all data stored on a volume is contained in a file. This includes the file allocation tables and volume table of contents structures used to located and retrieve files, boot data, and the allocation state of the entire volume. Storing everything in files allows the data to be easily located and maintained by the file system, and a security attribute or descriptor can protect each separated file. If a particular part of the physical disk becomes corrupt, the file system can relocate the metadata files to prevent the disk from becoming inaccessible.

Note *There is an important exception to the preceding statement that "all data stored on a volume is contained in a file." The exception is the allocation of disks using raw partitions where an application will bypass the file system and manage the raw storage segments. This is common for many relational database products.*

Types of File Systems

Windows utilizes several types of file systems that support both client and server operations. Most client OSs only need to support fundamental volume and file allocation functions. This is handled through its ability to initialize and partition volumes with formatting and file allocation through a simple file allocation table. However, within server products, a more robust file system is required, as shown in Figure 8-2. Windows server products provide a NT File System (NTFS), which provides a robust file system that supports enhanced volume and file allocation functions. These products include volume fault resiliency features for partitioning volumes with redundancy features, thus providing a subset of RAID features through software. Also supported is recoverability through logging functions. Enhanced security attributes are provided to support multiuser environments with levels of data protection for both user access and file and volume protection.

UNIX has several variants; however, most offer a POSIX-compliant file system that is a "bare-bones" component of the operating system. Enhanced and recoverable file systems are available through third-party products. These add-ons provide both enhanced performance and journaling. In UNIX, recoverable file systems are referred

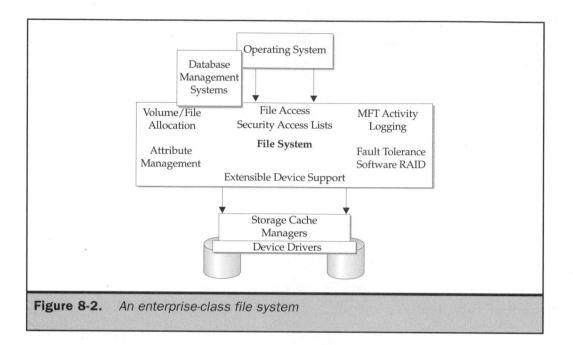

Figure 8-2.   *An enterprise-class file system*

to as "journal" file systems, e.g., logging being synonymous with journaling. More importantly, the UNIX markets have the availability and legacy of network file systems, where files are shared across a network through a common file system and access protocol.

Note   *The POSIX Standard, also known as the IEEE 1003.x POSIX standard, is the result of working groups under the auspices of IEEE. It describes a set of standard operating system interfaces.*

Access to information via the Internet and through World Wide Web interfaces has produced yet another variant of the file system, the Hyper Text Transport Protocol, or HTTP. Although more of a common file access protocol, it does define a file structure, within the web-based environments depicted in Figure 8-3. Because it is supported across both UNIX and Windows, it provides a common protocol for accessing files through a network.

Another advancement in common file protocols is the Common Internet File System (CIFS), as shown in Figure 8-4. Starting as a Microsoft initiative, it has now become an open standard. Based on the need to provide file sharing among a diverse set of operating system environments within a network setting, it is a model derivative of NFS that allows Microsoft Operating Systems to access shared files on Microsoft servers, UNIX servers, the Web, and most recently, Apple servers. CIFSs are based on

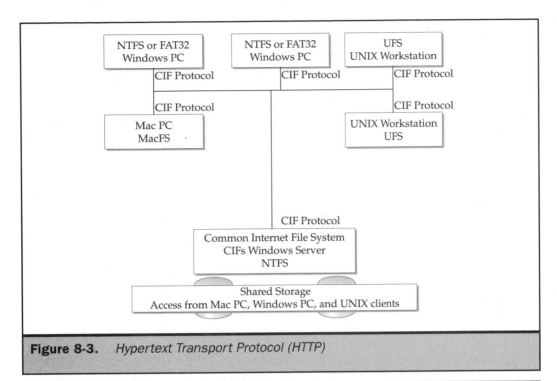

Figure 8-3.   *Hypertext Transport Protocol (HTTP)*

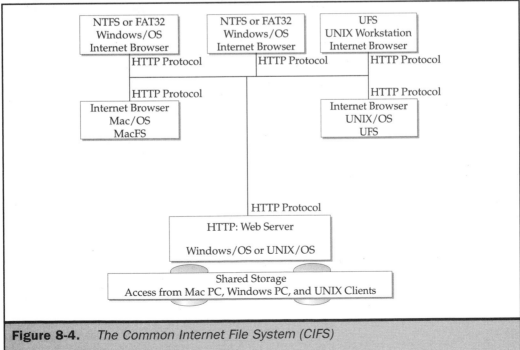

Figure 8-4.   *The Common Internet File System (CIFS)*

a Microsoft networking protocol of Server Message Block (SMB), and have both advantages and limitations compared to NFS.

Other file systems are generally derivatives of UNIX variants and are used for specialized applications, such as scientific and academic/research applications. However, one alternative system (as shown in Figure 8-5) has produced a new type of access, especially within networked environments. This is the Direct Access File System, or DAFS. DAFS can be especially important given its use of Direct Memory Access (DMA) functions for transferring data. Future DAFS products will have extremely fast access times given their capability to transfer data between memory locations.

The importance of file systems as they relate to storage systems and infrastructures is straightforward and should not be overlooked. As you encounter more detailed discussions in Parts III and IV regarding NAS and SAN, we will discover another dimension to the importance of file systems and their capability to operate within storage networked environments. As you may have already discovered, NFS, CIFs, and HTTP all play a big role in these environments.

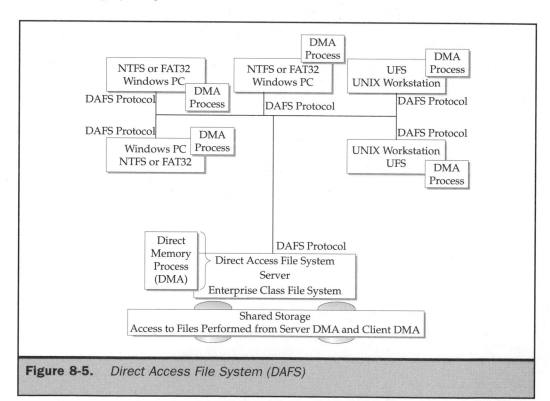

Figure 8-5.   *Direct Access File System (DAFS)*

Databases

A database system is made up of individual software components that interact with each other and with other system components, enabling applications access to various abstractions of physical data. Some of the external components include the functionality of file systems, storage cache, and resource manager functions. Other database system components work as an interrelated system of functions to process data requests on behalf of applications. The database's sole purpose is to provide consistent, efficient, and reliable data to end users.

I suppose it's politically correct to substitute "information" for "data" here. However, end users today manipulate more data than the average application programmer did ten years ago. The point is, I don't think end users are intimidated any more regarding the handling, manipulation, and "programmed" access to computer data. The sophistication of computer usage among "smart" users, the available tools to extract, manipulate, and process data, have placed many users into the category of "Super-User," "Query Monster," or "Departmental Programmer." The innovation and continued evolution of the database system has almost singularly provided the impetus for these changes. Fueled by the standard query language, SQL, and its derivatives, where programming has been taken to more accessible levels for all computer users to understand and manipulate on their own, the world has seen an explosion in database implementation, population, and usage.

Looking for Data

A major purpose of a database system is to provide many users with an abstract view of the data. Depending on who you are, you need different levels of abstraction when accessing existing data. IT professionals obviously require different types of access than end users who assume enterprise OLTP and batch applications will provide them with the right information (sorry, I mean data) at the right time. Underlying both IT professional and end-user activities, designing applications, data models, and required maintenance activities is a diversity of data access procedures. The various levels of access and abstraction are described here:

- **Physical Abstraction**   Used primarily by system database administrators (DBAs) and system administrators (storage administrators are slowly coming on board with these concepts), physical access is the lowest level of data abstraction. This allows complex low-level data types and structures to be described. It also provides a means to describe how the actual data is stored.

- **Conceptual Abstraction**   Used by programmers, application designers, and application DBAs, this is a level of abstraction up from the physical level that describes what user data is actually stored in the database. This also describes relationships that exist within and among the data elements. The conceptual level allows IT professionals to describe the entire database in terms of simple structures or data models. The physical level uses data models, structures, and descriptions to invoke complex physical structures to develop the database.

■ **View Abstraction**   Driven by those who derive value from its usage (usually the end user), views are the primary level of abstraction for development of graphical user interfaces (GUIs). End users are not concerned about the entire set of information within the database, or the complexities of its internal structures. As such, view levels become the highest level of abstraction of the data and describe only one part of a database, simplifying the interaction of end users with the database. Depending on the levels of abstraction required, most users require multiple views of the data.

From a storage point of view, it is important to understand not only the physical abstractions of the data, but also the database components that interact with native operating system functions and storage drivers. This becomes increasingly important as database systems push the limits of storage infrastructures unlike any other system or application. However, it is also important to study the translations of abstractions to understand storage-related problems as System and Application DBAs, Administrators, and end users encounter them.

The following are the typical components of a database system:

■ **Database Manager**   Functions that provide the interface between the physical data and the application programs, integrated application functions such as search and mathematical algorithms, and physical access to the data.

■ **File Manager**   Functions that allocate space on storage systems and manage the data structures used to represent the conceptual abstraction of data. This component, in many cases, is integrated into the database manager, bypassing the operating systems file system for these functions.

■ **Query Processor**   A component that translates statements from a query language, such as standard SQL, into low-level instructions that the database manager components will execute on behalf of the end-user query or application program.

■ **Preprocessor Compiler**   A component that translates database language queries, such as SQL that are embedded in application programs. The compiler turns these into instructions for the query processor, which, in turn, processes it and passes it on to the database manager.

■ **Data Language Compiler**   Functions that convert data language definitions into data structures called metadata . The Metadata table entries are then stored in a metadata database, sometimes called a data dictionary or repository.

Additional data structures are necessary as part of the physical implementation of the database system. These are the data dictionary or data repositories, as we just discussed.

Finally, index structures provide enhanced search access to data when searching for particular values or data files.

Databases change as data is added and deleted. The collection of data in the database at any given time is called an instance, while the overall design of a database is called the database scheme or schema. The latter is expressed as a conceptual abstraction, and is specified through a data definition language. The results of a data definition schema are placed into a data dictionary or metadata table. A data manipulation language is a set of procedures to access and manipulate the data such as the standard query language or SQL.

Database Systems: Different Animals

There are only a few popular database models that have survived the mainframe-to-client/server-to-Internet evolution. Interestingly, some of the older models continue to process workloads today, albeit mostly on mainframe processing complexes. Databases can be developed from a simple collection of sequential files, sometimes called flat files because of their non-dimensional access restrictions, to the most complex mainframe hierarchical databases. Regardless of implementation, major database management systems have evolved from three conceptual models.

These are the networked databases based on a network data model. Characterized by its capability to provide links within its fields of database records. The hierarchical data model is used by many file systems in their functions to provide faster access to directories and file indices. These are recognizable through their use of tree structures, such as the B-Tree and B+Tree data structures. The third and most popular model is the relational model, which forms the structure for all popular relational databases systems, such as Oracle, Sybase, IBM's DB2, Microsoft's SQL/Server and others. The database model that provides the most challenges, problems, and headaches to storage infrastructures today is the same one that provides the most challenges, problems, and headaches to storage networking infrastructures: the relational database.

Relational database systems consist of a collection of tables, each of which has a unique name. Each field in the table is considered a distinct entity with attributes and has relationships to other entities within its own table as well as to others in the collection of tables that make up the database. User data is populated throughout the tables by individual records. This forms the basis for the tremendous power of a relational database, the ability to compare data elements to perform set mathematical functions, or "What if" questions. From an overall systems perspective, this provides two challenges:

- First is the compute-intensive nature of relational processing. Because relational processing utilizes set mathematics to find the answer to a database query, the data necessary to construct the sets and processing to compute the answer is one of the most resource-intensive activities within data processing.

■ Second is the I/O-intensive nature of relational processing. I/O content and activity becomes intensive as the rows of data from tables are loaded into memory to build set constructs to compare data elements until all relational operations are complete. With a database of any size, the compute requirements coupled with the I/O requirements render relational database processing one of the most resource-intensive activities for commercial data processing.

Consequently, the relationship with storage for databases becomes very special. Although there are several considerations when maintaining a storage infrastructure for RDBMS, here are some particularly important points to consider as we move into the area of storage networking.

Relational databases have a legacy from UNIX and mainframe environments. This has resulted in a design whereby most relational database systems (RDBMS) contain their own I/O processing and file management functions. This means that when installed, they bypass the operating systems' file system and utilize their own. This is referred to as an RDBMS that uses a raw disk partition. In effect, they are performing their own I/O and substituting their own file system, essentially mapping the raw disk to their own to enable low-level access. Historically, they had to do this to provide acceptable levels of performance and reliability in the days when UNIX did not have an optimized file system, much less a journaling file system. Given the resource-intensive nature of these relational operations, early RDBMS vendors developed their own I/O systems.

Another important factor to keep in mind is the nature of the relational data structure. It is a table, not a file, a table. The physical data is stored in native block formats for those RDBMSs that use their own I/O and file system, or for those whose physical data is masked from the system when using a standard file system. This means that without special utilities and knowledge of the database, its state, and its metadata, that the ability to reconstruct the data structure from a disruption is impossible. Therefore, databases are difficult, at best, to maintain from a data maintenance aspect (for instance, backup/recovery operations, archival, and volume management).

Databases, especially the relational model, are a challenge to maintain and manage. They have a close relationship with storage systems given their own processing characteristics and development legacy in the area of I/O technologies. Storage networking adds new dimensions to the existing challenges in data organization models and methods. We will explore the role of databases in the world of NAS and SAN in the upcoming sections.

The
Complete
Reference

Storage
Networks

Part III

Network Attached Storage

The
Complete
Reference

Storage
Networks

Chapter 9

Putting Storage
on the Network:
A Detailed Discussion

131

Network Attached Storage (NAS) is the evolution of network servers. It was developed from efforts to configure, optimize, and operate a server directed only toward one thing: providing shared storage for users on a network. NAS is one of two pillars that make up storage networking infrastructures in today's data centers. It has evolved into a class of storage devices that address storage needs from departmental storage appliances to enterprise-class storage servers managing multiterabytes of data. This section will explain, discuss, and evaluate the NAS architecture, from the hardware and software required, to the necessary connectivity components. Developed using concepts from Part II, and expanding the NAS overview from Part I, this information will encompass a detailed view of the NAS internal structures.

The NAS Architecture

NAS is a specialized computer that provides file access and storage for a client/server network. Because it is a specialized solution, its major components are proprietary and optimized for one activity: shared file I/O within a network. NAS is considered a bundled solution consisting of prepackaged hardware and installed software regardless of vendor selection. The bundled solution encompasses a server part, a computer system with RAM, a CPU, buses, network and storage adapters, storage controllers, and disk storage. The software portion contains the operating system, file system, and network drivers. The last element is the network segment, which consists of the network interfaces and related connectivity components.

Plug and Play is an important characteristic of the NAS packaged solution. Given the bundling and configuration that comes with the product (which is dependent on the class of NAS solution you are implementing), it's out of the box and attached to the network in less than five minutes. Although this may be a fairly accurate portrayal for installation and identification to the network, the Plug and Play value must be considered in context with the size and scope of the NAS device. There are many implementation caveats to consider and ample thought should be given to existing server clusters and storage systems already in place.

However, for most small networks, providing a Plug and Play NAS solution is a productive solution. Though more sophisticated departmental solutions will take longer, the bundled characteristics of the NAS devices save considerable time in planning and implementation. Of course, enterprise-level solutions should have much more thought put into their planning and implementation. Obviously, with this class of storage, care should be taken not to fall prey to the "five-minute" Plug and Play temptation which could result in much larger infrastructure problems.

NAS can be a productive solution. Its simplicity is one of its greatest strengths. The entire perspective of the NAS phenomenon, however, should be considered prior to any implementation. The following points summarize the issues that are important to know and understand to facilitate a long-term productive configuration:

- NAS is a specialized server solution with proprietary hardware and software.

- NAS is optimized for file I/O; support of any other types of workload I/O will prove problematic.

- NAS is one of he easiest ways to accommodate increases to storage capacity for LAN-based shared files.

- NAS can be one of the most difficult to administer and manage when numbers of boxes exceed reasonable complexities.

- NAS uses existing network resources by attaching to Ethernet-based TCP/IP network topologies.

- Although NAS uses existing network resources, care should be taken to design expansions to networks so increases in NAS storage traffic do not impact end-user transactional traffic.

- NAS uses a Real Time Operating System (RTOS) that is optimized through proprietary enhancements to the kernel. Unfortunately, you can't get to it, see it, or change it. It's a closed box.

The NAS Hardware Architecture

NAS is a specialized server solution with proprietary hardware and software.

NAS products provide a *black box* style of computer externally configured as a server with extensible internal components configurable to the class of storage requirements you need. The black box computer style is available in both RISC and CISC or Intel processing chip sets. The computer system's hardware is proprietary to the manufacturer in terms of the internal component standardization, assembly, and the lack of interchangeable components.

The Server Part

Figure 9-1 is a generic layout of NAS hardware components. As you can see, they are just like any other server system. They have CPUs built on motherboards that are attached to bus systems. RAM and system cache, meanwhile, are the same with preconfigured capacities, given the file I/O specialization. What we don't see in the underlying system functionality are the levels of storage optimization that have evolved. NAS internal hardware configurations are optimized for I/O, and in particular file I/O. The results of this optimization turns the entire system into one large I/O manager for processing I/O requests on a network.

Given the black box orientation of the internal server components means you don't have to worry about further optimization and tuning for file I/O processing for the NAS solution. However, time spent on evaluating the hardware components of the vendor's solution is important, because once you install it, further changes will be only up to the manufacturer's extensibility of the model. Additionally, all file I/O workloads are not alike, as much as we would like to think so (see Part VI). Given the various and diverse products that exist, the evaluation of the speeds and capacities of the NAS hardware configuration are critical factors contributing to the effective storage and application performance.

Figure 9-1 shows the components that are optimized for file I/O, but does not speak to how they are optimized. This is done in the combination of the internal hardware and the proprietary operating system software as illustrated and discussed later in the software part of this chapter. However, it is important to note that extensive efforts have gone into the design and layout of the NAS internal hardware that provides the optimization for file I/O. It is unlikely we can find out how this is done unless we work for the particular NAS vendor. Needless to say, this work is proprietary to each vendor and is a significant part of the value proposition of their products.

The Storage Part

NAS is a storage solution, and as such, perhaps its most important aspect is the storage infrastructure it provides. NAS supports multiple storage types, capacities, and configurations, including select levels of RAID at the top end (for example, enterprise class NAS devices). However, support for RAID levels 1 (mirroring) and 5 (striping with parity) is beginning to become available already preconfigured in low-end NAS appliance devices. Support for incremental storage capacity upgrades depends on the vendor and flexibility of their models for upgrading.

Figure 9-1 is a generic representation of the storage part of the NAS configuration. Note that the proprietary nature of the hardware continues through to the storage connectivity and storage devices. Again, this part of the value proposition of the NAS bundled solution is optimized for I/O operations. There is an important design distinction to point out. Although largely assumed given the traditional I/O operations of the

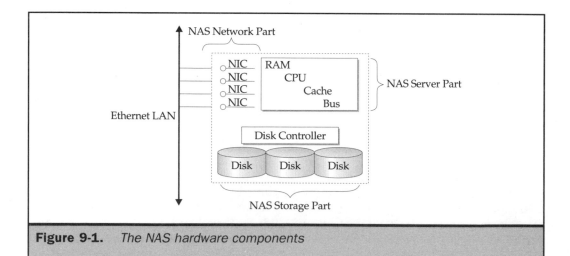

Figure 9-1.   *The NAS hardware components*

NAS device as a server, it becomes lost in the focus on file I/O operations. The NAS device processes file I/O requests from clients within a network. As with any computer, these are processed into read/write requests through the OS and file system. Ultimately, this results in low-level disk operations performed at a block level, which means the NAS device still performs normal block level I/O operations within its internal processing configuration.

The sophistication of the storage system itself, and how it performs block I/O processing, depends on the type and class of NAS system. However, the storage infrastructure (the storage system, temporary locations, connectivity, and so on) is tightly coupled with the server part as well as the reconfiguration and capacity upgrades that depend on the flexibility of the vendor.

NAS devices are managed differently both internally and from an administrator perspective. The formatting of NAS disk devices is performed under the control of the proprietary operating system and, more importantly, its file system component. Consideration for cluster or block size may be out of the hands of the administrator, and thus limits the flexibility to the types of files the storage system will handle. Monitoring device activity is dependent on the tools provided by the vendor. Although additional third-party tools support limited levels of NAS activities, tools for the internal performance of system, storage, and network parts are lacking.

The Network Part

NAS supports Ethernet-based network connections, with all released standards supported (for example, 100-baseT through Gigabit Ethernet). Connectivity to the server bus is through standard NIC-type connections, however the bus connectivity from the adapter to the system bus is proprietary to the vendor. Most will find PCI connectivity standard even though processing chip sets vary from RISC-based systems to CISC-based Intel systems.

The NIC network components are available from single adapter configurations to extensible configurations that support multiple NIC connections such as those depicted in our generic NAS component diagram, shown in Figure 9-1. The adapters will support standard TCP/IP stacks with most connections being offered by NAS vendors through OEM products from various suppliers. Because of this situation, network performance can vary given the capacities and functionality of the NIC.

Departmental solutions are offered with only single NIC adapters, while mid-range NAS solutions offer multiple connections. However, even network connections for extensible mid-range solutions generally don't exceed a maximum of four NIC adapters. Enterprise NAS solutions will be extensible according to bus structures that are available from the vendor. This NIC connectivity and performance can be a limiting factor in deploying NAS in high growth areas. However, this is generally addressed by adding multiple NAS solutions. (More about these considerations is discussed in Parts V and VI.)

The NAS Software Architecture

NAS is optimized for file I/O; support of any other types of workload I/O is problematic.

NAS software consists of three major components: the micro-kernel OS part, a proprietary file system, and the network software drivers. These are depicted in Figure 9-2.

The Micro-Kernel OS Part

The operating system for NAS is a UNIX kernel derivative, as indicated in the server discussion. The system is developed with only OS components that enable effective file I/O operations. Components such as memory management, resource management, and process management are all optimized to service file I/O requests. This implementation as a black box architecture renders extreme limitations to initiating other processes, jobs, or activities through the OS. Besides the management tools that the NAS vendor or third-party independent software vendor provides, other processing activities within the server are not available.

Process management is programmed to handle the file I/O processes as the highest priority. Interrupt processing queues and handles other requests secondary to the I/O manager. Various scheduling methods and algorithms are used to optimize these tasks, such as "first-in, first-out" and random selection by queue. In this manner, all file I/O processes are completed prior to starting any new overhead tasks that the system may

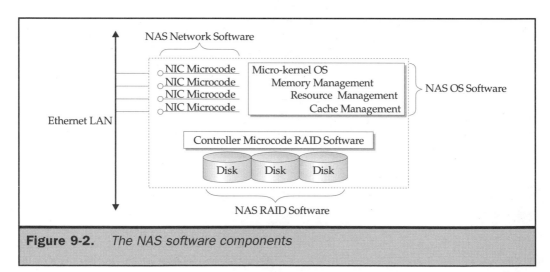

Figure 9-2. *The NAS software components*

require. Balanced among these is the need to manage network processes, as well as handling the overhead of the TCP stack. Given its reentrant functions, several network requests should be processing at any given time. This becomes a balancing act for the OS to handle sufficient network requests with I/O manager activities in order to complete block I/O operation to the storage.

Memory management will be optimized to handle as many file requests as possible—that means sufficient buffer space and cache management to facilitate the process management schedule. Capacity will play an important role in the capability of the OS to handle interactive requests. Most will be set for read-only operations to cache as many requests on the up-side (network input), and read-ahead buffer on the down-side (storage reads). Interchange will take place as the network process is completed in encapsulating the read request and passing control to the IP process and transmission. As we can see, a significant amount of time is used with TCP and IP process management.

Given the focused job the OS has to do, resource management is fairly static. I/O operations take over all the resources necessary to complete its tasks. Therefore, resource availability takes on a greater level of importance. In addition, the level of controller processing not only plays a significant role in completing the operations but is also fundamental in making resources available to the greatest number of processes. The operations of disk controllers and the further enhancements to controller processing, such as RAID levels and cache management, play significant roles in completing the I/O tasks.

NAS File Systems

The standard file systems included with NAS devices will support one of two types: the Common Internet File System (CIFs), the Network File System (NFS), or both. In many cases (as shown in Figure 9-3), the standard network file system interfaces with the NAS proprietary file system. Most NAS devices need to do this to manage their own storage. According to the vendors, the implementation of other types of connectivity protocols is supported inherently. As an example, the heterogeneous use of NAS devices to support multiclient access is evolving beyond CIFs through protocols such as SAMBA. Other proprietary network protocols such as Direct Access File System (DAFS) are beginning to emerge as well (see Part II).

 Note   *Samba is a freeware program that provides end users access to commonly shared resources, and is used primarily to share files and devices between Windows and UNIX systems.*

NETWORK ATTACHED STORAGE

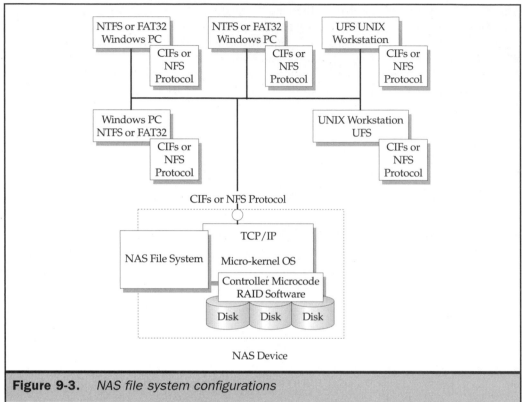

Figure 9-3.   *NAS file system configurations*

Network Connectivity

The third of the three major NAS components supports standard TCP/IP communications within a diversity of transport media. The most popular topology remains Ethernet. Support here is evolving with increasing bandwidth in light of Gigabit Ethernet standards, sophisticated participation within enterprise networks with quality of server (Qos) and routing participation, and advancements in coexistence with other storage models, such as FC SANs.

A limiting factor of file I/O processing with NAS is the TCP/IP network environment and the processing of TCP layers. As we discussed, the communication between client applications and server I/O is processed within the encapsulation layers. Within the

NAS architecture, these layers (which are normally processed within the server) are now processed within the NAS box. To address these challenges, the TCP/IP overhead should be given great thought when implementing a NAS solution. However, TCP/IP performance issues are difficult to address, given the black box nature of the NAS software and the OEM supplier relationship of the NIC components.

An advancement that may help this condition is the development of TCP off-load engines (TOE). These are special NIC cards that off-load much of the TCP encapsulation processing onto the NIC card itself. Although this solution is just emerging, it reflects evolving technology directions that optimize latency within IP networks.

Note   *TCP off-loads derive their value by processing TCP layers within the NIC card. Anytime software instructions are downloaded into lower-level machine instructions, it becomes highly optimized, operating at machine speeds. However, this is done at the sacrifice of software flexibility, given it's much harder to change micro-code or ASIC instructions than software that's operating under a high-level language within the OS.*

NAS as a Storage System

Putting all the parts together allows a highly optimized storage device to be placed on the network with a minimum of network disruption, not to mention significantly reduced server OS latency and costs, where configuration flexibility and management are kept to a minimum. The NAS solutions are available for a diversity of configurations and workloads. They range from departmental solutions where NAS devices can be deployed quickly and in departmental environment settings to mid-range and enterprise-class products that are generally deployed in data center settings.

The Departmental NAS Architecture

NAS is most often used to support the high growth of file servers that populate Windows client-based networks. An example is shown in Figure 9-4. It's an almost perfect solution for consolidating unoptimized file servers (for instance, Windows NT or Windows 2000 servers that operate only as network file servers for clients on the network).

The Internet NAS Architecture

An optimized solution is a more scalable and cost-effective answer as multiple servers can be consolidated into a single NAS device. NAS is also heavily used and is a good solution for interoperable access to files within web environments, as illustrated in

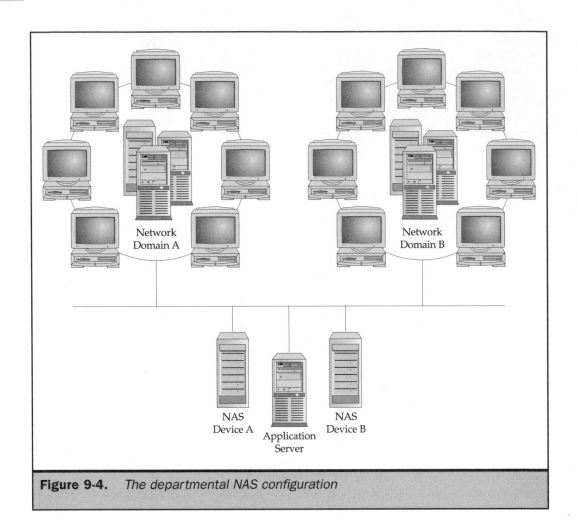

Figure 9-4.   *The departmental NAS configuration*

Figure 9-5. NAS is the perfect storage solution for Internet connections to web-based files accessed through HTTP.

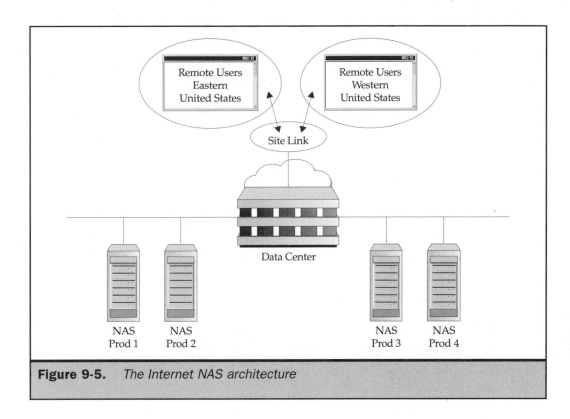

Figure 9-5. *The Internet NAS architecture*

The Enterprise NAS Architecture

At the high end are solutions that support large capacities of data, usually having reduced user transaction rates yet high I/O content. The storage and usage of unstructured data characterizes these workloads, although other structured data exhibiting these same characteristics can be NAS candidates. Figure 9-6 shows a specialized application being supported though high-end NAS devices.

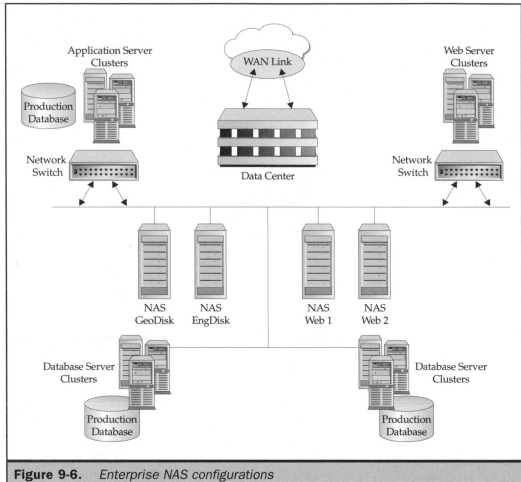

Figure 9-6. *Enterprise NAS configurations*

The Complete Reference

Storage Networks

Chapter 10

NAS Hardware Devices

143

NAS devices form an effective Network I/O manager for remote applications. From the perspective of the NAS hardware, functioning as an I/O manager, careful consideration should be given to the components and their corresponding characteristics that provide this complex functionality. This chapter will discuss NAS hardware components and their characteristics along with the issues that will confront these elements. Within these discussions will be definitions of key hardware components of the NAS device, configuration and capacities, and typical NAS I/O workloads as they relate to NAS hardware.

NAS hardware working in conjunction with related components function as an I/O manager. The NAS hardware components described in this chapter are the processor elements, RAM and related buffer management, and, of course, the storage system elements. We cannot overlook the communications and input-processing components largely made up of NIC interface elements and related bus connectivity options. These elements will be described and discussed in Chapter 12, which deals with NAS connectivity options, but it is important to recognize them in relation to the NAS hardware.

Closely related to NAS hardware are the effects of NAS processing models. Three models of NAS processing exist which drive NAS configurations and related component capacities:

- Simple extensions of a client's file system, as a shared storage resource, make up simple file processing (Sfp).

- Remote file acquisition with added reliability from a heterogeneous set of clients constitute quality file processing (Qfp).

- Enterprise-level processing of files using NAS within a transactional type of system with heterogeneous access and multitier applications form a complex file processing (Cfp) configuration.

With the NAS hardware functioning as an I/O manager, the performance of its components will be characterized by the workloads it processes. NAS workloads are made up of file-oriented processing activities performed on behalf of various applications. These workloads consist of I/O operations with disparate I/O content. Client network files transferring office application files offer a dramatically different I/O content contrasted against the unstructured data such as image, video, and audio. On the other hand, web-based and other specialized application file structures exhibit everything from variable length files to compressed and encryption-encapsulated, structures.

NAS Hardware as the I/O Manager

As we discussed in the previous chapter, the NAS devices perform a singular directive with a duality of function, network file I/O processing and file storage. A more concise term would be that it functions as an I/O manager. So, what is an I/O manager?

The I/O manager is a major component of computers and is made up from a complex set of hardware and software elements. Their combined operations enable the necessary functions to access, store, and manage data. A discussion of many of these components can be found in Part II. A comprehensive view of the internals of I/O management is beyond the scope of this book, however an overview of a theoretical I/O manager will help you understand the hardware operations of NAS.

Figure 10-1 shows the typical components that make up a theoretical I/O manager.

The I/O subsystem is made up of hardware, the processor instruction sets, low-level micro-code, and software subroutines that communicate and are called by user applications. The I/O manager is, in effect, the supervisor of all I/O within the system. Some of the important aspects of the I/O manager are the following:

- **Hardware Interrupt Handler**   Routines that handle priority interrupts for hardware devices and traps associated with error and correction operations.

- **System and User Time**   A system clock that provides timing for all system operations. I/O operations called by the user and executed in kernel mode take place in system time and are performed by the clock handler routines.

- **I/O Device Addressing**   A system whereby hardware devices are addressed by a major and minor numbering scheme. Major device numbers are indexed to a device table. The minor device number identifies the device unit number. For disks, the minor number refers to the device number and the partition number. For tapes, the major number refers to the controller slot number, and the minor number refers to the drive number.

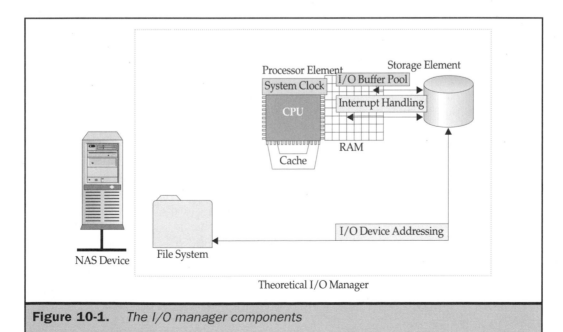

Figure 10-1.   *The I/O manager components*

- **I/O Buffer Pool**   Retaining data blocks in memory and writing them back only if they are modified optimizes disk access. Certain data blocks are used very frequently and can be optimized through buffering in RAM.

- **Device I/O Drivers**   Block I/O devices such as disk and tape units require instructions on how they must work and operate within the processing environment. Called device drivers, they consist of two parts. The first part provides kernel service to system calls, while the second part, the device interrupt handler, calls the device priority routines, manages and dispatches device errors, and resets devices and the status of a device.

- **Read/Write Routines**   System calls that derive the appropriate device driver routine, which actually performs the read or write operation to the device.

- **I/O Priority Interface**   System routine that handles requests for the transfer of data blocks. This routine manages the location of the block, making sure it is handled properly if in the buffer, or initiates an operation to locate disk address and block location within a device.

- **Raw I/O on Block Devices**   A system call and method used for very fast access to block devices, effectively bypassing the I/O buffer pool. These types of low-level operations of the I/O manager are very important in order to better understand the architecture and usage of database implementations using I/O manager functions.

NAS Hardware I/O Manager Components

If we view the NAS hardware functioning as an I/O manager, the critical components will be the processor element, the memory/cache elements, and the storage element. Certainly, the connectivity to the outside world is important and as such will be handled through its own chapter (Chapter 12 in this book). However, the internal hardware aspects of the NAS devices determine how fast it can process I/O transactions, how much data it can store, the types of workloads it can handle, and how it can recover from failing components.

The NAS Processor Element

The NAS processor component is critical to the power required to handle specific types of workloads. Although most vendors have moved to a CISC model (for example, using Intel chips to keep costs down), many of the leading vendors offer RISC-based processor components. The difference, although seemingly slight, can be substantial when evaluating the performance required for complex workloads.

RISC (Reduced Instruction Set Computing) versus CISC (Complex Instruction Set Computing) continues to be an on-going discussion within chip designers and system vendors. The differences are based upon different architectural designs in how the CPU component processes its instructions. The differences are depicted in Figure 10-2, which shows that RISC uses simple software primitives, or instructions, which are stored in memory as regular programs.

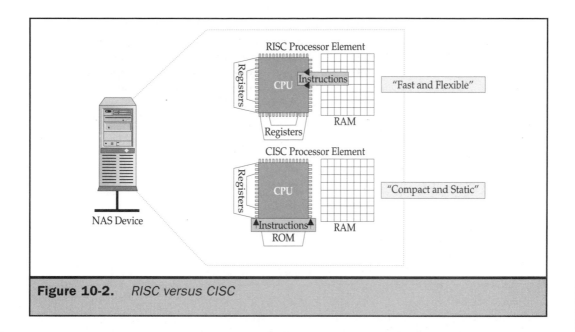

Figure 10-2.   *RISC versus CISC*

CISC provides the instruction sets using micro-code in the processor ROM (read-only memory). The RISC processors have fewer and simpler instructions and consequently require less processing logic to interpret—that is, execute. This results in a high execution rate for RISC-based processors. Consequently, more instructions will produce a gross higher processing rate with everything being balanced at a higher throughput. Another important characteristic of RISC-based processor architecture is that they have a large number of registers compared to CISC processors. More instructions that are closer to the ALU unit means faster gross processing and processor throughput.

Given the architectural differences, the capability to provide high system performance, with repetitive instructions, against a focused workload puts the RISC-based system on top. However, this is not achieved without cost. RISC-based systems are more costly than CISC-based systems, specifically Intel commodity processors. Therefore, a balance must be achieved between the performance sophistication of the NAS device versus the processing complexities of the I/O workload.

This is important as decisions made on cost alone result in non-scalable CISC-based NAS devices, or devices that may have a short-term usefulness in supporting a complex I/O workload. On the other hand, making a purchase based on performance alone may lead to an overallocation of processor performance which could be handled just as effectively with CISC-based systems performing in multiples (for example, deploying many NAS devices).

This is also important because it defines the type of Micro-kernel operating system the vendor supplies. All RISC-based systems are UNIX-based micro-kernel systems, while the CISC-based systems are a combination of both UNIX and Windows micro-kernel systems.

When evaluating NAS devices, you should at least know the type of processor architecture that's being used. Looking at technical specification sheets beyond the capacities of the disks and storage RAID capabilities, it's important to understand the scalability of instruction set computing for the workload being supported. You will find that all CISC-based processing will use Intel-based processors with the most recognizable RISC-based processors being offered through Sun, HP, and IBM.

The NAS Memory Element

RAM is an important factor in processing I/O requests in conjunction with available cache and cache management. Caching has become a standard enhancement to I/O processing. Cache management is a highly complex technology and subject to workload and specific vendor implementations. However, most caching solutions will be external to the processor and utilize cache functionality within the storage array controllers. As NAS solutions are bundled with storage arrays, any caching will be integrated into the NAS device using both RAM and storage controller cache. Caching solutions within the NAS hardware will remain vendor specific and available through the configurations. Note that some vendors have included a NVRAM (Non-Volatile Random Access Memory) solution that will provide a level of performance enhancement but a significant safeguard in data integrity to writes that occur within the workload.

The functions of the I/O hardware manager enable buffer management, which is a key element in the effective handling of I/O requests. As requests are passed from the TCP stack to the application, in this case the software components in the I/O manager, they are queued for processing through buffer management. Given the slower performance of the disk elements compared to RAM, the RAM I/O buffers provide an important element to quick and orderly processing of requests that may come in faster than the disk I/O can handle. Therefore, the more buffer capacity you have, the more requests can be processed in a timely fashion.

For data operations inside the processor element, the functions of system cache can also provide an additional level of efficiency. Our discussion regarding RISC versus CISC showed the efficiencies of having software instructions loaded as close to the CPU as possible. Having a combination of RISC-based instructions and user data blocks can provide additional levels of efficiency and speed. This can also prove effective in CISC architectures given the cache usage for user data blocks and the redundant nature of the I/O operations performed by the processor element within the NAS devices.

A popular solution to the esoteric I/O bottleneck problem is to add memory. Although this is an overly simple solution to a complex problem, in the case of NAS simple file processing (Sfp), it can generally be effective. The caveats (refer to Chapter 17) are many and lie within the read/write nature of the workload. Given that many NAS implementations are for read-only high-volume I/O transactions, the RAM element is an important part of the solution for increasing capacities for I/O buffer management.

The other effect RAM has on NAS devices is on the input side (for example, TCP/IP processing). Given that similar requests may develop faster than the processor element can execute them, the capability to queue these requests provides a more efficient environment in processing the TCP stack. In addition, the same will be true on the outbound side as requests for data are queued and wait their turn to be transmitted to the network.

NAS devices are configured with static RAM/Cache options in the low-end appliance level devices. Sizes of 256MB are common and are balanced to the small workloads these devices are configured for. Sizes and options increase dramatically in the mid-range and high-end models, with RAM options able to reach limits of one to two gigabyte levels. The configuration of system cache is highly dependent on the vendor and their proprietary implementation of the hardware processor elements.

The NAS Storage Element

Being that NAS is a storage device, one of its most important elements is the storage system element. As stated earlier, NAS comes with a diverse set of configurations for storage. These range from direct attached disk configurations with minimal RAID and fault resiliency support to disk subsystems complete with FC connectivity and a full complement of RAID options. Again, choice of NAS type is dependent on your needs and the workloads being supported.

At the appliance level there are two types of entry-level configurations. First is the minimum Plug and Play device that provides anywhere from 100 to 300GB of raw storage capacity. These devices provide a PC-like storage system connected to an Ethernet network using IDE connected devices with no RAID support. These configurations provide a single path to the disks, which range anywhere from 2 to 4 large capacity disks. As shown in Figure 10-3, the system provides support for a workgroup or departmental workload as Windows-based network file systems. However, these limited devices also do well with applications that support unstructured data (for example, image and video) within a departmental or engineering workstation group. Given their price/performance metrics, their acquisition and usage within an enterprise can be very productive.

The other ends of the appliance spectrum are the entry-level enterprise and mid-range NAS devices, as shown in Figure 10-4. These devices are also Plug and Play. However, capacities start to take on proportions that support a larger network of users

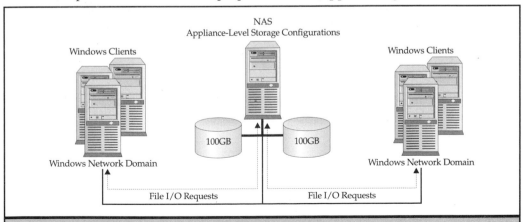

Figure 10-3.   *NAS appliance-level storage configurations*

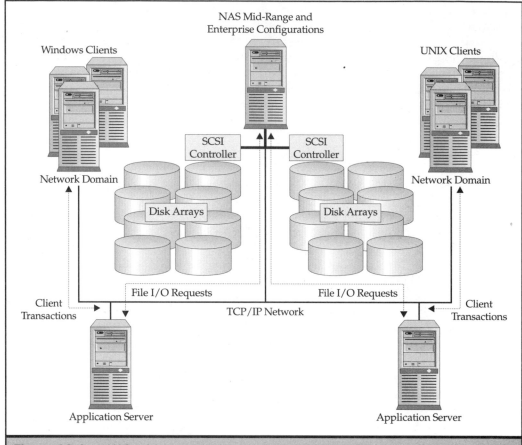

Figure 10-4.   *NAS mid-range and enterprise storage configurations*

and workload types. Storage systems capacities range from 300GB to 1 terabyte in size with RAID functionality at levels 0, 1, and 5. At these levels, the storage system is SCSI-based with options for the type of SCSI bus configuration required. With this, SCSI controller functionality becomes increasingly sophisticated. Although most use a single path into the SCSI controller, the SCSI bus functionality, because of its architecture, has multiple LUNs connecting the disk arrays.

The enterprise NAS devices extend the previous configurations with storage capacities, SCSI controller functionality, SCSI device options, and extensibility. Capacities extend into the terabyte range with multiple path connections into the disk arrays. The number and density of disks will depend on the array configuration. However, the top NAS configurations can support over 1,000 disk drives within a single device. At this level, RAID functionality becomes common place with pre-bundled configurations for levels 1 and 5, depending on your workloads.

Across the mid-range and enterprise offerings of NAS are three important hardware factors worth considering. These are fault resilience, FC integration, and tape connectivity. The NAS architecture renders these devices as functional units operating in a singular and unattended capacity. Therefore, the capability to provide a level of hardware fault tolerance particularly for the density and operation of the storage system has become a characteristic of the NAS solution. While Storage Area Networks provide another pillar to the storage networking set of solutions, the requirement for NAS to interoperate with SANs is increasing as related user data becomes interspersed among these devices. Finally, one of the key drawbacks to keeping critical user data on NAS was its inability to participate in an enterprise (or departmental) backup and recovery solution. This deficiency has slowly abated through the increased offerings of direct access to tape systems bundled with the NAS devices.

The ability to recover from a disk hardware failure has become sophisticated and standard among enterprise storage systems. These features have become integrated into the higher mid-range solutions and enterprise NAS devices. Look for full power supply and fan redundancy at the high end, and elements of both as these recovery options evolve from appliance-level solutions. This can be beneficial, as the environmental factors will differ greatly from closet installations to crowded data center raised-floor implementations. As one failure perpetuates another, this is an important place to consider fault-tolerant elements, because the inoperative power supply will bring the entire disk array down and potentially damage disk drives in the process. On the other hand, an inoperative or poorly operating fan will allow drives to overheat with potentially disastrous effects.

Another important aspect to the fault-tolerant elements is the capability to recover from a single inoperative drive within one of the disk arrays. NAS devices at the mid-range and enterprise levels will offer hot-swappable drive units. Used in conjunction with RAID functionality, either (software- or hardware-based) will allow the device to be repaired without the data being unavailable. Performance, however, is another consideration during a disk crash recovery period and is dependent on the workload and I/O content (additional discussion on this condition can be found in Part VI).

As with any recovery strategy, the importance of backing up the data on the storage system can't be underestimated. As stated previously, this is one area that has been lacking in the configurations and operation of NAS devices: how to back up the data within existing enterprise backup/recovery operations. Look for NAS devices to provide attachments to tape units. These will be offered as SCSI bus attachments where enterprise-level tape devices can be attached directly to the NAS device. Although a step in the right direction, there are two important considerations to make before launching into that area. First is the transparent implementation of yet another tape library segment. Copying data from the NAS device to an attached tape unit requires some level of supervision, ownership, and operation. In addition, the software required to provide the backup, and more importantly, the recovery operation has to run under the micro-kernel proprietary operating system of the NAS device. So, be prepared to support new tapes and new software to leverage this type of backup and recovery. (Additional discussion of this condition can be found in Part VI.)

NETWORK ATTACHED STORAGE

User data is now stored on disks directly attached to servers, using Storage Area Network and NAS devices. The applications using the storage infrastructure will largely ignore the specifics of the device infrastructure being used. That means that more interplay will happen with data that is stored between these different architectures. This condition is accelerating the need for NAS and SAN to communicate and provide some level of data access of each other's device. Look for high-end NAS devices to provide additional enhancements to participate within an FC-based storage area network. This will be offered as a host bus adapter from the NAS device with the appropriate software drivers running within the NAS OS. Using this type of configuration, the NAS device can service a file I/O and a block level I/O into the SAN. (Additional discussion on FC and Network connectivity can be found in Chapter 12.)

The sophistication and operational usage is just evolving for these types of integrated I/O activities. Data integrity, security, and protocol considerations (to name a few) are being developed as of this writing. In Chapter 17, we'll discuss some of the factors driving these requirements and various considerations to take note of when implementing applications within these configurations.

The NAS Processing Models

NAS uses three modes of processing. Understanding these modes helps determine and identify the growth of NAS workloads from the appliance level into the enterprise solutions. If we continue to view NAS as the I/O Manager for file-level processing, the modes in the following sections can be expressed.

Simple File Processing (Sfp)   This mode of processing simply extends the client's F/S and storage capacity into the NAS device. As depicted by Figure 10-5, this provides a simple transactional level of communication through a single type of protocol. Generally supporting Windows-based systems that require additional storage capacity for shared files or multiuser access to workgroup files, Sfp is handled by appliance-level type NAS devices with capacities that range up to 300GB at the high-end with minimal RAID support. Due to the limited transactional level (for example, access to shared files versus number of application transactional users), levels of RAM at or above (but not below) 512MB will generally support and balance the I/O operations for these configurations. Said configuration cross over to entry level and mid-range NAS devices as two things evolve: first, the number of users and consequently the size of user data; and second, the number of protocols supported. This can manifest itself in the heterogeneous support of client computers (for example, the addition of UNIX and Mac clients).

Quality File Processing (Qfp)   As user requirements move into supporting multiple protocols and increasing data capacities, the capability to provide quality processing increases. Quality processing, as shown in Figure 10-6, is defined as the capability to provide a level of data reliability to withstand component hardware failures, as well as support transactional level processing and heterogeneous sets of users. Qfp is supported

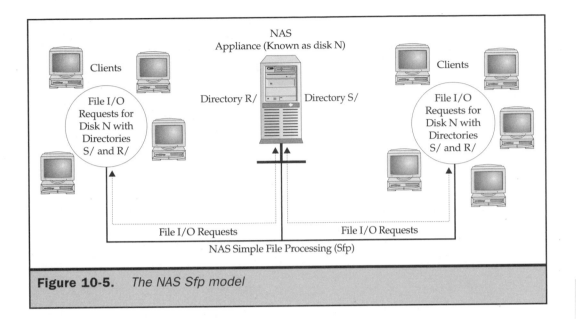

Figure 10-5. *The NAS Sfp model*

from entry level and mid-range level NAS devices with components such as fault-tolerant hardware components (power supply, fan redundancy, and hot-swappable drives), RAID functionality, and multipath disk array extensibility. Qfp is depicted in Figure 10-6 where a larger user base is supported along with transactional-like support through protocols such as HTTP. Storage capacities range from 300GB to 1TB, with RAM moving into the gigabyte range. These configurations cross into the area of enterprise level NAS solutions as the work begins to scale into multitier client/server applications with a heterogeneous user base and multiprotocol support.

Complex File Processing (Cfp)   Figure 10-7 illustrates the complexity of requirements that NAS can grow into. The multitier processing of application servers and the capability to service high volume Internet traffic forms the basis for Cfp. Within these configurations, the NAS devices must support quality processing and handle the transparency of transactional redirection. User requests coming into an application server that provides web services are redirected to the NAS devices where the files are physically stored. A more complex processing configuration is the integration of storage area networks. In these configurations, user transactions must be redirected to NAS file systems and further into the level of database block I/O contained in the SAN storage network. Cfp will clearly stress the high end of NAS devices and push the limits of what vendors offer. Clearly, this requires the features of fault-tolerant hardware given its participation within a highly available transactional system. The terabyte levels of storage capacities and RAM gigabyte levels notwithstanding, the uniform and reliable performance becomes paramount in Cfp. Consequently, additional importance will be placed on recovery options (for example, tape connectivity and backup/recovery software, management tools, and overall enterprise data center integration).

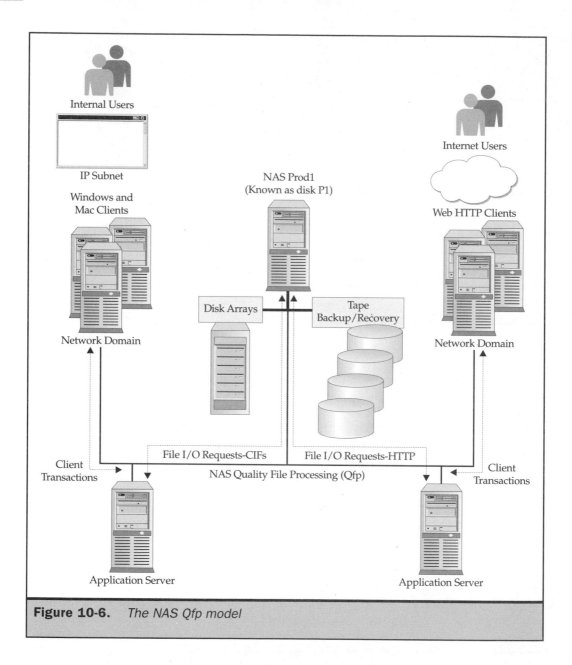

Figure 10-6. *The NAS Qfp model*

NAS Workloads and NAS Hardware

The NAS workload is characterized as file-oriented processing for various applications that end users require. Typical among these are Windows client files using personal applications such as office applications, shared forms, and templates. Other typical applications can manage unstructured data such as image, video, and audio files.

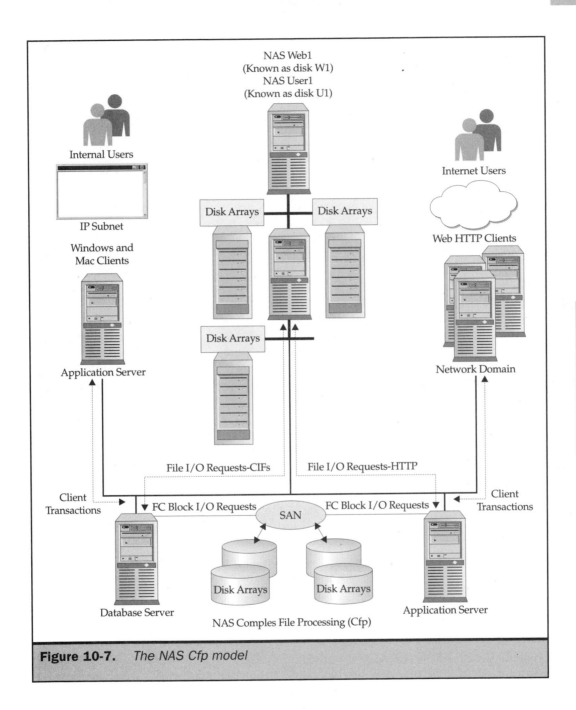

Figure 10-7.   *The NAS Cfp model*

Larger scale enterprise applications are centered on relational database tables while enterprise Internet applications are grounded in new web-based file formats. The application notwithstanding, the workload that NAS has to contend with centers on the characteristics of the files they are storing, or to put it another way, the I/O content they have to satisfy.

Within the context of NAS, the I/O content is determined by the type, format, and characteristics of the file. For example, the content of a word document is very different than the content of a JPEG image. The reason is not only self-evident but also simple: the size and structure of the data. If we look at the access of these contrasting file types, we see the effect each has on the NAS hardware components.

If we take the next step and observe the I/O operations necessary to access these diverse file types from the NAS storage system, we find that the data content transferred within each I/O operation can differ greatly. Contrasted against the operating system, we find that the I/O operation is dependent on many things, such as the number of paths to the controller, the number of LUNs, and disk density. Consequently, the number of I/O operations, commonly referred to as IOPS, is a number without a corresponding level of efficiency.

> **Note**   *IOPS is defined as the number of I/O operations performed per second by a computer system. It's used to measure system performance and throughput.*

It's possible, as we illustrated in Figure 10-5, that the transfer of a large text document can theoretically take more I/O operations, resulting in an inefficient transfer of data with each I/O. Conversely, the I/O operations for the JPEG could be done with less I/O operations, resulting in an efficient transfer of bytes of data with each I/O—very efficient! The difference is not only the density of the disk, the cluster size as set with the operating system, but also the capacities of the internal components of the NAS hardware elements themselves. The point is that the workload determines the capacities for individual, as well as groups of, NAS hardware specifications. Ensure that workloads and relative I/O content are given due consideration prior to setting the record for the fastest NAS install.

Given the black box orientation of the NAS device, look for efficiencies in the I/O manager that will provide levels of flexibility in these contrasting workloads. Operational evaluations of NAS devices should also cover the effects of a *black box* architecture on other data hierarchy locations, including system-level cache, RAM, and types of processor architecture.

Additionally, careful evaluation is necessary in maintaining the NAS devices for data recovery, disaster recovery, and data archiving. Operational discussions should also cover the challenges involved in participating in larger storage infrastructures, where NAS must interface with various storage devices such as tape, optical, and other server disk storage systems.

NAS hardware constitutes commodity components bundled into a Plug and Play storage solution. However, the evaluation of NAS devices requires some level of diligence in understanding the processing model used, the need for particular NAS components, such as processor types, device extensibilities, and capacities. More important is the type and extensibility of the storage system used with the bundled solutions. Given the rapid growth of end-user storage, configurations should ultimately be scalable to both the enterprise and workload.

Chapter 11

NAS Software Components

As discussed in Chapter 10, NAS hardware works like a Network I/O manager for remote applications. From the perspective of the NAS software, which functions as the I/O manager, it essentially becomes a remote file system with attached storage. As such, similar consideration should be given to the software components that utilize the corresponding NAS hardware features. Working together, they form the complex functionality that facilitates Network Attached Storage. This chapter discusses the software components and their sometimes-eclectic characteristics. Given the bundled architecture of the NAS devices and the black box orientation of NAS, nee storage appliance, each component will confront different issues as they perform their primary functions as a remote file system and attached storage.

NAS software can be categorized into three major components, as shown Figure 11-1. The first is the NAS micro-kernel, an optimized operating system. Working with the micro-kernel is file system software and file communication protocols that provide the NAS with its remote file capabilities. The foundation for the NAS solution is the storage software itself, made up of device drivers, RAID software, and other feature enhancements provided by particular vendors.

Although a fourth category exists, defined as the connectivity component, we defer discussion of this until the next chapter. The importance of networking and connectivity issues demand enough attention that in-depth discussions need to be dedicated to these subjects alone. Consequently, this chapter will deal with the internal software components of the NAS devices, with network communication factors being addressed only in a high level.

A Remote File System with Attached Storage

As stated in the previous chapter, the NAS devices perform a singular directive with a duality of function, network file I/O processing, and storage. Their directive as a remote file system or network file system has a colorful legacy enhanced and developed though multiple projects that span many academic and commercial computer research environments.

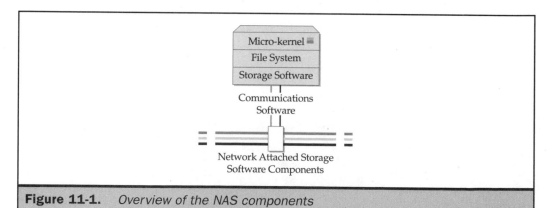

Figure 11-1. *Overview of the NAS components*

UNIX, having long been the mainstay of scientific, academic, and research computing environments, evolved as an open system with enhancements coming from these communities on a continual, although discretionary, basis. The need to share data in some organized yet distributed fashion became a popular and increasingly important development effort. Projects at AT&T labs and several major universities began to research this need in the late 1970s. UNIX became a viable offering to both the scientific and business community during the distributed systems revolution in the early 1980s, at which time data sharing really became predominant due to the exponential growth of users and open networks.

The problem of data sharing was addressed in two ways: First, by AT&T labs through their development of the RFS file system; second, and more importantly, a development effort by SUN using the inherent components of UNIX developed a Network File System (NFS) as the standard we know today. NFS was based upon the use of the UNIX remote procedure call (RPC). An RPC is a programming term for a "remote procedure call," where one system can execute a program on another system and return the results. Implemented on all open UNIX code bases, this formed the basis for allowing a user on one system to access files on another (see Figure 11-2, which shows how the UNIX RPC function allows a user to execute UNIX commands on a second system).

Although many of the academic projects provided alternative ways of using the RPC function, the basis was the same in terms of providing access between UNIX file systems. The implementation differences were characterized by the diverse levels of file systems, functions performed by the file system versus activities on the client, and the sophistication of administrative and housekeeping functions. It's important to point out that in some sense parallel development took place in providing solutions for Windows-based systems as Novell took a similar path in providing a file server solution with its Novell Netware Network Operating System. Although similar to what was happening in the UNIX environments, it went further as it developed a proprietary communications protocol creating a local network of computers based upon the Windows operating system.

Other functions were also developed around the open characteristics of the UNIX operating system. These were concepts of file and record locking, security, and

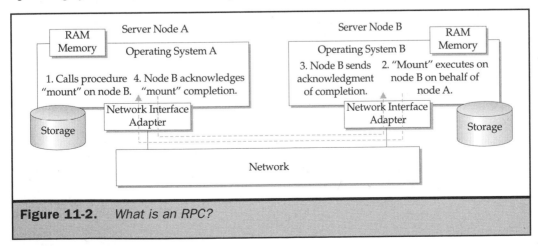

Figure 11-2.   *What is an RPC?*

extensions to the UNIX I/O manager. Unfortunately, these functions were open to compromise given the lack of enforcement of operating system standards, processing activities, and core UNIX functions. Operating within these environments, users were confronted with unexpected file deletions, records modification and corruption, and security violations. In many cases, this was predicated by the system security level perspective of UNIX academics that security was the responsibility of the user.

Sun's Network File System became an enabling component for specific vendors looking for ways to provide a specialized solution for file sharing with networked environments. The idea grew out of customer NFS configurations in which general purpose UNIX workstations were used only for storing common data within a network and making it accessible through the server's UNIX file system, something which had been set up to export portions of the file system to authorized clients. (Figure 11-3 shows the initial configurations of UNIX workstations and the designations of storage workstations—for example, the server.)

These vendors developed small footprint servers running a specialized UNIX kernel optimized for I/O and network connectivity. Its only job was to provide shared access to files within a network, where any client computer attached to the network could store and access a file from this specialized UNIX server. Given that the sole component visible to the network was its storage, the only appropriate acronym was Network Attached Storage, vis-à-vis NAS. (Figure 11-4 shows the initial NAS configurations with UNIX workstations, with a close-up of an early NAS system.)

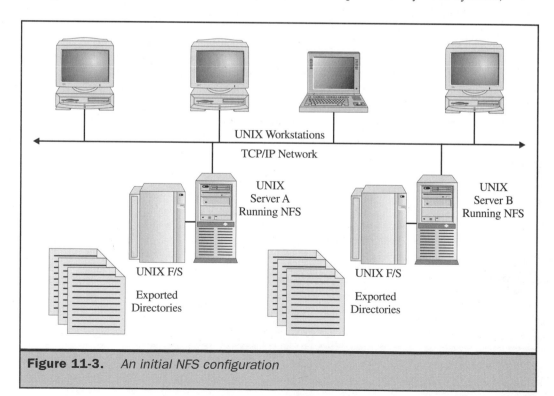

Figure 11-3.   *An initial NFS configuration*

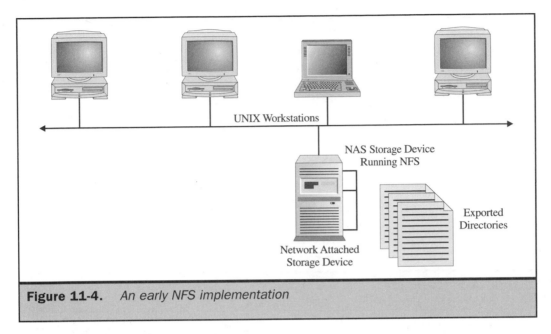

Figure 11-4.   *An early NFS implementation*

The NAS Micro-Kernel OS

The NAS legacy relies heavily on UNIX operating system foundations and functionality as it evolved to support distributed computing and networking. The NAS device operates from a micro-kernel operating system and although most NAS vendors offer their products with UNIX-based micro-kernels, it's not offered by everyone. As we'll discover, the positive aspect of standards with UNIX and Windows plays an important role in the heterogeneous functionality of the NAS devices. For example, the POSIX standard has provided a level of commonality to key operating system components and has become important as NAS devices expand beyond their native UNIX families to support other operating systems, communications, and file protocols.

Note   *POSIX (Portable Operating System Interface) standards were developed by IEEE for the purpose of cross-platform interoperability.*

Core systems functionality within an operating system is contained in the kernel. This consists of a collection of software that performs the basic functions of the computer and interfaces with the lower-level micro-code and system ROM facilities provided by the hardware vendor. Although this core-level software of the operating system will be called different names in different implementations, such as the nucleus in IBM's MVS OS, the term "kernel" has become synonymous with the core functionality of the operating system used by both UNIX variants and Microsoft Windows.

Within the kernel are the routines that manage the various aspects of computer processing, such as process management, scheduling, memory management, and I/O supervision by the I/O manager (refer to Chapter 10 for more information). The kernel also operates in a supervisory manner and services the requests of applications that operate in user-mode, thereby forming the fundamental cycle of processing depicted in Figure 11-5.

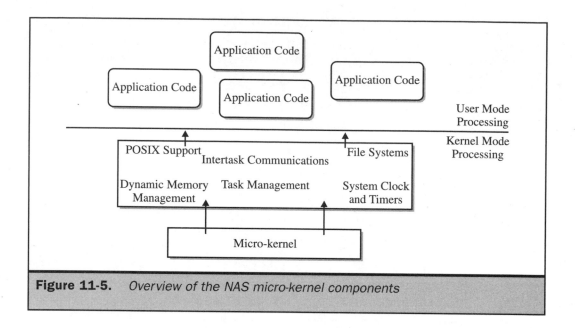

Figure 11-5. *Overview of the NAS micro-kernel components*

An interesting aspect of the UNIX kernel is the open nature of the UNIX operating system and the user's ability to modify the kernel code and rebuild it to suit their particular needs. This created a chaotic systems administration problem. However, outside the bounds of a stable environment, it did provide the basis for enhancements that solved particular problems. This flexibility provided the best platform for those individuals and companies that had to provide a special operating system for embedded or specialized applications.

These applications generally required operating a computer as a transparent entity where the OS supported a singular application such as mechanical automation, monitoring, and process control. This required the OS to be small, reliable, and transparent to the end user. The development of the OS for these particular applications was built from UNIX kernel code that had been modified to suit the specific needs of each application. Given that these applications had to run in real time, controlling equipment and monitoring machines, they became known as Real Time Operating Systems or RTOS.

All NAS devices in today's world are based on some type of RTOS. Given their highly customized ability to facilitate the OS for a single application, the RTOS offerings were highly compartmentalized, allowing vendors that used the OS to customize the components they needed. Most special applications did not require the entire functionality of the UNIX kernel and needed both performance optimization and limited overhead customized for the particular application. This resulted in the more common term of "micro-kernel." Even though I have used this term previously and many reading this section may have encountered the term before, the importance of accurately describing the micro-kernel cannot be overlooked given its relation to NAS devices.

A typical micro-kernel is shown in Figure 11-6. We can see that the selection of components depends on the application; however, there are multiple components to choose from that provide vendors with complete flexibility in how they customize the OS. Important NAS components include the following:

- Task management, multitasking, scheduling, context switching, priority levels
- Intertask communications, message queues, interrupt and exception handling, shared memory
- Dynamic Memory Management
- The system clock and timing facilities
- A flexible I/O and local file system
- POSIX support
- OS hardware targets, PowerPC, MIPS, SPARC, NEC, 80x86, Pentium, i960

The customization of the micro-kernel in NAS devices centers on effective and efficient storage I/O, its compatibilities to remote file systems, and its effective task processing for file-level operations. Given these tasks, the NAS micro-kernel will look like Figure 11-7 and contain the necessary components. On top of the micro-kernel are the embedded applications each vendor supplies in addition to the unique I/O processing through customization of the kernel. Key areas within these applications are the storage and network device drivers, file systems, and buffer and cache management.

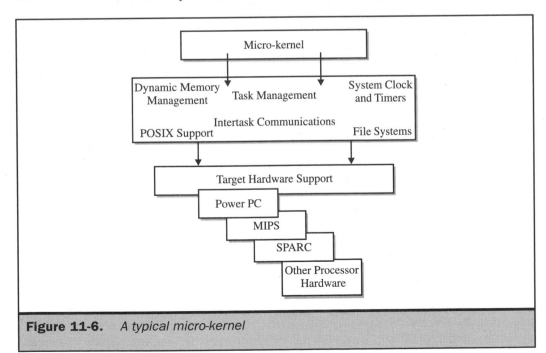

Figure 11-6.   *A typical micro-kernel*

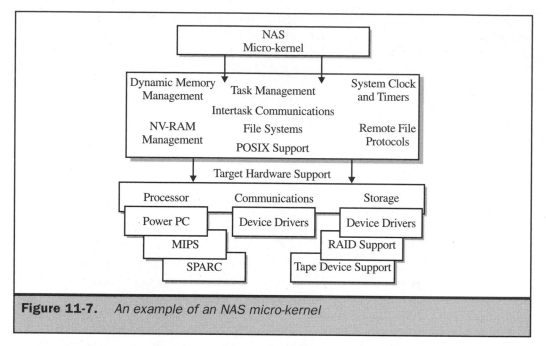

Figure 11-7. *An example of an NAS micro-kernel*

Another key area to introduce is the implementation of non-volatile RAM used in many NAS devices (for example, NV-RAM). Implemented through the physical RAM capacities, it is driven through specific memory management routines that allow these buffer areas to be used for checkpoints in the status of the file system and related I/O operations. This is memory that is protected through some type of battery backup so that when power is off, the contents of memory are not flushed but are available when the system is restored. This makes temporary storage less sensitive to system outages and permits recovery to take place quickly using routines built into the micro-kernel proprietary applications.

NV-RAM becomes an important factor when working with both device drivers and RAID software.

Not all micro-kernels are based on UNIX. The Windows NT and Windows2000 I/O managers form the basis for NAS micro-kernels used by an assortment of large and small vendors, through the Storage Appliance Kit (SAK) offering. Although the importance of POSIX compliance pays off, with Microsoft providing levels of compatibility, the characteristics of NT and subsequent Windows 2000 I/O manager derivatives have different architectures and the following additional components.

The Microsoft OS model is an object-oriented architecture. This is characterized by its use of layered architectures and I/O synchronicity (for example, the employment of file handles as compared to virtual files used in UNIX). The encapsulation of instructions, data, and system functions used in the object models provides programming power and flexibility; however, it comes with a higher cost of processing and resource overhead.

Micro-kernel communications with device drivers operate with a layered architecture. This condition allows operating subsystems such as a file system to call services to read a specific amount of data within a file. This is accomplished by the operating system service passing this request to the I/O manager, who calls a disk driver. The device driver actually positions the disk to the right cylinder, track, and cluster and reads the specific data and transfers control and data back to the I/O manager. The I/O manager then returns the requested data to the file system process that initiated the request on behalf of the application.

The Microsoft model uses mapped I/O in conjunction with its virtual memory and cache manager. This allows access to files in memory and manages their currency through normal paging activities of the virtual memory manager.

Although both UNIX and Microsoft architectures support synchronous and asynchronous I/O processing, the level of processing affinity is consistent within the Microsoft model. The asynchronous model used for many years in mainframe multitasking systems allows applications to continue to process while slower I/O devices complete their operations. This becomes important in processing scalability as more CPUs are added to the processor component.

Given its multilayered architecture and its ability to shield the developer from many of the OS internals, the Microsoft model comes with additional overhead. Considering the increased levels of abstraction of object orientation resulting in multilayered functions (for example, device drivers calling device drivers and file handles as virtual files or representations of the files in memory), it remains difficult to minimize the extra processing inherent with any of its OS RTOS derivatives.

The NAS File System

NAS uses a network file system or NFS. The implementation of NFS works by the use of the RPC, or remote procedure calls, to manipulate a UNIX file system existing on a server. The system encapsulates these functions to allow remote users on a network to issue commands to the server's file system. However, in order to understand the internal happenings of the system, we must look briefly at UNIX file systems.

The UNIX File System

The file system is one of the major components of an operating system. It is responsible for storing information on disk drives and retrieving and updating this information as directed by the user or application program. Users and application programs access file systems through system calls such as *open*, *create*, *read*, *write*, *link*, and *unlink* commands. The UNIX system consists of several different types of files. These are Ordinary files, Directory files, Special Files, and FIFO files.

For our discussion, the most important are the Directory files that manage the cataloging of the file system. Directories associate names with groups of files. Ordinary files are generally reflected through directory names created by users and applications. Special files are used to access peripheral devices. FIFO files are used by UNIX functions called PIPES that pass information and data from program to program.

The UNIX system contains a multilevel hierarchical directory structure set up as an inverted tree with a single root node (see Figure 11-8). When the system is booted, the root node is visible to the system; other file systems are attached by *mounting* them under the root or subsequently under the current directory known to the system. While

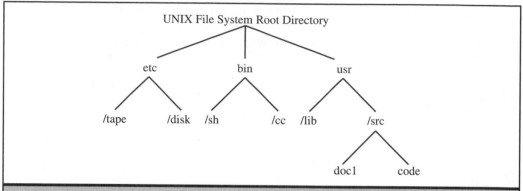

Figure 11-8. *The UNIX hierarchical directory system*

directories cannot be split across file systems (they're restricted to a single reference of a physical disk or logical disk partition), files can appear in several directories and may be referenced by the same or different names.

The directory entry for a file consists of the filename and a pointer to a data structure called an *inode*. The inode describes the disk addresses for the file data segments. The association between a file and a directory is called a *link*. Consequently a file may be linked to a number of directories. An important feature of UNIX systems is that all links have equal status. Access control and write privileges are a function of the file itself and have no direct connection with the directory. However, a directory has its own access control and the user has to satisfy the directory access control first, followed by the file access control in order to read, write, or execute the file.

Figure 11-9 shows an example of how the *mount* command works as users mount file systems for access. A formatted block device may be mounted at any branch directory level of the current hierarchy.

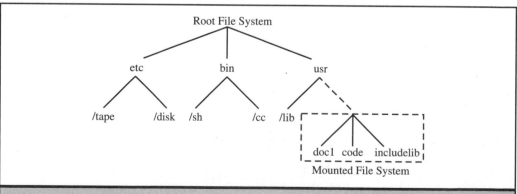

Figure 11-9. *Mounting a file system*

Since file systems can be mounted, they can also be unmounted. The unmount system call handles all the checking to ensure that it is unmounting the right device number, that it updates the system tables, and that the inode mount flags are cleared.

Internal Operations of NFS

The implementation of NFS is supported on a number of UNIX implementations. These installations support transparent network wide read/write access to files and directories. Workstations or file servers that allow their file systems to be accessible for remote access accomplish this through the *export* command. The export command allows these file systems to be sharable resources to the network. Workstations, or clients, wishing to use these files import the file systems to access the files.

Let's follow an example of a user requesting access to data within an NFS configuration. User "A" requires engineering drawings and a specifications document in the /Eng folder that is supposed to be shared by all in his department. Here is what has to happen for him to access this in a transparent mode.

First, as indicated in the following illustration, the system administrator has to set the /Eng directory as exportable to the network. They do this by using the export command, which allows users who have access to the network to share this directory and the files associated with it. Secondly, the user has to initiate a *mount* command that allows the server side to issue a virtual file system, consisting of directories as indicated in Figure 11-10. Although simple in an external representation, the internal activities provide us with a better indication of the complexities involved in using NFS.

The functions associated with this illustration are broken down as activities on the server file system. This is both in the form of local commands to the file system and remote commands via RPC. The server RPC sends out the acknowledgment any time

NETWORK ATTACHED STORAGE

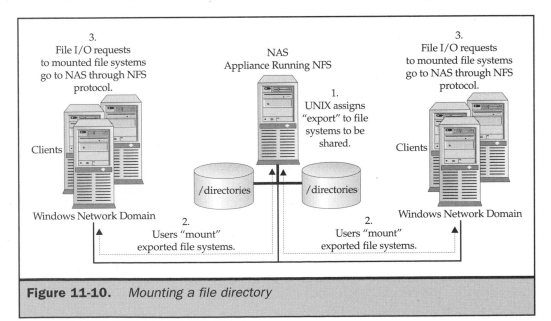

Figure 11-10.   *Mounting a file directory*

a client wishes to mount the NFS file system (sometimes referred to as mounting the NFS device), given that the UNIX file system refers to a logical disk. Consequently, the client sends initial requests to the server in the form of RPC to initiate the import, linking, and access to the NFS file system. Once this connection is made, the client then communicates via RPCs to gain read/write access to the associated files.

Although transparent to most users, all this takes place under the cover of UNIX and the application, the configuration and processing sequence provides an affordable storage network using general purpose hardware, operating systems, and networks.

The Storage Software

The third major component is the storage software consisting of device drivers and RAID support. Most prominent for consideration are RAID support and the relative inflexibility outside of pre-configured arrays, as well as the use of different levels such as RAID 4. As discussed in Part II, RAID storage systems are offered in various levels depending on the workload supported and fault resiliency required. This is important when considering NAS storage software options and their relative RAID support because NAS is a bundled solution and the level of RAID support may not be easily changed or upgraded.

Device driver support is also important, as the flexibility to upgrade and support new types of devices is driven from this element of NAS software. As stated previously, NAS supports enhanced disk hardware and is starting to offer support for attached tape drives for backup/recovery and archival operations. Within disk support are drive connectivity options that are now being offered in both SCSI and FC disk arrays. FC support should not be confused with storage area network connectivity or with functionality as a switched fabric. Additional information about NAS-SAN integration can be found in Chapter 20.

Support for RAID is determined by the NAS solution. Entry-level appliance devices come with little to no RAID support (for example, disk mirroring, both protected and unprotected). On the other end, enterprise multiterabyte NAS solutions have a pre-configured RAID selection ranging from level 1, disk mirroring, to level 5, disk striping with protection. Other vendors offer levels of RAID that best support their file system and processing architecture.

RAID level 1, disk mirroring with protection, is configured to provide a redundant file system. Figure 11-11 illustrates this point as the file system data is effectively duplicated within the storage arrays. Actually, the file system processing knows that two systems exist and each will be updated as files are updated and changed. Protection is provided by way of the storage software's ability to synchronize its processing so that in the event of a failure on any of the arrays, the other set of files can continue processing. This poses a problem when it comes to the resynchronization of both file systems after a failure. The functions of synchronization become a feature of the NAS solution. As stated previously, the entry level NAS solutions provide just straight mirroring with no synchronization. This is considered a RAID 0 or disk-mirroring solution without the benefit of continuous operations. The data would be protected but the system would become inoperative while the duplicate mirror is switched to become the primary file system.

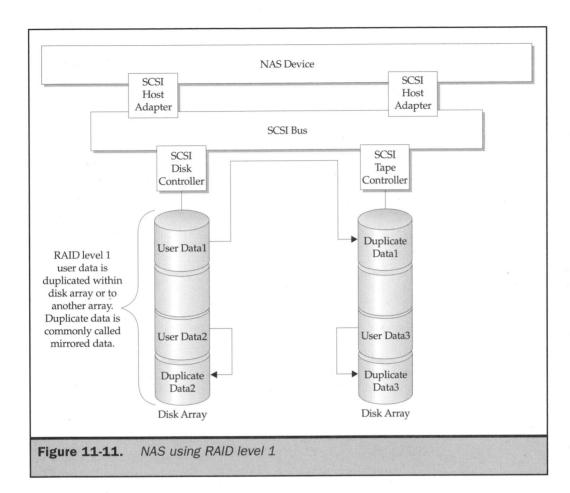

Figure 11-11. *NAS using RAID level 1*

As the NAS solution assumes a larger role in transactional types of processing (for example, multiusers and OLTP-type transaction support), the need for continuous processing becomes more defined. In these cases, the NAS solution offers RAID level 5 support. This provides the file system with the ability to strip its files throughout a storage array. To provide data and continuous operation protection, parity data is created on each device across the array.

The storage software uses the parity information, which is also striped and distributed across each drive, allowing it to recover from disk failures within the array. Recalculating the parity information and rebuilding the lost data and information onto the remaining disks accomplishes this. Figure 11-12 illustrates the same file system functioning within a RAID 5 environment.

RAID 5 works well in processing models where transactions are small and write operations are limited. As we can conclude, the RAID 5 software and related disk operations in providing parity, file, and data currency across the storage array

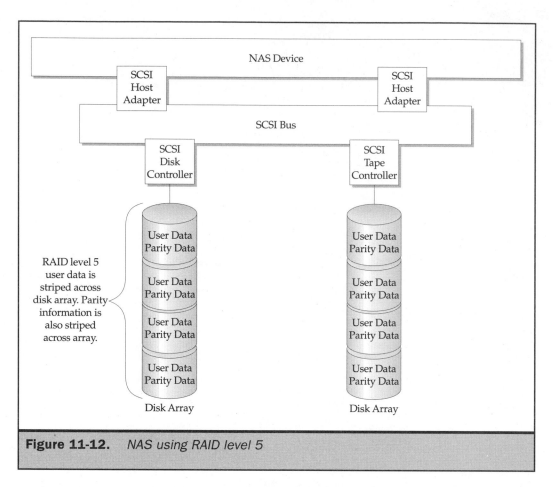

Figure 11-12.   *NAS using RAID level 5*

can be intensive when performing transactional work with heavy updates. However, this should be balanced with the read/write ratio of the workload and the ability to provide NV-RAM for operational efficiencies.

A relatively unknown RAID level you will encounter with NAS is RAID level 4. Similar to level 5, RAID 4 provides data striping across the array; however, it reserves one disk within the array for its parity, as shown in Figure 11-13. This offers a level of efficiency for write-intensive operations, but sacrifices operational protection in the event the parity disk becomes inoperative. Again, this level of RAID should be balanced against the workload and the quality of the NAS solution. Given the reliability of disk drives in today's market, the likelihood of the parity disk becoming inoperative within a multidisk array becomes statistically non-existent. However, for the workload that demands a fully redundant 99.999 percent uptime, this may become an issue.

Regardless of the RAID level, the workload and subsequent service level dictates the type of storage protection required. NAS offers a complement of RAID protection strategies such as popular levels of disk mirroring with protection or RAID level 1, and

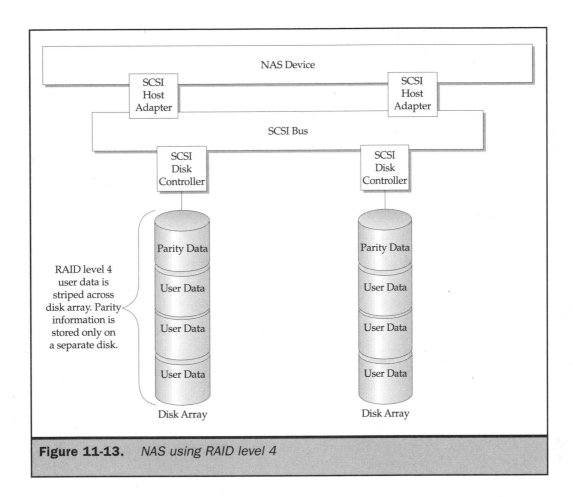

Figure 11-13. *NAS using RAID level 4*

data striping with protection offered though levels 4 and 5. It's important to keep in mind that many of these storage protection offerings are bundled and pre-configured with the NAS solution. Flexibility to change or upgrade to other levels of RAID will be at the discretion of the NAS vendor.

NAS Software as an I/O Manager

If we view the NAS software components—micro-kernel, file systems, and storage software—as a composite I/O manager, similar to how we viewed the NAS hardware, we uncover a tremendous value bundled into a single device. Along with a composite of I/O related functions is the value of providing a distributed solution as complex as file I/O through existing networks. This is an important distinction to identify as the difference between a NAS product is compared to a Do It Yourself (DYI) commodity server being retrofitted to function as a shared file server. Consider the following major functions that the NAS device provides, which the user consequently doesn't have to worry about.

- **Remote File Processing**   The ability for an application's file I/O requests to be handled through the network and serviced by a multipurpose file system.

- **Operating System Optimization**   The functions of an I/O optimized OS that is pre-configured, bundled, and RAID ready. Includes I/O optimization for task, memory, and scheduling management.

- **File System Ubiquity**   Provides the levels of support necessary to process multiple file protocols and is optimized within a single file system.

- **File Read/Write Processing**   Provides the ability to effectively, reliably, and securely store and retrieve application data from a remote network location.

NAS Software and NAS Processing Models

In the previous chapter, we defined three NAS processing models. These were contrasted with NAS hardware considerations which provided some insight into the general hardware requirements and capacities for each. The following discussion can be used in conjunction with this information to balance the software considerations and requirements for each of the NAS processing models. Support for each of these models stresses particular elements of the NAS software and, as such, should be evaluated carefully as workloads increase with each model and as software requirements grow from Sfp processing into enterprise-level Cfp models.

The following represents some key considerations as simple file processing grows into more complex processing requirements. Using these categorizations as guidelines, they can provide valuable insight into the types of NAS devices required for departmental and data center file processing workloads.

- Simple File Processing (Sfp) essentially extends the client's F/S, which should be accomplished with as little overhead as possible. This requires a simple micro-kernel implementation with the minimum enhancements. Processing is characterized by read-only synchronous processing with minimum queuing; however, with this processing model effective buffer and cache management is noticeable.

- Quality File Processing (Qfp), which processes files with added value for more reliability and integrity, adds extra overhead as activity builds the importance of effective interrupt processing, device drivers, and interaction among user-mode, kernel mode, and device-driver processing. Also, the sophistication and usage of Authorized Control Lists (ACL) for security and the ability to provide significant reliability with asynchronous processing and RAID levels is an important consideration of the NAS software for this processing model. Increased transactional workloads now point to additional TCP processing, which will leverage effective redirector functions.

■ Complex File Processing (Cfp) is the processing of files with the added value of user/application-defined prioritization as well as access to other file and storage systems. As with hardware components, this will be the greatest challenge as all elements of an I/O manager are stressed to their limits. Consequently, the ability to provide effective and efficient storage protection, device driver communications, queue management, and complex redirector processing is paramount.

I/O Workloads and NAS Software

The workloads for NAS devices have been characterized as file-oriented I/O operations performed on behalf of remote applications executing somewhere within a network. An important distinction in considering these workloads is the evolution of NAS devices as they take on a wider scope of I/O operations in supporting applications that require more than just file access. These workloads have been traditionally difficult for appliance- or black box–oriented RTOS machines, given their limited flexibility in performing operations outside of file access and I/O. Two major areas that NAS is beginning to support are database products and native data protection products.

Database processing, both in the context of the relational model and static model, typically exists where the database engine executes on a local application server and the user data exists on the same server using directly connected storage systems. When the user data in the form of tables are moved to a remote server or storage system, this becomes problematic given the integrated processing that occurs within the database engine and its associated tables (see Chapter 8). Making things more complicated in a remote setting are the required components to support transactional type processing in the form of log files and lock management.

Note   *The Static Database Model defines a database system that is distributed with a specific application. These bundled databases operate only with the application they are distributed with and consequently are closed to modification and use as a general purpose database. They are often referred to as embedded databases, or runtime databases, and are used with business applications that range from e-mail, Enterprise Resource Planning (ERP), to Customer Resource Management (CRM).*

Activities have been underway to ease the restrictions of running databases on NAS devices. First are the combined efforts of the NAS vendors and database companies. This has resulted in configurations where the database engine continues to reside on a commodity server; however, the data tables are remotely stored on the NAS device. This comes with many caveats, such as the support of these configurations by the database and NAS vendors, given the complexity of the solution and limited user expertise. Another major consideration is the limitations of database processing that can be sustained in these configurations. Additional discussions in Chapter 19 will provide more detail on these implementations.

NETWORK ATTACHED STORAGE

Data protection products such as backup and recovery software, mirroring, and data archiving are all used to support integrated data center maintenance functions. These functions are integrated into data protection activities and policies supported through software that function throughout a wide segment of operational environments—for example, mainframe configurations, UNIX configurations, and Windows network server environments. If a device doesn't easily fit into one of these categories, the likelihood that existing software products will effectively support it is low. Such has been the case for NAS devices. The reasons are straightforward given the RTOS nature of the NAS device and the additional processing that has to take place when executing data protection software on any server. Optimized NAS devices do not have the capacity and functions to run general-purpose backup and recovery as well as other data-protection solutions.

To overcome the limitations of data protection within NAS environments, NAS vendors and third-party storage software vendors have been working to provide native NAS solutions—that is, solutions that are integrated into the NAS devices. From the NAS vendors themselves, they have been enhancing their enterprise-level devices to provide physical connectivity to tape devices, allowing the ability to copy and archive data to tape directly from the NAS device. Although this is an effective way to handle the protection of data stored on the device, the consideration is the integration or new development of an IT tape library. Will the new tape units integrate into an existing tape library and how will they be protected and accessed are two questions for consideration regarding this NAS data protection solution.

There are two other enhancements to the integration of data protection activities for NAS that increase its level of enterprise reliability and availability support. These are mirroring and snapshot. Mirroring, a level of RAID storage functionality previously discussed, allows NAS devices to participate in a high availability processing strategy by providing the necessary support for real-time backup of data. This can be done locally or configured remotely to function as a disaster recovery solution. The snapshot function allows similar operations, however it provides a level of data redundancy, usually locally, that permits the processing of applications to continue even as the data is copied for backup purposes. The snapshot function essentially takes a "snapshot" of an existing file system and maintains this copy according to the timing of the snapshot itself. This can work in conjunction with other data protection methods, such as mirroring, to ensure multiple data protection strategies are implemented.

The Complete Reference

Storage Networks

Chapter 12

NAS Connectivity Options

NAS connectivity characterizes the real power of network storage. Connection directly to existing networks allows the NAS devices to function as network I/O managers. However, the ease of implementation within a network is a double-edged sword, providing administrators with an easy mode of implementation that masks the serious implications of the network storage traffic driven by NAS workloads. The use of Ethernet network topologies provides an effective and proven infrastructure when it comes to planning and implementing appliance, mid-range, and enterprise NAS solutions.

From a software perspective, the use of TCP/IP allows configuration and support to be easily integrated into existing IT knowledge and support structures. With the number of tools available to monitor networks and network infrastructures, the ability to manage the connectivity of NAS devices is far more advanced than any other storage networking methodology. However, the inherent nature of TCP/IP stack processing provides a challenging mix of performance and configuration issues once connectivity transfers from the network to the NAS server. These issues are still evolving as NAS workloads become more complex and network connectivity extends beyond the Ethernet and TCP/IP infrastructures.

Connectivity plays a very visible role as NAS devices become integrated into other storage systems. The evolution of storage networking is eliminating the boundaries between direct attach, Fibre Channel networks, and many sophisticated WAN configurations. Although many of these external connectivity issues will be addressed in Parts IV and V regarding integration with other storage models, we will discuss the effect and conditions surrounding LAN and WAN connectivity issues.

Putting Storage on the Network

A major benefit of NAS devices is that they utilize existing Ethernet resources and additional high-speed connectivity hardware. NAS vendors support all levels of Ethernet including 10 to 100 based T media to Gigabit standards. The connections are enabled through industry standard NIC cards that offer both concurrent Ethernet support and high-speed connections. Most vendors will offer various configurations regarding the type of connections, number of NICs supported, and related TCP/IP drivers. However, most devices will remain limited in the appliance and entry-level NAS solutions, with additional enhancements and offerings through mid-range and enterprise level NAS servers.

NAS Connectivity Architecture: Hardware

Bus connectivity for the NICs become proprietary as they attach through the I/O adapters of the NAS server bus. Most vendors adhere to the PCI standard; however, this is difficult to determine without specific inquiries to the vendor. This becomes an important aspect given that the number of transactions supported depends on the performance of the NICs and their respective bus interfaces.

NAS and LAN Topologies

The following discussion illustrates the various LAN topologies where NAS configurations are installed. Each offers a set of challenges and considerations, and in order to effectively understand these, we offer a summary overview of LAN fundamentals.

Understanding the fundamentals of network hardware devices is important to how the NAS solutions will perform in any network topology. Network connectivity devices such as bridges, hubs, routers, and switches operate at specific levels of the OSI reference network model while performing their duties. As you may recall, the OSI network model forms the layers for TCP/IP processing. The most important layers to consider for network devices are the physical access layer (layer 1), the datalink layer, (layer 2), the network layer (layer 3), and the transport layer (layer 4). They are depicted in Figure 12-1 and described below through their connection proximity and processing responsibilities.

- **The Physical Layer (Layer 1)**   The physical layer provides the direct mechanical and electrical connection to the network media (the wires and cabling that sends the data in bits throughout its physical interconnections). Layer 1 interfaces directly with the data link layer through the media access control (MAC) sublayer.

- **The Datalink Layer (Layer 2)**   The datalink layer separates the transmitted data into frames for transmission over the physical media, such as 10 base T5, 10 base T2 cable, or UTP wiring. This layer performs error-checking and is responsible for retransmitting frames. It provides a direct channel to the network layer through a logical link control (LLC) sublayer and a lower sublayer which connects to the transmission media called the media access control layer (MAC).

- **The Network Layer (Layer 3)**   The network layer provides information on the routing of data transmitted from sender to receiver. This layer ecncapsulates the user data through routable network protocols such as, IP, IPX, SNA, or AppleTalk.

- **The Transport Layer (Layer 4)**   The transport layer provides information on how a point-to-point connection is developed. Layer 4 utilizes the network layer to determine the type of connection between computers. This is based upon TCP or UDP protocols. These two connections set up sessions between computers, and determine the protocol under which they will operate. However, it should be noted that TCP is a connection-oriented protocol while UDP is connectionless, which characterizes their performance and error recovery. This facilitates the use of Remote Procedure Calls between operating systems (refer to RPCs in Chapter 11).

NETWORK ATTACHED STORAGE

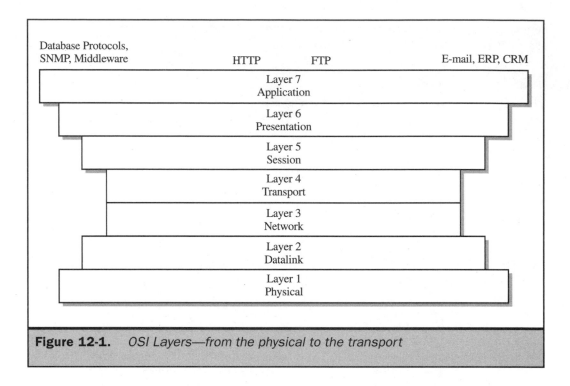

Figure 12-1. *OSI Layers—from the physical to the transport*

Using the OSI model, network devices operate using layers 1 through 3 to develop a local area network (LAN). The network devices used to leverage each layer of the OSI model in building a campus network or LAN is diverse, sometimes interchangeable, and can be confusing if you are inexperienced in network administration and management. However, they are illustrated in Figure 12-2 and categorized into the following segments.

- **Repeaters, Concentrators, and Hubs**   Although most are becoming obsolete given the evolution of LAN switching devices, many still exist, and all operate at the physical level. Repeaters provide a retransmission of signals in order to increase the range of physical segments of wiring. They continue to be used to extend the physical distance capabilities of LAN wiring segments. Concentrators and hubs provide the same services—that is, the connection of clients and servers through one wiring segment. This results in all servers, PCs, and workstations on the segment sharing the bandwidth and forming a single collision domain, as it relates to the machine access layer (MAC) algorithms that use the Ethernet Carrier Sense Access/Collision Detection (CSMA/CD) protocol.

- **Bridges and Layer 2 Switches**   Bridges interconnect different types of physical network topologies such as FDDI, Ethernet, and token ring, and operate at layer 2: the data link layer. They also can be responsible for filtering network traffic

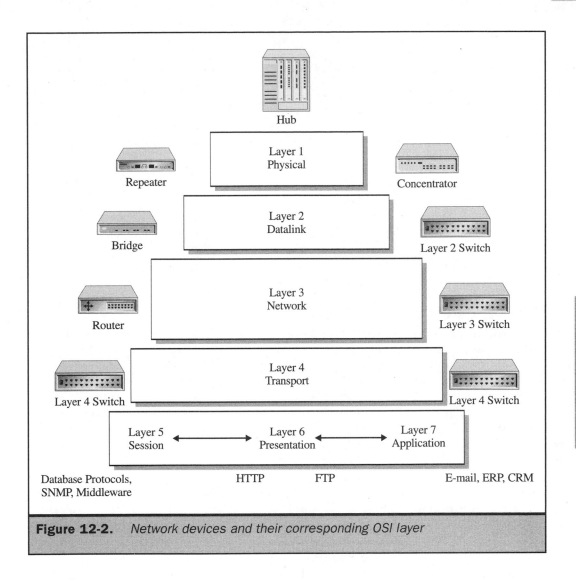

Figure 12-2.   *Network devices and their corresponding OSI layer*

using the layer 2 MAC addresses. Layer 2 switches connect different port connections and enable the transfer of data by destination address. They are commonly used to provide a backbone network connection where clients can reach servers outside their domain and interconnect to outside WAN services.

■ **Routers and Layer 3 Switches**   Routers or layer 3 switches forward data packets based upon IP address, link, or network availability and performance. Layer 3 switches perform similar functions as routers. They provide this service from two distinct architectures, both operating under layer 3 information. Port switches operate at the hardware level of the switch by directing network traffic from port to port according to layer 3 information. They also perform at chip speeds. The follow-on from port switches are frame switches that operate from layer-3 information; however, they perform port traffic direction by examining the data packet and providing the most effective routing to the destination.

■ **Layer 4 Switch**   These switches make connection decisions based on information in layer 4 regarding session and application layer information. This allows them to provide such services as load balancing across servers and broadcast services.

We can view the placement of NAS devices within two major topologies: appliance placement and enterprise placement. Appliance placement facilitates the placement of data as close to the user as possible. This requires the placement of an NAS device within a hub or single-network segment. The enterprise placement provides greater access to data through multiple segments of the network. Given the variability of the network designs and topologies, there are many ways of implementing these configurations. We will discuss these two major approaches and their related considerations.

NAS Network Deployment

To discuss the NAS deployment in as much context as possible, we offer a typical network infrastructure, as illustrated in Figure 12-3. This conceptual network supports a theoretical business that is populated with a headquarters staff within a three-story building, and a data center which is housed in a separate building. The business is externally connected to the Internet and outside leased lines. External sales and marketing personnel utilize the network through Internet connectivity and servers connected through outside dedicated leased lines. This conceptual network does not illustrate particular topologies, but is designed to represent major components that will both influence and pose deployment challenges to NAS devices.

As mentioned previously, there are two categories of deployment: appliance level and enterprise level. Although derived by various requirements, including the network infrastructure, initial deployment decisions center on data ownership and access. This means the user community may feel they own the data, such as an accounting and finance department, and have characteristics of homogeneous access (in other words, only persons within the accounting department can access the information).

Another perspective is data that becomes developed from multiple sources and accessed by multiple user communities. Often characterized by marketing and sales departments that utilize multiple sources to build data bases, data access profiles become very complex. User access can be on multiple levels (say, for sales people, executives, and order-entry administrators), and therefore requests for data may traverse multiple network segments. More importantly, answer sets tend to move through multiple network segments.

Yet another view of external access within the data center comes from using combinations of homogeneous and heterogeneous access. The most obvious are facilities that store web-based data for access to companies outside sales personnel,

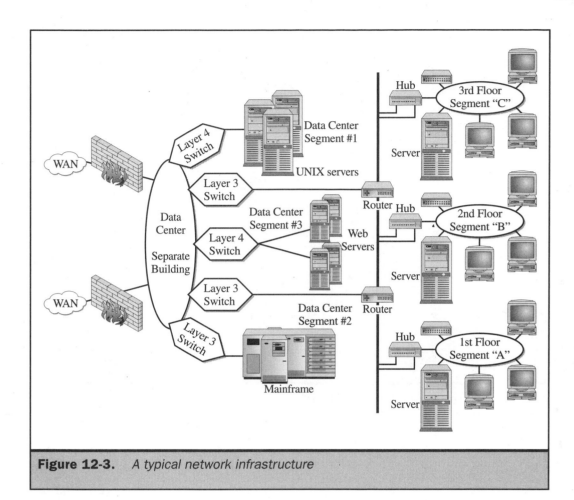

Figure 12-3.   *A typical network infrastructure*

partners, and customers. An important aspect of this data placement is, of course, security; however, data integrity and availability is paramount as well.

NAS Appliance Network Deployment   Given our typical company, let's analyze the homogeneous access of data. This type of access and data placement easily justifies the appliance level of NAS solution. A subset of our large network infrastructure is illustrated in Figure 12-4, where the Accounting department has installed an NAS appliance, and access is contained within the network segment handling the first floor. Note that this segment is configured with a hub that provides a connection between the PCs and workstations used in the finance department, as well as the main server handling the finance client/server financial applications. The NAS device handles the I/O load of the financial application server and performs very well as long as the traffic is contained with the network segment.

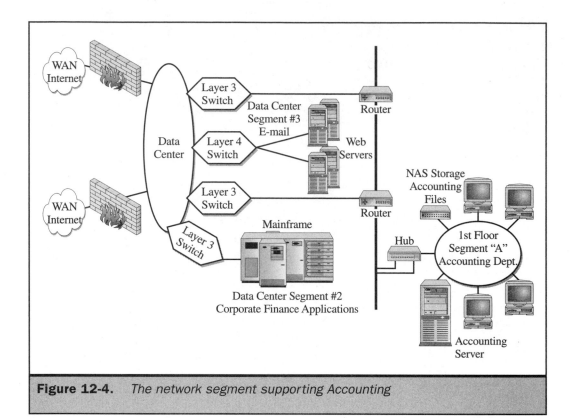

Figure 12-4.   *The network segment supporting Accounting*

The challenges and performance issues begin to show up as users from other network segments begin to access the NAS device. Outside users degrade service by adding additional traffic that is serviced by a hub device which must share its bandwidth within the network segment. Secondly, as users outside the network segment access the NAS accounting data, they must traverse several jumps from one network segment to another. These are referred to as "hops." The more "hops" the more network latency is built up, adding to aggregate traffic on the network backbone.

Finally, the type of I/O workload also determines the placement factors and, more importantly, the required bandwidth for network segments and the capacities of network devices. Consider our example of the accounting data. One reason this works well is the financial planning data that's used within this area. These worksheets can be extremely large and I/O-intensive as they are processed by the financial application server. The answer sets and results of these financial planning programs are extremely I/O-intensive, however, when handled within the limits of the hub and configured connections (for instance, multiple ports for the server and multiple ports for the NAS device).

NAS Enterprise Network Deployment   Certainly, not all data access is contained within a network segment. As a matter of fact, many corporate applications must be accessed through the data center. Figure 12-5 shows the network segments within the data center. This portrays a more complex set of segments than the local user networks. Considering that the data center must support multiple user access, applications, and data, its requirements for network segmentation become comprehensive. If we add external access to the Internet as well as dedicated leased lines, the network infrastructure becomes the focal point for corporate data access and makes data placement a more daunting task.

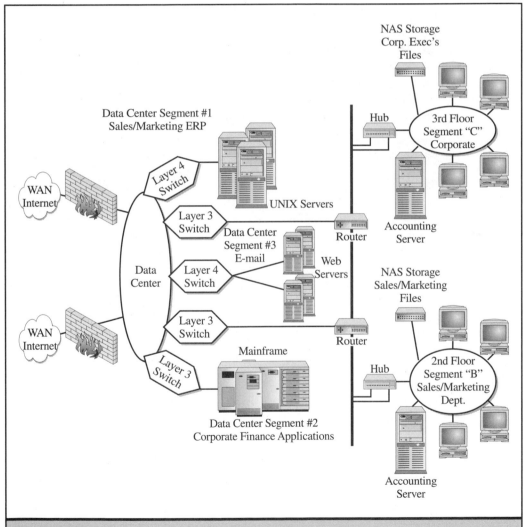

Figure 12-5.   *Network segments within the data center*

NETWORK ATTACHED
STORAGE

Let's take our example of sales and marketing data that must be accessed by multiple users, and which is then developed from multiple data sources, both internal and external. Although this is also a good candidate for NAS solution, placement and capacities become key to a successful implementation. Without restating discussions that will be covered in Part V, let's assume that the sales and marketing data have the following characteristics.

- **Sales Data**   Sales orders, tracking, and customer information are contained in the ERP system, which is processed and accessed through the UNIX servers within the data center. Data access is handled by sales administration through the third-floor network segment, outside sales people from the web sites, and finally by limited users that work in branch offices and access the ERP system through the dedicated leased lines.

- **Marketing Data**   Marketing information, product information, brochures, market analysis, and data mart analysis are contained in every system in the data center, the mainframe, the UNIX servers, and the web servers. The information used to build market and customer analysis data marts are copied from sales orders, customers, customer tracking, and products.

Two solutions are productive in these situations. First, is the use of NAS devices for the collection and storage of web data. Second, is a large NAS device to hold the sales data that is accessed by sales personnel in the field. An additional important installation would be the use of NAS devices to hold large data base tables that make up the marketing datamart (for example, market and customer analysis data). Each of these solutions can be placed within the data center for general access. Given that the data center connects to the network backbone and contains a secondary network backbone within the data center (as shown in Figure 12-3), the bandwidth to handle multiple user access can be configured with high-speed network resources and devices.

Although on the surface it may appear that the installation of these large NAS devices should be on the data center backbone, when we look closer at the network's makeup, we find that each segment within the data center is handled by a layer 3 layer 4 switch. Each of these devices provides additional flexibility in the placement of NAS devices given their I/O responsibility. For example, the NAS sales data device could be placed within the UNIX segment given the network access from both internal and external users. The NAS device could be placed within the web segment given that access, security, and sourcing can be managed with existing web workloads. (We placed a layer 4 switch in our example shown in Figure 12-5; this could leverage workload balancing effectively, however, from a newer layer 5 switching device.)

NAS over WAN Topologies

Part of our discussion has touched on network challenges and various issues with LAN topologies. However, as Figure 12-5 shows, there are outside network connections that influence various NAS configurations, along with their placement and opportunities. Each configuration discussed earlier offers a set of challenges and considerations which effectively utilize WAN connections.

To facilitate this understanding, we offer a summary overview of WAN and LAN-WAN fundamentals. Figure 12-6 shows the external connections from the data center into the outside world. There are two major types depicted, Internet connections and dedicated leased-line connections. The Internet connections are leased lines that attach to an Internet service provider (ISP) where additional connections provide external Internet accesses. These lines are dedicated and depend on the grade and capacity of the line, the capacity and resources of the ISP, and the type of service the company has contracted for. In any event, it is outside the control of the NAS device and internal network infrastructure. Basically, you have to deal with what you have available, in Internet terms.

The second external connection is through dedicated lease lines that are available through the long distance carrier, IXC, and local exchange LXC carrier. They provide dedicated lines and services through a wide variety of telecommunications transport technologies that include frame relays, ATMs, and other communications protocols.

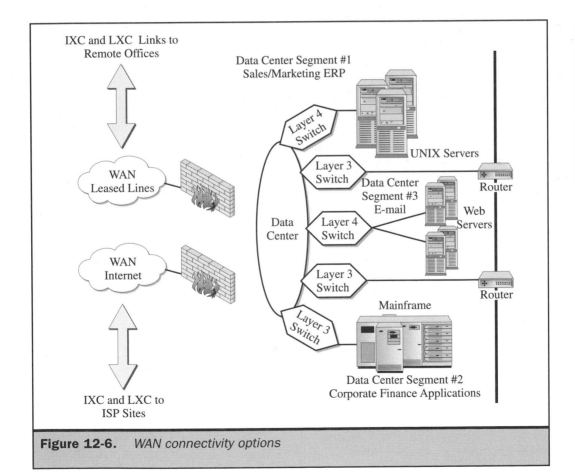

Figure 12-6. *WAN connectivity options*

Actually, once it leaves the confines of the data center, the data being transferred is within the control and management of the IXC or LXC, which could mean, and usually does mean, multiple communications protocols, circuits, and equipment. Basically, you have to deal with what you have available, in long distance and local carrier terms, same as the Internet.

The point is that when you leave the data center and transmit data either through a myriad of Internet connections and equipment or the IXC and LXC set of circuits and equipment, it is out of your control. This requires that you compensate for each of these conditions and deploy the NAS devices with due consideration for the issues of each. Essentially, these are areas of security and recoverability. Given that you are dependent on the availability of specific communications vendors as well as bandwidth and service levels from these local and long distance vendors, your confidence and history with vendor services should drive your deployment choices.

From the NAS perspective, there are two considerations for deployment that facilitate access and data placement. These are access to data from the remote branch locations that require application access and specific services of the data center. Secondly, the ability to provide levels of application and data recoverability in a disaster recovery scenario is a major consideration for remote offices. Each of these deployments utilizes dedicated leased lines. These solutions are depicted in Figure 12-7, where a NAS device is deployed within the data center attached to the data center backbone that the remote offices utilize to back up their data. This is followed by a more complex deployment where production NAS devices hold sales and order data which are mirrored into a disaster recovery site where a similar NAS device holds the synchronized data.

The second D/R deployment employs the ability to utilize RAID level 1 functions of the NAS devices to provide an asynchronous link between the data center NAS device and the D/R site NAS device (see Figure 12-7). This solution utilizes an asynchronous update process that does not require the production NAS device to wait or hold I/O processing before the D/R site commits to writing the same data. The setup compensates for the availability and reliability factors within the WAN connection to minimize disruption with production processing.

The backup deployment for the remote sites is less complex and, although performed in an asynchronous manner, is generally done at night on an automated basis. Backup processes are run at the remote sites that transfer copies or backups to the NAS backup device attached to the data center network backbone in order to facilitate the greatest level of bandwidth and throughput as possible (see Figure 12-5). This compensates for the WAN connection being consumed during the daytime with user transaction traffic and minimizes the disruption of production processing within the data center during prime usage.

Internet access is the other major category for NAS placement that has WAN effects—although in many cases it is secondary given the typical placement of the NAS device. NAS provides an excellent solution for the storage of web files that are dynamically created through user access to web servers. In Figure 12-7, our theoretical company provides web servers that link to the outside world through a firewall and

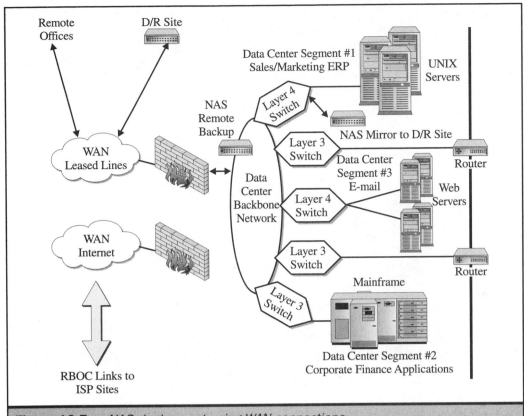

Figure 12-7. *NAS deployment using WAN connections*

then switch to the ISP. The ISP then supports global connectivity to the root servers of the Internet, sometimes referred to as the "13" root servers. This connection enables the global communications that allow data to flow in and out of the web servers. Consequently, this becomes a critical point for managing traffic access and security with which the NAS devices become integrated.

In any event, the WAN access as it comes in from the Web is in the form of presentation layer commands, or HTTP requests. However, the resolution of IP addresses, and then subsequent network and computer addresses, are provided by the switch connected to the ISP circuits; this is often called an "edge" switch. Given the transmission of packets from the edge switch, additional direction is provided, vis-à-vis our example in Figure 12-7 through the layer 4 switch where load balancing is facilitated to balance access among the web servers. Finally, the redirection will take place to initiate the file I/O to the appropriate NAS storage device.

Figure 12-8 illustrates this in more detail. The importance of the transmission path plays an important role in the placement of the NAS devices within the data center segment. More importantly, placement within the subsegment provides additional functionality with handling the type of traffic that may be expected with web access. Our example also points out that there is a scalable path for growth as both web servers and associated NAS storage devices will undoubtedly grow within the network segment in conjunction with the network itself (in other words, as web access grows, network bandwidth needs increase along with layer 3 and layer 4 switching and the need for NAS storage). Given NAS placement in this scenario, the NAS boxes follow a logical path that is associated with related network infrastructure components.

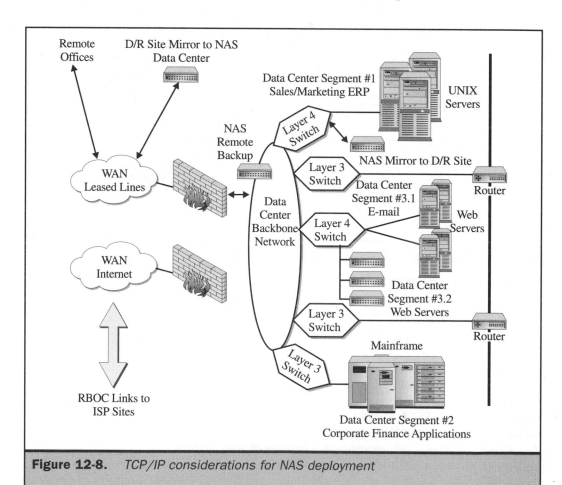

Figure 12-8.   *TCP/IP considerations for NAS deployment*

NAS Connectivity Architecture: Software

TCP/IP is the third of the three major components supporting communications within a diversity of transport media; however, the most popular data communications protocol remains Ethernet. Support here is evolving with increasing bandwidth to support Gigabit Ethernet standards, sophisticated participation within enterprise networks with quality of service (QoS) and routing participation. However, it should be noted that one of the limiting factors of file I/O within a TCP/IP network environment is the processing of the TCP layers for communications between client and server (for example, NAS device) elements. Note that this should reflect the TCP Off-load Engine (TOE) technology and other initatives such as InfiniBand that are evolving to optimize this latency.

To understand the relationships of network software and NAS we must describe the basic concepts behind the transport software that support the transmission of data throughout a network. As we discussed in Part II, the blueprint for open networks is the OSI layers of network processing. Parts of the OSI layers have been discussed in the previous sections of this chapter in explaining how the network devices work within LANs. We left that discussion within the transport layer, or layer 4.

We will begin the software discussion at the network layer and move up through the additional layers of the OSI model, discussing transport layer, session layer, presentation layer, and application layer. Most of our time will be spent on network, transport, and session layers due to their contribution to TCP/IP processing and their effect on I/O processing within the NAS model. However, it is important that we also mention the session and presentation layers and their effect in transporting the file level protocols, such as HTTP and FTP, and the subsequent interchange between applications and presentation layers.

The OSI model represents all the required processing for making a connection within a network as well as the necessary connections to applications that occur within a client/server computing model. Figure 12-9 shows layer 3, the network layer, and the remaining layers of the model: transport, session, presentation, and application. Each represents an important aspect of processing applications within the client/server model. More importantly, they represent a focused set of activities as they relate to NAS devices, along with their integration and interchange with the NAS micro-kernel.

An Overview of TCP/IP Processing

We begin the following overview by taking a look at how TCP and IP work to encapsulate and transport both data and messages throughout a network. TCP/IP supports data transmissions and functions within a switched packet network. This means that IP provides the packets and associated delivery information to the network. As discussed in the network device overviews, many of the switch and router devices derive their function from IP addresses.

Although we have already referenced IP in association with TCP/IP, the function of the Internet Protocol (IP) component is critically important to the transmission of data. IP functions as the envelope for application communications within a network. To that

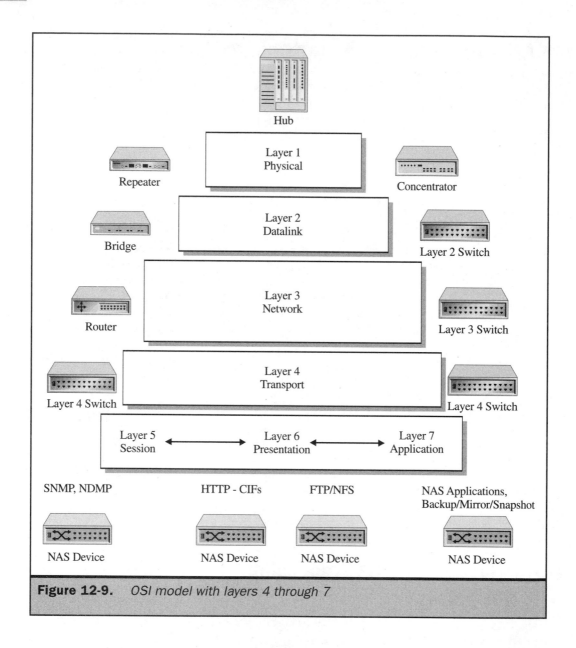

Figure 12-9.   OSI model with layers 4 through 7

end, it provides an address, consisting of both network and computer addresses, for delivery within the Internet networking topologies. Using the IP address provides a means of locating any computer within the universe of the Internet and local networks that is designated to receive the IP packet.

All computers running TCP/IP software have IP addresses. These are assigned when the TCP/IP software is installed and initialized. The IP assignments become part of the computer's network name and specific address within the network. The addresses, being a collection of numbers, rely on processing by the network devices to evaluate the IP address and route the IP packet to the appropriate network, and subsequently to the specific computer.

NAS functions on a TCP/IP communications basis. Therefore, NAS devices run TCP/IP and consequently play by the same rules as other computers that are addressed through IP address schemes. There are several considerations to this, however—the most important being the placement of NAS within the network segments due to its IP addressability and transmission of I/O file content within the IP packet.

The considerations are the placement and usage of the layer 3 and layer 4 network devices which can have a positive or negative effect on an NAS device. We'll look at specific performance conditions in Part VI, however it's important to understand these devices as they operate with an NAS device. Figure 12-10 further illustrates our example network with NAS being fronted with both the layer 4 device, supporting UNIX applications servers, and the layer 5 device, supporting e-mail and web servers. The layer 4 devices examine the IP packet as it comes into the network segment, and then route it according to the routing tables it maintains. This allows some requests to be transmitted directly to the NAS device for I/O file processing without them being redirected from the server. Such well-performed tasks illustrate the real value of the NAS solution. Some requests, however, are more generic and are sent to the application server where they're redirected to the NAS device. This is a function of the application and its related request.

Also a function of the NAS device to support the application server I/O requests, some degree of network efficiency can be derived by processing I/O requests directly through to the NAS device. However, layer 4 network devices only route the IP address and don't provide any additional intelligence as to its routing processes.

Layer 5 network devices may be more appropriate when trying to mediate complex data access requirements regarding application servers supported by NAS devices. One way this is done is through load balancing, where layer 5 network devices working at the session and presentation level can derive information about its network traffic and route accordingly. Therefore, in some instances, NAS devices can participate in load balancing by routing all explicit or some masked inexplicit I/O file requests directly to the NAS server.

A client request for data uses TCP to encapsulate and break the request into packets and then passes them to the IP functions. IP provides addressing information in the form of headers regarding the destination of the packets. Another important distinction of the TCP processing is the error checking it provides, especially for datacentric requests.

TCP uses a common error algorithm called "checksum" to calculate the data within the packet. When the packet has reached its destination, the IP functions verify the correct address and pass the packet to TCP. TCP, on the receiving end, breaks the packet and

NETWORK ATTACHED
STORAGE

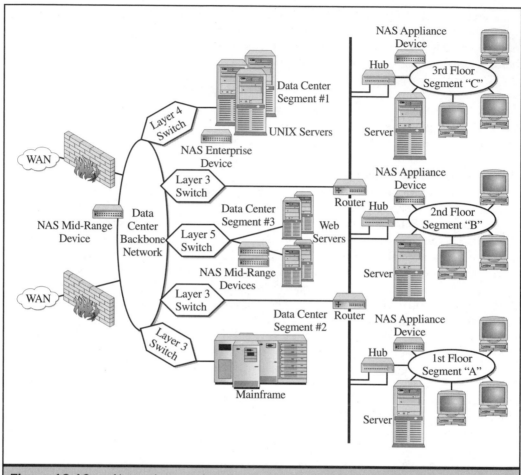

Figure 12-10. *Network operational aspects of NAS deployment*

reassembles the initial client request. On the receiving end, the TCP "checksum" error routines verify that the correct amount of data was sent. If not, TCP returns the packet to IP, which requests a retransmission from the sending client.

The effect of the IP and subsequent TCP processing places an additional workload on both the sending and receiving computer. In the case of a server, the overhead can be extremely high given the amount of TCP/IP processing required with multiuser access. Given that the majority of overhead occurs within the TCP and IP software running on a particular server, this can become critical when considering the case for NAS.

There are important points regarding NAS that need to be thought through when working with TCP/IP processing. First, is the number of concurrent users possible with the workloads. This is actually the number of client or server redirect I/O requests planned for the NAS device. Placement within a network segment must balance the capabilities and resources of the NAS device. An obvious example would be the placement of an NAS appliance device in a network segment that handles an enterprise workload. In addition, placement within a network segment is imperative given it could easily become overloaded if the workload expanded beyond the capabilities of the NAS device. This is characterized by the placement of NAS appliance devices in network segments served by hub devices which are extended by additional client PCs or servers. The shared bandwidth of these segments can quickly overwhelm a network segment with NAS workloads.

NAS Connectivity in Operation

Our previous example of a sample network illustrates NAS I/O operations as they relate to connectivity. Figure 12-8 shows how the network operates, using sample workloads that take place in the user departments as well as in the data center. The Accounting and Sales departments are good examples of NAS appliance deployment, while the more heavyweight workloads in the data center depict mid-range and enterprise NAS solutions.

Operational aspects of Figure 12-8 include the following:

- **NAS Appliances** These devices are placed within network segments that contain traffic within the local users. The devices also can be reached through administrators and support personnel for problem and maintenance activity. They become problematic with data protection (for example, backup and recovery), and are scalable within their segment.

- **NAS Mid-Range** Data center devices that support the Sales and Marketing departments are greater in both capacity and data access resources (that is, the number of network interfaces). These devices also support inquiries through WAN connections and, therefore, must have additional security both prior to access and as the requests are processed within the NAS device. The scalability is much greater here given the layer 3 and layer 4 switch and router processing, not to mention the bandwidth of the data center backbone. Also, the mid-range NAS appliance can be upgraded in place to achieve larger storage capacities and data access network interfaces.

- **NAS Enterprise** The other data center device supports more intense workloads by housing the data tables for data mart processing of the marketing applications. Although the access is limited to marketing and executive users, the complexity of the processing and size of I/O access is much greater than what we see with both NAS Mid-Range and NAS Appliances. Again, the scalability is handled through the bandwidth of the data center backbone, the limited number of users, and layer 3 routing. However, this solution becomes problematic with backup and recovery given its relationship to database systems running on an application server. A related problem is the capability to provide an effective disaster recovery solution of this magnitude over WAN mirroring functions due to bandwidth and size considerations.

■ **NAS Web**   This solution, although similar to the mid-range NAS devices, is singled out due to its ability to respond quickly to the Internet type of data access, as well as the volatility of storage requirements. This solution is well placed to take advantage of both layer 3 and layer 4 network devices by providing levels of workload balancing and caching throughout the web server configurations.

Network Configurations and Workloads

The previous sample network also provided a basis to illustrate NAS placement as it relates to I/O workloads. Figure 12-11 shows how the I/O workloads operate within their specific placements. Our sample workloads form an important aspect to NAS placement decisions as they relate to user departments or placement within the data center. The accounting and sales departments are good examples of simple file processing (Sfp) using NAS appliances, while the more heavyweight workloads in the data center provide examples of both complex file processing (Cfp) and network file processing (Qfp) using a depiction of the mid-range and enterprise NAS solutions.

The workload aspects of Figure 12-11 include the following:

■ **NAS Appliances**   Workload descriptions using Sfp

■ **NAS Mid-Range**   Workload descriptions using Qfp

■ **NAS Enterprise**   Workload descriptions using Cfp

■ **NAS Web**   Workload descriptions using Qfp and Cfp

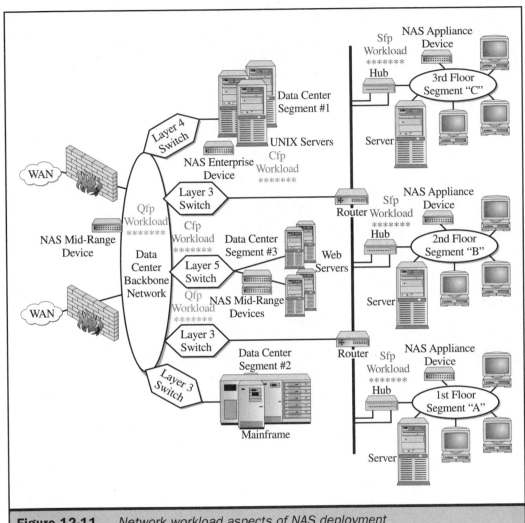

Figure 12-11. *Network workload aspects of NAS deployment*

The Complete Reference

Storage Networks

Part IV

Storage Area Networks

The
Complete
Reference

Storage
Networks

Chapter 13

Architecture Overview

In 1993, the largest data warehouse application supported only 50GB of aggregate data. Although this appears trivial by today's standards, it drove the client/server and mainframe computing infrastructures to support larger and larger data capacities. Both mainframe and open server vendors responded by increasing the number of processors, channels, RAM memory, and bus capabilities. However, these technologies had reached a level of maturity in their development that limited dramatic improvements in many of these areas. Coupled with the momentum of online transactional workloads driven by Internet access, web applications, and more robust Windows-based client/ server applications, the network began to play an increasing role in supporting the larger data-centric platforms. However, the distribution of work through the network only found the LAN to be challenged by its own data-centric traffic congestion.

In a different response to this challenge, both new and established vendors moved toward hybrid types of computing platforms, while methods appeared to handle the growing data-centric problem (see Chapter 8). These were parallel processing and high-end SMP computing platforms using high-performance relational database software that supported increased degrees of parallel processing. Vendors of systems and databases were thus caught in a dilemma, given that applications requiring data storage above 100GB capacities needed very costly high-end solutions.

Driven by the sheer value of access to data, end-user appetites for data-centric solutions continued to grow unabated. However, these requirements proved increasingly difficult for IT organizations as they struggled to supply, manage, and integrate hybrid solutions into their data centers. Obviously, one of the main areas experiencing dynamic growth within this maelstrom of datacentric activity was storage and storage-related products. This was an interesting dilemma for the storage vendors, given that the key to any enhancement of the data-centric application rollout revolved around a high-end I/O system. This drove storage vendors to the same traditional solutions as their mainframe and open-server brethren: enhance the existing infrastructure of disk density, bus performance (SCSI, PCI), and array scalability.

As the conservative approach from mainframe and open server vendors drove innovators offering alternative solutions to start their own companies and initiatives, a similar evolution began within storage companies. Existing storage vendors stuck to their conservative strategy to enhance existing technologies, spawning new initiatives in the storage industry.

Several initiatives studied applying a network concept to storage infrastructures that allowed processing nodes (for example, servers) to access the network for data. This evolved into creating a storage network from existing architectures and technologies, and interfacing this with existing I/O technologies of both server and storage products. Using the channel-oriented protocol of Fibre Channel, a network model of packet-based switching (FC uses frames in place of packets, however), and a specialized operating environment using the micro-kernel concept, the architecture of Storage Area Networks came into being.

This was such a major shift from the traditional architecture of directly connecting storage devices to a server or mainframe that an entire I/O architecture was turned upside down, prompting a major paradigm shift. This shift is not to be overlooked, or taken lightly, because with any major change in how things function, it must first be understood, analyzed, and evaluated before all its values can be seen. With Storage

Area Networks, we are in that mode. Not that the technology is not useful today. It can be very useful. However, the full value of Storage Area Networks as the next generation of I/O infrastructures still continues to evolve.

Creating a network for storage affects not only how we view storage systems and related products, but also how we can effectively use data within data-centric applications still in demand today. Here we are, ten years from the high-end data warehouse of 50GB, with today's applications supporting 500GB on average. This is only a ten-fold improvement. What can we achieve if we move our data-centric applications into an I/O network developed specifically for storage (perhaps a hundred-fold improvement)? Hopefully, ten years from now, this book will reflect the average database supporting 5 terabytes and being shared among all the servers in the data center.

Creating a Network for Storage

Network attached storage is very different from a Storage Area Network on many levels. First, SANs denote an entire infrastructure supporting storage systems. Secondly, (and maybe this should actually be first) SANs function on their own network developed specifically for shared I/O processing, enhanced storage devices, and scalability within a data center infrastructure. Thirdly, SANs operate on a protocol different than NAS (NAS integrates into traditional TCP/IP networks and associated network topologies) by using Fibre Channel. Lastly, SANs offer complete flexibility within their infrastructure by maintaining the intrinsic I/O communications protocols inherent with directly attached storage.

Whereas NAS remains a retrofit to existing computer networks, SANs offer an entire I/O infrastructure that breaks the storage boundaries of traditional storage I/O models and moves the support for data-centric applications into a new generation of computer processing models.

Several things happen when you create a storage network. The storage becomes accessible through a network model—for example, nodes logging in to the network can communicate with other nodes within the network. Nodes operating within the network offer a diverse amount of function depending on their device types—they can be storage devices, servers, routers, bridges, and even other networks. You can transfer data faster, with more throughput, and with increased flexibility. Managing the resources in a storage network can be performed from a centralized perspective across sharable domains.

This results in an inherent value to the Storage Area Network. Servers can now share the resources of storage systems such as disk arrays and devices. Conversely, storage arrays can be shared among the servers consolidating the number of devices required. This means increased access to centralized data by large numbers of applications, with support for larger storage capacities through increased ways of providing I/O operations.

Storage Area Networks are made up of four major parts. As we discussed with NAS, these parts cover the major areas of I/O operations, storage systems, and supported workloads. In SAN technology, however, there are more seemingly disparate parts that must be integrated to form an entire solution. With NAS, most of the products available are offered as bundled solutions. Not so with SANs. When considering SAN infrastructure, we must ponder more carefully the separate components that make up the infrastructure, because each operates independently and interdependently with the Storage Area Network they participate in.

Given that consideration, we can discuss and consider the major components of a Storage Area Network and resulting architecture. SAN components include the following:

- **Network Part**   SANs provide a separated network over and above what the client/server or mainframe networks utilize in connecting clients, terminals, and other devices, including NAS. This network, as mentioned, is based on the Fibre Channel protocol and standard.

- **Hardware Part**   SANs depend on specific hardware devices just like other networks. Given that SANs provide a packet-switched network topology, they adhere to a standard layer of processing that the hardware devices operate within. Again, to avoid confusion between data communications packet topologies, the FC protocol relies on frames and an architecture more compatible with I/O channel operations.

- **Software Part**   SANs operate within a separate set of software called a fabric that makes up the FC network. Additional software is required at the server connection where the average Windows or UNIX OS drivers must communicate within a SAN environment. The same thing is true for storage devices that must communicate with the SAN network to provide data to the servers.

- **Connectivity Part**   Much of a SAN's value derives from its connectivity, which is made up of several hardware and software functions. Given the complete shift in I/O operations from bus level communications to network communications, many components must change or be modified to operate within this environment. Connectivity options within the SAN determine performance and workload applicability.

Figure 13-1 offers a glimpse into the SAN infrastructure.

The Network Part

SAN is a network and, as such, its main task is to provide communications among devices attached to it. It does so through the FC standard protocol, denoted by the FC standard and relative T-11 standards committee that maintains the protocol. The FC protocol offers a layered approach to communications similar to TCP/IP, but through a smaller set of processing layers. The FC layers are illustrated in Figure 13-2, showing functions FC-0 through FC-4. (More detail on FC layers can be found in Chapter 16.) However, what's important is that each layer is leveraged through different hardware components within the SAN.

What facilitates the network is the switch component that provides a set of circuits making up the communications paths for the devices attached. The communications paths are accommodated through the addressing associated with the devices' communications layers. Therefore, the FC switch device can provide an any-to-any connectivity matrix that allows communications from one device to another.

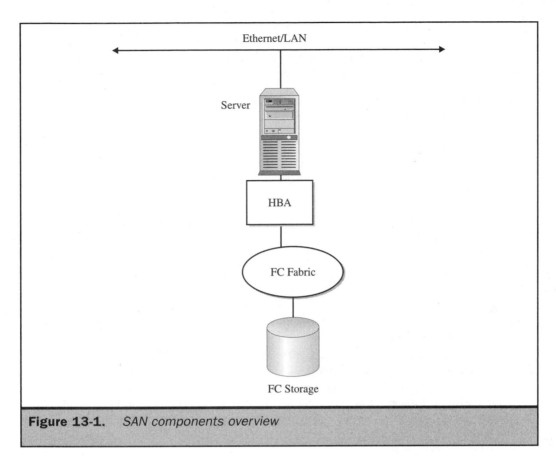

Figure 13-1. *SAN components overview*

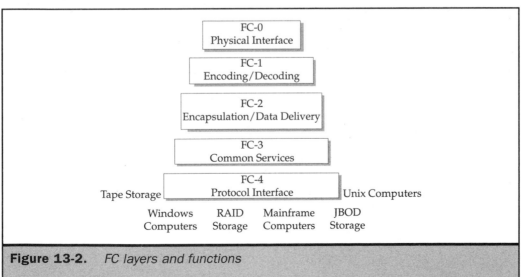

Figure 13-2. *FC layers and functions*

For example, a server may require a read from a particular disk. The server's I/O request provides the address for the requested device, the network fabric develops the connection, and that passes the read I/O to the storage device. Conversely, the storage responds with the same type of process, whereby the storage device requesting a connection with the server address returns the block of data from the read operation, the switch fabric makes the connection, and the I/O operation is completed.

It is important to note that one of the particular values of SANs, and specifically Fibre Channel, is its capability to provide a way for existing protocols to be encapsulated within the communications. This is especially valuable, as the SCSI commands for disk operations do not have to change. Consequently, disk and driver operations can operate within the FC protocol unchanged.

However, it is also important to note that in developing the SAN network, additional components are required beyond the FC switch for both the server and the storage devices. These are depicted in Figure 13-3, as we see the effects of our read I/O operation within the switch. These components—HBAs, FC switches, hubs, and routers—will be discussed in more detail in the section titled "The Hardware Part" in this chapter, as well as in Chapter 14.

Inside the FC network, the fabric software operates on a frame-based design. Similar to concepts used in TCP/IP packets, communications within the network are performed by transmitting FC frames throughout the fabric. The frames are composed of header, user data, and trailer information. FC layers determine the operations responsible for the frame development, frame addressing, and transmission (see Figure 13-3).

We would be remiss if we did not mention other ways the FC network can be configured. This is important because many of these configurations are still operating and some offer specific solutions to particular situations; they're also cost-effective. However, most can be attributed to implementations that occurred prior to the development of the FC Switched fabric solutions.

These solutions include the following:

■ **Point-to-Point**   This uses the FC to connect one device to another. Employed in initial FC implementations of FC disk arrays, it leveraged the increased bandwidth, but remained a direct attached solution. Also, tape devices could be used with an FC point-to-point configuration, increasing the number of drives supported from a single server.

■ **Hub**   This uses FC to connect in a loop fashion. Basically, the initial network fabric supported an arbitrated loop arrangement whereby, like SCSI bus configurations, the devices were configured in loop topologies which not only shared bandwidth but had to arbitrate for network communications, like a SCSI bus. It leveraged the speed of FC and the capability to place additional disk arrays within the network allowing connection of additional servers. FC-AL, however, provided latency issues that never fully facilitated the bandwidth and performance of FC-switched fabric implementations.

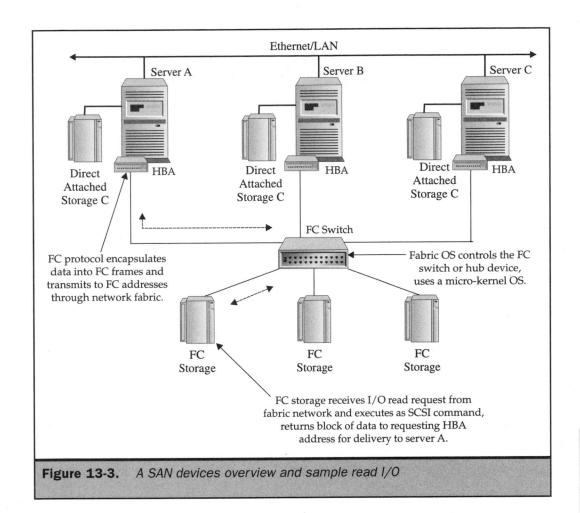

Figure 13-3. *A SAN devices overview and sample read I/O*

The Software Part

The central control of a SAN is contained within the Fabric Operating System functions (sometimes called the SAN OS, or just the fabric). Like micro-kernel components, SAN fabric utilizes the micro-kernel implementation as the basis for its operating system.

The Fabric OS runs within the FC switch. Figure 13-4 shows the typical makeup of the Fabric OS. As we can see, it truly is an effective implementation of a micro-kernel, supporting only the required functions of the fabric. This is good news for performance, but bad news whenever future enhancements and management functions are considered. It has similar limitations to the NAS bundled solution—a micro-kernel conundrum shared among storage networking solutions.

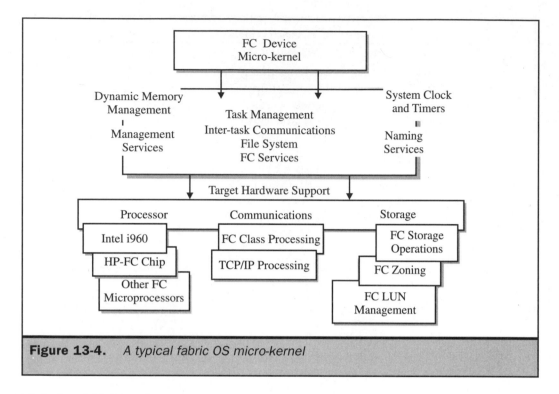

Figure 13-4. *A typical fabric OS micro-kernel*

Fabric OS Services

The Fabric OS offers a common set of services provided by any network. However, it also provides services specific to Fibre Channel and I/O operations. These services are summarized in Figure 13-5 and described next:

■ **OS Services**   Required functions configured with micro-kernel, such as task, memory, and file management, are included within these services. These form the basic OS functions that provide the core-level processing specific to supporting a fabric.

■ **FC Services**   These functions interact closely with OS services to facilitate the FC layer processing of frame management within the switch. The FC services provide both switched fabric and arbitrated loop modes of processing, as well as frame processing and protocol routing for the complex interconnections that occur within the switch.

■ **Simple Name Services**   The FC network works on the basis of a naming convention that identifies devices (such as HBA port and storage adapter port) by their names as they are attached to the fabric. These services provide a rudimentary database (for example, a file that supports the SAN naming conventions, the status of device connections, and so forth) and functions to identify new devices as they are attached.

■ **Alias Services**   The fabric provides functions that allow particular devices to broadcast frames to a set of aliases as noted within the naming conventions (for instance, a generic set of names that one device can broadcast to).

■ **Management Services**   FC switches that provide startup and configuration utilities allowing administrators to set up and configure the switch. These utilities range from direct attached access through a PC attached to a serial interface of the switch to web browser-based access if the switch is configured with an Ethernet interface. The management functions over and above configuration and setup consist of status and activity information stored and accessed through a Simple Network Management Protocol (SNMP) database. This database referred to as a MIB (Management Information Base) is specific to SNMP and requires this protocol to extract or store any information. Additional information and discussion of SAN management can be found in Part VI.

Fabric APIs and Applications

FC-switched fabric systems operate similar to other software operating environments by providing a set of basic services to the supporting hardware (refer to the previous bullet points within the OS services discussion). However, like any base operating environment, it must have interfaces to the outside world for access from administrators and other software. These access points will come from application programming interfaces, or APIs. This software interface will provide third-party software vendors, or any systems administrators brave enough to try, the specification for writing

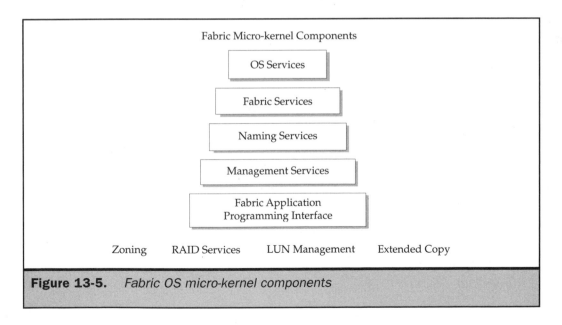

Figure 13-5.   *Fabric OS micro-kernel components*

a program to work with the fabric OS. We provide an overview of both API and fabric applications below.

- **Application Programming Interfaces** FC switch vendors all include various levels of Application Programming Interfaces created specifically to allow other software vendors and complementary hardware vendors to develop applications that enhance the operation of the switch. These interfaces are generally so complex that it is beyond most IT administrators to leverage, nor is it recommended by the switch vendors to facilitate local API utilization by customers. Regardless of complexity, this does provide an important feature which enables software vendors—mostly management vendors—to supply applications that interface with the switch and therefore enhance its operation.

- **Fabric Applications** FC fabric supports specific applications that adhere to the vendor's API structure. Applications generally provided by the switch vendor are characterized by their close operation of the switch through facilities such as zoning, hardware enclosure services, and advanced configuration features. Third-party tools, offered as products from software vendors, will interface with the switch to offer mainly management services such as backup and recovery, device and component monitoring, and storage services.

Server OS and HBA Drivers

Dealing with I/Os generated from servers requires that the server operating systems be SAN-compliant. This generally means that the OS is able to recognize the FC Host Bus Adapter driver and related functions necessary to link to SAN attached disks. Although mostly transparent for disk operations, this aspect of the software dependencies and functions supporting the SAN configuration is becoming increasingly complex as file and database management becomes more compliant with SAN network functions.

Most system vendors offering operating systems support SANs. However, it should be noted that further diligence is necessary to identify specific OS release levels that support a specific SAN implementation. Given the variety of hardware and network devices supported through operating system compatible drivers, the support for particular SAN components requires detailed analysis to ensure the attached servers support the SAN infrastructure.

All HBA vendors provide drivers to support various SAN configurations and topologies. These drivers are matched to a specific level of OS. Given most SANs are available as a packaged solution, it is critical that the driver software provides sufficient flexibility to support not only the FC switch configuration, but also the storage arrays and other devices attached, such as routers/bridges, tapes, and other server HBAs. Refer to the OS macro guide to cross reference the SAN support for a particular configuration. As with the server OS consideration, more diligence is necessary to identify specific driver release levels that support a specific SAN implementation and set of hardware components and fabric.

Storage Intelligence

An additional area of software to note is the functional area inherent with particular storage systems. Storage arrays are all delivered with particular implementations of FC, SCSI, and added utility applications. These software implementations must be compatible with both the server OS and fabric OS, as well as the HBA drivers.

Other Networks   As a final note on software, we must recognize the effects SAN fabrics are having on TCP/IP and their integration into other enterprise networks. We noted previously that the integration of NAS devices with FC storage components is now available. This configuration does not require a FC switch to support Ethernet attachment. However, it does not develop into a storage area network despite the fact that FC storage can be accessed through TCP/IP stacks and compatible file protocols supported by the NAS device. The capability for a fully functional SAN to participate within the IP network remains problematic.

This also provides a method for switch-to-switch connectivity, thus allowing remote connectivity from one SAN configuration to another. This should be given due consideration, given its ability to execute a block I/O operation through an IP network, something which impacts security, performance, and loading. We examine this in more detail when discussing SAN Connectivity in Chapter 16.

The Hardware Part

The most striking part of a storage area network is its diversity of components. NAS, as we have discussed in Part III, is almost polarized in the opposite direction given its bundled and simplistic structure. The SAN, on the other hand, must have a central network of new devices as well as supporting network appendages attached to the storage and servers it supports. This is most apparent in the required hardware of switches, HBAs, and sometimes bridges and routers. In support of our discussion on the SAN, the following overview will further familarize you with these components.

The Fastest Storage Possible: 100MB/sec

The hardware part of the SAN is made up of components that allow a complete storage network to be enabled. The minimum devices necessary are an FC switch, an FC-enabled server, and FC-enabled storage systems. Although the FC switch could be replaced by a FC hub to facilitate the storage network, we will address it separately (in the section titled "The Unusual Configuration Club, Optical, NAS, and Mainframe Channels" later in the chapter), given its legacy position and its enhancement of switches to handle both FC fabric and arbitrated loop operations.

Figure 13-6 illustrates the minimum components necessary to configure a simple SAN. The FC switch centers the network as it connects the server and storage array. The FC server is connected through an FC Host Bus Adapter (HBA). The FC HBA provides the necessary FC protocol processing and interfaces with the server's operating system. The FC storage array is connected through an integrated FC port attachment that injects the necessary FC protocol communications into the storage controller's mechanisms.

STORAGE AREA NETWORKS

This forms the simplest SAN configuration. However, it is the one that facilitates the FC SAN architecture and provides the basis for additional SAN configurations no matter how complex. In addition to the basic devices, Figure 13-6 also shows the type of connections required for implementation into an existing data center.

The Usual Configuration Gang, RAID, Disk Array, and Tape

Figure 13-7 takes our simple SAN configuration and places into a data center setting. As we can see, the SAN has been enhanced to include additional servers, two storage arrays both supporting RAID levels, and a tape device connected through a FC bridge. This characterizes a sample configuration that supports all the necessary data center operations including database, backup and recovery, and shared access.

The Unusual Configuration Club, Optical, NAS, and Mainframe Channels

Figure 13-8 takes our simple SAN configuration and provides some interesting twists. Although these are unusual implementation scenarios, they are important to point out because they show the increasing levels of flexibility SANs have. Note that there is FC optical storage involved, as well as connection to file storage systems through an IP

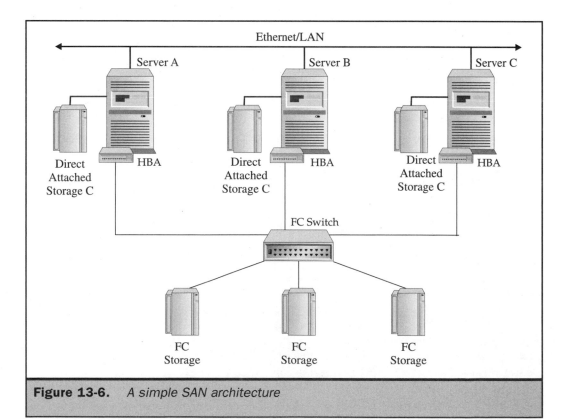

Figure 13-6. *A simple SAN architecture*

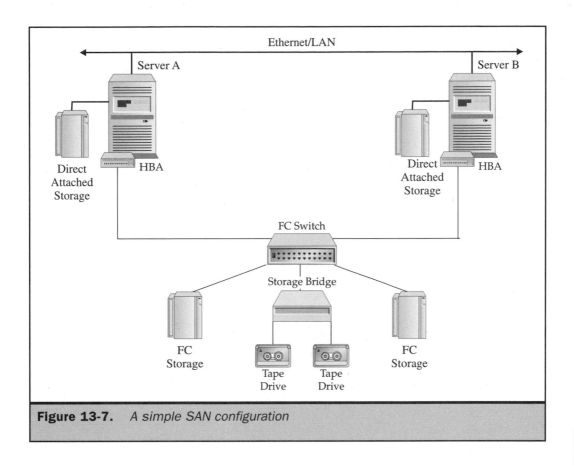

Figure 13-7. *A simple SAN configuration*

connection, and, finally, the connection to alternative servers such as mainframes supporting FC connectivity, like IBM's FICON.

The Connectivity Part

If we further analyze our simple SAN implementation, we find that switch connections come in two forms: the physical connection and the logical port configuration. The physical connection supports both optical and copper connections. Obviously, most switch products operate at optimum using the optical connections; however, the capability to support several connectivity schemes can be important when integrating into existing cabling structures.

The logical connection requires understanding the type of port configuration the switch provides. Ports can be configured as particular types of connections. These are defined according to topology and class of processing. In some switches, these are performed automatically per port, as different types of processing configurations are defined for the fabric—for instance, Classes 1, 4, and 6 for connection types of circuits, and Classes 2 and 3 for connectionless circuits or frame switching (that is, packet-switched networks).

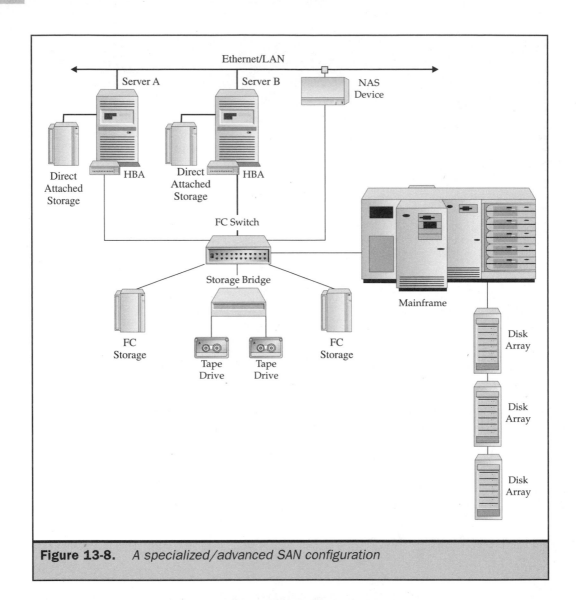

Figure 13-8.   *A specialized/advanced SAN configuration*

Connecting the Server: The Host Bus Adapters

Connecting the server requires the use of a Host Bus Adapter (HBA). This is a component similar to the Network Interface Card (NIC) discussed previously in Chapter 8 as network fundamentals in storage connectivity options, and in Chapter 12. It essentially performs the same function as the NIC in terms of providing a physical connection to the FC network, using either copper or optical connectors. In addition, it provides the software functions that translate the FC protocol communications and interfaces these commands with the server operating system. This is provided (similar to NICs) with a set of drivers and is configured according to the type of FC topology the SAN is operating with.

Connecting the Storage: The SCSI/RAID Operations

One of the most effective architectural design strategies within the FC protocol and FC fabric elements is its ability to frame higher-level protocols within communications processing. This means that the SCSI commands that communicate disk and tape operations can continue to operate. These commands are packaged within the Fibre Channel frame and transmitted. Upon delivery, the FC frame is translated and the SCSI commands are reassembled for delivery and execution on the target device.

This is not only effective for server operations, which have historically interfaced with SCSI bus technologies in direct-attached disks, but also for the disk and related controllers themselves. As the SCSI commands are developed from I/O operation activities within the server OS, the I/O operations at the disk controller perform as if they continued to be directly connected. However, this begins to become complex as the reference to logical units (LUN) within a bus are tracked and configured for an FC network. This then becomes a process that grows more challenging when operating with LUNs that are dynamically modified or hidden by layer 2 or 3 processing—say, in the case of a bridge or router.

SAN Configurations

SANs evolve within data centers from simple configurations using single switch or hub operations with a limited number of disk devices. These are often limited traffic projects that provide an entry level of operations and proof of concept for targeted applications. However, they soon grow to configurations with multiple FC switches that are interconnected to optimize the reliability or availability of the applications. The following three levels of configurations best characterize the types of configurations IT will become familiar with.

Entry Level

An entry-level configuration will basically be a proof of concept or beta installation to prove the reliability of the SAN project. As stated earlier, these are often limited projects handling limited user traffic and designed to support a targeted single application. The entry-level SAN configuration can also allow IT personnel to become familiar and comfortable with the new types of hardware, give them some experience with the new software fabric configurations and operation, and let them experience real traffic within the SAN.

Figure 13-9 shows an example configuration of an entry-level SAN. Note this configuration contains a single FC switch, two storage arrays, and a tape device. There are three Windows-based servers attached to the switch which complete the SAN network. In this example, anywhere from three to five relational database systems provide production test beds for application testing. Each database has its aggregate data stored across the storage arrays. The storage arrays themselves are configured for RAID level 5 and level 1. This allows several databases to share storage in a single array; in this case, array A using RAID level 5, while array B is configured for RAID level 1.

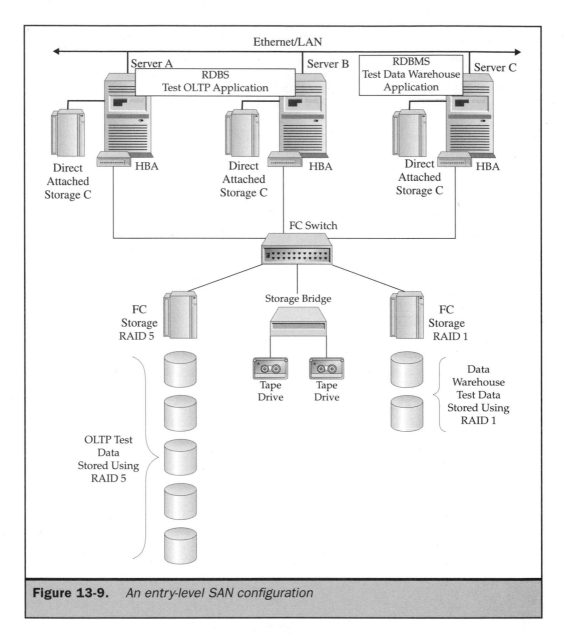

Figure 13-9. *An entry-level SAN configuration*

This configuration provides an entry-level SAN that provides a test bed for three database applications; some are for typical OLTP workloads while the third is for a data warehouse application. The systems are set to allow applications and DBAs to test new query applications against test databases. The SAN configuration replaces the six servers used to support database testing and the six storage arrays directly attached to their respective servers.

Consequently, even for an entry configuration, the architecture of the SAN can consolidate a considerable amount of hardware and software.

Mid-Range: Production Workloads, Multiple Switches

If we move up to supporting production workloads, we must consider all the necessary reliability and availability configuration requirements. Figure 13-10 shows an example SAN that supports production applications with ten servers using Windows OSs. The servers are attached to three FC switches configured in what's called a *cascading arrangement*. The multiple storage arrays support both RAID 5 and RAID 0 in our example set of applications. Our production configuration also has the addition of backup with the attachment of a tape library.

Our production workload supports several database applications that utilize five of the ten servers. These transactional OLTP-type requirements utilize the storage arrays configured for RAID 5. Our other workloads are a combination of an intranet for internal users of the company's internal web application. This application utilizes the storage arrays configured for RAID 0, which has the data stripped but has no failover capability.

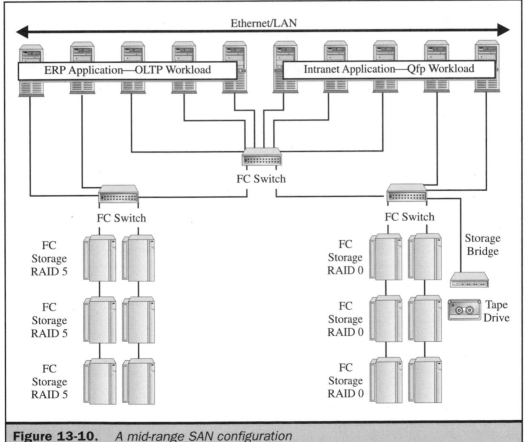

Figure 13-10.   *A mid-range SAN configuration*

STORAGE AREA
NETWORKS

Enterprise: Director-Level with
Duplicate Paths and Redundancy

Moving up to the support of an enterprise level and the support of multiple applications, we have an example enterprise configuration in Figure 13-11. This much larger configuration shows 20 servers, consisting of both UNIX- and Windows-based OSs, attached to six FC switches. Storage arrays support 2 terabytes of both file- and database-oriented data models, given that the workloads range from OLTP database applications to web servers, and data-centric datamart applications. A datamart, incidentally, is similar to a data warehouse with limited subject scope; in some industry sectors, however, datamarts have proliferated faster given their singular and more simplistic database design. This allows for faster design and implementation activities, which makes them demanding in their storage capacity, access and data sourcing requirements from larger data warehouses, and operational databases.

The storage arrays are configured in RAID levels 5, 1, and 0. As with any production workloads, appropriate failover has been configured with a more complex cascading switch configuration. There is a new twist, however—a remote connection within the switch that allows for a disaster recovery operation to be in place. The usual configuration of a tape library to facilitate the backup strategies of various workloads and applications is also in place.

As demonstrated here, SAN configurations have an inherent value to storage network architecture. Even though the architecture reflects a new model of processing, SAN configurations provide the most effective and efficient method of server consolidation, storage consolidation, improved data access, and scalability of data storage.

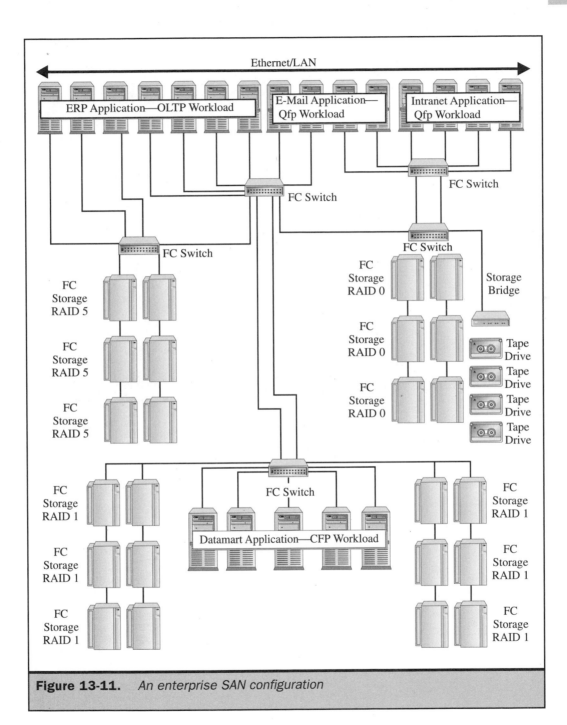

Figure 13-11.   *An enterprise SAN configuration*

Chapter 14

Hardware Devices

AN hardware is divided into three distinct parts: the Fibre Channel switch, the Host Bus Adapter (HBA), and the storage device itself. In addition, one must consider bridging, or routing, solutions. Chapter 13 is the continuation of the detailed discussion of SANs started in Chapter 12, which covered their specific architecture. This chapter will explore the hardware components that make up the SAN, a summary of what they are and how they operate, and a view of fabric operation from a hardware perspective.

The switch part is a discussion of the Fibre Channel (FC) switch component that essentially becomes the heart of the SAN. Included will be a discussion of the device attachment options, a brief explanation of operation, and the role they play in the configuration of the switch, consisting of the foundations for configuration, port identification, and interswitch links.

The FC Host Bus Adapter (HBA) is a necessary component to attach servers to a SAN. HBAs have ports that connect to the switch, which play a pivotal role in communicating with the SAN fabric on behalf of the server. There are also considerable differences in HBA software drivers and OS support, as well as options for HBA functions and their interaction with FC switch.

Perhaps their most important aspect, given that SANs are "storage" networks, is the FC-enabled storage itself. Storage devices for SANs require that they communicate using the Fibre Channel networking standard, consequently their roles and various operations differ in comparison to direct attached storage devices. Included with this discussion will be an orientation to tape media into the SAN, where we identify an additional supporting component, the FC bridge/router, which is necessary in developing a fully functional FC-based storage area network.

We will conclude the chapter with a brief discussion on several important points in the operation of the SAN fabric. From a hardware perspective, the modes of processing and the functions of the physical ports become required knowledge when designing and implementing the SAN. Given that the SAN's heart is the FC switch, the operational aspects of how the switch provides a circulation of data throughout its system cannot be overlooked. SAN switches will be used in multiple configurations (covered in detail in Chapter 18). This requires an initial understanding of the switch-linking functions used for expansion, redundancy, and recovery configurations. Discussions of such can be found in this chapter, as well as in Chapter 15.

The Fibre Channel Switch

The Fibre Channel switch is the heart of any Storage Area Network configuration. It connects the user to the data being stored in the SAN. Like a heart, all information traveling through this closed system will sooner or later pump through the switch. Within the switch are connections, called ports, which function in different ways depending on the type of device connected. There is an effective Fibre Channel standard, called the T11.3 standard, which is the ANSI standard governed by the X3T11 group and defines the usage of the port via the Fibre Channel protocol. The T11.3 standard provides a set of guidelines for vendors to follow—a common language, so to speak. The Fibre Channel standard defines three types of ports:

- **The F_Port**   Used to attach nodes. In storage networking, nodes refer to a network logical term for attached devices (for example, servers, storage devices, routers, and bridges, which are attached to the switch).

- **The E_Port**   Used to connect one switch to another switch.

- **The G_Port**   A generic port that can be pressed into service as an F_Port or an E_Port depending on the vendor's implementation.

It should be noted that, in general, Fibre Channel switches are categorized in terms of port capacity and their capability to sustain port failures. Low-end switches, while cost-effective, support only a base set of functionality in connecting devices to the network; moreover, the ability to connect to other switches or fabrics is minimal. Low-end switches offer no real port failure tolerance. The class of switches defined for entry level and mid-range usage is referred to by the generic term *Fibre Channel switch*. A glass ceiling of port counts exists that separates the FC SAN switch from the *Director* level products. With port counts at or above 64, including internal path redundancies for fault tolerance, the Director class storage switches are used for large enterprise class storage configurations. Feature function notwithstanding, there is a clear cost difference between low-end Fibre Channel switches and Director Class switches. The difference is not only clear, it is quite large.

Unless a user has a high-end requirement, most users start with a handful of low-end switches, as well as the myriad problems associated with them, and end up very quickly needing to bump up to Director Class switches. The point is, you may not need the ports now, but you may very well need the functionality depending on the service level requirements of the applications being supported.

The F_Port

As stated previously, the F_Port, also referred to as a Fabric Port, connects server and storage devices to the switch itself. A device plugged into the switch's F_Port is referred to as a *node*, and, in FC terms, is identified as an N_Port. If used in an arbitrated loop topology, it becomes an NL_Port. For instance, a server, when plugged into the switch, creates an N_Port, whereas a storage device using an arbitrated loop is recognized as an NL_Port. A basic F_Port is shown in Figure 14-1. Operating as FC nodes, they are identified by the switch as their particular N_Port or NL_Port designation.

All devices attached to a Fibre Channel switch must log in. When a device is attached, it accesses a file in the Name Server database within the switch that contains information explaining to the server just what this device is. The Name Server informs the switch of the device's name, address, type, and class of service. It is the formal introduction between switch and device. Anyone putting together a Storage Area Network must make sure the devices they are planning to attach (or are going to attach in the future) are supported by the switch. If a device is not supported, it becomes all

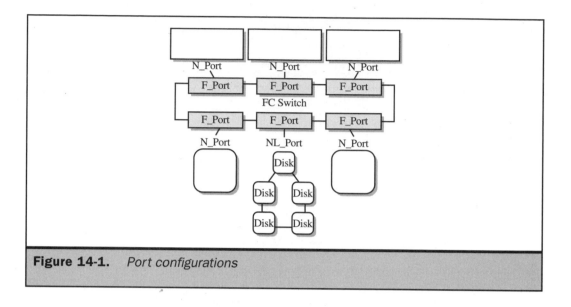

Figure 14-1. *Port configurations*

but useless to the SAN. Keep in mind, too, that arbitrated loop login will take longer than general fabric login or import login, given the extra loop and device assignments.

The Name Server, shown in Figure 14-2, registers a device's port address, port name, node name, class of service parameters, and the Fibre Channel layer 4 (FC-4) protocols it supports, as well as the type of port. The Name Server also provides the information one device, like a server, needs to find another device on the network, like the storage. Port name and port address are contained within a single table so that a device can be referred to by its name or by its address, much the way a web site can be called up by its URL or IP address. This is helpful as Storage Area Networks increasingly have IP ports made available to them. The Name Server supplies a method of recognition between the two types of ports, regardless of the protocol. When connecting switches, it is paramount that each switch's Name Server be synchronized and consistent with one another.

Any changes made to the devices attached to the switch are handled by either voluntary or involuntary services provided within the switch. As devices or connected switches are upgraded, port usage can become volatile. This is an important aspect in change management within the port itself. How these changes are made is dependent upon vendor service and implementation. Certain vendors automatically update the Name Server using State Change Notification (SCN) or Registered State Change Notification, which is an example of an involuntary change. A voluntary service consists of, you guessed it, using the two preceding methods to update the Name Server yourself. At this point, you may be asking yourself—and rightly so—just how is that voluntary?

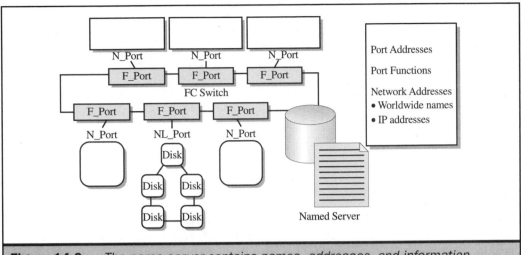

Figure 14-2.   *The name server contains names, addresses, and information on nodes.*

The E_Port

E_Ports, also referred to as expansion ports, connect one switch to another. These switch ports have become critical given the rapid expansion of multiple switch configurations needed to support larger and larger server and storage capacities. E_Ports are now fundamental to the operation of a Storage Area Network and should be considered carefully when designing and implementing any SAN configuration.

The E_Port, as shown in Figure 14-3, provides the means by which one switch fabric communicates with another switch fabric. For this to happen, a compatible connection is required. This allows the E_Port to successfully coordinate with the Name Servers within each switch, synchronize frame transfers between switches, and facilitate interswitch access to storage resources. Utilizing arbitrated loop configurations between switches, while possible, increases the overall risk factor in the efficiency of an E_Port because of the increased overhead and treatment of the NL port as a separate network, which dramatically increases the number of addressable units and decreases bandwidth utilization.

The G_Port

The G_Port is a generic port and, depending on the vendor's implementation, can be used as either an F_Port or an E_Port. In other words, G_Ports are universal ports that can be used for a combination of functions. Although we haven't covered the necessary overhead in implementing a port configuration for issues such as recoverability and

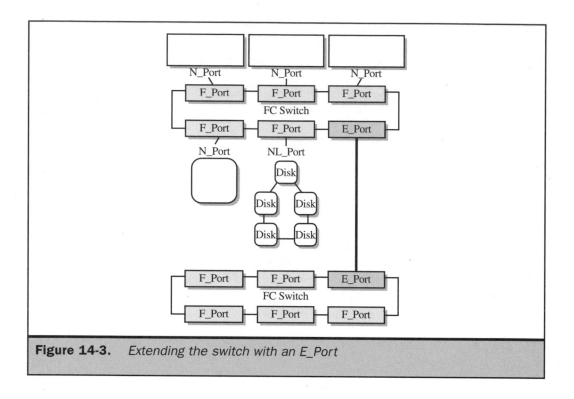

Figure 14-3. *Extending the switch with an E_Port*

redundancy, G_Ports are likely candidates for recoverability and redundancy usage in light of port failure.

G_Port populations will dramatically increase, as ports become multifunctional and autosensing becomes more prevalent. Switches will come equipped with 64 so-called generic ports, and will distinguish themselves as either F_Ports or E_Ports when a device or an additional switch is attached. This adds critical switch flexibility when configuring multiple switch operations—all of which increases the cost per port.

Host Bus Adaptors

Simply put, the Host Bus Adapter (HBA) is the link between the server and the Storage Area Network. Similar to the Network Interface Card (NIC), HBAs provide the translation between server protocol and switch protocol. HBAs connect to a server's PCI bus (see Chapter 7) and come with software drivers (discussed in greater detail in the following chapter) that support fabric topologies and arbitrated loop configurations.

HBAs are available in single port or multiple port configurations. Multiple ports allow additional data paths for workloads moving between the server and the switch via a single HBA. In addition to containing multiple ports (a maximum of four, at this point), a single server can hold, at most, four HBAs. Today, any single server can possess 16 ports (four ports times four HBAs), or 16 separate points of entry into the switch. However, keep in mind that four discrete ports on one HBA increases the risk for single point of failure along those data paths.

In providing the initial communication with the I/O from the server, HBAs encapsulate SCSI disk commands into the Fibre Channel layer 2 processing. HBAs communicate within the FC standard through the class of service defined by the Name Server at the time of login. As such, the HBA plays a key role in providing levels of efficiency in executing the operating system's I/O operations. Figure 14-4 illustrates an HBA's basic functions.

One key duty of any HBA worth its bandwidth is discovering and mapping the storage resources available to it within the switch fabric. This mapping is critical to the devices that are available to any particular server. As will be discussed in the next chapter, there are various ways to restrict access to storage resources, such as zoning. It is important to note here, though, that HBAs must deal with this issue in an effort to understand the devices it must contact on behalf of the server, which it ultimately works for.

As you might expect, all of this becomes even more complex in supporting arbitrated loop devices on the switch.

Depending on the vendor, additional functionality is bundled with different HBAs. These functions range from software RAID functionality to advanced management functions (for example, diagnostic functions and the new enclosure services provided by many vendors). In the future, additional functionality will come to include a virtual interface that bypasses much of the layered processing currently required. For more

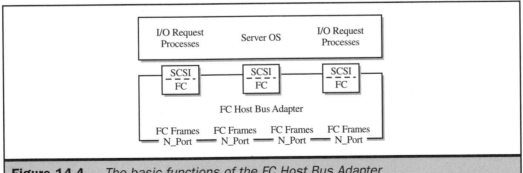

Figure 14-4.   *The basic functions of the FC Host Bus Adapter*

information on this, check out the discussion on InfiniBand in Chapter 20. But don't say I didn't warn you.

The major reliability questions of any HBA are twofold. First, the HBA's compatibility with its server's operating system is key to the effective operation of the FC network in total because each operating environment has unique differences in how it handles base I/O, file system, and buffering/caching methods. It is important to understand at a macro-level the differences between a UNIX integration and implementation of an HBA versus integration and implementation within a Windows environment. The second factor is the compatibility, at a software level, of the switch's fabric operating system and the HBA's software drivers. This requires an understanding of the supported release levels of any given switch vendor against any particular HBA vendor. Since many SAN components are acquired through OEM relationships, compatibility can become sticky when intermixing equipment from different vendors. As shown in Figure 14-5, HBAs play a critical role in the interoperability of a SAN configuration.

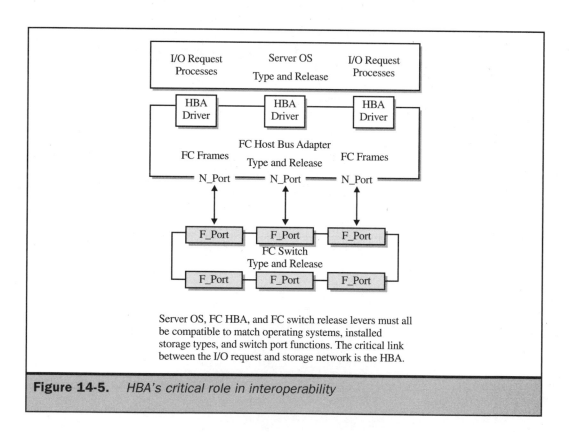

Figure 14-5. *HBA's critical role in interoperability*

Putting the Storage in Storage Area Networks

Given that SANs are *Storage* Area Networks, perhaps the single most exigent component in the configuration is the storage itself. SANs require storage that is Fibre Channel-enabled. In other words, FC disks must be connected to the switch via an FC topology. Fibre Channel-enabled disks come in two configurations: JBOD, Just a Bunch Of Disks, and RAID, Redundant Array of Independent Disks. Each configuration maintains its own set of FC features and implementations.

FC storage arrays, which are multiple disks hooked together, are connected in a loop configuration, as depicted in Figure 14-6. Loop configuration allows each disk to be addressed as its own unique entity inside the segment. FC storage arrays (depicted in Figure 14-6 as well) also provide additional functions, such as the stripping of data across the units, which allows a single outsized file to be spread across two, three, or even four drives in the array. In addition, most provide low-level enclosure management software that monitors the device's physical attributes (its temperature, voltage, fan operation, and so on).

JBOD

A typical JBOD configuration is connected to the switch through an NL port. Most implementations provide dual loop capacity whereby redundancy protects against

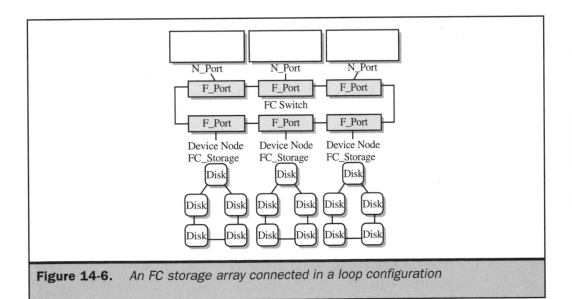

Figure 14-6.   *An FC storage array connected in a loop configuration*

single loop failure. In other words, should one loop go down, the information on the storage device can be retrieved via the second loop. A dual loop requires four of the switch's ports. Another, less typical method of attaching a JBOD array to a switch is to split the devices into separate loops. A JBOD array of eight drives could have one loop serving drives 1–4 and a second loop for drives 5–8. This method also requires four ports on the switch. The benefits of splitting the devices into several loops include shorter path lengths and less arbitration overhead within the loop itself.

The disadvantage of any JBOD implementation is its lack of fault resiliency, though there are software RAID products that allow the stripping of data with recovery mechanisms encompassed in the JBOD enclosure. Given the number of disks and the transmission of SCSI commands to multiple targets, using RAID software in conjunction with a JBOD implementation presents its own problems. It is important to keep in mind that while these are Fibre Channel-enabled disks, the disk drives themselves execute a SCSI command set when performing read/writes.

RAID

A Fibre Channel-enabled RAID storage array places a controller in front of the disk array that provides and controls the RAID level for the disk array (RAID 1–5). RAID offers a way of protecting the data by creating an array of disk drives that are viewed as one logical volume. Inside this logical volume, which may consist of seven drives, data is partitioned, as is recovery information. In the event of a single drive failure, the array reassembles the information on the remaining drives and continues to run. The RAID controller uses either an N_Port or a NL_Port depending on how the vendor put the disk enclosure together.

Because the RAID controller stands in front of the array, the FC-enabled disks, regardless of their configuration, become transparent. The switch only sees one device, not several linked together. A single RAID controller can also control several arrays, as indicated in Figure 14-7. For example, four volumes, each volume containing seven disks, would equal a RAID system of 28 disks. Still, the switch only sees the RAID controller—just one device. In this scenario, more often than not, the RAID controller will utilize an N_Port, not a loop.

The key advantage of Fibre Channel RAID is its ability to provide levels of fault resistance for hardware failures, a feature not found in JBOD configurations. For enterprise-level workloads, this feature is all but mandatory.

Just as the HBA is the critical point between a server's operating system and the switch's operating system, RAID controllers require a level of specific Fibre Channel software that must be compatible with the switch and the HBA. As noted previously, it is the HBA's job to inform the server which disks are available. In a JBOD configuration, this is pretty straightforward. Each disk is an addressable unit. In a RAID configuration, it becomes the controller's duty to specify which disk is addressable. The RAID controller, via the software contained within it, has to identify itself to the switch, specifically the Name Server within the switch, as well as the HBA,

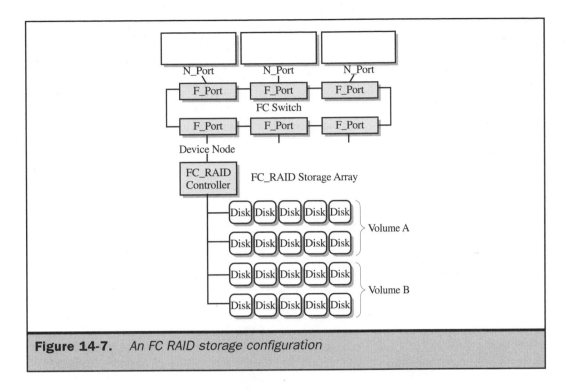

N_Port   N_Port   N_Port

F_Port   F_Port   F_Port

FC Switch

F_Port   F_Port   F_Port

Device Node

FC_RAID
Controller   FC_RAID Storage Array

Disk Disk Disk Disk Disk

Disk Disk Disk Disk Disk   } Volume A

Disk Disk Disk Disk Disk

Disk Disk Disk Disk Disk   } Volume B

Figure 14-7.   *An FC RAID storage configuration*

in order for the server to know which disks it has access to on the network. This can quickly become confusing, given that RAID deals in logical units, not independent addressable disks.

One last word about Fibre Channel storage, and this goes for RAID and JBOD configurations: when assigning multiple servers to the switch (via the HBA), the servers have to be told which storage resources they are allowed to play with. And this can quickly become tedious. For example, each server has its own file system, and that file system must reflect the location of the files the server has access to. Problems arise when two or more servers have access to the same files. What happens when two servers reach out for the same file? You guessed it… trouble, headaches, and a whole lot of shouting. File sharing between servers attached to a Storage Area Network remains a tedious and problematic issue. Consequently, zoning and masking each server's authorized resources continues to be a prerequisite for effective operation. Before *you* start shouting, and reach for the aspirin, have a look at Chapter 22.

Bridges and Routers

In addition to the challenges posed by file sharing, data sharing, and device sharing, there are standard data center practices that are required for any type of storage model. Every data center must protect the data stored within the arrays. Most accomplish this using backup/recovery software and practices, which entails the use of tape devices as the primary media for archival copy and data copy functions. In a SAN environment, however, this is easier said than done. Fibre Channel-enabled tape devices have been problematic in their support of this new storage model.

To overcome this hurdle, a new type of device was required to bridge the FC protocol into a SCSI bus architecture used in tape media. Because of tape technologies' sequential nature and the resulting complexity entailed with error recovery, tape media has been difficult to integrate. Solving these difficulties required a device that not only bridged the Fibre Channel into the tape controller/drive bus system, but also further required the management of the logical unit numbers (LUNs) that were utilized in the tape's SCSI configuration. The solution was found in bridges, or routers, for Fibre Channel. This is illustrated in Figure 14-8.

Although they are compatible with other SCSI devices, routers are primarily known for their capability to facilitate the operation of tape media within a SAN. Routers provide an effective means of establishing a tape media library for SAN configurations. The alternative would be to copy data from the FC storage arrays onto the LAN and shoot it off to a backup server with a directly attached SCSI tape drive. Considering the

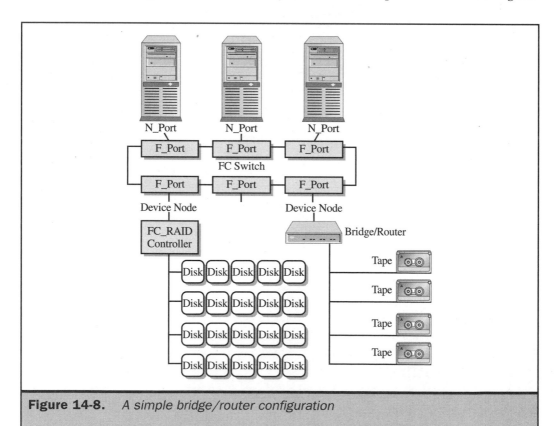

Figure 14-8.   *A simple bridge/router configuration*

overhead required, routers provide a much sleeker configuration for data protection. As always though, even the sleek solutions have their drawbacks. Fibre Channel to SCSI routers bring their own performance issues in matching the switch's port performance with the SCSI bus attachment at the other end of the bridge. Due to SCSI transfer rates, speeds across the router will be constantly slower and throughput will be compromised.

When integrating a router solution, it is important to understand what is needed, whether it's a discrete component or one of the integrated solutions that are increasingly creeping into tape subsystem products. In looking at either of these solutions, you'll have to distinguish other protocols besides SCSI that may be necessary to bridge into your SAN configuration. Router technology is beginning to move toward a gateway type solution where Fibre Channel integrates additional I/O and network protocols.

An additional word of caution: routers add yet another level of microkernel operating environment that must be compatible with all of the components across the Storage Area Network. Routers must also be compatible with a significant number of tape systems, which only adds to the complexity of implementation. The surest bet is to approach the integrated solution supported by the tape manufacturer.

Fabric Operation from a Hardware Perspective

The SAN's fabric operates through, and is governed by, the logical components of the Fibre Channel standard previously mentioned. The standard is broken down into logical constructs of frame, sequence, and exchanges. FC provides its storage flexibility through the ability to transport other protocols, such as the SCSI protocol.

- **Frame**   The logical construct of transporting data through the switch.
- **Sequence**   A block of numbered or related frames transported in sequence from initiator to target. Error recovery takes place as the receiving port processes the sequence.
- **Exchange**   A number of nonconcurrent sequences processed bidirectionally (it should be noted, however, that a port can only process one sequence at a time). Although a single port is limited to single sequence processing, it can process multiple simultaneous exchanges.

Within the overall FC protocol standard are embedded the primitive sequence protocols used for error recovery during exchange processing. Fabric login is used to communicate the port's operation characteristics. Operations are directed by the N_Port login and logout commands, which provide session-level parameters as ports issue and exchange sequences. The exchanges are made up of frames (as shown in Figure 14-9) and indicate the large user data area or payload that allow FC protocols to transmit at gigabit speeds.

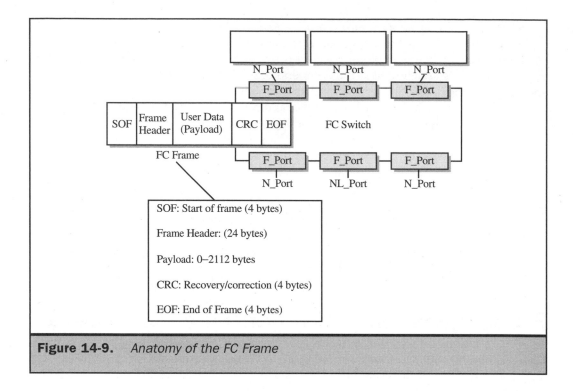

Figure 14-9.   *Anatomy of the FC Frame*

Selected by the port at login, the class of service and other parameters the switch will support directs flow control of the frames. Flow control is determined by connection attributes between communicating devices. This process is similar to network operations where connections are either mindful of their state and acknowledge transmission and receipt, or disregard their state, acknowledgment, and effective frame recovery. Although there are six classes of operation defined by the FC standard, only three are useful to data storage operations, and therefore worthy of mention.

- **Class 1**   A dedicated connection in which two devices establish complete control and dedicated bandwidth of the link. Until they complete their transactions, the ports remain busy and unavailable to any other traffic. Although useful for batch type operations and data streaming when the complete bandwidth of the link can or must be used, Class 1 operation performs best in transactional-intensive workloads like OLTP, web, or data warehousing.

- **Class 2**   A switched bandwidth sharing connection (considered connectionless) providing a form of time-slicing algorithms that share bandwidth, thus enabling multiple exchange activities to take place. Although Class 2 service does have acknowledgment of frame delivery, frames do not have ordered, guaranteed delivery, and thus must wait their turn in the linking schedule to perform the reordering of frames within the routing mechanism set up by the vendor. Class 2 (illustrated in Figure 14-10) demonstrates its value in typical application I/O workload situations. It can handle the transaction rates an OLTP or time-dependent system might throw its way.

- **Class 3**   A connectionless buffer-to-buffer flow mechanism that offers a quick way to broadcast messages within a multicast group. However, cutting out the recipient acknowledgment and buffer coherence means introducing a high risk of frame loss. Class 3 works well for specialized applications that broadcast requests to devices. Without the retransmission of the request in other class processing, this limits the useful value to simple data replication and browsing/searching acknowledgment.

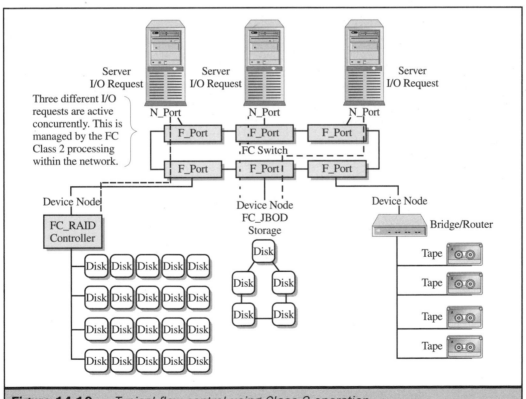

Figure 14-10.   *Typical flow control using Class 2 operation*

SAN Hardware Considerations

As you might have gathered by this point, SAN hardware is made up of multiple components with many variables, specifications, and options unique to each. Most hardware decisions are made based on the features and standards supported by a particular component's vendor. It is important when heading into a purchasing decision that you eliminate as many unknowns as possible.

Of the billions of things to keep in mind, first and foremost will always be ensuring that total I/O workload matches SAN resources. (Chapter 17 lays the foundation for I/O workload planning, while Chapter 18 sets out some guidelines in estimating basic SAN resources.) Consider the following.

Match server hardware- and software-supported releases with proposed storage and SAN configuration components. This will ensure the correct operating system level, HBA, and switch fabric release levels for compatibility. Also, verify the compatibility and features of the switch against the type of I/O workload you are supporting. Ensuring you can configure Class 2 support, at a minimum, will be important as you implement the workload processing into the environment.

It is paramount that a planned SAN configuration be compatible with the operations you are planning. If you are going to use an external tape library, ensure sufficient port and network resources for transmitting data across the SAN and LAN network. If instead you are going to employ an integrated tape library, understand the compatibility issues surrounding the additional equipment. Whether integrated or discrete, routing hardware must come under the same scrutiny as every other component in the configuration.

The Complete Reference

Storage Networks

Chapter 15

Software Components

The era of client/server computing ushered in the challenge of dealing with multiple operating environments. The need for operating systems to communicate has only grown and become more sophisticated. As discussed earlier regarding NAS hardware and software, its architecture of effective OS communications is at the heart of what it delivers. Fortunately for IT professionals, the NAS devices were efficient, encapsulated product bundles and didn't require an in-depth configuration integration effort with other operating environments. This isn't true of SAN technologies (as Chapter 14 illustrated) with their various hardware components.

This chapter will cover the multiple software components that make up the SAN, a summary of what and how they operate, and a view of fabric operation from the software perspective. At the forefront of this discussion will be the FC switch's operating system, a discussion of the microkernel-oriented set of software services that provides the base functionality for creating the SAN network and switched fabric of interconnections.

The device driver discussion will cover the necessary software drivers that must be available to allow the external node devices to connect to the fabric. Their functions, and how they operate, are integral to the complete configuration of a SAN. Due to their distributed nature, their considerations for design and implementation are dependent on server, storage, and fabric software components.

The most important is the SAN storage software part, given that the entire value of the SAN components leverage a stronger storage position. The SAN infrastructure provides a transparent implementation of most storage media, especially in the area of disk storage arrays and the use of external controller functions necessary in RAID and tape media functions. These include RAID recovery functions, internal array caching, and fault-tolerant features that are integrated with the storage component. Their interaction with the switch's OS, as well as the FC HBA drivers, are critical to the effective configuration and operation of the SAN.

Supporting components part: Additional features inherent with the SAN, but which require additional components to leverage, are data sharing, device sharing, management, and special routing software functions. Although supplied by third-party vendors, the milieu of interrelationships with the Fabric OS and device drivers becomes problematic when implementing these advanced SAN functions.

The Switch's Operating System

If a Storage Area Network's heart is the switch, continuously pumping data between the storage and the servers, then the network's brain is the switch's operating system. Switch operating systems are similarly configured to the microkernel RTOS used in NAS solutions. In fact, the operating systems, in many cases, are a derivative of the same technology used by certain NAS vendors. Switch operating systems, regardless of implementation, operate with the same core-level operating systems that support other embedded options.

Figure 15-1 illustrates the basic components of a typical switch operating system, the foundation of which is the core-level, or kernel-level system calls that provide basic

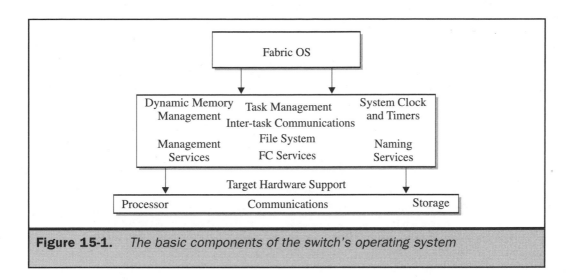

Figure 15-1.   *The basic components of the switch's operating system*

system-level functions, such as interrupt processing, memory management, and task prioritization. The ability to execute Fibre Channel commands through low-level system calls to the FC chip-set is the specialization encapsulated in the switch, given that microkernel performance of the switch's operating system is paramount to the successful operation and effective utilization of switch hardware.

There are two major issues that impact the operation and performance of the switch's OS. The first is the extensibility of the system's functions to successfully execute existing functionality while being able to encompass new levels of applications which have become increasingly important to the operation of the SAN as a whole. Surrounding this level of compatibility and scalability is the microkernel's capability to coexist alongside a commodity-level chip and Fibre Channel microprocessor. Consideration must be given to the addressability of the operating environment and its ability to multiprocess and multitask the network linking functions of the switch. The second issue is the operating system's capability to provide reliable yet efficient Name Service functions for intraswitch operations and interswitch communications. The inherent danger in mixing and matching different vendor's switch components should be duly noted, and strongly heeded.

Figure 15-2 illustrates the importance of add-on applications that must also utilize the operating system's resources—for example, recovery services, management services, external API, and communication components.

The following list discusses the additional components that process under the control of the fabric operating system. The specific processes will be implemented differently depending on the vendor selection of FC switch products; however, the common functions as explained here should be included to achieve a complete operational SAN fabric.

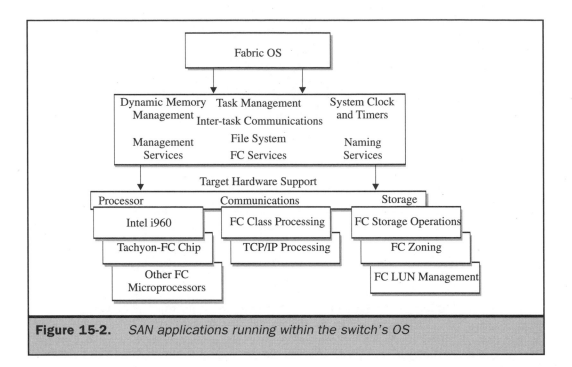

Figure 15-2. *SAN applications running within the switch's OS*

- **Recovery** Core-level services that provide specific class processing within the switch, including link recovery, sequence retransmission, and frame recovery of, specifically, class 2 processing. This also includes class 3 and 4, not to mention the added value functions related to Fibre Channel that enable disk-to-disk communications. These leverage node functions from layer 3, 4, and upwards, along with the extended copy command that allows devices to communicate without a third-party supervisor. As you might have guessed, recovery functionality is essential. For additional information, see Chapters 21 and 22.

- **Management** Not an easy one. The big difficulty with any embedded system is its inability to be seen within the environment it operates. SAN configurations are just about the least visible to existing server-level applications, so it falls to the switch's operating system to provide some level of visibility. This is accomplished through the use of a Management Information Base (MIB). Given its network-centricity, MIBs, and its subsequent access method of Simple Network Management Protocol (SNMP), are the foundation components monitoring the SAN. These unwieldy components are difficult enough within a network environment, and have proved to be just as obtuse in storage network environments. As hard as they are, though, MIBs have provided management vendors and those users intrepid enough to brave the waking nightmare that is SNMP an opportunity to gather information about the operation of the switch. So, choose the fabric component, but please make sure the operating system is compatible with third-party management tools. *Please...*

■ **External Application Programming Interface (API)**   Most switch operating system implementations will make some accommodation for an API to facilitate third-party programs that enhance the operation of the SAN. APIs include data sharing software, management software, and communications software.

■ **Communication components**   A way to get from the switch to the outside world. This is yet another important duty of the switch's operating system, given that port communications are encapsulated within core-level functions, outside communication to IP networks, serial communication to console functions, and the leveraging of E_Port switch-to-switch communication. The switch's capability to direct these functions is dependent on size and scalability. IP overhead communication through a G_Port provides sufficient latency to affect the performance of the switch. E_Port interswitch communication stacks additional processing cycles that subtract from the core functionality of the switch itself. As a result, console configurations through a serial port should have sufficient low-level prioritization to interrupt kernel functions in order to reconfigure or solve a problem.

Taking all of this into consideration, it becomes plain that the concurrency of port-to-port communication, outside communications, switch-to-switch communications, and the latency factors for the microkernel can, and will, quickly become overwhelming.

At the end of the day, the microkernel operating system is not likely to handle a lot of other work on top of what its core-level job is, which is the linking of ports. Low-end, generic switches of 8 to 32 ports aren't likely to support additional data sharing, management, or switch-to-switch latencies without taking away from core-level functionality. These switches are designed to provide a switch fabric set of operations for hooking switches to storage, and that's it. Microkernel operating systems just weren't designed to be general operating systems. So why are we asking them to be general operating systems?

Device Drivers

Communicating externally with the switch's operating systems requires the use of software drivers that allow the devices to operate as either N_Ports or NL_Ports. Each type of device requires a specific kind of driver to enable this functionality. In a Storage Area Network, the two big ones are the HBA's interface with the switch, and the storage's connection.

As discussed in Chapter 14, the HBA provides an FC-interface from a computer device, typically a server, to a Fibre Channel switch. In addition to the hardware adapter that must be physically connected to the server's bus interface, the software contained in the HBA must translate the file I/O request and device command set into Fibre Channel commands. For this to happen, software drivers are installed on the system that execute as device handlers at the kernel level, requiring a change to the ROM configurations, as well as additions to recognize the new interface that exist within an HBA. In essence, an application takes SCSI commands found for particular

STORAGE AREA
NETWORKS

file destinations and translates these commands into specific requests through the FC protocol as it logs in to the switch and executes the appropriate services.

HBAs are critical for two reasons. First, for their capability to shield the server from the specifics of the addressing encapsulated in the Fibre Channel (not to mention in managing the actual physical and logical units they're authorized to use within the fabric). The HBA maintains the logical unit numbers (LUNs) for the devices it can access. It works in tandem with the operating system to determine the bounds of the devices it has access to, thereby initiating the first level of device virtualization to the server.

The second critical function is providing the server with an effective transmit and receive data path into the switch, which supplies a way of leveraging the flexibility and bandwidth of the FC network it is connected to. Figure 15-3 shows both the logical and physical functions that are controlled by an HBA's device drivers.

Given an HBA's critical proximity to the I/O path, performance is a direct result of the addressability of the server's bus interface bandwidth. Providing a high-end HBA interface to a low-level bus won't buy you much performance. Similarly, hooking

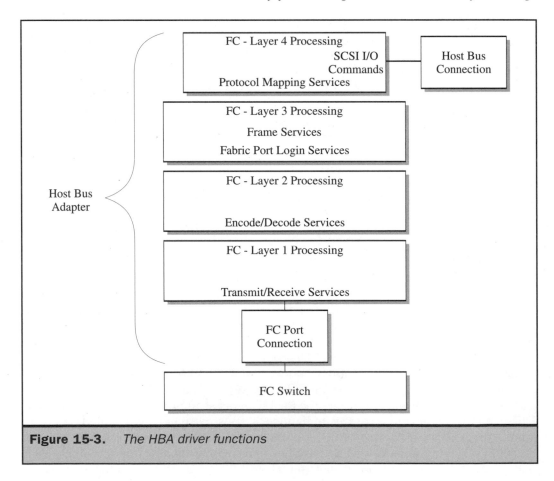

Figure 15-3.   *The HBA driver functions*

a legacy bus into an HBA is only asking for trouble. The additional features found in today's HBAs parallel much of the added functionality mentioned earlier in our discussion of the switch's operating system. Some of these features are unique to the device drivers themselves, including software RAID, support for virtual interface protocol (see Chapter 8), and service features like enclosure management.

Fibre Channel storage arrays, discussed in the previous chapter, provide yet another embedded system for consideration when it comes to compatibility, functionality, and servicing. The big hardware vendor feature offers the capability to differentiate on the basis of software, which means that all storage arrays, whether JBOD, RAID, tape, or optical, have some level of secret sauce that must be downloaded in order to gain bonus levels of functionality. In the Fibre Channel arena, it becomes super challenging in just trying to access the storage array through the FC network on a native basis. This is a required step in configuring either JBOD or the RAID controller with the proper software (we're really talking firmware here). As a result, another configuration utility must be used against the storage array as it becomes implemented. Having said all this, never fear, once you work through this a first time, the process can generally be proceduralized into the functions and servicing of the SAN. Now, here's the fly in the ointment. Each vendor's implementation is different. A heterogeneous storage array installation, as you might have guessed, can become mired in inconsistencies, incompatibilities, and 25 different ways of doing the same thing.

RAID configurations pose the biggest problem, but also provide the biggest buyback. Given that RAID software shields, or manages, the local devices it is connected to, it directs through its parameters read/write operations within the disk subsystems. This is an example of level 2 virtualization. Coupled with level 1, which has already occurred on the HBA, we're then forced to contend with two levels of virtualization. Even after configurations, care should be taken as to the level of logical unit numbering that occurs when defined within the RAID configuration chosen.

The Supporting Components

Even with the previous components of switch OS and its multitude of functions, there are yet additional supporting components that have become increasingly important to the SAN software. The following are critical to SAN configuration and operation:

- **Data sharing**   Still problematic because a global file system operating across a set of servers doesn't yet exist. Although some existing software products can be employed, they provide an increased level of latency in switch processing and external server processing. They also require additional hardware resources which provide a centralized locking mechanism.

- **Device sharing**   Less problematic than data sharing, device sharing can be used effectively to some degree in homogenous environments (for instance, in all Windows servers). By allowing the devices to be controlled by the operating system, they will not be able to communicate altogether effectively.

■ **Management**   This continues to evolve as a discipline. Because SANs are still a new technology, no one's quite sure what to manage, or what to look for, actually. Problem uniqueness, driven by the overwhelming configuration options, thus makes management a site-specific discipline.

■ **ISL functions**   The Achilles heel of SANs. This type of implemented configuration drives interswitch communication. Core-edge configurations, meanwhile, demonstrate different switch-to-switch communications than cascading configurations. As additional hops are needed from switch to switch, processing latency builds, and performance becomes non-linear with respect to resources applied (see Chapter 1).

Device Sharing

One of the first dilemmas faced in working with SAN hardware is sharing devices within the fabric. Device sharing frustration rivals the initial learning curve of setting up network fabric, connecting the devices in the SAN, or even coming up with a suitable cabling strategy. Device sharing requires the knowledge of switch software, HBA parameters, and OS storage access.

The problem boils down to sharing devices between operation systems. NAS environments provide this level of sharing because they separate the native I/O from the application infrastructure (see Chapter 20 for additional information on the differences between SAN and NAS I/O operations). This separation does not happen in SAN configurations. The servers communicate through native I/Os (say, block I/O requests) with the storage devices. This makes the switch, and the switch's operating system, the fundamental global access supervisor in which the storage administrator is used as the key in establishing who can access what.

Although this could be construed as a hardware function, device access within the switch fabric is handled through the configuration parameters of the switch OS. This is known as *zoning*, a control function that specifies at switch startup time and device initialization time what devices the node login can access. This happens logically through a set of port addresses associated with a particular server. When implementing a SAN configuration, careful thought should go into planning the "who's who" of SAN storage access. Most SAN switch vendors recommend that the user develop a matrix of server-to-storage access required for SAN design and implementation.

Figure 15-4 shows the zoning function in partitioning the storage arrays within a simple SAN structure. Sever A has access to devices on storage array "prod" and "test." Server B, however, can only access "QA," with shared access for both occurring through the "test" array. Zoning, at what is considered the hardware level, restricts the access of one device to another, and becomes further complicated when individual devices within the arrays need to be zoned within the configurations.

The zoning process requires the mapping of LUN addressing at the server (and, by default, the HBA) level, the array level, and the bridge/router lever, which only makes the whole process that much more complex. Further LUN zones take place within existing zones, something called LUN masking, which masks off access of specific LUNs to the nodes. Operationally, this provides a lower level of device sharing and partitioning within a storage array, or in the context of a tape unit. This process is shown in Figure 15-5, where zoning with LUN masking accommodates further sharing of the "QA" array along with the installation of the tape drives, which can be used by both servers, though only with specific tape drives.

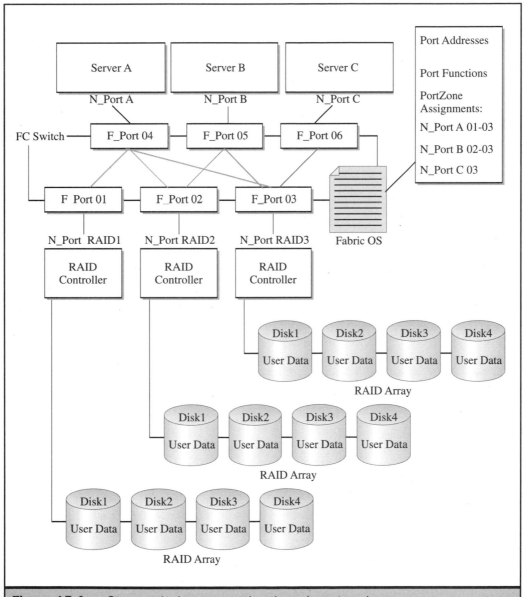

Figure 15-4. *Storage device segregation through port zoning*

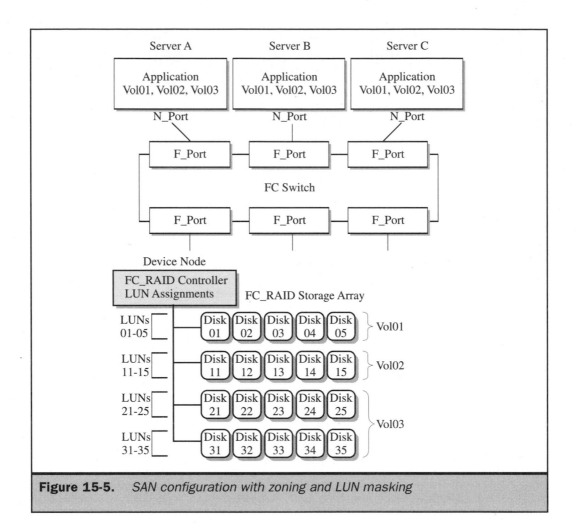

Figure 15-5. *SAN configuration with zoning and LUN masking*

Data Sharing

Device sharing naturally suggests data sharing. NAS allows a level of sharing because it separates the data from the actual I/O, allowing ownership and access to the data. SAN, however, as we have discussed, provides native access to the data from several servers. As such, data sharing is problematic, to say the least. The major reason is that within a SAN software environment there is no global supervisor to monitor and control access to shared data. As Figure 15-6 shows, through unrestricted access or liberal zoning, two servers can access the same data block for write access, which spells significant data integrity trouble.

Data sharing in a SAN environment is tricky, and, depending on the server operating environment, can be assembled using multiple components of the server OS, switch-zoning functions, and LUN masking. This level of complexity within a heterogeneous server OS-SAN environment can be challenging and problematic, given the differences of file access between UNIX and Windows-based operating systems.

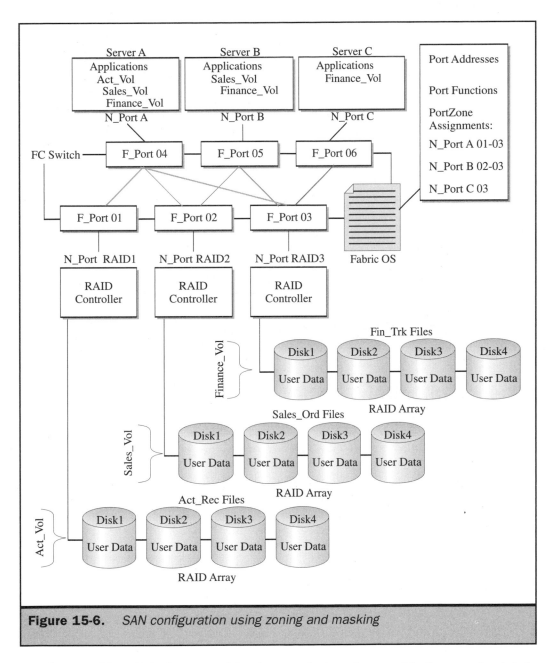

Figure 15-6. *SAN configuration using zoning and masking*

STORAGE AREA
NETWORKS

There are a handful of commercial software solutions that provide the psuedo-global file manager to monitor and control shared data access. Although these products are becoming more robust, mature, and reliable, they supply an overhead to the processing requests that are subject to data sharing restrictions. Figure 15-7 shows how these products operate in an out-of-band processing mode with the SAN.

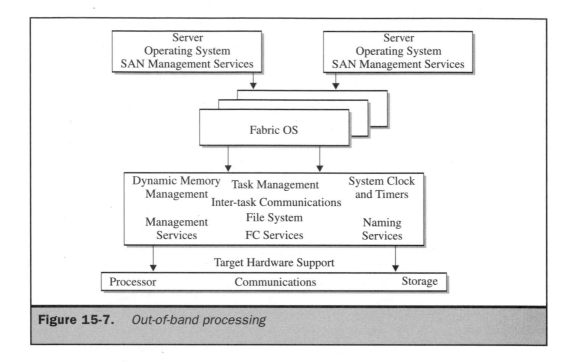

Figure 15-7.   *Out-of-band processing*

SAN Management Applications

While device sharing and data sharing could be considered management applications, they are directed from both the switch OS as well as from external devices, such as attached servers and contollers. These applications run on external devices and only communicate with the switch to obtain specific data for their processing requirements.

This also characterizes a SAN's management software components, which are categorized from an external and internal perspective of the switch. Management components are considered out-of-band when processed external to the switch and in-band when their functions process within the switch. Both sets of software, whether in- or out-of-band, access the switch OS for their particular function. As you can see, management functions are quickly becoming imperative to the effective operation of the SAN.

In-Band Management Functions

In-band management functions are distributed within FC switch application functions. However, several provide base functionality, including activities such as configuration and maintenance. Other functions allow add-on type applications, like performance, change, and problem management. Several of the functions generally available through in-band management applications are discussed next. Keep in mind that vendor selection and third-party availability play a key role in what is actually configured in the switch or SAN product set.

Console or Workstation Access   Console, or workstation, access is the initial entry to the switch OS, requiring a direct connect console or workstation, and is used in communicating changes through the OS. This interface provides a base-level entry into the initialization and configuration of a SAN fabric, as well as the set up of switch parameters and operating specifications.

Configuration Utility   Defining fabrics, assigning worldwide names, domain names, port ID addresses, and IP addresses are just a few of the initial activities performed through the configuration utility console. Others (although vendor-dependent) include license verification, ISL operation and verification, and FC fabric validation.

The Console Boot Process   The console boot process is very important, unless you're installing or operating a single-point SAN. The order in which you reboot the switch operating systems is critical. Most vendors provide some form of boot utility that allows the specification of boot sequencing. Also, given the critical nature of console boot processing, the configuration must be able to provide alternate paths for redundant configurations, such as core/edge installations.

Maintenance   Loading new firmware releases will exercise boot processes, given that the operating environment of the switch is no different than any other computer. Most configuration utilities have an integrated function that loads new releases of the switch OS, service patches, and other new or upgraded functions. In some cases, this may be a separate function of an application accessed through the console. However, this brings up an important point of change management, one that is central to OS maintenance in general, and imperative to SANs. The sophistication of this type of management application is just beginning to evolve and change. Management is largely a manual tracking process, albeit an important one (see Chapter 22 for a more detailed discussion of management applications that affect SAN availability).

Monitoring Functions   Monitoring functions provide a window in which to view the performance of the SAN components. These same functions can also be accessed through the console and configuration utilities. Like change management, don't expect much. The ability to view port operations is usually on an "on-off" status level, which can also be done by looking at the port status LEDs. Port activity, in terms of I/O workload performance, is left to third-party tools that process on an out-of-band device. However, ISL operation and status functions can be found with most switch in-band applications. A separate discussion later in this chapter, in the section titled "ISL Functions," will cover ISL components.

Out-of-Band Management Functions

Managing the SAN externally will require functions and processes that are executed from attached devices. These, for the most part, will be enabled from attached servers, although some supporting functions will be necessary for functions that bridge, route, or provide an external process. The following discussion highlights some of the major functions that should be considered in design and configuration of SAN solutions. These become critical once the SAN configuration becomes operational.

Configuration Management   Configuration management is perhaps the most widely available function, even though it's probably the one that does the least. It scans a name server and configuration files on the switch and renders a picture of the total SAN environment. Given additional sophistication, the SAN diagram can become an active diagram in providing a "rear view" elementary monitor function based on information from the switch's MIB. Added sophistication or no, it is still a "rear-view," so there's not a whole lot you can do having used it. (Imagine trying to drive using only your rear-view mirror.) The ability to shield the SAN administrator from the complexities of the line-command configuration utilities or the obtuse nature of the Windows-based "GUI" is still evolving. It's great for having a pretty picture of the SAN to show your boss, or downloading it to his PC so he can show his boss.

Performance Management   Like the other five management disciplines, performance monitoring of the SAN is very elementary. Given the complexities of the switch configuration, fabric software, and diversity of device attachments, this is a difficult task, one that will require additional development and maturity within SAN technology and vendor areas before reaching a real-value proposition. However, I remember what the old IT manager once said about availability of systems information, "In the land of the blind, the one-eyed man is king." Given that analogy, any insight into these complexities will provide a piece of the puzzle, which will help accurately manage performance. However, be prepared to manually correlate the information from the application on down to the device.

Note   *Systems management has been categorized into five management disciplines that are used to maintain computer systems regardless of vendor class or technology. These are performance, change, problem, configuration, and capacity management.*

Storage Management   Many SAN-specific storage functions that interact with the switch and related software are becoming increasingly available—for example, storage applications that provide device and disk management solutions like volume managers, disk utilities, and failover solutions. This type of software, in the case of volume managers, executes on the server and interacts through the switch to manage disks into volumes, providing a level of virtualization for applications. Other software products manage the backup/recovery processes that handle data protection strategies. They can also execute on an attached server, and leverage a device-to-device copy operation. Known as server-free or server-less backup, such operations allow the backup application to turn control of the copying operations over to an FC device such as the FC switch. Without the extra resource utilization normally imposed by the controlling server's involvement, the results are a highly optimized data backup operation (see Chapter 22 for more on backup/recovery and the extended copy operation).

Considerations for Integrated Management Functions

Here's the problem. Each application running as an in-band operation on the switch's operating system takes away from the processing dedicated to the operation of the switch, as well as the movement of data within the fabric on behalf of the attached devices. Likewise, any time an out-of-band application accesses the switch, it too takes away from processing power. As Storage Area Networks are very often built with entry-level switches, and continue to experience growth through incremental switch upgrades, supporting applications can easily overrun the switch's operating system's capacity to perform, even at minimum levels. Additionally, as out-of-band applications become more sophisticated and contact the switch with increasingly complex requests, major latency issues are going to pop up with greater frequency. Left unattended, this will put the SAN into a gridlock of overhead versus primary processing responsibilities.

ISL Functions

Interswitch linking (ISL) functions are integral to implementing scalable and highly available SAN configurations. ISL functions are a combination of hardware and software functions, though software functionality quickly becomes the predominant component in enabling switch-to-switch connectivity. Be warned though, ISL functions continue to limit the heterogeneity of configuration flexibility and design due to the proprietary implementation employed by various vendors. The bottom line is that highly scalable multiswitch SAN configurations are best built from homogeneous products.

ISL functions provide a communications link between switches and fabrics, which allows switches to be configured to meet the needs of the I/O workloads they are supporting. Simple cascading connections provide a way of attaching multiple device nodes within an extended fabric, or among disparate fabrics. Figure 15-8 shows the ISL functions required to support a three-switch configuration. The server's I/O requests for switch "A" are processed through the switch it is directly connected to. If the server requests data from storage array "Prod2", though, it has to connect through switch "A", then reconnect to switch "B" through ISL 1 port. The I/O request is then serviced and the response from the "Prod2" storage array is sent back along the same route, using ISL 1 to return to the server via switch "A".

Taking this a step further, switch "C" can be accessed via switch "A" through the ISL 2 port. This configuration continues to expand using ISL functions to provide additional access to storage device nodes. Additional operational characteristics to this switch configuration include dynamic switch configuration, cross connections (also referred to as trunking), fabric recognition, ISL device recognition, and performance.

Many switches support dynamic configurations, where, upon initialization, the switch automatically recognizes and logs in attached device nodes and E_Port ISL functions, thereby identifying the ISL connection as well as the devices connected to both.

STORAGE AREA NETWORKS

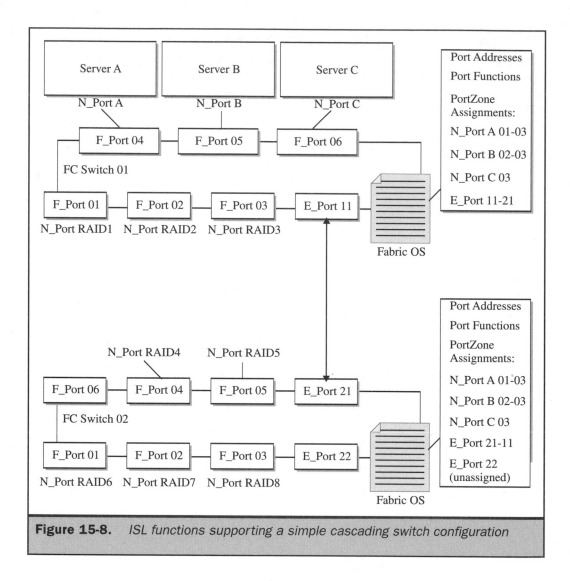

Figure 15-8. *ISL functions supporting a simple cascading switch configuration*

In many cases, the use of an ISL facilitates the basic connectivity to other node devices, but may not possess the necessary performance or failover requirements for the workload. Should this arise, multiple ISL functions are paired to facilitate throughput requirements and act as a backup if one ISL port becomes inoperative. This is illustrated in Figure 15-9.

The final factor is the switch's capability to dynamically recognize storage devices. In many cases, this is performed automatically when the switch configuration is initialized. Sometimes, though, the device nods might drop off and not be recognized by the primary switch, as in cascading configurations. If this happens, caution must be taken in analyzing the requirements for the storage device and the switch through which recognition is passed to the owning server.

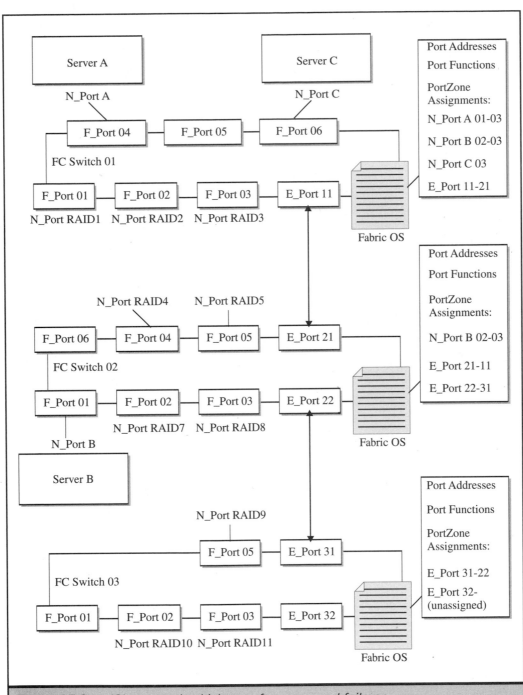

Figure 15-9.   *ISL supporting higher performance and failover*

Considerations for SAN Software

SAN software components can form a complex set of functions. SAN configurations, given their multicomponent assembly, require software that provides the distributed communications capabilities of the fabric, as well as the core-level functionality that drives the internal routing and linking of FC frame processing. The bottom line to all this is that SAN software supporting a new infrastructure (for example, a Fibre Channel storage network) is much more complex than NAS environments. Additional discussions regarding these differences in terms of applicability can be found in Chapters 17, 18, and 19.

Many SAN software functions are accessed outside the switch operating system, which makes the configuration more complex as processing takes place both externally (out-of-band) and internally (in-band). The switch, although similar to the internal RTOS in NAS solutions, is not accessible except through the configuration process. Configuration complexities require that some training be made available prior to the design and implementation of the SAN software.

The
Complete
Reference

Storage
Networks

Chapter 16

Configuration Options
for SANs

A s was shown in Chapters 14 and 15, Storage Area Networks can be assembled and connected in a variety of ways. Switch options and device configurations are dependent on I/O workloads and recovery requirements. Once assembled and connected, the network as a whole has to be integrated into the data center infrastructure. Chapter 16 moves SAN configurations out of the abstract and into the data center.

Regardless of connectivity or configuration, viable SAN solutions are moving from single switch configurations to multiswitch configurations with numerous device attachments designed to deal with increasing workloads and even the simplest recovery and redundancy requirements. And though there are many ways to configure a switch, the basic starting-point configurations remain core/edge, meshed, and cascading configurations. All three present their own unique challenges when integrated into an existing infrastructure.

This chapter delves further into an external SAN connectivity beyond the node devices, which become the drivers for application usage. Storage configurations, the workhorses of SANs, are often called upon to provide multiaccess for the server population within the data center. One of the biggest integration challenges is in trying to throw the configuration into the support of heterogeneous storage components. Additionally, external forces driving new and enhanced storage media waiting to be included in the SAN can play a part in connectivity.

Connecting into the Data Center

Connectivity refers to how the SAN as a whole integrates into the data center. In this discussion of connectivity, we will draw a theoretical line between SAN components and server processing. As such, the SAN as a whole includes the components that connect to the FC switch with a dotted line drawn at the HBA. This allows us to position the FC SAN in a set of server populations and existing configurations. Even if only used as a logical model, it helps us visualize the inevitable problems. Figure 16-1 shows the logical demarcation line we will use throughout the chapter.

Implementing a SAN configuration into a data center presents three challenges right off the bat. The first challenge is the need to configure a multiswitch SAN. As I/O workloads, driven by supporting applications, are applied, the need to provide multiple connections, discrete zones, and paths for performance drive the configuration into multiple FC switches. There's just no way around it. Over and above this is the need to provide some level of recovery and redundancy for data availability and protection scenarios. Existing policies and practices will drive this challenge; if not, it's good to start thinking about recovery, redundancy, and single point of failure—of which, a single switch strategy presents.

The second challenge is in providing support to the server population within the data center, which can be driven by the justification for the SAN in terms of server consolidations and supported applications. Note, though, that it also moves into the

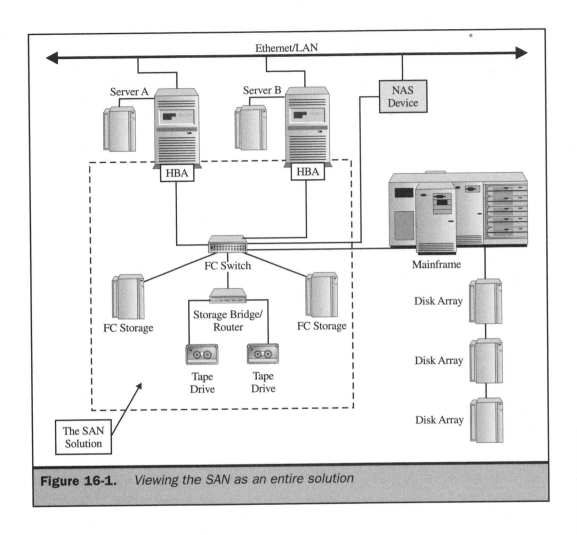

Figure 16-1.   *Viewing the SAN as an entire solution*

realm of data ownership, production cycles and processing, and data sensitivity. More importantly, it pushes the need for a heterogeneous SAN supporting more than one operating system at the attached server level. In many cases, this becomes the big SAN imbroglio in which implementation becomes political and ceases being productive, or relatively anxiety-free—or, for that matter, fun in any way.

The third challenge is supporting external networks, which encompasses all of the issues mentioned previously. The ability to provide the data stored within the SAN to corporate networks is dependent on the external network points within the data center, as well as the capability of the attached server to distribute this data within the infrastructure it is connected to.

Implementing Multiswitch Configurations

The need to configure a multiswitch SAN solution will become evident when designing your first solution. Any solutions should encompass a rationale for the configuration orientation used (for example, cascading, core/edge, or mesh). Initial implementations often move from a simple cascading architecture to a multilayered cascading architecture without the benefit of, or options for, moving into a more complementary configuration. Keep in mind that SAN configurations are driven by supported I/O workloads. As such, the need to provide recovery and redundancy should play a significant role in the design. Here are a few ideas to chew on.

- **OLTP Workloads**   Using a core/edge configuration enhances performance through storage access at the edge, while reducing instances of single point of failures for high availability transactions accessing multiple I/Os through the SAN configuration (shown in Figure 16-2).

- **Web Applications/Messaging Workloads**   Using a mesh design provides alternate paths for high traffic, asynchronous I/O processing, while reducing instances for single point of failure. It relies on effective switching methods for high traffic management within the SAN configuration (shown in Figure 16-3).

- **Data Warehouse/Datacentric Workloads**   Using a cascading design provides the necessary access and performance of datacentric transactional workloads. Here, availability requirements are reduced, but access to large data bases remains paramount when it comes to processing time and I/O intensive transactions (shown in Figure 16-4).

Coming up with the appropriate SAN design for I/O workloads also requires some thoughts on recovery. Though driven by the application's needs, a working design should encompass current backup/recovery processes that are in place within the data center. It's good to reconsider recovery issues relative to the storage capacities of the SAN and the recovery requirements of the data. In a normal backup situation, data is copied from the storage arrays to an attached server and shuttled onto the network so it can get to the backup servers attached to tape drives. In all likelihood, these are located close to the tape library. However, if the SAN starts out with capacities over 500GB of user data, this scenario might just overcome existing backup practices.

Consideration should be given to backup/recovery within the SAN infrastructure, which means the addition of external tape media—tape drives and tape libraries providing backup/recovery operations integrated into the SAN. Designs will have to be modified, regardless of configurations (core/edge, mesh, cascading), in order to accommodate the backup traffic and backup/recovery software—meaning the addition of a bridge/router component. This setup adds another benefit (which is largely dependent on recovery requirements and storage capacities): the evolving capabilities of FC fabric to provide a direct copy operation in support of backup software will eliminate a significant amount of I/O overhead. Often referred to as "server-free backup" or "server-less backup," these configurations will be covered again in Chapters 22 and 23.

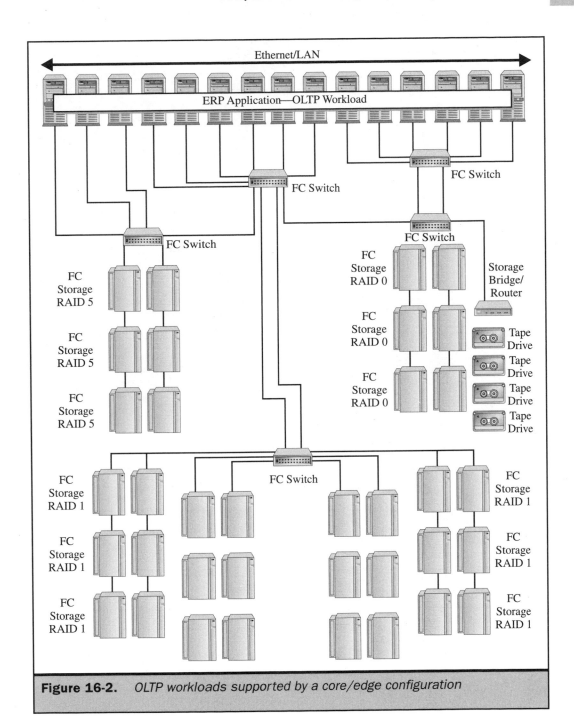

Figure 16-2. *OLTP workloads supported by a core/edge configuration*

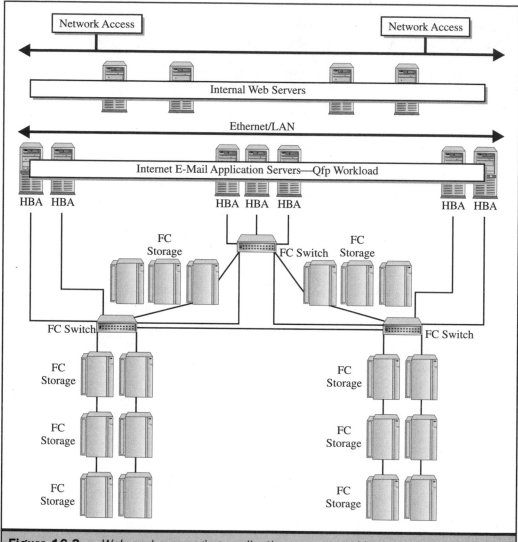

Figure 16-3.   *Web and messaging applications supported by a mesh configuration*

Supporting the Server Population

The next challenge is determining which servers to support. Not only is this driven by what applications are moving over to the SAN, but also what strategy justified the SAN in the first place. If consolidation justified the SAN, then someone will be looking to retire or redeploy a number of servers through the consolidation efforts, which brings up an interesting set of activities.

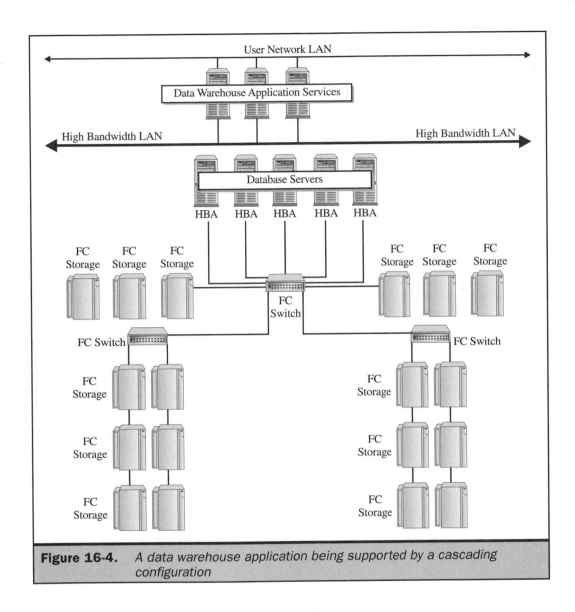

Figure 16-4.   *A data warehouse application being supported by a cascading configuration*

First is the modification of existing capacity plans to calculate the requirements of new or redeployed servers, and to calculate the necessary I/O workloads as they contribute to the design of the SAN (some examples and guidelines for estimating I/O workloads are upcoming in Chapter 17, with specifics for SANs following in Chapter 18). This will very likely make you have to think about moving applications that are running on both UNIX- and Windows-based servers. And though this is possible, and many vendors provide a mountain of literature on the theory and ability to support this configuration, it significantly raises the cost of the SAN, not necessarily in terms of added hardware or software, but in complexities encountered implementing and supporting these configurations. Consider the following, carefully.

UNIX- and Windows-based servers do not access or handle storage in similar fashions. Even though there are multiple solutions based on POSIX standards, the capability to share devices within the SAN is not yet a reality, which means strict segregations have to be enforced with system-level zoning and LUN masking strategies that are both time-consuming and complex.

Applications supported by UNIX- or Windows-based servers have drastically different service levels. Design and configuration of the SAN will either add resources to the Windows area, which don't need it, or compromise the UNIX environment by not providing sufficient SAN resources. Plus, recovery requirements are going to be different, which means they will either share the tape media, likely to result in problems, or they will have to have their own tape media for backup.

We should stop here and make sure we're not overlooking one of the big-time workhorses within the data center, the IBM and IBM-compatible mainframes. The need to interconnect a mainframe to open computing has been with us since the first UNIX server deployed its data throughout the enterprise, and the Windows PC began to develop its own legacy data, while needing to be integrated with the corporate record on the mainframe. Unfortunately, mainframe solutions continue to elude vendors, IT systems organizations, and research agendas—not that disparate and site-specific solutions don't exist, they do, if only in order to support specific business applications. Integration of IBM mainframes into server environments remains elusive, even counting all the money IBM has thrown at making the old, but reliant, MVS operating system both compliant with POSIX as well as available to networking infrastructures like Ethernet and TCP/IP.

To its benefit, and its everlasting detriment, IBM mainframe-processing models predate many of the innovations we are now working with, including storage networking, data sharing, device pooling, and scalable configurations—both internally at the high-end SMP level as well as in the multiprocessing, multitasking, transaction performance that no other processing platform can beat. Sadly, and perhaps tellingly, the IBM mainframe-processing model was a proprietary system that resisted evolving into the client/server architecture too long and was thus eclipsed by its own inability to deploy and support new and distributed applications in a cost-effective manner.

There is, however, hope on the horizon, in the form of a serious revolution in the IBM mainframe world. The traditional operating environment has given way to a new operating system: the zOS. This next step in the evolution of MVS provides a multipartitioned operating environment in which you can run an IBM Linux system on user-defined partitions that leverage the power of the mainframe while ensuring that it remains cost-effective.

So what does this have to do with storage and, specifically, integrating a Storage Area Network into the data center? Quite a bit, if you want the truth. Because here's the first question you're going to hear: "Great! When can we connect to the mainframe?"

The ability to share storage resources within the complete populations of servers, keeping in mind that zOS facilitates a logical set of servers, is a big-time perk for data center managers. Now, here's the flipside. IBM mainframes are moving toward their own orientation to storage area networking and are connected to their data paths by a fiber optic connection, which the IBM folks refer to as *channels*. This evolution from legacy bus, tag cables, and enterprise connectivity (or ESCON cabling: a parallel bus implementation), not to mention the low-level channel link protocols to Fibre Connectivity (or FICON), supplies the first real direct connect to the IBM mainframe usable by other open storage networks.

This level of service in SAN requires a FICON connection at the FC switch port level. IBM has been the pioneer in connecting storage through a switched environment, having integrated director-level switches for some time. At the end of the day, providing switch-to-switch communication with IBM storage switches may be an alternative to the evolving mainframe connectivity conundrum. Entry through an IP address will also provide connectivity, but the bandwidth restrictions make this alternative unlikely.

Figure 16-5 illustrates the many alternatives to supporting a heterogeneous OS data center through a SAN infrastructure.

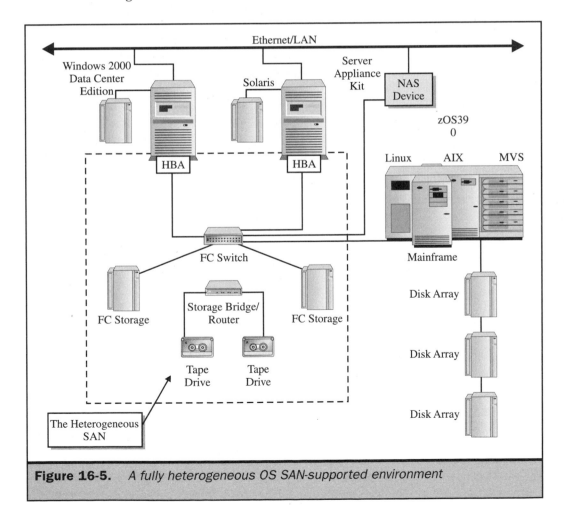

Figure 16-5. *A fully heterogeneous OS SAN-supported environment*

Supporting the External Networks

What if a SAN has to support an OLTP application for a highly available business process in three time zones? Not a problem. At least it's not *my* problem. I'm just a little ol' Storage Area Network.

Though maybe not.

The ability to access the SAN remotely, instead of going into the data center every time you need to access SAN operations and information, can be configured to meet administrators' needs through external network access. The SAN configuration discussed in Chapter 15 required that SAN operations be performed through a dedicated workstation that is directly attached to one of the SAN switches. Given this is where software configuration tools can be directly accessed for setup, maintenance, and initialization activities, most switch products are enabling users with IP access points that allow some of the SAN operational tools to be available remotely.

There are several innovations waiting in the wings that will drive advanced connectivity options for the SAN. Key among these is the need to further integrate IP-based storage solutions with FC networks. However this will require a more sophisticated usage of storage systems driven by user data that is increasingly distributed throughout a corporation. By analyzing current data usage scenarios, iterations of data must make several stops within an enterprise infrastructure in order to satisfy distributed application requirements.

The Evolving Network Connections

There are several innovations waiting in the wings that will drive connectivity options for the SAN. Among these is the need to further integrate IP-based storage solutions into FC networks, which will be largely driven by the integration of more sophisticated usage of storage as data is distributed throughout the enterprise. If we look at current data usage scenarios, data still has to make several stops within an enterprise infrastructure.

For example, many organizations still take it upon themselves to distribute data to remote locations, something largely accomplished by a series of data subset deployments that are both time- and location-dependent. Using a combination of data replication software services and remote storage devices, these configurations depend on general-purpose servers to communicate within the enterprise network so they can ship current data to remote locations. And though some of these can be cleaned up smartly with a NAS configuration, many remain datacentric and rely on sophisticated RDBMS functions at the corporate data center, as well as the distributed location. Figure 16-6 is a conceptual picture of how this works and how it lays the groundwork for future deployments and connectivity strategies for SANs.

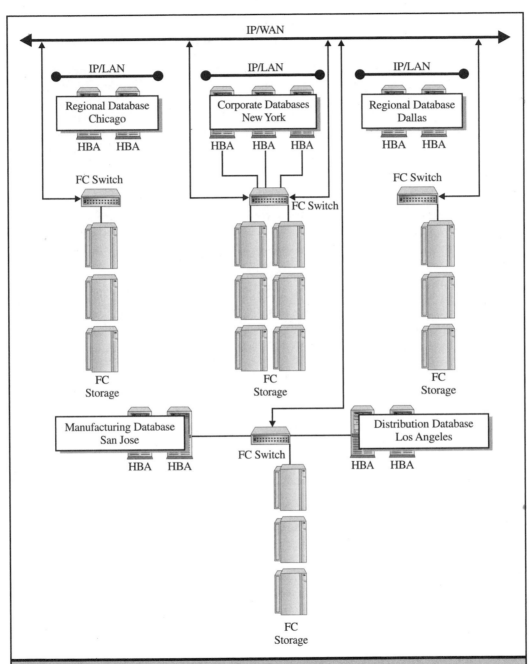

Figure 16-6.   *A data replication strategy and potential SAN solution*

There are two basic scenarios that will push these networks into integrated, global SAN infrastructures. First is the integration through IP storage devices, which offer the capability to store data without the latency and overhead general-purpose server deployments and direct-attached storage components required. This is handled in two ways, either through an enhanced NAS device that supports direct communication with the SAN infrastructure, or with an iSCSI device that supports direct I/O communications with the SAN infrastructure. Either way, the devices have to be linked through an existing IP connection and be viewed as a node device within the SAN, which means additional port functionality at the SAN switch to handle the IP file or block I/O over the IP network.

The second scenario involves the installation of SAN configurations that are both local and remote and can communicate and be controlled remotely. Figure 16-6 also shows a conceptual view of how this is accomplished, facilitating timely data replication throughout a typical corporation. Remote configurations need further extensions of fabric software to encompass remote fabrics as extensions or as recognized external fabrics.

This SAN-to-SAN scenario assumes that switch port evolution will continue to support the extended functions of an E_Port communicating with a remote switch. As noted earlier, vendors must further enhance the switch as users demand full IP connectivity and FC processing between the storage node devices. Users will also require a management scheme to operate these configurations in a physically distributed fashion.

However, once this is established, the capability to provide a vast infrastructure of storage will be in place, providing yet another step in the ubiquity of data for applications. This will further enhance effective web services, thus allowing applications to be synchronized with data.

The feasibility and availability of these solutions is now becoming based on enhancements to existing network standards, including the addition of Fibre Channel throughout the enterprise, IP standards, and SCSI integration into IP specifications. All of which have added up to an initial wave of solutions that lead to the extension of SAN technology. Figure 16-7 shows the potential future IP storage integration and SAN-to-SAN communications supporting advanced data management strategies.

The Evolving Device Connections

Along with network connections, SAN connectivity options continue to evolve, encompassing more storage devices. In fact, integrating FC communications with the myriad tape solutions available has been underway for some time. Further enhancements to tape media will likely come in the form of optical and solid state disks, as well as advanced forms of caching mechanisms.

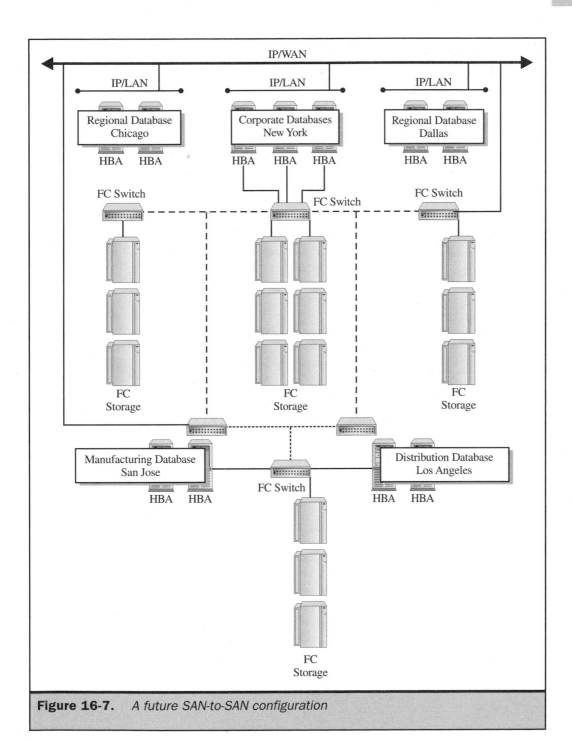

Figure 16-7.   *A future SAN-to-SAN configuration*

Integrating Tape Solutions

Tape media is currently integrated using an external bridge/router solution (see Chapter 14). Bridge/router connections are increasingly integrating solutions whereby FC connectivity is built into the tape controller devices, allowing for a cleaner installation, not to mention a closer integration into the controller mechanism that takes advantage of individual tape manufacturer's differentiators and functions. This level of integration comes closer to allowing tape to function more efficiently by talking directly to the switch port. Developing tape media is an ongoing effort of the FC standards groups.

Tape media remains a particularly sensitive area within data centers, given the large investments that must be made in these realms. The capability to change and start additional library areas that support additional media is no small undertaking. One of the largest bottlenecks in support processing within data centers is backup, which gets performed on a daily, weekly, and monthly basis. This takes up an inordinate amount of time compared to the production processing that takes place in direct support of the company's business. (Additional details on backup/recovery processes are covered in Chapter 22.) Integrating tape library functions into the SAN is a significant task. Even though it may seem trivial at the beginning, the importance of the complete analysis of this integration greatly impacts the backup cycle—both positively and negatively.

The positive aspect is enhanced performance when moving backups to FC speeds. Even though you're throttled by the limitations of the tape device, it remains significantly faster than a slower and copy-redundant direct-attached model that can quickly congest an IP-based network infrastructure. There is also the potential value that a "server-less" backup scenario can be supported within your SAN configurations. Here, the elapsed time savings in running backup jobs can be as great as 50–75 percent, meaning that a typical backup cycle which runs seven hours would now take only three and a half. Because of this, significant overhead savings can be obtained over and above the amount of production processing time placed into the cycle.

The negative aspect is the increased cost to the facilities and recovery operations that result from integrated SAN tape configurations. The additional costs are needed to allocate tape drives for the FC SAN switch. More than likely, these will be dedicated given the non-sharing that FC SANs are currently encumbered with. In addition to this are the extra facilities necessary for extending the tape library functions—even though it may integrate into the current library system.

Another negative aspect is the consideration of the recovery operation that will ultimately have to take place. This requires the ability to locate proper backup tapes, log tapes, and control tapes. The tapes have to be dumped to the appropriate volume within the devices from the attached server, and then applied in the event of database recovery (which most may be). This isn't necessarily any different than normal recovery, other than that all of this has to be performed within the SAN environment, which, unless it's taken into consideration beforehand, can very quickly get out of hand.

Looking for an Optical Connection

Another popular media that will potentially integrate into the SAN is optical, or CD and DVD drives and libraries. Historically, these devices have seen limited usage as removable media libraries within enterprise network environments because of their performance as a write-once disposable media and physical read/write performance at the optical device level. Both of these conditions have improved to the degree that optical media and drives can be used for special applications of information distribution, reference, and, in some cases, effective backup media.

Optical devices can be integrated into a SAN using a bridge/router device to perform the same interconnection as Tape media. The use of SCSI optical drives with a SAN router can integrate the CD and DVD media sufficiently for production processing. The production of CD or DVD for distribution from digital sources, such as post processing of entertainment and educational packages, can benefit from the increased speed of SANs and allow it to process in a connection-oriented environment to facilitate the total bandwidth of the SAN.

Front-end processes of these applications, the preprocess production, where digital entertainment and educational products are edited and produced, have been an early adopter of SAN technology. This is largely due to bandwidth and storage capacities, as well as the ability to provide a Class 1 connection, which facilitates the streaming media production requirements for digital video files. These configurations can form either the production system for manipulating and creating digital video/audio effects, or the distribution system to move entertainment or educational files out to a network.

Actually, optical drives and autoloader packages have recently become available in NAS configurations. The NAS device is bundled with optical media drives and an autoloader system while maintaining the NAS file access front end and Plug and Play connection to an IP network. Given the future integration of NAS and SAN, the integration of NAS optical systems into SAN will become another alternative to SAN/ NAS integration and optical media usage with the SAN environment.

Connecting to the Future

Over and above the connectivity of SAN into existing data center infrastructures, SAN will soon need to integrate into the continuing evolution of external processing technologies, such as advanced clustering, InfiniBand, and blade-level computing. Each of these will require the SAN to address the compatibility issues of how the FC network interfaces with these evolving technologies.

Clustering has been an emerging solution for highly available configurations and is now employed to address availability levels for real-time transactional workloads. Although clustering solutions utilize the SAN in an effective manner, the ability to support both sides of a cluster is problematic, causing most configurations to support two distinct SAN configurations, which provides two distinct system images, with a SAN fabric supporting each.

The consideration regarding these configurations is the expense in doubling the processing environment to ensure that upon failover the supporting system can take over the workload and synchronize the data and continue processing. Secondly, the protocol used to communicate between the two systems, TCP/IP, adds quite a large overhead for the short communication paths between servers. Finally, the complexities of synchronizing the databases and data for continued processing upon recovery makes these solutions expensive and difficult to configure and maintain.

Look for clustering to take advantage of two systems sharing the same fabric, reducing the complexity of totally discrete systems to failover at the processing level with shared SAN access. This allows the data to be protected through a RAID-level mirror within the SAN, should it be needed at the storage level. Additional protection for hardware and data redundancy within the SAN configuration provides for failure recovery within the storage infrastructure, as shown in Figure 16-8.

If we take our clustering discussion and replace the system-to-system communications (now using TCP/IP) with a switched fabric network implementation using the InfiniBand protocol, we begin to see the benefits of InfiniBand. Let's take that one step further and implement a fabric-to-fabric interconnection, tying our SAN configurations together. Now we're really seeing the benefits of InfiniBand.

An InfiniBand configuration allows system-to-system communications to scale beyond the current 2-, 4-, or 8-way clusters that are expensive and unwieldy, but nonetheless available, and replace this with low-cost process node servers communicating through a switch fabric. This allows an infinitely larger number of servers to effectively communicate. In addition, the ability to tie in storage devices, such as the SAN, through an InfiniBand fabric to FC fabric interconnection allows some or all the servers to share the storage resources being managed by the SAN fabric.

InfiniBand technology allows for the creation of both a process infrastructure and a storage infrastructure, each with the capability to communicate though a common scalable interconnect in order to develop a dense computing and storage fabric.

If we take our Infiniband and FC SAN fabrics and key in on the process nodes, the application of a switched fabric internal to the process node provides yet another scalable resource within the process fabric. The use of internal switched fabrics, such as Rapid I/O and HyperTransport, form a foundation that allows internal components of the process node to scale new heights, bumping up the number of CPUs and addressable storage levels.

Given this configuration, we can begin to visualize the requirements for an internal storage function within the process fabric to support the internal functions of the process node. The communications between storage and process fabrics are enabled by the InfiniBand protocol.

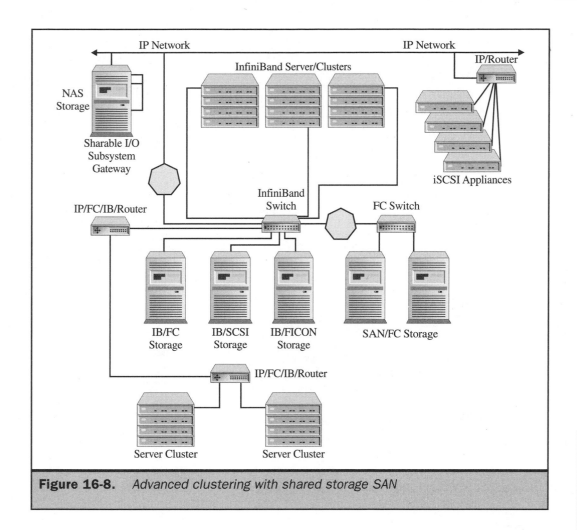

Figure 16-8. *Advanced clustering with shared storage SAN*

In conclusion, network technologies will continue to decouple the traditional computing configurations into process and storage networks. The data center is headed toward the next level of computing, driven by storage area network technologies that support all aspects of application sets and process environments: business, academic, scientific, and personal. The future data center is likely to become a logical set of storage and process fabrics, as illustrated in Figure 16-9, communicating through a public and private network infrastructure.

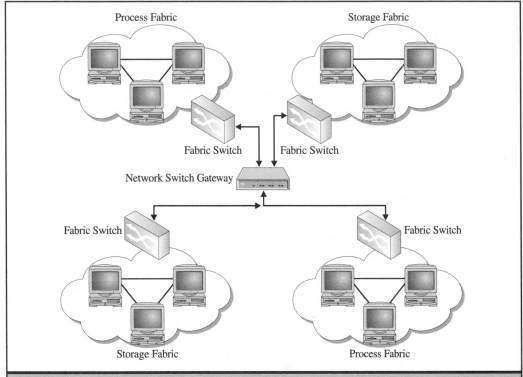

Figure 16-9. *The future: process and storage fabrics with a common interconnect*

SAN Configuration Guidelines

The capability of Storage Area Networks to integrate into the data center can become more complex than expected. However, given the right orientation, and a realistic view of current solutions, SAN offers a compatible solution to both UNIX and Windows environments. Not without its challenges, the ability to move beyond the homogeneous implementation can be successful, though more expensive and encumbering than the original SAN justification may have entailed. With the current set of products and solutions available, the data center can expect the following when connecting the SAN into the data center:

■ *Multiswitch configurations will be a way of life.* Be prepared to work with multiple switch configurations. Again, there's just no way around this. Even if the simplicity of a single switch configuration may suit your requirements, the minimum attention to recovery and availability requirements will force a move to at least two switches for some level of continuous operations.

■ *Matching I/O workloads to compatible configurations will require additional planning.* Part of the justification for the SAN will likely be server and storage consolidation. As you consider the combined workloads and their relative I/O, you will begin to see port count requirements, HBA data paths, and storage sizes themselves moving beyond a simple solution. However, for performance and availability, it is best to implement a SAN configuration that facilitates your workloads. Given the flexibility and numerous variables to work with, be prepared to spend considerable time upfront considering these design activities carefully.

■ *SAN configurations will be subject to rapid change and enhancement.* One of the most important practices to consider is staying flexible, especially considering the evolutionary tracks SANs are on. Major enhancements will continue to be announced on a constant basis, so a reliable and consistent view and monitoring of the SAN industry will be an effective tool to understanding the evolution of SAN connectivity.

As Storage Area Network technologies and solutions continue to evolve, connectivity of components to key elements within the data center infrastructure can be terribly disruptive to existing operations. However, this same connectivity can also be the most productive in facilitating the scalability of a storage infrastructure as well as establishing a foundation for the evolving enterprise storage fabric.

STORAGE AREA
NETWORKS

The Complete Reference

Storage Networks

Part V

Application—Putting It Together

The Complete Reference

Storage Networks

Chapter 17

Defining the I/O Workload

Capacity planning has always been something of a black art. Commodity-level distributed computing has driven IT to conduct a simplistic set of activities meant to plan and implement computing resources. Any discussion on applying the concepts of storage networking must touch on key workload definition concepts that are part and parcel to an effective capacity plan and to the possible rejuvenation of a more effective capacity planning model. Part V orients the reader towards applying storage networking concepts by way of an initial discussion and overview of workload definition and planning. The following chapters contained herein focus on identifying existing and anticipated workloads where storage networking solutions can be implemented for maximum value and productivity to the data center. SAN and NAS configurations will be addressed in analyzing the particular workloads of each.

We have explored and used the term workload many times already, and in Part V, it remains important to our discussion. Chapter 17 provides a detailed examination of workload definitions, identifications, and planning. Workload guidelines will be placed into a real-life context that characterizes both business applications and support activities, as well as the maintenance of capacity strategies as they relate to storage networking. Many of the activities that you manage on a daily basis may be enhanced or hurt by the new technologies involved in SAN and NAS solutions. In an effort to provide as much relative information as possible, generic descriptions and examples are used in Chapters 18 and 19 to cover several specific workload characterizations.

Part V addresses the usage of SAN and NAS as an integrated solution. Chapter 20, for instance, explores situations based on current IT experiences and also looks at future uses of integrated SAN and NAS solutions. This becomes a complex exercise when multiple workload scenarios are cast within the same environment. The ability of microkernels to communicate effectively and for storage caching mechanisms to operate in tandem becomes a challenge when considering the future of heterogeneous storage operation. This is compounded by the ability to maneuver within a distributed file system that incorporates optimum support for both traditional workloads yet sustains the proprietary nature and operation of database technologies. The current evolution of common application services through enhancement of web-enabled solutions will incorporate all the attributes of OLTP, batch, and data-intensive I/O, and will play a key role in these discussions.

Moving storage networking into the future requires an analysis of integrated storage networking solutions, using both FC- and IP-based connectivity schemes. Because of this, Chapter 20 addresses key future technologies, showing how they may affect IT storage networking solutions. Such technologies and standards include iSCSI, the Internet SCSI standard that allows SCSI commands to be encapsulated and transmitted through an IP network. In addition, we address the slowly evolving InfiniBand standard and infrastructure advancements that will result. Finally, we'll look at some of the internal bus connectivity standards and strategies that could have a dramatic effect on the data storage hierarchy as we know it today (see Chapter 5) exploring products such as AMD's Hyper-Transport, the industry standard VI transport mechanisms, and Intel's next bus technology, Rapid-IO.

Storage Planning and Capacity Planning

Planning and installing applications continues to require a big effort within IT, especially when it comes to applications that are considered *enterprise-level* (a term which has never seemed appropriate, by the way). Nevertheless, the term was employed by large system players (read mainframes) to differentiate their solutions from those of the small system players (read PCs) in the early days of the user revolution. Commonly known as the PC "wars," it was a time in which many business users made attempts to buy their own IT infrastructures for pennies on the mainframe.

It was about this time that sophisticated capacity planning and workload management started to go out the door—out the door, out the window, and out of IT standards and practices. All in all though, those tools and activities provided a certain amount of pride and gratification when the systems (read mainframes—again) were upgraded and everything not only worked, but worked the same as it had before, and had improved user response time, balanced utilization, and a batch window that was completed two hours earlier.

Well, we traded those simple days for ubiquitous and prolific computing resources based on everyone's desktop, job, travel agenda, and meeting rooms. We traded the security of centralization that made the capacity planning a manageable and gratifying entity for a Wild West distributed environment that reflected the scalability of the *box* we were operating on, be it UNIX or Windows. The mantra was: If the ones we're running don't work, are too slow, or can't support the network, we can always get new ones. What could be simpler? A capacity plan based at the *box* level. If it doesn't work, just get another one. They don't cost much. We don't need to consider no stinking workloads, we can process anything, and if it grows, we'll just add more *boxes*. The same goes for the network.

A wonderful idea, and to some degree it worked—until the applications started to take advantage of the distributed network features of the boxes, as well as the increasing sophistication and power of the boxes. Yes, the little *boxes* grew up to be big boxes. Others grew to be giants, the size of mainframes. It should be pointed out, however, that many boxes had genes that stunted their growth, keeping them from becoming *enormous* mainframe-like boxes. Even then the *box* applications grew in sophistication, resource utilization, and environmental requirements.

Note *The "gene" mentioned here was referred to as the Gatesonian gene, whose scalability would not grow beyond the confines of a desktop.*

Interestingly enough, we seem to have come full circle. Although nothing essentially duplicates itself, our circle of activities has landed us back near the realm of the—gasp!—workload. It's not like workloads ever really went away, we just haven't had to recognize them for a while, given we all got caught up in the *box level capacity planning* activities, known as the BLCP practice.

BLCP is not unlike the IT practice of going into installation frenzy during certain popular trends—for example, ERP, relational databases, e-mail, office automation, web site, intranet, and now the dreaded CRM. Such things cause us to be driven by current application trends, leaving us to distinguish between CRM performance, ERP utilization, and e-mail service levels. To a great degree, we handled these installation frenzies with the BLCP (box-level capacity plan); we can implement anything by using the right box, as well as the right *number* of boxes.

Several things within the applications industry have rendered the BLCP practice obsolete. First and foremost is the sophistication of the application. Today, applications are distributed, datacentric, hetero-data enabled, and, the up-and-coming process, de-coupled. Second, the infrastructure has become specialized—for example, there is the network, the server, the desktop (for instance, the client), and the storage. Third, the infrastructure itself is becoming further de-coupled. More specifically, storage is taking on its own infrastructure, with storage network freeing its processing bounds and restrictions from the logic of the application, as well as the network overhead of the client/server model, becoming itself immunized against the Gatesonian gene.

Note	*Hetero-data is the characteristic of an application that requires multiple data types to perform its services.*

Finally, the common services that support the application logic infrastructure are quickly becoming both commodity oriented and public in nature. We are moving into a future where applications are programmed by end users to employ web services. These services access lower level infrastructures and subsequently complex and proprietary support products operating within a particular information technology structure. Users will likely take it for granted that adequate resources exist.

These conditions will further render the storage entity with its own operating infrastructure. However, this will require that it evolve as a more complex structure, supporting an even more complicated set of common services that includes application logic, network processing, and common I/O facilities. Each of these entities will have to understand and configure themselves to effectively operate with existing and future workloads that will dictate the processing and physical requirements necessary for just minimal performance.

That's why workloads are important.

The Definition and Characterization of Workloads

Workloads are traditionally defined as application processing modules that exhibit similar resource requirements, processing characteristics, and user expectations. Figure 17-1 further depicts this definition with its characterization of banking transactions. For example, at one time or other, we've found ourselves in a bank line with someone who's balancing their bank statement, applying for a car loan, and/or trying to find a missing check from, say, 1982, all at the same time. Their transaction, obviously, is much more resource-intensive than the deposit of your Grandma's birthday check.

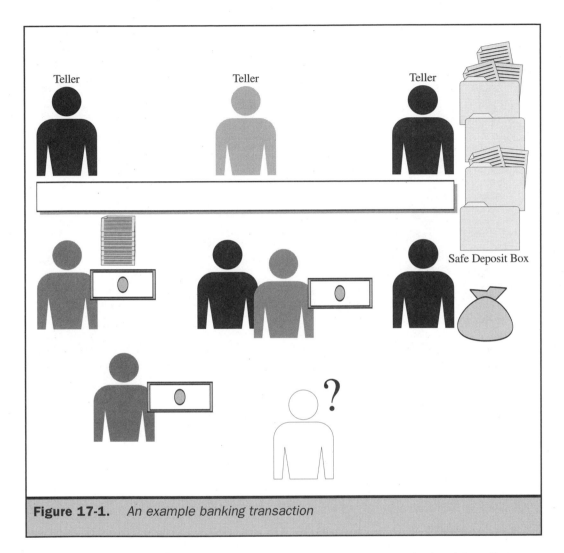

Figure 17-1. *An example banking transaction*

So, if there were a categorization for the types of transactions the bank handles, everyone would get serviced more efficiently within a prescribed set of expectations. However, this would require the tellers to be categorized by the type of transaction they perform. Tellers would have appropriate resources at their disposal to deal with the transactions they service. There you have it, a simple workload categorization for the tellers, who, in this example, can also be characterized as servers (depicted in Figure 17-2).

The tellers have a set of resources and types of transactions they work on, giving certain kinds first priority. However, since these are all general-purpose tellers, they can work on any transaction should they run out of the particular type of work they are optimized for. Keep in mind that they are optimized for a particular type of workload and prioritize their work on that basis. Because of this, they may not handle a different workload as effectively as a peer teller that is optimized for a different type of transactional processing.

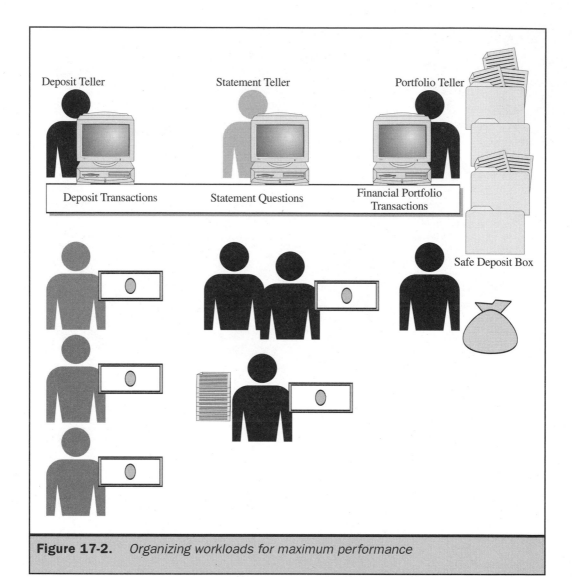

Figure 17-2. *Organizing workloads for maximum performance*

In this example, a simple transaction like depositing your Grandma's check can be taken care of by a teller, who functions similar to a computer transaction server that specializes in, and is optimized for, checking deposit transactions. The teller has the appropriate resources to process your deposit within a service time you are expecting. Other tellers process different transactions, such as safe deposit transactions (very physical, employing various resources), bank statement questions (very process-intensive, requiring much data), and financial portfolio transactions (multiple processes, compute-intensive with high priority).

The Business Application

By using the banking example, we can determine all the necessary considerations for identifying, describing, and characterizing the workloads. We first define the banking activities as the business application. Within the application are several subsets of activities, which can be directly related to application programs that support the banking business application. We will now convert our abstract teller infrastructure, supporting the banking application to a computer infrastructure with servers and related components that allow users to perform transactions. This is illustrated in Figure 17-3 and will serve as our basis for workload considerations for this chapter.

Using Figure 17-3, we see that identifying parts of the application becomes fairly straightforward, as an application development group defines the functions performed by the business application. This provides an inventory of application programs that have been developed and need to be available for meeting the users' needs through their transactions. We evaluate each function, or program, to our computer configuration, as indicated in Figure 17-3.

We do this by understanding the data organizational structures required for each application program, the data paths it uses, and the user access requirements for each. For example, our checking deposit program uses a database and related log files to handle its processes. The user access demands that the deposits be reflected in the daily database but also in the statement of record for the customer, which is in another database. Further subsets of this information go toward an activity log used for updating other applications within the banking business application.

Deposit Application—Workload Attributes

The previous information describing the banking transaction pretty much defines the data paths required for the deposit program. We then coalesce this information into a set of workload definitions for the deposit application. Based upon the organizational

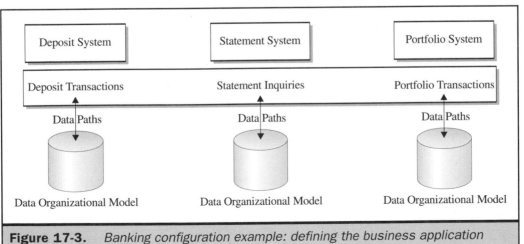

Figure 17-3.   *Banking configuration example: defining the business application*

and user access information, we can define additional attributes of the data path. This allows us to describe the deposit application with the following attributes and begin identifying it as a workload.

- **Data Organizational Method (DOM)**   Relational database, flat files, and temporary suspense files.
- **User Access (UA)**   Online transactions that require immediate update to daily customer tables, with conditional processing based on secondary transactions to customer system record tables and log suspense files.
- **Data Paths (DP)**   Macro data paths require update access to daily customer tables, read access to daily suspense tables, and a system of record tables. In addition, there are multiple paths required to facilitate the reliability, availability, and serviceability of the application.

By further defining the technical attributes of the workload, we begin to make decisions on where this particular program will be placed within our infrastructure. These are illustrated in Figure 17-4, which are depicted as updates to our initial Figure 17-3. We can now overlay workloads within this configuration. What we have in our sample banking application is a classic OLTP workload that supports the deposit subset of functions. The OLTP workload dictates several configuration characteristics at a minimum, with additional considerations based upon estimated traffic and growth.

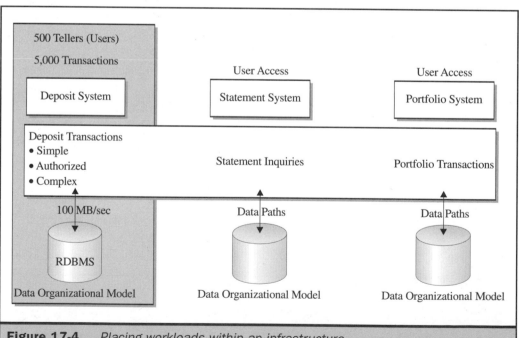

Figure 17-4.   *Placing workloads within an infrastructure*

This defines a simple model for identifying and describing a macro set of attributes for the workload. Having done this, there are additional details that become necessary as we move to place the application into our sample configuration. Now it becomes necessary to further understand the resource utilization, traffic arrival rates, and environmental conditions surrounding the support of this workload. However, before we proceed with deriving additional details from the deposit application, we must address in summary fashion the analysis of the complete inventory of the Banking Application. This requires using the same process that created our initial workload definitions for the deposit application.

Given this iterative process, the importance of analyzing the entire Banking Application in context cannot be overemphasized. During this process, we find that many of the applications within the Banking Application have similar workload characteristics, such as same database, similar user access demands, and process requirements. On the other hand, we also recognize that many applications have completely diverse sets of attributes. Our example shows two other distinct workloads for placement within our configuration— a batch workload and an archival workload—each of which has a unique set of user transactional requirements.

 It should be noted that such "distinct" workloads were chosen to reflect the ubiquitous nature of each configuration. These can be found in almost all IT data centers and remain applicable across business and scientific applications.

This requires an accumulation of resource, access, and environmental elements to derive a total picture of the workload. As such, our original example of the banking deposit becomes only a part of the Banking Online System, which we have concluded from its accumulated characteristics to be an OLTP workload, with a set of requirements designed to meet user expectations. Figure 17-5 offers guidelines for identifying workloads and defining their characteristics.

Another interesting aspect to this exercise is something you may have already concluded as we moved through our workload identification and definition stage. That is, with few exceptions, the majority of resource requirements and characteristics center around the I/O of the workload. Certainly I/O plays a pivotal role in processing transactions, given the necessity of timely execution of data acquisition and transfers in relation to response time. Within this simple concept lies an interesting conclusion: over 90 percent of the workloads that IT professionals deal with are I/O-intensive transactions. In other words, the majority of activities encapsulated within commercial processing consist of I/O-related activities.

The corollary to this observation is that the majority of workload planning and implementation centers on the I/O system that supports the processing infrastructure. A further realization is the importance storage architecture plays within the infrastructure and the tremendous impact putting storage on a network will have. Why? Because it changes the implementation strategy of the workload so dynamically that workload identification and definition becomes paramount. Otherwise, just throwing disparate workloads within a storage networking infrastructure can be a hit or miss affair—one with a low probability of success. However, making it too simple and only implementing homogeneous workloads may not leverage the real value of storage network technology in how it supports disparate workloads.

The conclusion is that workload identification, definition, and planning are critical activities to the effective application of storage networks.

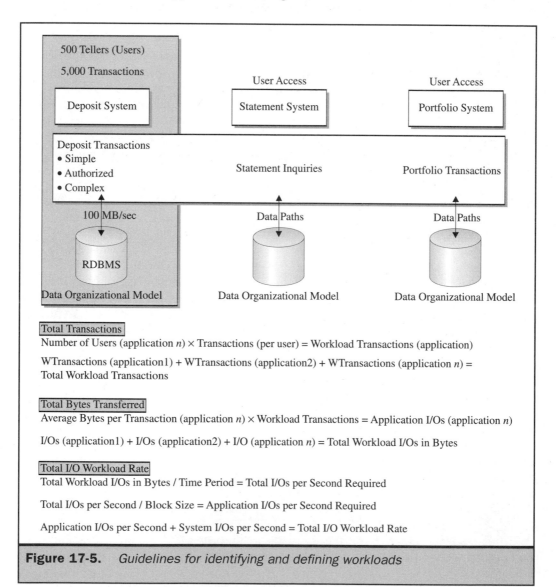

Figure 17-5. *Guidelines for identifying and defining workloads*

I/O Content and Workloads

Potential resource utilization and traffic arrival rates play a very important role in integrating the workload into an existing infrastructure, or in building a new infrastructure, for that matter. As discussed previously, the categorization and accumulation of workload attributes provided the definition and requirements for the workload. Continuing with our banking application example, Figure 17-6 illustrates the final inventory, categorization, and definition of the workloads. This allows us to accumulate a set of estimates of resource requirements for each workload and provide an estimated sum of the entire set of workloads. In order to accomplish this, we must look closely at each category of workload.

The resource requirement details are contained in the major areas of I/O activities, data organization, data paths, and user access. Putting these areas together forms a picture of the required infrastructure for the workload and, as we will see, a picture of the total infrastructure.

The Data Organizational Model

The most important aspect of the workload is the data organizational model it uses. In today's inventory of applications, both internally developed by IT application groups or IT implemented through application packages, the majority are based upon a relational model. The use of relational database technology (RDBMSs) defines the major I/O

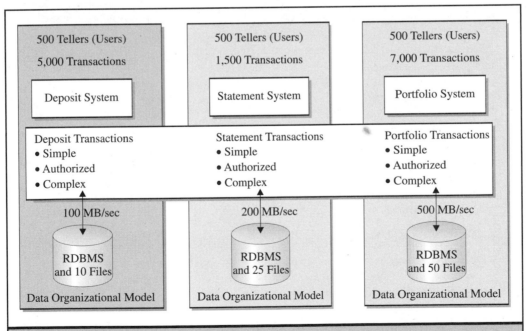

Figure 17-6.   *The workload inventory, categorization, and definition of the Banking Application System*

attributes for commercial applications. This is a good thing because it provides those workloads that use RDBMSs a set of processing metrics for estimating I/O behavior and utilization. The use of the relational database has become so accepted and widespread its macro behavior is very predictable. Additional resource utilization is provided by the workload characteristics that define internal processing requirements such as caching, temporary workspace, and partitioning.

Don't make the mistake of overlaying the storage infrastructure too quickly—the consideration of recovery scenarios and requirements needs to be considered at the macro level first and then decisions made to handle specifics of the workload or particular subset of workload (for example, the specific application program). Therefore, we will have all our workload consideration taken into context before we make any conclusions about storage system features such as RAID, cache sizes, and recovery strategies.

The data organizational model provides the following sets of information to the workload behavior:

- **Block Size**   The size of the block of data moving from the application transaction is dictated by the setup of the database. This can be either file or database attributes.

- **Partitioning**   This attribute defines behavior regarding user access patterns in relation to the data itself. It influences decisions regarding the type of fault resiliency strategy for the workload (for example, RAID levels) and software recovery mechanisms.

- **Physical Design**   The physical design of the database drives how a supporting file system is used. This is perhaps one of the most important attributes to consider given the type of database and its performance when using a file system.

> **Note**   *Relational databases continue to prefer the use of raw disk partitions. This is important given the performance penalties one may encounter when performing I/O operations that are duplicated through the file system and passed off to the RDBMS system for further read/write operations. Referred to as the "double-write" penalty, this will be covered in more detail in Part VI.*

- **Maintenance**   Probably the most overlooked attribute in today's implementation-crazy environments, this defines workload behavior itself and includes requirements for backup/recovery, archival, and disaster recovery.

> **Note**   *Regarding the use of RDBMS technology, the backup/recovery group not only includes basic backup operations but more important recovery operations that have to occur within a transactional basis. They must therefore include the necessary log files and synchronize the database to a predefined state.*

This articulates a macro view of workload considerations and attributes supported by the analysis of the data organizational model.

User Access

User traffic defines the data hi-way attributes for the workload. Notice that we address this set of information prior to our topic on data paths. Obviously, we need to know the estimated traffic to understand the type, number, and behavior of the data hi-ways prior to associating that with the workload expectations. We basically need three types of information from the end users or their representatives, the application systems analysts. This information is shown in Figure 17-7 and consists of a number of transactions, the time-period transactions needed to execute, and the expected service level.

This activity is the most challenging. Trying to get either end users or their application representatives (for example, application system analysts) to estimate the number and type of transactions they will execute is difficult and, although important, can and should be balanced with a set of empirical information. Let's look at our banking application example and the deposit transactions. If we query the user community, we find that each teller handles approximately 100 deposit transactions per day. There are ten branch locations and, on average, five tellers per branch working an eight-hour shift. This results in an estimated 5,000 deposit transaction per day that need processing between the hours of 9 A.M. to 5 P.M.. Tellers expect their deposit transactions to be available during the entire eight-hour shift and have transactional response times ranging from subsecond processes to those lasting no more than five seconds.

However, the deposit transaction comes in three forms: simple, authorized, and complex. Simple requires an update to a customer table, authorized needs an authorized write to the permanent system of record for the account, which requires a double-write to access more than one database table. The complex, meanwhile, requires the authorized transactions but adds an additional calculation on the fly to deposit a portion into an equity account. Each of these has a different set of data access characteristics yet they belong to the same OLTP workload.

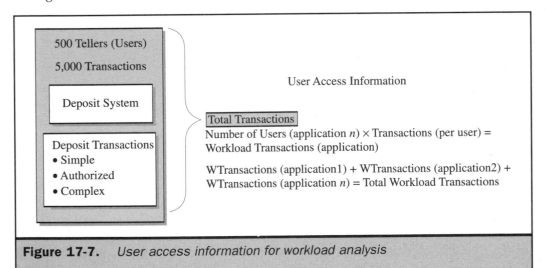

Figure 17-7. *User access information for workload analysis*

This is important given the potential for performance degradation if the appropriate data access points are not taken into consideration. Not all of this information can be expected to come from the end users, although we can estimate by analyzing the transaction history to determine the mix of subtransactions and thus plan accordingly. Consequently, the importance of fully understanding the transactional estimates generally goes beyond the end user or even the application developer's estimates, providing critical information regarding decisions in I/O configuration.

However, it's also important because it defines the I/O content of the transactions. I/O content is defined as the amount of user data transferred during an I/O operation. We have discussed previously that both bus and network transfer rates differ in the amount of bytes transferred. However, this is dependent on several variables including operating system, file system, and data partitioning in RDBMSs. Consequently, it is not always the case that the bus is full when executing an I/O transaction. Therefore, the more intensive the I/O content, the more throughput occurs, and the less time it takes to complete a transaction based on obtaining the amount of data needed.

An example is the deposit transaction set where the simple transaction only requires access to a database record within the database table. Even though this customer record only consists of a small amount of data, it still requires the server OS to execute an I/O operation. This design hardly makes the trip productive given the system overhead of the I/O operation using SCSI/PCI configurations or the larger amount of system process overhead necessary to leverage the tremendous payload of Fibre Channel. However, if the application design requires that each separate transaction is provided a single transfer packet or frame facilitated by the I/O operation, then the efficiency of the I/O must be considered to understand the necessary system requirements to support the I/O workload. Although this may provide an extremely fast I/O operation and subsequent response time, the amount of system resources dedicated to accomplishing this limits the number of transactions supported.

Using this example analysis of a single I/O per transaction, the number of transactions processed within the stated time period becomes very important. In the case of the example deposit application, the simple transactions make up the bulk of the workload. This leads to the conclusion that the capacity of the system is simply based upon the number of I/Os required for processing. Nevertheless, we know that the efficiency of the I/O system is highly inefficient and subject to non-linear response time service should any anomaly in increased transactions occur. Consequently, basing a capacity estimate simply on the number of I/Os a system is capable of is not necessarily the only metric required for balancing or building an effective and scalable I/O infrastructure.

The final piece of critical information regarding user access is the expected service level. This places our eventual, albeit simple, calculations into a framework that defines the resources needed to sustain the amount of operations for the OLTP workload. From our initial information, we find that there are two goals for the I/O system. First, the banking application's data needs to be available from 9 A.M. to 5 P.M. each workday. Second, the transactions should complete within a time frame ranging from subsecond response times to those lasting no more than five seconds. For the sake of our example, we will not address the networking issues until later in Part VI. However, it is important to note that although the I/O can, and will, take up a great deal of response time factors, network latency issues do need to be considered.

By adding our service-level expectations to the mix, comparing these to user transactional traffic estimates, and considering the detail of the subset of deposit transactions, we find that the deposit transactions require a system that enables a transaction rate of 5,000 transactions/8 hours, or approximately 10 transactions per minute. That adds to our cumulative amount, which provides the capacity for the entire banking application. The cumulative analysis further concludes that a 500-MBps transfer rate is needed to successfully meet user expectations.

In addition, the infrastructure must support the 100 percent uptime that users expect in terms of data availability. This is a foundational requirement for meeting response time (for example, the data must be available to process the transactions). However, this begins to define the type of storage partitioning and structure necessary to provide this. Consider also that in meeting these goals the system must continue to process in the event of error—an area handled by RAID. In particular is the decision to provide level-1 or level-5 solutions necessary for efficient response time even during recovery processing.

Data Paths

Now, let's look at the data hi-way required for this workload. From an analysis of our first two categories we create a picture of the logical infrastructure necessary for the workload. By comparing the data organizational model (for example, the type of database and characteristics) and byte transfer requirements with something called the concurrent factor, we can begin to formulate the number of data paths needed to meet workload service levels. The concurrent factor, as mentioned previously during the user access discussion, determines the minimum, logical set of paths required to sustain our service level given the probability that all tellers at some point may execute deposit transactions simultaneously.

This calculation provides a more accurate picture of the resources needed to sustain the service level in real time. In reality, the probability that all the tellers will execute a deposit simultaneously is actually quite high and is calculated at 90 percent. Therefore, for each time period, 90 percent of the total tellers would be executing a deposit transaction. From our previous calculation, we estimate a mix of simple, authorized, and complex deposit transactions, which would be something like 80, 15, and 5 percent, respectively. This calculation provides for the average number of bytes transferred while taking into account the different I/O content of each transaction.

Figure 17-8 illustrates the accurate requirement for our workload. With this I/O workload analysis information, we can evaluate existing configurations to see if any of them will sustain the load, or develop a new model to configure a system that *will* sustain the load. Most likely you will want to do both. As in our sample case, we can see that we need a large amount of sustained workload I/Os for the entire business application. If we overlay this existing solution of direct-attached SCSI storage systems with capacities of no more than 50 MBps and arbitrarily-based device execution, it is likely this will be completely deficient in meeting workload service goals.

However, if we develop our own model, we find that a simple FC SAN solution with a 100-MBps rate through a frame-based transport will likely sustain the workload and support the concurrent transactional workload I/Os. If you add storage controller

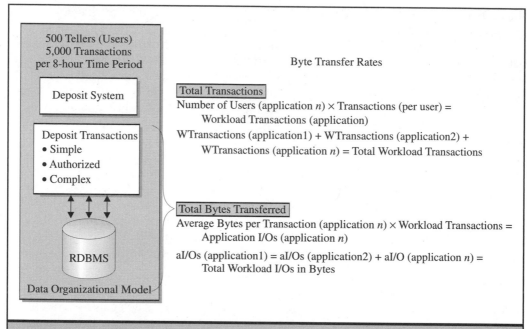

Figure 17-8. *Calculating workload requirements for byte transfer rates*

requirements of RAID, data maintenance, and recovery applications, we can estimate three data paths totaling 300MB burst rates. An estimated 240MB sustained rate thus will not only provide sufficient transfer rates but also a safe zone to compensate for peak utilization and growth factors before additional paths are required. Figure 17-9 illustrates a logical model built from our calculations.

Note *The 240MB transfer rate referred to previouly is calculated at 80 percent of total capacity (2,000 bytes × 80% = 1,600 bytes), which provides for switch and device latency.*

From this model, we can begin to assign specific technologies to find the most appropriate fit. Cost will certainly be a factor in determining the best solution for the workload. However, cost notwithstanding, the value of workload identification, definition, and characterization starts to become evident when moving the workload analysis into real implementations.

Considerations for I/O Workloads in Storage Networking

Implementing a solution that meets a set of business applications requires a workload analysis, as we have demonstrated. It then becomes necessary to analyze an existing configuration or develop a new configuration that can sustain the workload and meet user service levels. However, in the world of storage networking, IT faces additional challenges.

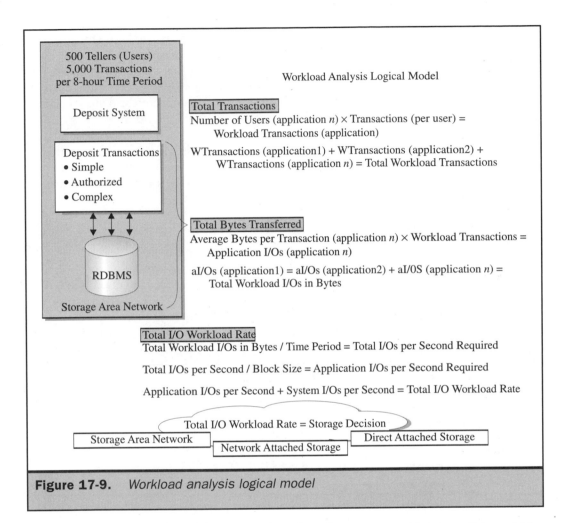

Figure 17-9. *Workload analysis logical model*

These issues focus on the increasing separation from the server complex, something which becomes an infrastructure in and of itself (such as a storage network infrastructure).

The most visible issue will be the discrete activities necessary to analyze the I/O infrastructure. Even though it must be taken in context with the business application and subsequent workload analysis, I/O becomes its own entity when moved into a storage networking model. Therefore, it is imperative to plan, model, and configure storage networking solutions with sufficient detail and I/O specifics that are consistent with the workloads you are supporting.

In some cases, the I/O workload is only part of a larger capacity planning exercise. Consequently, I/O workload planning needs to become integrated into existing planning activities and be driven from workload estimates that have been previously discovered. If that is the case, the minimum elements of I/O workload planning, as indicated in the earlier section "Deposit Application—Workload Attributes," are still required and should be discovered even though they may come from an existing capacity planning exercise.

The ability to support multiple workload types cannot be overlooked. This will probably be the most challenging activity required. Certainly SANs and, in some cases, NAS solutions will be required to support workloads that are disparate in their characteristics and processing service levels. This makes workload analysis imperative when planning the I/O infrastructure so workloads can be identified and sized before implementation takes place. This is also necessary in order to defend existing configurations when planning upgrade strategies.

This leads us to the next two chapters in this part of the book, which concern the application of storage networking solutions and technologies. Given that we have already identified, described, and characterized our workloads at a macro level, the right solution should become evident.

SAN or NAS Solutions

With current information, you can decide pretty early whether you're looking to leverage an IP-based NAS solution or a more comprehensive FC SAN configuration. The decisions based upon workload analysis will provide accurate direction when it comes to choosing a storage networking solution. Keep in mind, it will also provide accurate justification if staying with current direct-attached storage solutions looks to be the best alternative. Figure 17-10 offers some guidelines on initial workload analysis when macro decisions need to be made regarding SAN, NAS, or direct attached.

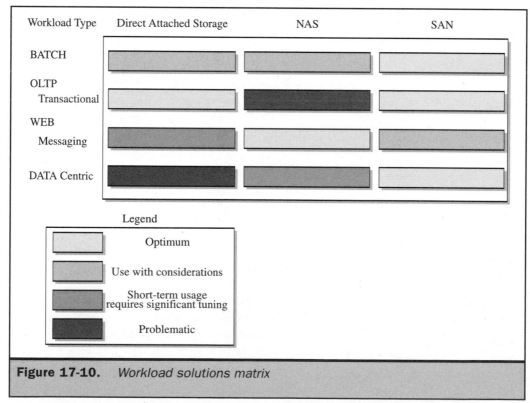

Figure 17-10. *Workload solutions matrix*

Chapter 18

Applying the SAN Solution

The SAN architecture, as previously discussed in Chapter 17, provides a level of storage scalability and capacity beyond traditional I/O infrastructures. SANs provide a rich set of opportunities to apply to several workloads that are standard within today's data center. Among these workloads are OLTP, web services, and data warehousing. OLTP, a foundation of most businesses by supporting their daily operations, is a significant consumer of storage capacity with strict access requirements. The increasing use of web services to provide an array of Internet transactional messages between customers, retailers, and suppliers, enables a significant value benefit to all involved; however, it pushes the performance and scalability envelope of the traditional I/O infrastructure. Data warehouse applications and their related brethren, the data mart, always move the storage capacity bar to its limits as the movement of data within these applications accelerates the need for wider access bandwidth.

This chapter will discuss the guidelines for estimating SAN configurations and explore key concepts concerning the deployment of SANs into these standard workloads. Key among these will be the identification of port requirements necessary to sustain a particular workload, as well as particular issues associated with the often-disparate processing characteristics of OLTP, web services, and data warehousing applications.

SAN Workload Characterization

When characterizing workloads for a SAN, it's helpful to consider the inherent value that Storage Area Networks bring to the data center. This cross-application infrastructure enhancement may be the overriding factor in the justification of an initial SAN configuration that on the surface could be handled by direct connect architecture. This further demonstrates the importance of defining I/O workloads, as discussed in Chapter 17.

When describing SAN I/O workloads, it is also important to be aware of the possible integration of system-level capacity planning as well as network capacity planning for the obvious reason that the SAN architecture represents a combination of computer system and network characteristics that must work together to sustain the workloads. This requires that workloads be evaluated with both I/O processing and network configuration metrics. Even though SANs are young by contrast to other technologies, standard configurations have emerged that can be applied to most common workloads. The major categories, excluding a single switched environment, are cascading, meshed, and core/edge configurations.

These categories provide starting points for data center–specific customization and specialization. SAN expansion and derivations will likely come from one of these three configurations. A brief overview follows.

- **Cascading SAN Configuration**   This configuration provides a switch-to-switch connection that allows the number of server and server devices to scale quickly. Figure 18-1 shows a simple cascading configuration with three servers and multiple storage devices using three FC switches.

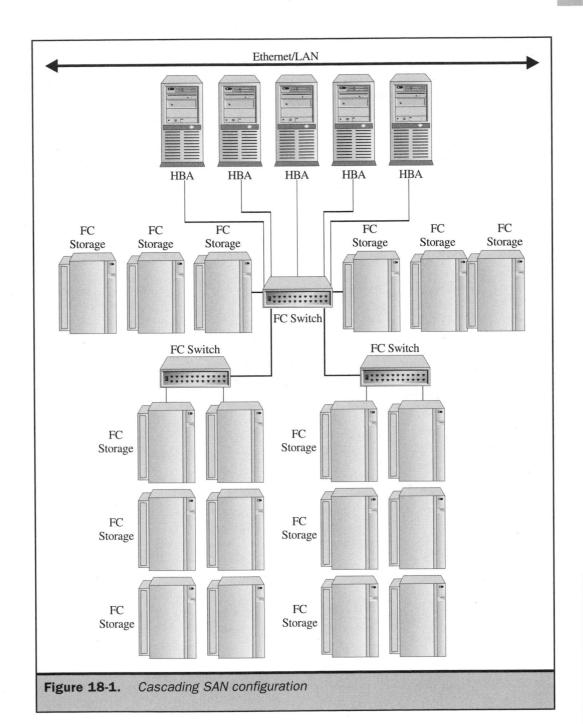

Figure 18-1. *Cascading SAN configuration*

■ **Meshed SAN Configuration**   This configuration provides a performance-oriented system that allows for the quickest path from server to data. Figure 18-2 illustrates how an I/O's path is reduced as it can reach the storage array without traversing multiple switches. However, it also provides the multiple connections to connect to the storage array using alternate paths in the event of heavy traffic or switch disruption.

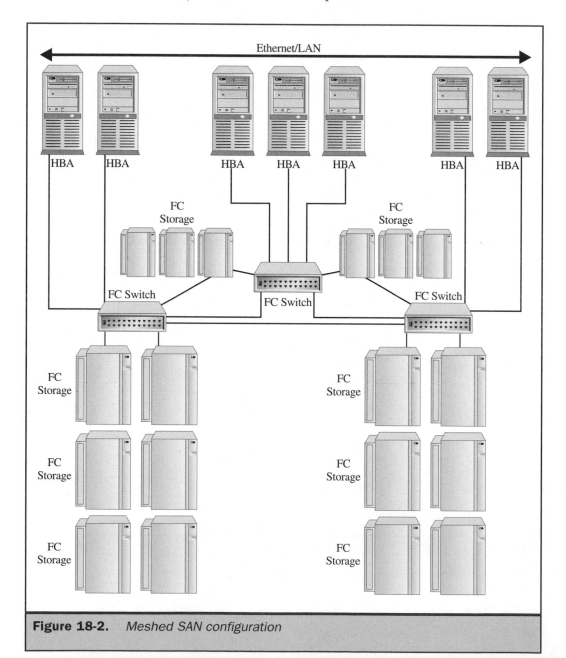

Figure 18-2.   *Meshed SAN configuration*

■ **Core/Edge SAN Configuration**   This configuration takes into account I/O optimization, redundancy, and recovery, as shown in Figure 18-3. By far the most performance oriented, it is also the most complex in implementation and configuration.

These are all important considerations as you begin to evaluate your SAN design and implementation. Some words of caution, however, before the details of configuration complexities overcome your planning and design:

■ Identify and describe the I/O workloads of the applications you expect the SAN to support.

■ Understand the strengths and weaknesses of each of the major networking configurations.

Reviewing Chapter 17 will help get you started on I/O workload analysis. Assuming you have completed a general workload analysis and have a total I/O workload transfer rate (see Chapter 17 for guidelines on estimating I/O workloads), we can estimate the number of ports required to support the I/O workloads. The sidebar "Guidelines for Estimating the Number of Ports Required to Support I/O

Guidelines for Estimating the Number of Ports Required to Support I/O Workloads

The assumptions to consider in viewing these guidelines include the following:

■ The I/O workload transfer rate is available and accurate.

■ The base configuration consists of FC switch ports using switched fabric.

■ The base ratio available from the server to a number of data paths (for example, the number of HBAs for each server connected to the SAN configuration).

Guidelines for estimating SAN port requirements include:

■ Total I/O Workload Transfer Rate (I/OWTR) / Maximum Port Transfer Capacity (MPTC) = Number of Port Data Paths (PDPs) required

■ PDPs × Redundancy/Recovery Factor (RRF) = Number of ports for Redundancy and Recovery (RRPs)

■ PDPs + RRPs = Total Data Path Ports required

■ Total PDPs (with RRF) + Server Ports (SPs) {number of servers × number of HBAs) = Total Switch Ports required Where RRF = 30–40%; SPs = 1–4

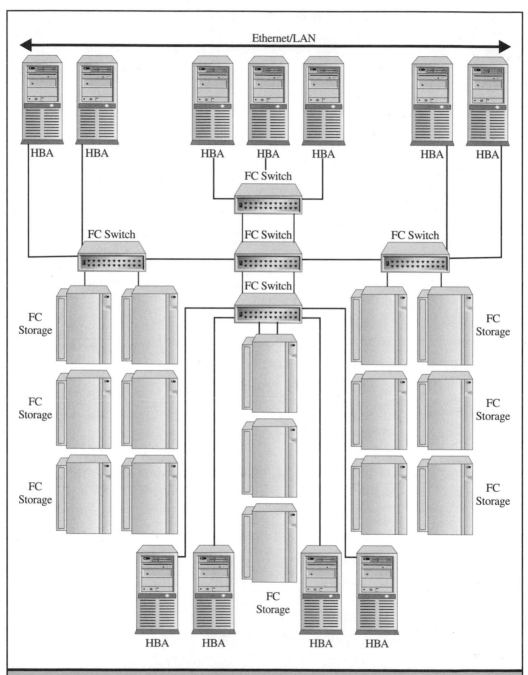

Figure 18-3. *A core/edge SAN configuration*

Workloads" describes a set of activities helpful in estimating the number of ports required.

Once the total estimated numbers of switch ports are calculated, the workload characteristics can be applied to determine the type of access and performance factors necessary. As shown in our examples, this can be an OLTP-type application, such as our banking example in Chapter 17, or a typical web transactional workload that may be used for processing warranty and service information. Finally, the ubiquitous datacentric application, the data warehouse, demonstrates unique processing characteristics and is enhanced by the basic architectural value of SAN architectures.

Switch port estimates are applied to each of these workloads, which drives the configuration into connectivity schemes that best suit the workload. As discussed previously, we then configure and distribute the port count into a cascading, meshed, or core/edge configuration. Through examples, we apply an I/O workload for each configuration and discuss the rationalization for our decision, first using OLTP to demonstrate a core/edge solution. We then move to web transactional applications supported by a meshed configuration, and finally a data warehouse using a cascading architecture.

Applying the SAN to OLTP Workloads

What are OLTP workloads? Multiple users performing a set of consistent transactions characterize online transaction processing workloads. The transaction mix will be simple to complex, but consistent in its processing requirements, usually applying an 80/20 rule (that is, 80% simple, 20% complex). The transaction type identifies its nature in terms of resource utilization, I/O content, and I/O utilization. If we use our banking application as an example, the tellers perform most of their transactions using the deposit transaction. This transaction verifies a customer account and adds the deposit to a suspense balance. The suspense files would be used as input for later off-shift processing during a batch cycle to update permanent customer records and accounts.

In this case, the simple transaction's I/O content is approximately 80 bytes of customer and account information. This is accomplished with a minimum of simple math additions and balance calculations within the application. Although small, these are executed on a transaction-by-transaction basis and require an existing file or database table be updated. Given that profile, each transaction generates an I/O operation to complete the transaction process. Meanwhile, every associated I/O completes a read/write operation to a specific disk within the supporting storage array. In the case of RAID implementation, the physical I/Os will increase based upon the type of RAID level in operation within the storage array.

Consequently, the I/O workload is characterized by many small transactions where each will require an I/O operation—multiple I/Os as RAID is introduced. As the transaction rate builds during peak utilization, the workload is further characterized by additional simple transactions adding multiple I/Os, all requiring completion within a three- to five-second time period (essentially the service level for the deposit transaction). The workload and service level demands a configuration that can handle the peak load. This requires a large number of data paths to handle the I/O transaction rate.

SANs are excellent choices for OLTP workloads because they can provide more data paths than any other storage model. Given the flexibility of the storage network, the scalability of the I/O workload can be enhanced without the addition of server resources.

SANs also provide the additional benefit of data partitioning flexibility. Given that most OLTP applications leverage the services of an RDBMS, the ability to utilize the database's partitioning schemes intra-array and inter-array provides the additional balance necessary to physically locate data for OLTP access.

Most OLTP applications support an operational aspect of a business. Therefore, data availability is important given that the day-to-day activities of the business depend on processing transactions accurately. Any downtime has an immediate effect on the business and therefore requires additional forms of redundancy and recovery to compensate for device failures and data integrity problems. SANs offer an environment that enhances a configuration's ability to provide these mechanisms in the most efficient manner.

Additional discussion regarding recovery and fault-tolerant planning can be found in Part VI of this book. However, it's important to note that each of the workloads discussed will have various degrees of business impact and therefore require different levels of recovery management.

The Data Organizational Model

The use of relational database technology (RDBMSs) defines the major I/O attributes for commercial applications. This provides OLTP workloads with a more defined set of processing metrics that enhances your ability to estimate I/O behavior and utilization. The use of the relational database has become so accepted and widespread that its macro behavior is very predictable. In recognition of this, additional consideration should be given to I/O workload characteristics relative to I/O processing requirements such as caching, temporary workspace, and partitioning.

Don't make the mistake of overlaying the storage infrastructure too quickly. The consideration of recovery scenarios and availability requirements should be considered at the macro-level first, followed by decisions on how to handle workload specifics. Particular subsets of a workload, such as a complex set of deposit transactions, may require different resources or configurations.

OLTP workloads using an RDBMS can be supported through RAID arrays using level 5 configurations. This provides both redundancy and fault tolerance needs. RAID 5 allows the storage array to continue to function if a disk is lost, and although running in a degraded mode it permits dynamic repair to the array, or, if needed, an orderly shutdown of the database itself. Additional storage system features, such as caching strategies and recovery models, require due consideration given the unique nature of the data contained within the relational database model.

User Access

User traffic plays a significant role in defining the number of data paths necessary for the OLTP transactions to be processed within the service level. Obviously, we need to know the estimated traffic to understand the type, number, and behavior of the data paths prior to assigning the configuration ports. We basically need three types of information from the end users or their representatives—the application systems analysts. This information consists of the number of transactions, the time period within which the transactions will be executed, and the expected service level.

The deposit transaction used in our example banking application comes in three forms: simple, authorized, and complex. Simple requires an update to a customer table, while authorized requires an authorized write to the permanent system of record for the account, necessary for a double write to take place when accessing more than one database table. Complex requires the authorized transactions but adds an additional calculation on the fly to deposit a portion into an equity account. Each of these have a different set of data access characteristics even though they belong to the same OLTP workload.

Service levels become critical in configuring the SAN with respect to user access. This places our eventual, albeit simple, calculations into a framework to define the resources needed to sustain the amount of operations for the OLTP workload. From our initial information, we find there are two goals for the I/O system. First, the banking applications data needs to be available from 9 A.M. to 5 P.M. each workday. Second, the transactions should complete within a time frame of 5 seconds. It is important to note that although the I/O can and will take up a great deal of the response time factors, network latency issues should not go without consideration.

In addition, the configuration must support a high availability uptime, usually expressed in terms of the percentage of downtime for a period. Therefore, 99 percent uptime requires the configuration to only be down 1 percent of the time. For example, if the OLTP time period is 12 hours each workday, the downtime cannot exceed 7.2 minutes every day. The users expect availability of data, which is a foundation requirement for meeting the response time (in other words, the data must be available to process the transactions, as well as be available during the batch cycle to process information for updating other database tables). This also forms the requirement for supporting the reliability factors and defines the type of storage partitioning and structure suited to providing this.

Data Paths

Next, we need to understand the data highway required for this workload. This necessitates breaking down our first two categories into a logical infrastructure for the workload. By comparing the data organizational model (that is, the database type and its characteristics, as well as the byte transfer requirements) with something called the *concurrent factor*, we can begin to formulate the number of data paths necessary to meet workload service levels. The concurrent factor provides us with a minimal and logical set of paths to sustain our service level, given the probability of all tellers executing deposit transactions at the same time.

This estimate provides a more accurate picture of the amount of resources needed to sustain the service level in real time. In reality, the probability of all tellers executing a deposit transaction is actually quite high during peak hours, and could be calculated at 90 percent. Therefore, for each time period, 90 percent of the tellers would be executing a deposit transaction. Using our previous calculation, we estimate the mix of simple, authorized, and complex deposit transactions to be 80, 15, and 5 percent, respectively.

We can develop our own OLTP SAN model by using the preceding considerations as well as the guidelines for I/O workload port estimates. With our banking example, we estimate that 116 switch ports are required to support the OLTP application. From this information, we can begin to model the appropriate design topology for the I/O workloads. Our previous definitions lead us to a core/edge configuration, which supports the maximum number of data paths into the storage arrays, while minimizing the length of each transfer for each I/O (for example, the number of interswitch hops is kept to a minimum). This is also the configuration that provides the best redundancy when alternative paths are needed in the event of a port interruption or switch failure. Cost not withstanding, we can now evaluate configuration options with this logical model in terms of switch types, port densities, and recovery options.

The value of workload identification, definition, and characterization becomes evident as we move into the OLTP SAN implementations.

The Design and Configuration of OLTP-Based Workloads

Figure 18-4 shows an example of our core/edge configurations supporting the OLTP application. This configuration is comprised of four FC switches, 15 disk arrays, intersystem-link ports, and an integrated FC-SCSI bridge into a tape library. This supports our workload analysis estimate of ports using three servers with two HBAs, respectively. It assumes a relational database that is capable of partitioning among the storage arrays and leveraging a RAID 5–level protection scheme within each array.

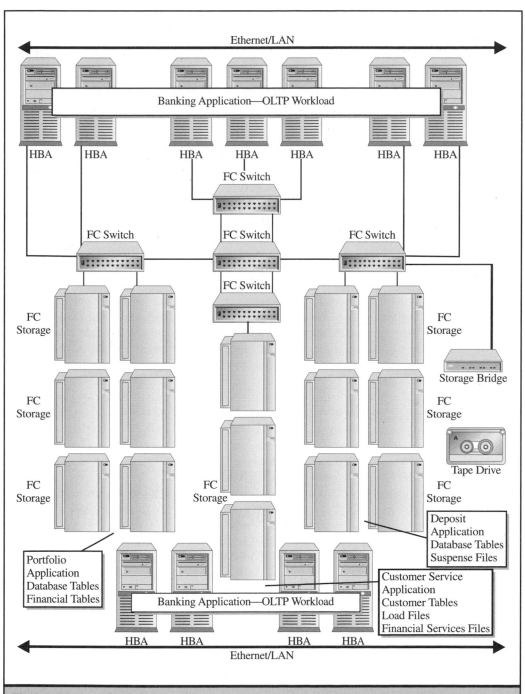

Figure 18-4. *An OLTP workload using a core/edge SAN configuration*

Applying the SAN to Web Transactional Workloads

Workloads generated from Internet or intranet sources can be very complex. Internet applications can generate transactions from simple reads of web pages to complex queries and updates of database structures. Based upon the processing architectures of web server software, which enable interactive web services, many of the workloads will be almost entirely transactional in nature. However, within this transactional model, another type of transaction type will emerge—the messaging transaction.

Though messaging transactions are processed in real time, they will have a different set of processing characteristics than typical OLTP transactions. Messaging provides an asynchronous form of processing where the client application who has submitted the messaging transaction relinquishes any synchronous connection with the corresponding application. The most familiar of these is e-mail, although many other Internet transactions are message-based. This produces a different set of processing characteristics and certainly a more complex set of I/O operations.

Note *The emergence of asynchronous processing of applications also produced an additional category of software termed middleware. The middleware, which has been used in both traditional interactive application processing architectures as well as Internet/web-based applications, provides the mechanisms for queuing a transaction for later processing. This can be for effective resource utilization or handling larger interactive transaction requests where synchronous processing is impossible. The use of middleware within applications can be a key indicator that storage networking can also be an effective supporting strategy given its architecture to handle multiple workloads and, in the case of middleware, handle multiple middleware queues.*

Messaging workloads generate asynchronous I/O operations. This is actually a very simple model where an application transaction is submitted, and a request is queued for later processing. The client, or *initiator*, of the request is notified that the transaction has been accepted for later execution. The processing is executed at a later time or when required resources become available or are provided. All this is accomplished in a manner that doesn't require the user, or initiator, to wait for the transaction to complete and can continue to execute other transactions. Although the characterization of the messaging workloads can be estimated similar to OLTP as we demonstrated previously, care must be taken to account for delayed I/O and resulting byte transfer requirements that may go unaccounted for when estimating total I/O for web transaction workloads.

Note *The difference between client and initiator is an important distinction because other software and internal storage bus processes operating on storage devices are initiators of messaging or asynchronous operations.*

Web Internet transactional workloads, which we'll refer to as WIT workloads, also contain typical synchronous transactions, much like those described in our OLTP examples. Many older WIT workloads use file systems for their data organizational models and specifically their web-based file formats. However, the RDBMS vendors have made significant advances in providing a relational model database for web servers. Consequently, many new applications utilize a relational database demonstrating characteristics similar to databases supporting OLTP processing. The fundamental I/O resource requirement details continue to be contained in the I/O activities relative to user access, data organization, and data paths. An analysis of each of these areas begins to form a picture specific to WIT workloads.

In general, WITs require flexibility and multiple paths to sustain their I/O workloads. However, they are not as sensitive to multiple hop degradation given the amount of messaging contained with the workload. Therefore, a meshed configuration can provide both transactional synchronous support through single-hop data paths while messaging data can sustain longer paths due to their asynchronous processing.

The Data Organizational Model

WIT workloads simply use the OS file system as the data organizational method. This provides a straightforward view when determining byte transfer rates for WIT I/Os given the format of web file structures. However, this must be augmented when considering the amount and type of delayed I/Os generated from messaging transactions. Similar to the transactional structure of OLTP, the typical WIT I/O may be small but the random nature of arrival rates and unpredictability regarding the number of users provides a challenging configuration problem. This defines the need for placing WIT workloads in the most flexible environments possible.

User Access

Defining user traffic is the most challenging activity in estimating WIT workloads. In web-based processing environments, the classic time periods do not apply. This is especially true in retail-oriented web sites that rely on customer interaction for sales and which are open 24/7. The requirement to provide adequate service levels in an environment where user interaction crosses worldwide time zones means estimating WIT workloads becomes problematic and challenging at best.

It is not impossible, however. Many software packages and services provide an accounting of user access and traffic analysis. Though most are oriented toward information access and purchase patterns, there is sufficient information to provide a macro estimate of I/O workloads. User access in terms of time periods, time zones, and further seasonal factors demonstrate a SAN configuration's ability to provide a flexible storage environment that supports OLTP and messaging types of I/Os.

Data Paths

The number of data paths, as with any workload, is key to the performance of WIT workloads. The influence of FC frame capacities may become a factor when analyzing switch port capacities, given that the nature of OLTP may prove to be overkill in some web transactions. However, in many cases, the FC frame capacity may become the required transport, given the increasing I/O content of web transactions which continue to grow with text, image, and other unstructured data needed for transport. Even though the SAN I/O comprises only a portion of the overall response time factor, given the move to larger Ethernet capacities in order to support client IP networks, the matching components have begun to come together.

Note	*FC frame payloads transport a maximum capacity of user data (approximately 2k).*

Data paths for the WITs in a complex web environment, comprised of both OLTP, messaging, and batch loads, will likely surpass the number for typical OLTP. However, the gating factor to this continues to be the reliance of the web server file system. It's important to keep in mind that the probability of multiple data paths may have little or no effect if client requests are queued at the file system. Consequently, there may be a need to consider the following:

- The ratio of channels per server (for example, the number of HBAs per server)
- The need for SMP-enabled servers (meaning more concurrent processing)
- Ensure workload balancing can be used in some form (for instance, in a workload balance software package, processing affinity options, or process prioritization)

More detail on these options can be found in Part VI of the book.

The Design and Configuration of Web-Based Workloads

Figure 18-5 shows an example of a mesh configuration supporting the web-based workload. This configuration is comprised of three FC switches, 18 disk arrays, intersystem-link ports, and an integrated FC-SCSI bridge into a tape library. This supports our workload estimate using web-based consideration and using seven servers with two HBAs, respectively. It assumes a combination of web-based e-mail files, a transactional relational database supporting customer retail transactions, and a complement of web pages. This supports both transactional activity through the meshed configuration where numerous paths exist to the data while the messaging workload is supported by sufficient data paths with consideration for delayed I/O.

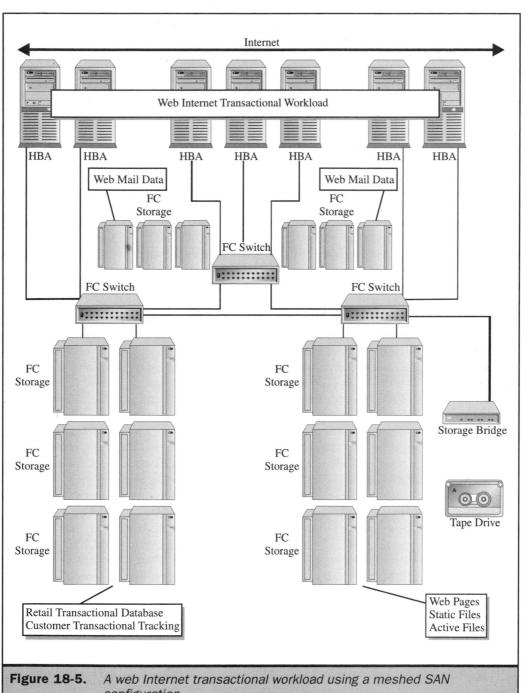

Figure 18-5. *A web Internet transactional workload using a meshed SAN configuration*

Applying the SAN to Data Warehouse Workloads

Data warehouses provide strategic and tactical business information used to direct business planning and forecasting analysis. Data warehouses are built from subsets of operational databases, typically OLTP workloads that form a historical database of various business activities. Users query these large databases in the form of "What if" transactions that range from simple to complex questions. The answer sets of these queries can be extremely large, complex, and form the basis for additional subsets of databases that warrant further analysis.

A spin off of data warehouses is the data mart. Theoretically, data warehouses are based upon corporate information and are used to drive corporate business decisions. Data marts are subsets of data warehouses that are used to drive lower-level business decisions within the divisional or departmental levels. This is important because the size and I/O content will be driven by use of the data warehouse at the corporate level or divisional or departmental level. Given that the true nature of data warehousing is tied to the functions of the relational database, there are many database rules, guidelines, and practices that determine its design, operation, and usage. However, most of these are outside the scope of this book and although important, only those that provide us with clues to their I/O workload analysis will be mentioned.

As you may have experienced or surmised, data warehouses can be very large. Given their sources are the continuing updates from daily business transactions, their storage utilization has been the most comprehensive. The capture of operational database records—known as the extraction, transformation, and loading activities— are driven by the complexities of the data analysis application. In other words, the more comprehensive the analysis application, the more data is required. Many data warehouse configurations are moving into the multiple terabyte range and, consequently, provide the foundation for why data warehouses and data marts are good candidates for SANs. Of all the workloads examined so far, the data warehouse provides the most complex I/O activities that we will discuss.

Data warehouses are built around relational databases; therefore, they are under the control of the user's database system of choice. Moreover, this defines the need to provide large storage capacities that scale well in terms of pure size and I/O content. This is due to the activity of the data warehouse transaction. The DW transaction in its simplest form accesses information from multiple database tables which span multiple records—For example, in order to analyze the number of customers with account balances over $1,000 for an entire year with credit card balances requires the database system to access a customer table, deposit accounts table, credit card accounts, and so on. Without going into the specifics of the database design, we see that even a simple query generates multiple I/Os, each with a large set of records.

DW transactions are serviced on a synchronous and asynchronous basis. Consequently, it's important to understand the mix of transactions and relative service levels. This brings up an interesting phenomenon as both online and batch-oriented operations can process simultaneously within these environments. Given that these are disparate workloads in terms of their resource requirements, it becomes a challenge to configure an I/O system capable of handling this set of complexities.

This is where SANs come in. SANs provide the most comprehensive solution for data warehousing since the MPP database machines. SANs, through their increased addressing capacity, provide an extensible and scalable solution to configuring a very large database. Moving well beyond the addressing limitations of SCSI bus configurations, the need to supply beyond 16 addressable storage devices has long been a requirement in DW environments. SANs support a comprehensive workload with considerable I/O content given the increased FC frame payload capacity for each I/O. Finally, the flexibility to isolate disparate I/Os through SAN operations and configurations can sustain a disparate and complex workload.

Consequently, taking into account the mix of disparate workload characteristics, there needs to be a balance between transactional activity, update activity, and data currency. These should be identified in the workload analysis. The subsequent resource requirement details can be estimated in the major areas of I/O activities (for example, the data organization method, data paths, and user access).

The Data Organizational Model

The use of a relational database system as the data organizational model for the data warehouse is guaranteed. This not only defines a set of metrics that allows for greater detail in determining the byte transfer rates, but also the physical placement of data within the storage devices. Working closely with a database administrator greatly enhances the SAN design and operational factors. As discussed earlier, there are three key database metrics to consider. These are database size, multiple table accesses, and updates.

Database size determines the number of storage devices necessary for pure capacity. Although important, physical placement becomes a critical factor. Partitioning within the database, meanwhile, is key to the type and transaction mix. Consequently, databases that span storage arrays have needed consideration in determining port capacities and access at the switch level.

Depending on the DW transactional mix, the ability to provide adequate performance for accessing I/O concurrently across the database is required. Databases partitioned within storage arrays (which is a given), and those that span storage arrays (a good possibility), need to be analyzed in order to provide sufficient data paths that meet required service levels. Just as important is the ability to isolate the data paths in terms of concurrent access to batch operations that may be taking place simultaneously.

The significant challenge is the configuration attributes that handle the updates. DW sources are operational databases that handle a company's day-to-day operation. Copies of subsets of data from these databases are used as updates to the DW databases. The operational databases may or may not be part of the SAN configuration. In most cases, they aren't; therefore, care should be taken in how the update process is executed. Usually, this is a batch process performed during an off shift. If this is the case, an analysis of the options for getting the data into the DW is key to the success of SAN operations.

User Access

The one break you can expect from DW configurations is that the user community supported is generally limited. Although somewhat obvious, since there are only a limited amount of company personnel assigned to strategic planning, the user base is likely to grow significantly as the success of DW applications demonstrate their value. Although user traffic may be limited, keep in mind that the I/O content of answer sets can be very large. This is one area where applications like DW push the boundaries of FC transfer rates.

If we consider our previous example of analyzing the number of customers with accounts of $1,000 for the year, with credit cards, and who have lived in the same place for more than three years, we may find that the answer set exceeds a gigabyte of data. Dealing with such a large transaction, the number of I/Os generated requires sufficient resources to meet the expected service level and that may be a real-time requirement. However, if only two users generate this requirement per day, this will begin to put the requirement into perspective in terms of analyzing the total byte transfer rates.

Data Paths

Processing transactions that have gigabyte requirements requires multiple data paths. In addition, the necessity to physically partition the database across storage arrays requires more data paths. If we augment the requirement further with database updates that may need to be performed in isolation, the number of data paths becomes significant.

Although the number of data paths needed is dependent on the service level, the ability to access multiple terabytes of data using complex queries in a reasonable time period will drive the number of data paths required by a SAN. The alternative is a highly complex MPP environment using sophisticated parallel processing functionality.

The Design and Configuration of Data Warehouse Workloads

Figure 18-6 shows an example of our cascading configuration supporting the data warehouse application. This configuration is comprised of three FC switches, 18 disk arrays, interswitch-link ports, and an integrated FC-SCSI bridge into a tape library. This supports our workload estimate using data warehouse metrics and considerations, and supports the five servers attached to the end-user LAN. It assumes three relational database systems supporting two warehouses, the Financial Analysis System and the Financial Planning System. Note that the Financial Analysis data is large enough that it is partitioned into North American activity and European activity. The outstanding issue in this configuration is the update process that occurs with operational databases that are not part of this SAN. Considering our initial example of the banking application from Figure 18-3, an interesting problem to contemplate is the operational activities necessary in updating the data warehouse from SAN to SAN. This will be discussed in Chapter 20, which concerns integration issues.

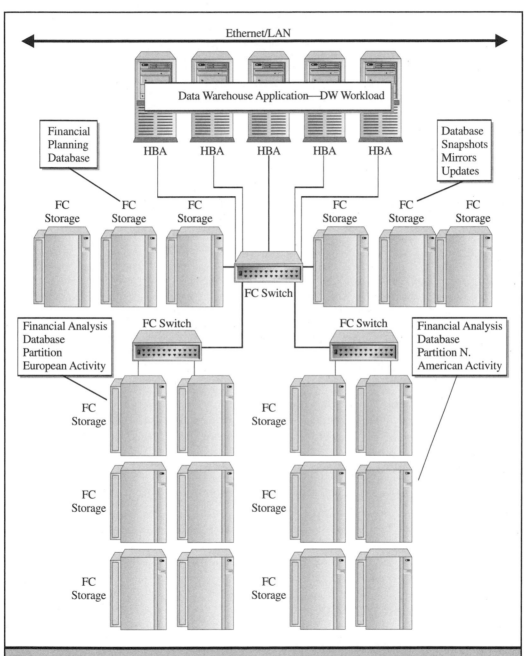

Ethernet/LAN

Data Warehouse Application—DW Workload

Financial
Planning
Database

Database
Snapshots
Mirrors
Updates

HBA   HBA   HBA   HBA   HBA

FC
Storage

FC
Storage

FC
Storage

FC
Storage

FC
Storage

FC
Storage

FC Switch

Financial Analysis
Database
Partition
European Activity

FC Switch

FC Switch

Financial Analysis
Database
Partition N.
American Activity

FC
Storage

FC
Storage

FC
Storage

FC
Storage

FC
Storage

FC
Storage

Figure 18-6.   *A data warehouse workload using a cascading SAN configuration*

Conclusions on Applying SAN Solutions

Three major points have emerged from our discussion of applying workloads to SANs. First is the SAN's scope of configurations needed to handle the most common set of workloads within the data center. Second is the flexibility of the configuration which enables both transactional, messaging, and batch types of workloads. In some cases, as in data warehouse datacentric loads, two diverse workloads can be processed concurrently while providing a manageable configuration necessary to meet service levels.

Points to Consider Before Proceeding

It should be noted that SANs consume both manpower and dollar expenses, which in many cases are over and above your existing direct-attached configurations. Cost notwithstanding, the following additional considerations should be analyzed when contemplating the use of SANs within a data center.

- **Enterprise Workloads**   SANs are justified using enterprise-level workloads that have resource requirements which exceed the scope and functionality of direct-attached solutions, or which exceed the capacity of a NAS solution.

- **Integrating Systems and Networking Skills**   SANs require existing personnel be educated about them—there's no getting around it. However, storage expertise, coupled with network expertise, will best facilitate capacity planning, design, and installation activities.

- **Plan for Open-Ended Solutions**   SANs allow the data center to design and plan for the long term, while making purchases for the short term. This leverages the SANs scalability and long-term viability as a storage solution.

Preparing for the Solution

All the solutions in these examples follow a macro plan. The following steps are recommended when implementing a SAN into a production environment. The macro plan is further defined by separate micro plans that describe actual task-level activities, IT assignments, and target dates. Additional steps may be required given the level of change control managed within the data center. (Refer to Chapter 23 for more details on change control processes and practices.)

Design and Configuration

Our examples show SANs supporting three common types of workloads: OLTP, web Internet-based, and data warehouse. It is beyond the scope of this chapter to illustrate the enterprise application, which will be defined by your workload planning. Typically, configurations are comprised of combinations of 8-, 16-, and 32-port FC switches, with disk arrays commensurate with storage capacities; however, it's not unlikely to surpass 20 distinct systems. Another important point we have focused on in configuration management is the inclusion of interswitch-link ports (ISLs), as well as an integrated FC-SCSI bridge into a tape library.

Test Installation

Define a test installation environment. Putting a small configuration in place provides essential first-case experiences useful in the configuration and operation of a SAN environment. This also provides a test bed for assessing future software and hardware upgrades while enabling an application testing facility.

Use the test installation to initiate a pseudo-management practice. Management becomes the most challenging activity when operating the SAN. It's also the fastest moving and most quickly evolving practice given the rapid change in software tools and accepted practices today. Detailed discussion of SAN management can be found in Part VI of this book.

Production Installation

Develop a production turnover activity where a formal change window is established. In many cases, this may need to be integrated into existing change management activity within the data center. Key among these is tracking the changes made to components of the SAN. It is particularly troublesome if you formalize changes to the switch configurations and don't upgrade critical components like HBAs, routers, and attached storage devices.

An important aspect of the production installation is the discipline surrounding establishment of a back-out practice. Because the SAN is an infrastructure in and of itself, its reliability can be problematic in the beginning, as with any new technology. However, being able to back out quickly and return the production environment to a previously existing state will save valuable time as you move into a SAN environment.

Production and Maintenance

If you have established a formal set of production turnover and change window practices, maintaining the SAN components should become manageable. The key area in providing maintenance to the SAN components is recognizing their complexities as interoperable components. Upgrading the fabric OS in a switch configuration may effect interactions with the server HBAs, which in turn may impact storage bridge/ routers and other attached node devices.

Further establishing a maintenance matrix of SAN components is your best defense against maintenance ricochet, where upgrading or changing one component affects the operation of others. However, SANs are no more complex than networks, and as we've discussed several times in this book, they share many of the processing characteristics of a network. The differences you encounter will be in the devices attached to the network (for instance, the switches, servers, routers, tapes, and so on). This means that the mean time to defect recognition is longer than in traditional networks, given the fact that there are no clients directly attached that will provide instant feedback if the network is down or not operating properly.

Consequently, there is a need to monitor the operation of the SAN in as active a fashion as possible. Although we will cover this in more detail in the management part of the book (Part VI), it is important that the information gathered during this activity play an important role in problem identification, tracking, and resolution.

Chapter 19

Applying the
NAS Solution

NAS is best known as a cost-effective, general-purpose storage solution. Although accurate taken from its legacy of initial deployment, the definition remains a misnomer as the evolution of this storage device has outgrown its provincial network orientation. NAS usage has expanded to include solutions ranging from departmental appliances deployments to strategic data-center solutions. NAS can contribute significant value within the data center supporting applications with over-1TB (terabyte) capacities and gigabit speeds, and outside the data center with its bundled nature that survives end-user environments in remote and campus settings.

NAS devices support an increasing breadth of applications as well as transparent infrastructure storage solutions. These range from specialized engineering, scientific, or academic applications to multiple device installations that have become standard in many Internet service provider data centers. Consequently, the selection of NAS as the best solution for the job requires a bit more effort than throwing NAS against a storage problem and seeing if it sticks. Applying NAS will require a similar characterization of workloads as we demonstrated in applying the SAN solution.

This chapter offers both insight into this process and an overview of typical data-center applications where NAS provides significant value. We'll set forth guidelines for estimating NAS resources and configurations, thereby establishing a foundation for demonstrating key configurations.

NAS Workload Characterization

When characterizing workloads for Network Attached Storage, the first step is to keep in mind the inherent value that NAS brings to application storage environments. As described in Chapters 3 and 12, these include the following:

- Compatibility with existing network resources
- Quick deployment with bundled packaging
- Support for multiple file protocols
- Cost-effectiveness

These characteristics appear to reinforce NAS as a general-purpose storage solution; however, it also places some parameters around what NAS can do—as well as what it can't do. Some of this was also covered in Chapters 3 and 12, which touched on processing environments with the following workload characteristics:

- An OLTP configuration supporting write-intensive applications
- A high-traffic transactional-intensive environment with high I/O content

- Messaging environments that use embedded databases
- Relational database systems supporting distributed environments

As we review each workload characteristic and environment, both pro and con, we'll begin to narrow our scope of supported applications.

What NAS Does Well

NAS provides one of the best solutions for departmental network storage requirements. In many cases, it can extend beyond these applications and move into an enterprise orientation where user access heads into the thousands and data size moves into the terabyte range. We examine each of these NAS characteristics next.

Attachment to Existing Network Resources

As discussed previously, this is NAS's capability to operate within an existing Ethernet LAN environment. This allows any server existing on the LAN to connect and utilize the NAS file server functions. It also allows clients who use network files to connect and utilize the file server functions as a general-purpose file server.

Deduction: A good file server at a greatly reduced cost.

Quick Deployment as a Bundled Solution

Quick deployment as a bundled solution allows NAS to be installed swiftly on a network, where it's defined as an addressable entity and made available for immediate use. In many cases, this can be done within a matter of minutes given the right network and network functions.

Deduction: A quick fix for storage capacity, once again at a greatly reduced cost.

Support for Multiple File Protocols

NAS supports most common remote file protocols, allowing many applications to exist transparently while application servers redirect I/O requests to a NAS device. More importantly, this allows both clients and servers to move storage requirements and I/O requests to an external device.

Deduction: A good device for separating storage requirements from application requirements, and if it supports HTTP, it can be used as a cost-effective storage device for Web Services.

Cost-Effectiveness

Although I think we have introduced this concept with each of our previous attributes, it can be further articulated in terms of the NAS bundled solution, which provides both hardware (processors, network attachments, and storage devices) and software (the OS, file system, and so on) with several alternatives to RAID protection.

What NAS Can't Do

It is also important to keep in mind what NAS can't do. Trying to get NAS to support things it can't undermines its value as a cost-effective solution and potentially renders it obsolete. Here are some things to balance against what NAS does well.

OLTP in a Write-Intensive Application

Remember two things: First, NAS is bundled with a file system; OLTP almost always requires an RDBMS that restricts NAS from fully participating in this application. The RDBMS engine cannot run on the NAS device because it has an RTOS and is closed to other applications. Second, the file system will hamper performance of tables that are stored on the device, and support from database vendors using NAS in this fashion is problematic.

Deduction: Be cautious when considering NAS storage for high-end OLTP applications supporting multiple remote end users. These are applications using traditional relational database solutions.

Transactional-Intensive Applications with High I/O Content

NAS devices, although offering multiple network access points and multiple SCSI paths to data, remain limited in their scalability to meet high-transactional traffic.

Deduction: You probably don't want to use NAS for your corporate data warehouse application, or any application that requires sophisticated RDBMS partitioning, updates, and complex data access.

Messaging-Intensive Applications Using an Embedded Database

The same can be said for messaging environments like e-mail, where high user traffic coupled with high I/O operations cannot sustain large user communities with additional deferred I/O operations that may require the remote execution of transactions.

Deduction: Be cautious when considering NAS for your e-mail operations. Although this is a matter of scalability, most e-mail systems continue to have a monolithic file architecture that makes remote partitioning of the data difficult, and scaling problematic.

High-Performance Relational Database Systems

The relational model has yet to fit well with NAS systems given the optimization at the file-system level and the singular nature of the storage array options. Relational databases at the high end of the product spectrum do not work well with NAS storage. Given there is some value to using NAS to store database tables in elementary RDBMS installations, enhanced performance options such as the parallel processing of queries, sophisticated table partitioning, and adding global table locking mechanisms remain beyond the capabilities of NAS.

Deduction: You should not consider NAS for applications that have database systems, which may extend their requirements into advanced RDBMS functionality. Although considerations of scalability is a factor, NAS storage servers do not have the processing services necessary to handle advanced database functions.

In conclusion, there are a number of applications to which NAS will provide significant value. These applications are not necessarily the most highly political or visible, but they make up much of IT's expenditures. Thus, our findings for NAS include the following:

- The NAS device can be used as a storage solution for Web Services, because it does speak HTTP, along with other remote dialects such as NFS, CIF, and future file transfer technologies such as Direct Access File System.

- NAS provides a quick solution for file servers whose storage capacity is constantly being upgraded within specific network domains.

- Given the flexibility in attachment to an existing Ethernet LAN, NAS can be utilized as a remote storage device while controlling it through the network and vice versa.

- NAS provides an excellent cost-effective storage device for archival- and HSM-type activities.

These conclusions establish disembarkation points for departmental solutions, data center–specific solutions, and application-specific solutions. Derivations of any one of these solutions will likely come from one of these three configurations. A brief overview follows:

- **Appliance/Departmental Configuration**   This NAS deployment provides a storage-centric solution to departmental file services. Figure 19-1 shows a simple NAS configuration supporting a network domain of two servers and multiple client devices that rely on NAS storage for networked file services, shared files such as application code libraries, and the download of business info (for example, results of large data warehouse operations).

- **Enterprise/Data Center NAS Configuration**   This NAS configuration provides a performance-oriented system that supports multiple web servers for both Internet and intranet storage requirements. Figure 19-2 illustrates multiple NAS storage devices supporting the Web Services servers which connect clients as they transfer data within their own network segment using high-speed gigabit Ethernet transports.

■ **Specialized Application Support NAS Configuration** This configuration supports the large storage requirements for special applications that store unstructured data in existing file formats, archived HSM data used for near real-time access, or image/video data used in streaming applications. (See Figure 19-3.)

The following are some important considerations as you begin to evaluate your NAS design and implementation. Keep in mind that although NAS is easy to implement, and in some cases can be installed as a quick fix to a critical capacity problem, a level of analysis may be helpful to avert potential problems.

■ Identify and describe the I/O workloads of the applications you expect NAS to support.

■ Understand the strengths and weaknesses of each of the major networking configurations.

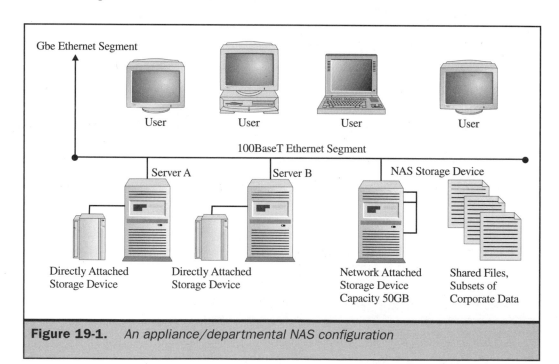

Figure 19-1. *An appliance/departmental NAS configuration*

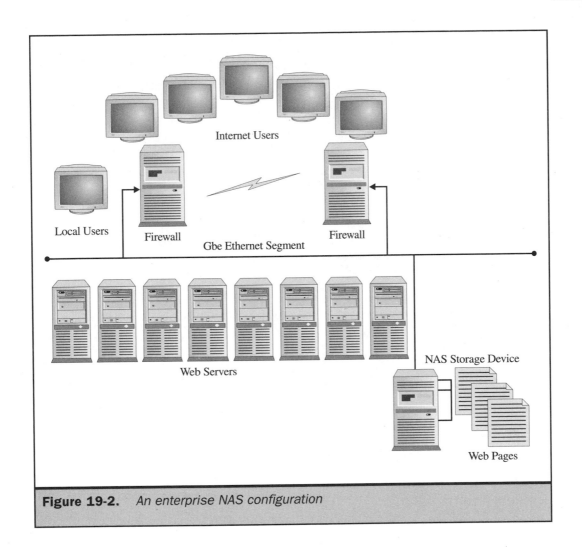

Figure 19-2. *An enterprise NAS configuration*

Assuming you have completed a general workload analysis and now have a total I/O workload transfer rate (see Chapter 17 for guidelines on estimating I/O workloads), you can estimate the number of ports required to support the I/O workloads. The sidebar "Guidelines for Estimating NAS Requirements" describes a set of activities that can be used to provide NAS implementation estimates given the size and scope of a potential NAS solution. These should be viewed as general guidelines and used as a worksheet when analyzing your potential NAS requirements. As always in capacity

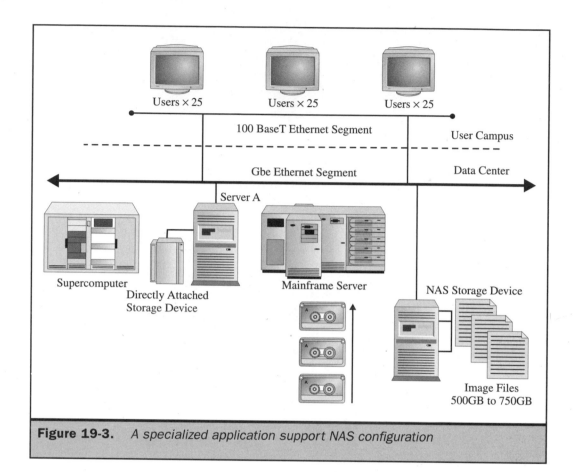

Figure 19-3.   *A specialized application support NAS configuration*

planning exercises, many data-center specifics should to be considered in context. Your results may vary according to those specific requirements.

Consider the following when contemplating specific NAS requirements:

■ The I/O workload transfer rate should be available and accurate.

■ The base configuration will be using LAN.

Conclusion   Use the guidelines to calculate estimates for data paths, (number of SCSI channels), network paths, (number of IP ports), and the NAS sizing factor. This will build in additional resources for redundancy and recovery operations/device transfers.

Guidelines for Estimating NAS Requirements

- $$\frac{(\text{Total I/O Workload Transfer Rate (I/OWTR)} / \text{Max Network Performance}[1])}{2}$$
  = Minimum number of Network Paths (NetPaths) required

- Total I/O Workload Transfer Rate (I/OWTR) / Max NAS Channel Performance[2] = Minimum number of data paths (DataPaths) required

- Add NetPaths to DataPaths = Total logical paths (Lpaths)

- Lpaths × Redundancy/Recovery Factor (RRF)[3] = Number of paths for Redundancy and Recovery (RRPs)

- Lpaths + RRPs = Minimum logical paths (Lpaths) required

- Calculate ratio of Lpaths to DataPaths – Lpaths/Dpaths = Size Factor (*sf* %)

- Compare *sf* % factor to NAS sizing table

[1] The MAX network performance is based upon the type of Ethernet network segment you install on the NAS device (ranging from a low-speed base 10 to high-speed 10Gb segments). A recalculation of bits to bytes is required to perform the calculation.

[2] Max NAS Channel Performance is the bandwidth MB/sec burst rate specification of the SCSI channels selected. This ranges from 10MB/sec to 50–60MB/sec, depending on the SCSI type selected.

[3] The RRF is made up of an average of 40 percent for transactional workloads, 20 percent for file servers, and 10 percent for archival and special applications.

NAS Sizing Factor Table

NAS Device Type	Data Capacity Requirement	Sizing Factor
Appliance	Aggregate Data is < 500GB	0 – 30%
Mid-Range NAS	Aggregate Data is >500GB <1TB	30% – 60%
Enterprise NAS	Aggregate Data is > 500GB <5TB	< 60 %

Use the NAS sizing factor table to find the NAS device most appropriate for your workloads by comparing your total data storage requirements to the sizing factor.

For example, if your total data required for NAS workloads is less than 500GB and your calculated sizing factor is under 30 percent, your best solution will be an appliance-level NAS device. Size the appliance-level device with estimates that provide the minimal number of data paths and network paths as estimated in your calculations.

Estimates that do not fit the table or cannot be sized with sufficient network or data paths are probably better suited to a more scalable solution such as a SAN, a high-end, direct-attached solution using SMP, a clustered system, or a combination of any of the three.

Applying the NAS to Departmental Workloads

Departmental workloads make up the bulk of NAS implementations. These workloads are defined as users and applications that are closely integrated in terms of physical office structure, network segments, or application usage. Most environments are a combination of all three of these attributes. This is characterized by a physical attribute such as all the engineers on the third and fourth floors, the entire set of architects within the building, or the customer support representatives in the basement. They share a common attribute in that they are physically located together and are serviced by servers that provide both network access and a shared storage space within that server, or a combination of servers supporting that physical area.

However, the physical factor may only exist in terms of network proximity, where all the sales people at the front of the building share a network segment with, say, the executive secretaries, and half of the customer service department, which is located in the basement. The common network segment provides an infrastructure again where these groups likely share file system servers that provide outside network access to the rest of the company as well as customers and shared files within their own organizational domains.

Certainly, many of the personnel with the same physical environment and network segment are going to share a common set of applications—usually the ones directed by the corporation, installed by the IT department, and used by the sales and support representatives in the front of the office and the customer service representatives in the basement.

Common activities within the shared environment just discussed are the continual additions, upgrades, changes, and enhancements to the departmental file servers that service the network segment. This is driven for the most part by the growing demand for storage on the file servers. Even though the applications are upgraded and enhanced, physical growth must increase alongside the data accumulated by the sales department, administration, and, yes, the guys in the basement.

This continual upheaval becomes costly, disruptive, and inefficient, adding, replacing, and enhancing general-purpose servers to accommodate additional and more sophisticated storage, just to access files.

The solution is a NAS appliance.

The Data Organizational Model

The data organizational model has a file system bundled into the solution (yes, that's right, a file system). File processing characteristics are based upon the requirements that workloads place on the file system and supporting file transport protocols. Characterizations of file system processing complexities, including simple file processing (Sfp), quality file processing (Qfp), and complex file processing (Cfp) can be found in Chapter 12.

User Access

User traffic always plays a significant role in defining the number of paths needed on a concurrent basis for a particular workload. The I/O content of the user's transactions compared to the total workload byte transfer rate will begin to determine the NetPaths required. These estimates are based upon the aggregate network speeds and the type and characteristics of the Network Interface Cards used in the proposed NAS solution.

Data Paths

Data paths must include the total number of paths that the data travels. Consequently, data paths are combined with the number of network paths from both servers and users (for instance, the NICs), and the number of SCSI channels for each storage array that has access to server processing.

Design and Configuration for Departmental-Based Workloads

Figure 19-4 shows an example of NAS appliance configurations supporting the departmental file server requirements.

APPLICATION—
PUTTING IT TOGETHER

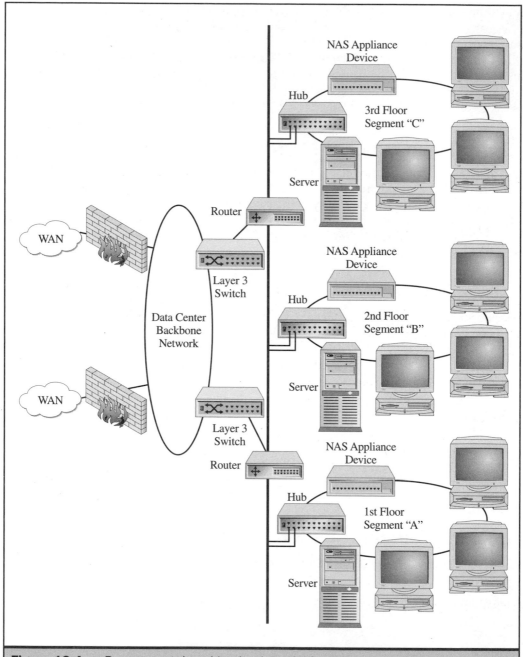

Figure 19-4.   *Departmental workload using a NAS appliance configuration*

Applying the NAS to Enterprise Web Workloads

Workloads generated from Internet or intranet sources can be very complex. Internet applications can generate transactions from simple reads to complex queries and updates of database structures. Built upon web software and providing interactive web services, many enterprise web-based workloads are almost entirely transactional in nature. However, within this transactional model much of the traffic is generated from the read-only access to web pages.

This plays into the strengths of the NAS model, which should provide storage for the rapidly growing number of web applications accessed only as read I/O and which are loaded on a remote client. Web servers provide the necessary infrastructure to redirect I/O to storage servers based upon a HyperText Transport Protocol (HTTP) universal resource locator address. Given that NAS boxes are able to speak HTTP, this client request along with the subsequent redirection from web indexing software can provide the requested web page, and thus free the web server for web transactional and indexing tasks.

In some cases, a web services provider may provide a heterogeneous set of servers for web service deployment. This is characterized by UNIX and Windows servers coexisting within the same data center. The inherent strength of providing heterogeneous support to both server operating environments through the NAS multiprotocol services allows us to use the NAS device as a storage solution for Web Services, given it speaks HTTP and other remote dialects (NFS, CIFs, and so on), as well as future file transfer technologies, such as the Direct Access File System.

The Data Organizational Model

NAS-WIT (Web Internet Transactional) workloads simply use the OS file system as the data organizational method. This provides a straightforward method of determining byte transfer rates for WIT I/Os given the format of web file structures. However, this must be augmented when considering the amount and type of delayed I/Os generated from redirected I/O transactions and asynchronous transactions (for example, messaging). Similar to the transactional structure of OLTP, the typical WIT I/O may be small but the random nature of arrival rates and unpredictability regarding the number of users provide a challenging configuration problem. In terms of NAS devices that are limited in their network and data path capacities per device, we are driven immediately into a multidevice configuration. Consequently, this requires a logical distribution of the total workload byte transfer rate among a set of NAS devices.

User Access

Defining user traffic is the most challenging part about estimating WIT workloads. In web-based processing environments, the classic time periods do not apply. This is especially true in retail-oriented web sites that rely on customer interaction for sales and are open 24/7. Providing adequate service levels across worldwide time zones makes attempts at estimating WIT workloads problematic.

Data Paths

The number of data paths, as with any workload, is key to the performance of WIT workloads. The influence of IP packet traffic becomes a defining factor in analyzing network interface capacities given the OLTP nature of the WIT workload. Given the rich I/O content of web transactions that continue to grow with text, image, and other unstructured data, a gigabit transmission may become the required transport, even though it's a read-only environment. NAS I/O comprises only a portion of the overall

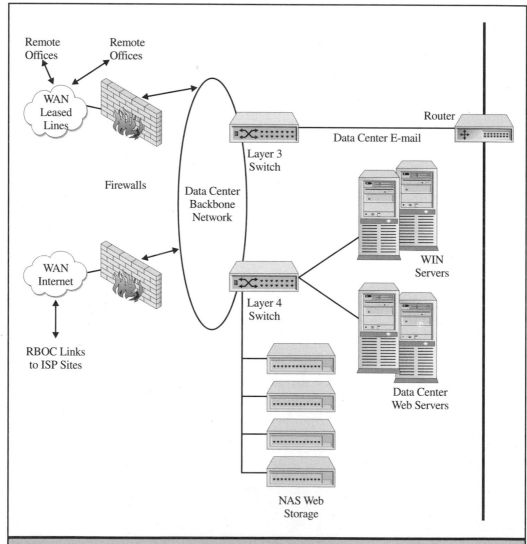

Figure 19-5. *A web Internet read-only workload using a mid-range NAS configuration*

response time factor; limiting network latencies with Gbe capacities helps bring the number of network paths and data paths into line.

Design and Configuration for Web-Based Workloads

Figure 19-5 shows an example of a mid-range NAS configuration supporting the web-based workload.

Applying the NAS to Specialized Workloads

Engineering, scientific, academic, and entertainment segments all demonstrate specialized needs given their increasing reliance on data that is characterized by its unstructured format. The data organizational model is an average file system and contains information used in GIS seismic applications, image and video streaming, and model simulations such as weather patterns and nuclear explosions. The files associated with these applications typically require large file sizes with multiple read I/Os from many users, both local and remote.

The additional characteristic of this data is the way it gets created. On the high end, the data may come from seismic studies and surveys where millions of digital measurements are contained within the data to simulate a geophysical structure. The measurements are contained in files, which are later used by simulation applications to visualize a projected oil deposit. Consequently, the data is larger and must be accessible to those engineers and scientists who analyze the visualization. Traditional client/server storage solutions become very expensive as storage capacities and resources beseech a general-purpose server that's beyond the necessary computer capacities required.

On the low end, data may be generated from the increasing amount of digital images used in governmental work. For example, images of land, land surveys, and improvements can provide a significant productivity improvement in many small governments. The problem is that storage of the images greatly exceeds the limitations of departmental servers employed at this level. Traditional client/server systems are very expensive, especially when purchased just to add storage capacity.

The Data Organizational Model

File systems continue to be the most common level of data organization for these applications. Given their straightforward access needs (no relational model is necessary to perform "What if" analyses on the data itself), the data is formatted to the mathematical/computational operations of the application. This characterizes a processing cycle of large data transfers followed by compute-intensive processing. Consequently, the arrival rate of large data transfers initiated by the user may appear to be random; however, further investigation of I/O activity may show processing trends defining the level of concurrency required.

User Access

User access is typically much smaller than traditional web, departmental, or general business OLTP applications, and is characterized by specialists that are processing the data. The major client change in these areas is the makeup of workstations for specialized end users with increased storage capacity at the client level. This extends the I/O content of the transactions that are executed as well as the requirements needed for file transfers between workstation and NAS storage devices.

Data Paths

Processing transactions that have gigabyte requirements necessitates multiple net-data paths. However, similar to the enormous database structures described in data warehouse applications, the need to physically partition the file system across storage arrays due to size requires more data paths. If we augment this requirement further with updates to the files that may need to be performed in isolation, stored or archived, the number of data paths becomes significant.

Design and Configuration for Specialized Workloads

Figure 19-6 shows an example of specialized NAS configuration supporting the seismic analysis application. An interesting problem to contemplate is the operational activities involved in updating the seismic files, archived files, or remotely transmitted files (see Chapter 20 for more on integration issues).

Conclusions on Applying NAS Solutions

Several major points have emerged from our discussion of applying workloads to NAS. Consider NAS not only for cost-effective departmental workloads but also for some enterprise-level workloads that fit the NAS profile. Integrating network skills and storage skills becomes the best educational platform for effectively supporting NAS environments. Even though NAS can be justified very simply, and installed quickly with immediate results, this does not relinquish your responsibility in planning out your NAS solutions.

Consider These Points Before Proceeding

It should be noted that NAS, while being a cost-effective solution, could consume both manpower and additional dollar expenses as your workload begins to grow. Cost notwithstanding, the following additional considerations should be analyzed as you contemplate using NAS within departmental, remote, or data-center environments.

- **Departmental and Enterprise Workloads**   NAS configurations are easily justified for departmental settings where storage resource requirements exceed

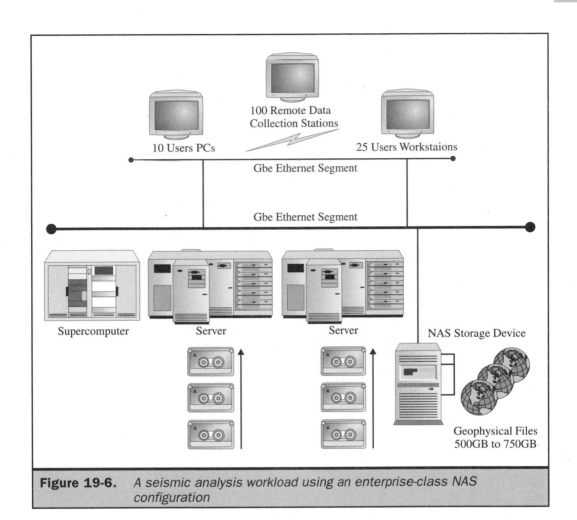

100 Remote Data
Collection Stations

10 Users PCs

25 Users Workstaions

Gbe Ethernet Segment

Gbe Ethernet Segment

Supercomputer   Server   Server   NAS Storage Device

Geophysical Files
500GB to 750GB

Figure 19-6.   *A seismic analysis workload using an enterprise-class NAS configuration*

the growth of general-purpose server processing elements. In some cases, departmental applications expand beyond the scope and functionality of direct-attached solutions by their increased I/O requirements. In these cases, consider bringing these inside the data center with consideration of a mid-range or enterprise NAS configuration. Don't immediately go to SAN justification unless the total workload I/O transfer rate and user access concurrency factors demand it.

■ **Integrating Systems and Networking Skills**   NAS solutions, like SANs, require an educational requirement for existing personnel. Although vendors would like to downplay this aspect, there's no getting around it. The problem is that there are few options for this type of storage networking education.

APPLICATION—
PUTTING IT TOGETHER

As with SANs, storage expertise—coupled with network expertise—best facilitates capacity planning, design, and NAS installation activities, and serves as a combined template for storage networking solutions supporting both SAN and NAS.

■ **Plan for NAS Integration and Migration**   NAS allows the data center to be implemented quickly and to be safely purchased for the short term without unduly lengthening the design and planning necessary for SANs. However, this doesn't mean planning or foresight isn't necessary when it comes to NAS. NAS should be viewed in the long term more critically as it migrates through various NAS capacities and sizes with consideration for integration. Integration eventually occurs as NAS workloads work in conjunction with SAN workloads, or as NAS workloads become integrated into a SAN solution.

Preparing for the Solution

All the solutions within these examples follow a macro plan. The following steps are recommended when implementing NAS into production environments. As we stated with plans for SAN implementation, a macro plan is further defined with separate micro plans, tasks, and assignments. Additional steps may be required, given the level of change control managed within the data center.

Design and Configuration

Our examples demonstrate an overview of how NAS can support three common types of workloads, departmental file systems, Web read-only workloads, and specialized engineering seismic analysis application. Guidelines used in these sections can provide general direction for specific design and configuration activities.

Test Installation

Although not as critical for NAS, it is helpful and productive to define a test installation environment. Putting a small configuration in place provides essential first-case experiences in the configuration and operation of a NAS device. This also creates a test bed for testing future bundled model upgrades while simultaneously enabling a risk-free application testing facility.

Use the test installation to initiate a pseudo-management practice. Remote management is the most challenging activity when operating the NAS. It is also the most rapidly evolving practice, with daily changes in software tools and accepted practices. A detailed discussion of NAS management can be found in Chapter 21.

Production Installation

Develop a production turnover activity where a formal change window is established. In many cases, this may need to be integrated into existing change management activities within the data center. Key among these is tracking all the changes within the TCP/IP network infrastructures that support the NAS device. This can save much time when formalizing changes to the NAS configurations and integrating these into server OS and application upgrades that modify or change file-level protocols. This includes tracking key components such as the server NICs, network routers, and attached storage devices.

Production and Maintenance

If you have established a formal set of production turnover and change window practices, maintaining the NAS components should become very manageable. The key area in providing maintenance to the NAS components is in recognizing the complexities of serving multiple file-level protocols. Upgrading the server OS, web software, or new storage management software may affect interactions with NAS NICs, file systems, and internal storage software.

Further establishing a maintenance matrix of NAS devices is your best defense in quelling maintenance ricochet, where upgrading or changing one component affects the operation of others. The mean time to defect recognition can be much shorter in the NAS configurations, given the fact that clients directly interact with the NAS devices. This provides an immediate feedback loop if the NAS device is down or not operating properly.

As with any active component within the network, there will be a need to monitor the operation of the NAS devices. We'll cover this in more detail in the management part of the book, Part VI, but it's important to note that the information gathered during this activity, regardless of product or NAS functions, plays an important role in problem management, capacity planning, and performance and fine-tuning.

Chapter 20

Considerations When Integrating SAN and NAS

Chapter 20 addresses the usage of SAN and NAS as an integrated solution. Discussions will cover current data-center realities and experiences but also look to the future uses of integrated SAN and NAS technologies. Because many of the challenges to integration are hidden in managing multiple I/O workloads, just the introduction of this subject can be a complex exercise. This chapter was developed with a broad scope in order to provide a meaningful orientation for those uninitiated to storage strategies as well as prove valuable to those experienced with enterprise storage and I/O workloads.

Integrating storage networking models is, in many ways, like developing a client/server-networking environment; it maintains some fundamental differences given the extreme architectures of SAN and NAS. The fundamental differences are block access in SAN operations versus file access in NAS—block I/O being an extension of the server OS, and file I/O as a functional extension to networking technologies. Beyond these visible differences, the challenges of microkernel compatibility, communications standards, and caching coherency issues will require server and storage vendors to cooperate with synchronization, technology integration, and yet-to-be-developed standards. The current evolution of business applications through the continuing enhancement of web-enabled solutions will incorporate all the attributes of OLTP, batch, and data-intensive I/O. These application attributes will be key drivers in the SAN/NAS product evolution. Taken in context with current data-center infrastructures, the evolution of comprehensive SAN/NAS integrated products will definitely be a future solution.

As combined SAN/NAS solutions support the drive to an application democracy existing in a universal network, the integration of major components of the I/O infrastructure becomes paramount with the development of integrated and faster I/O protocols. This chapter discusses some of the key future technologies that will begin to affect IT storage networking solutions, along the way viewing future I/O infrastructure technologies from two perspectives. First will be a view external to the server with innovations such as iSCSI and InfiniBand. This will be followed by a view internal to the processor components with advancements such as HyperTransport and Rapid I/O initiatives.

The Differences

This book, to a great degree, is about the differences between SAN and NAS architectures, technologies, and solutions. Looking at SAN and NAS products as an integrated solution within the data center, we must view both the differences and similarities from a different perspective—that is, how do we put such solutions together to provide value in the data center. Moreover, what are the applications and, more specifically, I/O workloads that would benefit from both technologies?

The most visible difference is the method in which SAN and NAS process an application's request for data. This represents the block I/O versus the file I/O orientation of each solution.

SANs provide a storage interconnection that enables an attached server to process an I/O as if it were communicating with a direct attached storage device. This allows the attached server's OS to execute a block I/O even though the operation is transported over the FC protocol within the storage network. Consequently, SANs enjoy the benefits and efficiencies of block I/O while enabling the flexibility and added bandwidth performance of being on a network.

From the perspective of the NAS device, the application's request for data is handled through a file request, which is in turn managed by the operating system, where the application is executed and the NAS operating system takes the file request. However, as the request is executed from the NAS operating system, it performs a block I/O to access the data on the NAS device. Block I/O is the native function in how the OS executes an application I/O, whether the application is local or remote (refer to Part II for more detailed information).

Figure 20-1 contrasts these differences to show SAN I/O as an *intra*system transaction and the NAS I/O as an *inter*system transaction. The SAN block I/O requires direct communication with the initiating operating system. The NAS file I/O does not require direct communications with the initiating operating system, but must communicate with another operating system where it obtains only the file attributes. Having accepted that information from the initiating OS, the NAS OS executes a block I/O on their behalf. When viewed from an application standpoint, the application program does not care where the data is, as long as there is some level of addressability to locate and read or write the data. The internals of that operation, which are a block I/O, are handled by the NAS OS where the data actually resides.

The other visible difference is the network where each solution resides. NAS uses existing Ethernet topologies and the TCP/IP-layered network software model, rendering it an IP-based storage transport. SAN, on the other hand, uses the Fibre Channel–layered network software model across a variety of media transports. Nevertheless, it remains a closed system that requires some method of translation to participate in other networks.

The differences of data encapsulation, speed, and reliability between transport protocols of TCP/IP and FC illustrate the challenges of integrating IP-based networks with FC-based networks. TCP/IP based upon data communications architectures is not well suited to the transmission of a native I/O, as indicated in Figure 20-2. The size of IP packets limits its value in the types of I/O workloads it can handle. Enhanced only through the increased media speeds, the limitations of TCP/IP for storage equate to many of the limitations of NAS products. However, the ability to leverage the wide area network capability of TCP/IP networks can provide access to remote storage locations.

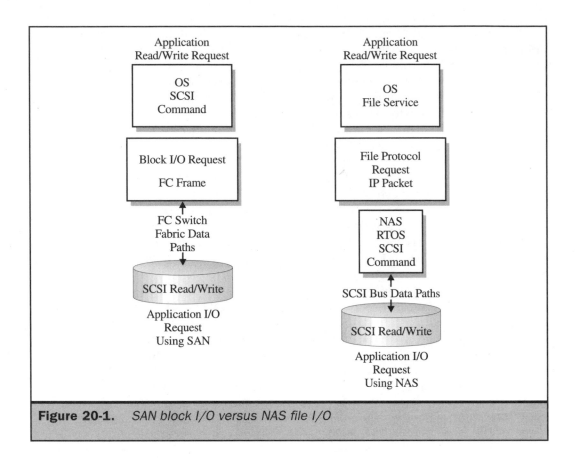

Figure 20-1.   *SAN block I/O versus NAS file I/O*

A SAN's use of FC provides the basis for a channel-oriented architecture that facilitates its use as a storage transport (shown in Figure 20-3). The FC classes of service provide the levels of reliability to perform in environments where data integrity is important (for example, most commercial data centers). The frame architecture of approximately 2KB and its transfer rate of 1 Gbps moving to 2 Gbps and beyond extends FC's ability to handle a larger set of I/O workloads. The FC protocol functions as a transport for block I/O within the limitations of SAN networks. The issue with FC SANs is its limitation in providing wide area network usage when accessing remote storage locations.

The Similarities

The need to provide access to more storage resources characterizes the similarities of both NAS and SAN solutions. Both solutions utilize a network to facilitate this requirement. The NAS and SAN products provide multidevice access that interconnects both servers

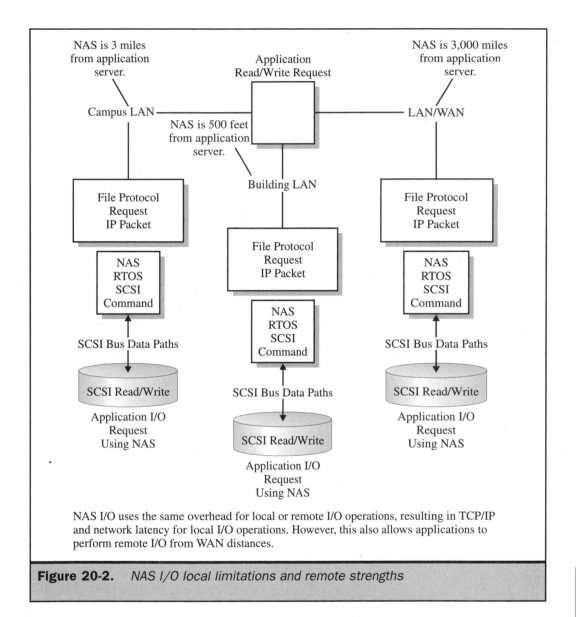

Figure 20-2. *NAS I/O local limitations and remote strengths*

and storage. With respect to their local operations, they both perform block I/O, as described previously.

The use of a network ties these storage models together and provides a foundation for integration activities. Despite the evolution of data communications networks, the integration of disparate network topologies and protocols remains with us today. Accomplished through the use of bridging mechanisms at the lower levels of the

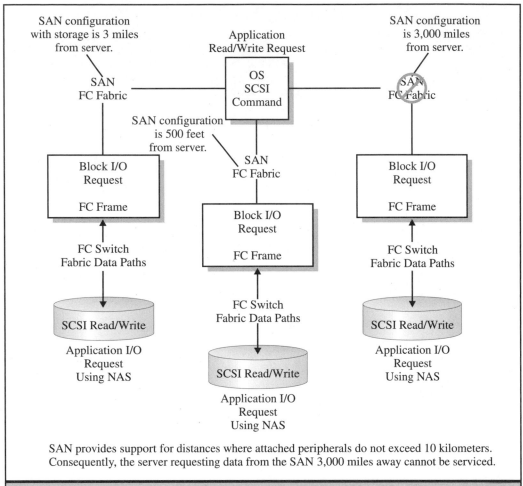

SAN configuration with storage is 3 miles from server.

Application Read/Write Request

SAN configuration is 3,000 miles from server.

SAN FC Fabric

OS SCSI Command

SAN FC Fabric

SAN configuration is 500 feet from server.

Block I/O Request

FC Frame

SAN FC Fabric

Block I/O Request

FC Frame

FC Switch Fabric Data Paths

Block I/O Request

FC Frame

FC Switch Fabric Data Paths

SCSI Read/Write

FC Switch Fabric Data Paths

SCSI Read/Write

Application I/O Request Using NAS

SCSI Read/Write

Application I/O Request Using NAS

Application I/O Request Using NAS

SAN provides support for distances where attached peripherals do not exceed 10 kilometers. Consequently, the server requesting data from the SAN 3,000 miles away cannot be serviced.

Figure 20-3. *SAN I/O local strengths and remote limitations*

network transport layers, data networks were able to interoperate, allowing the scalability of multiuser networks. The evolution of these elementary bridging technologies to router products facilitated the delivery of client/server data packets as well as sophisticated traffic management and communications reliability.

Although we have yet to see this sophistication within the storage networking world, the use of bridges and routers to accommodate disparate storage protocols in the SAN has been an accepted and widely used mechanism (see Chapter 15). Given their nature of communicating at the file level, NAS can leverage existing bridge, router, and switching technologies as an inherent characteristic necessary to utilize standard Ethernet TCP/IP networks.

In terms of value, they provide similar justification in what they offer—that is, storage consolidation, server consolidation, centralized management, larger storage capacities, multiple application access, and storage scalability. These value propositions center around the effective usage of each storage model, respectively.

This requires the ability to identify and analyze the characteristics of the I/O workload. As discussed in Chapter 17, specific I/O workloads are better suited to either NAS or SAN technologies. Which leads us to the underlying question: Why does anyone need to combine a NAS and SAN configuration? Part of the answer lies in the simple rationale as to why disparate data communications networks need to integrate. The reason is that those users with Macs need to access the same applications and data as PC users. Further, UNIX workstation users operating within an NFS environment need to access shared information on the PC networks. Users of mainframe applications require a separation of complexity from legacy applications that are increasingly integrated with front-end client/server systems. Ultimately, the Internet prompted uniform access to information both locally and worldwide.

The Need to Integrate

If we accept the premise that storage networking will evolve to some degree like data communications networks, then we have to accept the state of today's technologies as being at the forefront of this evolution. Consequently, elementary and sometimes proprietary and localized solutions give way to integration, allowing applications transparent access to storage resources regardless of the model.

If we view this from a pure user requirements perspective, the evolution of web services and the integration of local systems inside data centers to accommodate this will drive the need to integrate storage networks to a uniform access model. Not that any of the complexities will go away; actually, they will be more complex—just as they were with data communications networks. However, the necessity to consider lower-level access fundamentals, such as block I/O versus file I/O, will dissipate as increasing layers of storage access fold over the technical uniqueness of SAN and NAS architectures.

Web services will demand an integration of I/O workload types by their very make-up. Service that combines transactional synchronous responses will be coupled with secondary and tertiary transactions that respond with a series of asynchronous message-oriented requirements. Each of these will require a set of I/O workloads commensurate with its processing characteristics. However, each will be integrated in its application processing responsibilities. Thus, we may find the future of I/O workloads being driven by web services. Common personal and business applications will be executed by an integrated I/O system with the flexibility to route the appropriate I/O requests to the correct set of data using the correct access mechanism—for example, block, cache, or file.

These are the driving factors to integrate SAN and NAS. The flexibility to handle multiple workload requirements demands that storage networking have multiple access mechanisms. The industry is starting to experience this as NAS solutions begin to integrate both file access and block-level access. This is currently being accomplished through the integration of NAS server configurations with FC disk arrays. This sets the foundation for bilateral access to the data via file access through existing IP network requests and block I/O access through the FC disk array. There are many issues surrounding these early solutions, such as the need to provide extensions to OS and file system functions, application interfaces, and additional levels of standards, that are necessary to get everyone on the same page. However, it's a start.

Future Storage Connectivity

As the SAN/NAS core technologies evolve, they will be affected by additional external changes happening with the microprocessor and networking industries. These changes can be viewed from a perspective external to the server, many of which will be network driven. Other changes will occur from an internal perspective where technology advancements in chip-to-chip communications takes place within the microprocessor system.

iSCSI, LAN/WAN Storage

One limitation of the SAN I/O architecture revolves around distance. Performing a block I/O remotely requires the resources of the NAS solution and the inherent overhead of file I/O processing. If there was a method of extending the server I/O operation remotely, this would allow native I/O operations to take place without the necessity of an alternative network and required special devices, as in FC SANs, or the special server devices associated with NAS. This appears to be a very efficient and cost-effective solution for remotely accessing data in storage arrays.

This also describes an upcoming standard and product solution called iSCSI. The iSCSI solution (*iSCSI* denoting *Internet SCSI*) provides a standard for transmitting SCSI commands through an IP-based network. This would allow servers to send a block I/O request through an existing TCP/IP network and execute the SCSI storage read/write operations on a remote storage array.

The iSCSI configurations require special Network Interface Cards (NICs) that provide the iSCSI command set at the storage array end (as shown in Figure 20-4). This facilitates data and SCSI commands to be encapsulated into an IP packet and transmitted through an existing IP network, thereby bypassing file-level processing protocols and additional server-to-server communications inherent to NAS solutions. On the surface, this solution provides an effective mechanism for disaster recovery operations, data replication, and distribution.

However, this develops an increasing number of issues in implementing and managing an iSCSI configuration. First is the security of sending an unsecured block

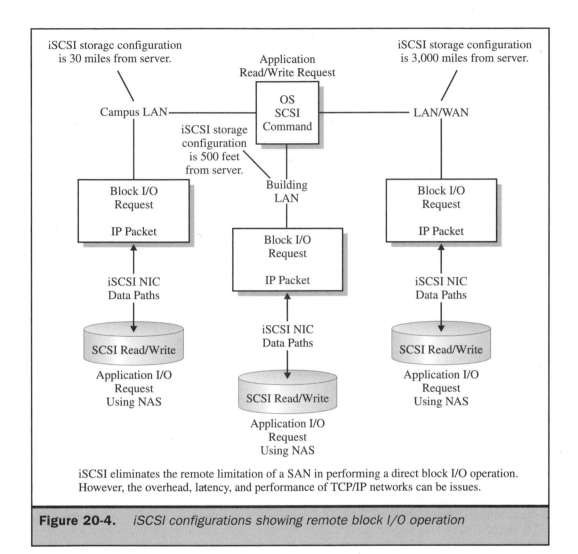

Figure 20-4. *iSCSI configurations showing remote block I/O operation*

I/O across a public network. An associated aspect is the reliability of the IP packet transmission process. Overall, the ability to access data within unsecured environments that can withstand packet transmission errors may be the I/O workload that suits this future technology.

Extending I/O functionality beyond the server has been a goal of system vendors for many years in their struggle to replace the aging bus mechanisms that form the foundation of our current computing platforms. Multiple initiatives suggesting that I/O should be disengaged from the computing elements have coalesced into the industry initiative of InfiniBand. InfiniBand provides a switched fabric environment very similar to the FC SAN switched-fabric environment. However, the InfiniBand standard encompasses all I/O from the processor into the external connectivity of networks and storage devices. InfiniBand on the surface can be viewed as a replacement for the aging PCI bus technologies (see Chapter 7). However, due to its scalable I/O infrastructure, it provides a shift in computing fundamentals by providing a switched-fabric architecture that allows devices to communicate with processor nodes with increased bandwidth, reduced latency, and throughput.

InfiniBand, the Universal Bus

InfiniBand is an I/O standard developed by seven of the computer industry's key players: IBM, Compaq, HP, Sun Microsystems, Microsoft, Intel, and Dell. InfiniBand replaces traditional PCI bus technology with a switched fabric (think network), which allows peripherals (such as storage and client/data networks) to communicate within a network (think switched fabric) of servers. It also allows InfiniBand-enabled servers to utilize the same fabrics (network) to communicate amongst themselves.

InfiniBand is poised to cause a fundamental change to the data center, as we know it. As its scalable I/O infrastructure is integrated, the total cost of ownership (TOC) models and metrics will change, as will how applications are deployed and managed. IT departments, especially IT management, must understand this infrastructure if they hope to leverage intelligent adoption strategies. InfiniBand vendors, on the other hand, must move toward systems solutions in order to overcome the initial wave of anxiety and reduce the complexities of integration and adoption.

As illustrated in Figure 20-5, the I/O fabric is connected from the server through a Host Channel Adapter (HCA), while connections to peripherals move through a Target Channel Adapter (TCA). These components communicate through a switch that routes to all the nodes that make up the fabric. In addition, the I/O fabric enhances communication within the fabric by using remote direct memory access (RDMA) methods to facilitate I/O applications operations. InfiniBand links are serial, segmented into 16 logical lanes of traffic. Given this architecture, the bandwidth for each link eclipses all other data transports now available.

Why is InfiniBand important? The traditional deployment of servers has come through vertical implementation. In most cases, expanding an existing application requires the installation of a new server. Each time this happens, total overhead and the latency needed to support the application increases. Left unchecked, the operating system services and network overhead required to support the additional servers can consume as much or more processing power than the application. Scalability of the application ultimately becomes non-linear as the number of servers increases.

From an I/O standpoint, the vertical deployment of servers poses additional problems. As application data grows, so must the required I/O bandwidth and paths needed to get to the data. If the server cannot provide either of these, the application suffers from having to wait on data to be processed. This same phenomenon happens when users are added to the application, or there is an increase in the users accessing

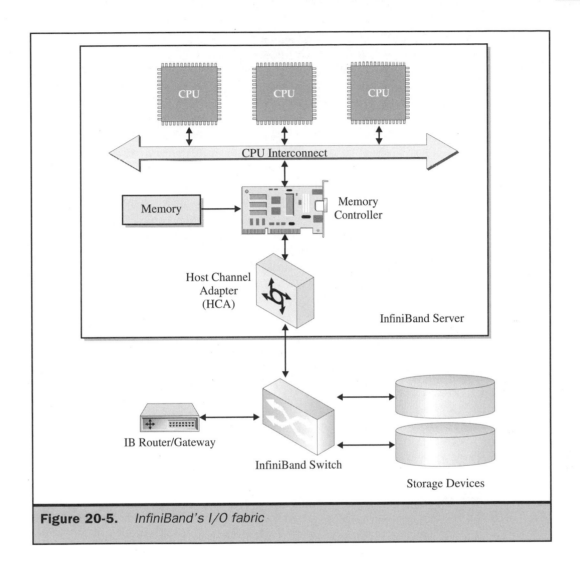

Figure 20-5. *InfiniBand's I/O fabric*

the application, as often happens with Internet applications. The required bandwidth and paths must be in place, otherwise the application suffers by having to wait on large queues of user requests.

These conditions are further exacerbated by the inefficient usage of resources—in both hardware and software—needed to provide an adequate configuration for supporting the workload. All of this places additional burdens on data-center personnel, who must handle the complexity of installation, maintenance, system upgrades, and workload management.

What we have achieved is a "gridlock" effect. Unfortunately, planning and implementing configurations for new applications is even more daunting.

However, InfiniBand's potential value can be significant. InfiniBand architecture addresses each of the challenges noted earlier. Scalability enhancements, in terms of link speeds, switched peripheral connectivity, and server-to-server connections, provide a significant boost to the scalability of an application. If we consider the prioritization and management within link technologies driven by fabric software, InfiniBand configurations can process multiple workloads within the same configuration, thereby reducing the vertical implementation required by traditional server technology.

Once vertical implementation has been addressed, a new model for TCO within the data center emerges. This is accomplished by utilizing two key characteristics of InfiniBand technology. First, InfiniBand servers only require a CPU(s), memory, and related interconnects, while using HCAs for outside communication. This reduces an InfiniBand server to a "Blade" computer (a computer the size of a Plug and Play board-level component). Smaller servers will significantly reduce required space, power consumption, and installation complexities. Secondly, InfiniBand configurations centralize the processing of applications and provide for more dynamic operations within the fabric. Management of applications and related resources is centralized, which means software and resources can be shared and used more efficiently as workloads demand.

What will the price be? In realizing an InfiniBand infrastructure within the Data Center, the following considerations should be noted. InfiniBand will require a learning curve—there's no way around this. InfiniBand configurations affect all major components within the Data Center. This is especially true in regards to storage and networking components. Product offerings must support systems adoption, distribution, installation, and support. Software, as usual, will be the significant detractor. Server OS integration and services and application optimization and compatibility are a must.

Inside the Box

This section describes the requirements for HyperTransport and Rapid I/O. There are two in-the-box initiatives, one of which connects processor modules, thus providing the ability to interconnect multiple CPU configurations. The complementary initiative is to provide a faster, more efficient interconnect between the CPU components within the constructs of the board.

Rapid I/O

Rapid I/O is an industry initiative that in some ways provides an alternative to the InfiniBand standard, moving the universal bus concept down to the microprocessor level. It provides a serial connectivity protocol and physical link standard in connecting processor board-level components. As shown in Figure 20-6, Rapid I/O provides an alternative to PCI or other bus-connectivity solutions that interconnect components through a Rapid I/O switching mechanism.

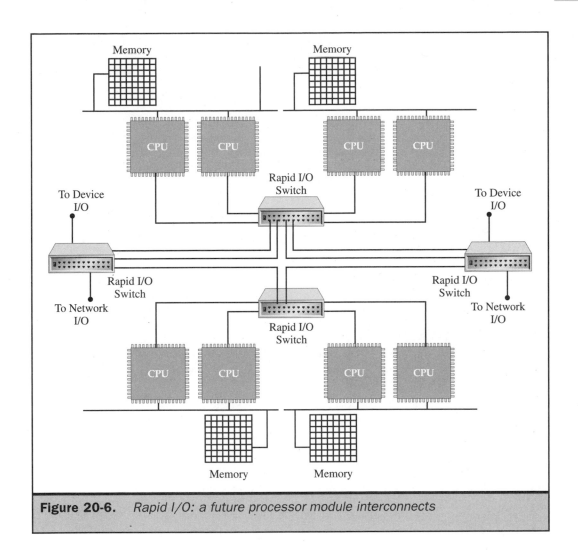

Figure 20-6.   *Rapid I/O: a future processor module interconnects*

Rapid I/O is used to facilitate connectivity of clustered systems, multifunction embedded systems, and general-purpose systems that must communicate within close proximity of each other (for instance, within the system chassis). The standard facilitates the connection of an extensive set of internal and external components. However, Rapid I/O remains one of the few future technologies that takes into consideration legacy components by providing parallel technologies that offer compatibility for those components which require multipin physical connections.

HyperTransport

Providing a high-speed interconnect between components within the processor module has long been a goal of microprocessor designers. The usual bus connections have been eclipsed by new serial connections that form a switched environment. HyperTransport is a vendor-sponsored initiative that proposes a standard set of specifications when building an internal switched bus to increase I/O flexibility and performance. Staging and moving data in and out of CPU processing units is just as important as the performance of external I/O.

The HyperTransport standard defines an I/O protocol that facilitates a scalable interconnect between CPU, memory, and I/O devices. As a switching protocol, the architecture is defined within a layered network approach based to some degree on the OSI network model. Consequently, there are five distinct layers of processing that direct how internal components communicate.

Figure 20-7 depicts an example of the deployment of HyperTransport architecture. In this type of configuration, an I/O switch handles multiple data streams and interconnections between CPUs and memory. The configuration is extended to support external bus and network connections such as InfiniBand, PCI, and Gbe Ethernet. This enables processing and memory components to have scalability and bandwidth flexibility similar to switched network environments like InfiniBand and FC SANs.

Storage Integration

Is it necessary to have a SAN and NAS model? In the near term, both storage networking models will be with us. As we continue to support the present application mix of OLTP- and batch-type workloads, it's necessary to provide an optimized access method. This will continue to drive the segregation of data between file and block level access and require increased duplication and overhead. The results will be a continuation of storage demand and growth, albeit an inflated use of resources.

The future of SAN/NAS integration will be driven by the increased need to utilize existing data for multiple purposes or applications. The slowing of duplication requirements is a critical requirement for any integrated front-end storage access method. As some applications require file access from remote locations, other local applications will require read/write access on a fundamental block I/O level. The ability to provide these access levels through a combined storage network utilizing a file or block access will be the next storage system.

What is missing today are the components to make that happen. Figure 20-8 shows a future configuration where an integrated file system serves as both file- and block-level access to a common storage network. Future components that will facilitate this solution will be a shared file system with storage network coherency, increased state-aware disk devices, and real-time fault resiliency in recovery fabrics. The storage network components will communicate with storage access appliances that serve

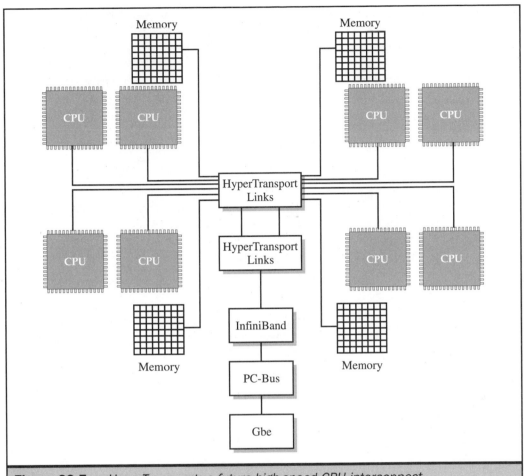

Figure 20-7.   *HyperTransport: a future high-speed CPU interconnect*

applications with either block or file access. Applications will log in and register with the storage network regarding their preferences for recovery, access, and security.

In looking toward the future, use caution when developing storage networking configurations. The useful life of storage networking technologies has only been a year and a half in the short end and three years in the long term. The point must be made

that we remain at the forefront of storage innovations that will be increasingly vulnerable to both changes in microprocessor technologies and the evolving universe of web services.

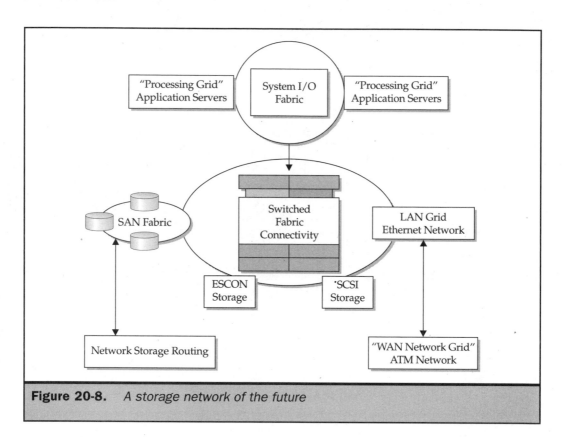

Figure 20-8. *A storage network of the future*

The
Complete
Reference

Storage
Networks

Part VI

Management—Keeping It Running

The Complete Reference

Storage Networks

Chapter 21

Planning Business Continuity

Computer systems depend largely on their keepers, whether they be embedded systems, the latest blade servers, or the largest super computer. Computer operators and systems programmers have largely given way to increased areas of specialization for administration, maintenance, and servicing. Although many mundane tasks have been automated, more complex configurations of distributed systems have increased the need for system-oriented personnel to monitor and keep the servers running. This is because, no matter how sophisticated they become, computer systems remain electronically controlled components, susceptible to both human and mechanical error.

The basis for these activities revolves around the accepted disciplines of managing systems. These are known as the five systems management disciplines and can be applied to any macro system in operation. These disciplines include the following:

- **Performance Management** The activities associated with the monitoring, tuning, and analysis of a computer system's (or subsystem's) performance.

- **Capacity Management** Analysis activities that drive the planning, design, and implementation of computer resources necessary to maintain established service levels.

- **Configuration Management** Activities that surround the design and implementation of a computer system; this includes ongoing support of system enhancements and upgrades.

- **Change Management** Driven by performance and configuration management activities, these practices monitor and supervise changes that occur to computer systems.

- **Problem Management** Activities that track, analyze, identify, and resolve system problems.

Before you object to the absence of applications management, security management, network management, web management, and others, I should first explain how these topics relate to the subject. The basic disciplines of systems management, as discussed previously, can be applied to any logical definition of a system. Consequently, targeting business applications for management can, and should, have the same disciplines applied to it—in other words, performance, capacity, change, configuration, and problem. By any other name, they usually do. However, particular topics, such as security, add a different dimension to management practices given they are so integrated with the supporting infrastructure. Security, which will be discussed in Chapter 25, should be regarded as a supporting system, like backup and recovery, or database administration. Even here, foundation disciplines can, and should, be applied.

As discussed in Chapter 1, the difference between enterprise applications and programs and utilities that support the systems' infrastructures cannot be overlooked. They form synergistic relationships between the productive and the necessary. Applications drive the business and form the primary components for workloads. However, the performance of computer systems depends on the effective interaction between productive work and overhead. Although many systems programs and utilities are referred to as applications themselves, they often offer productivity enhancements to the systems management activities and therefore to the effectiveness of the IT staff. However, they do nothing for the bottom line. In analyzing basic systems management disciplines, its important to remember that they do not exist purely on their own. Without the bottom line application of computing for some productive processes, the activities that monitor, track, and analyze computer systems would be non-existent.

Although we often consider the management of business applications to be the pinnacle of systems management, there are many other scientific, academic, and government endeavors that require activities just as stringent as general business computing. Consequently, the five systems management disciplines are not aligned to any vertical market or work orientation.

Computing continues to be a general-purpose discipline where applied technology and operational practices migrate within the society of computer professionals who perform management operations. Practices that worked well in scientific areas have migrated into business over time, with both government and military agencies using unique database management, just to name two.

The point is that computer system management is an iterative process and continues to evolve through cross-pollination with different application bases, such as storage networking. Given that storage networking is a different storage model, however, existing management practices, though relevant, need to be molded to support a new infrastructure, which is what storage networking creates, a new application of storage.

In evaluating management of storage networking, we must apply the five disciplines. Figure 21-1 shows how these trans-technology practices are applied to the ever-increasing diversity within the data center further separating the systems into specialized practices. However, as Figure 21-1 also points out, storage networking draws heavily from data center practices and interfaces with each in order to be an effective infrastructure.

Planning computer systems to meet business continuity requirements has been one of the most tedious jobs within Information Technology. In the past 30 odd years of established data centers, business continuity responsibilities were ill-funded exercises in theoretical computer systems planning. However, as the world's socio-economic conditions began immersing computer systems within business operations, whether

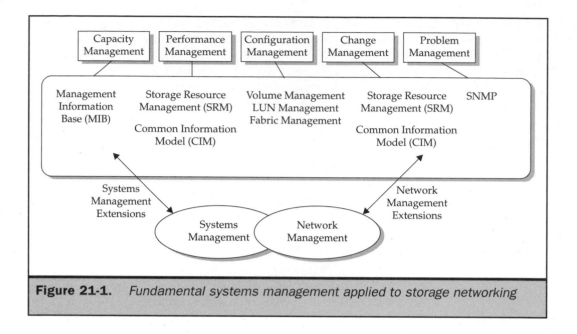

Figure 21-1.   *Fundamental systems management applied to storage networking*

for the sake of competitive positioning or national defense, the discipline of disaster recovery became a more imperative science.

Computer storage has always been the linchpin of any recovery scenario. From legacy systems to existing blade level embedded servers, all are linked to the vital circulation of data. Without it, the computer infrastructures they create would be worthless. Historically, the storage component was considered part and parcel to the holistic system that supported the evolving set of automation we have grown to depend on. Only recently has this link been recast into an infrastructure of its own. Storage networking in its inherent value has caused many to rethink their data center continuity plans, change their processes, and modify and enhance their solutions according to this new storage paradigm.

Defining the Environment (Putting Storage in Context)

The objective of business continuity is to facilitate uninterrupted business support despite the occurrence of problems. This depends on the problem, of course—it could be a small problem only effecting a single user application through an operative disk drive, or a complete system failure where the outage is caused by the entire SAN or NAS configuration being down. However, it could also be a site disaster affecting the entire data center. Certainly, the categorization of the problem is important, but the plans in place should be able to provide a road map, resources, and ability to hopefully recover from any incident.

Storage has traditionally played a key role in any recovery scenario. Without the data, the applications are useless. Consequently, most recovery scenarios center on making the data available as quickly as possible so business applications can continue the company's operations. Without stating the obvious, this requires the ability to replicate data throughout an infrastructure that enables everything from a micro recovery to a macro disaster site deployment.

Traditionally, with storage being tied directly to the server, this rendered storage problems and outages as associated problem instances—meaning they were viewed as a server outage and thus were combined with all the problems and outages associated with a server that's down or inoperative. As storage networking configurations create their own infrastructures, supporting more independent external components, they become active participants in the management disciplines. This redefines the data center environment and must be reflected in the continuity planning.

Figure 21-2 reflects the change from associated server/storage components to separate and discrete server, network, and storage components. This describes a data center that has divided its processing environment into three discrete infrastructures: servers, networks, and storage. Although many data centers have evolved into viewing and managing their environment this way, the separation of responsibility by operating environment (for example, UNIX, Windows, MVS, zOS, and Linux) must contend with the integration effects of heterogeneous storage networks.

Categorizing Interruptions in Service

The plans that are designed and implemented all depend on the magnitude of the problem incident. Therefore, it's important to distinguish and categorize the types of storage problems you are likely to encounter as well as larger problems that affect an entire infrastructure. This analysis provides a realistic view of the amount of insurance (redundancy, failover, and recovery methods) you need.

The interruptions in service that most commonly reflect outages can easily be lumped into two distinct categories: hardware failures and software problems. Hardware failures can be categorized through the inventory of storage networking devices and subcomponents, as well as the subsequent development of a matrix that reflects the causal relationship to each. Software problems can be organized the same way, although the causal relationships may assume complexities that are unnecessary to the task at hand. Because of this, it's best to be reasonable about what the system can and can't do when developing this list.

An enhancement to existing systems information will be to develop a matrix for SAN hardware components. Among necessary items such as component, name, vendor, serial number, and model, this type of list provides an excellent location to indicate a priority designation on the component in case of failure. Given our Plug-and-Play component-driven world, most problem resolutions fall into the category of a field

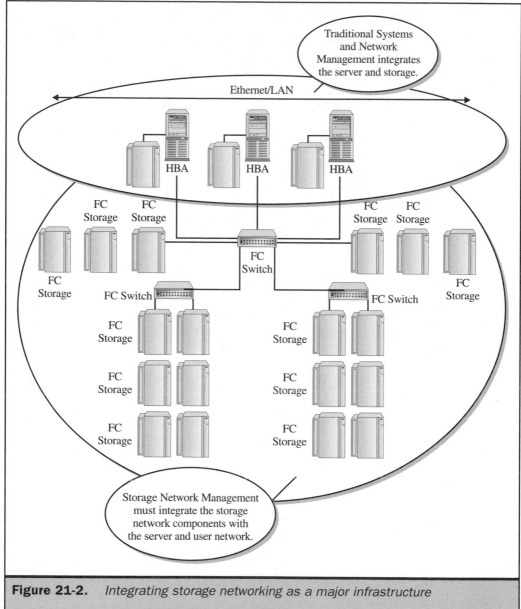

Ethernet/LAN

Traditional Systems and Network Management integrates the server and storage.

HBA   HBA   HBA

FC Storage   FC Storage   FC Storage   FC Storage

FC Storage

FC Switch

FC Switch   FC Switch

FC Storage   FC Storage

FC Storage   FC Storage

FC Storage

FC Storage   FC Storage

FC Storage   FC Storage

Storage Network Management must integrate the storage network components with the server and user network.

Figure 21-2.   *Integrating storage networking as a major infrastructure*

replaceable unit (FRU), which provides an excellent beginning point to the categorization of the list. The value of having readily accessible and up-to-date SAN hardware information will enhance all management activities associated with the SAN hardware.

A corresponding matrix for SAN software configurations can be just as important. The relationship between switch operating system releases, node firmware, and server OS releases is necessary for problem identification and resolution. Keep in mind the SAN and NAS will place the overall solution in a multivendor scenario. The more information you have at hand, the better you can facilitate the problem resolution activities. Like the hardware matrix, the software list and categorization can articulate a level of priority and failure relationship to software elements as well as affected hardware components.

Work from the Top Down

Laying the groundwork for business continuity planning in this manner allows you to view the enterprise in a macro level. This enables the identification of a set of requirements to determine how a storage networking infrastructure fits into the data-center environment. This guides the level of planning that needs to occur at the micro level of storage continuity as you deal with storage recovery and, more specifically, the details surrounding storage networking.

If we refer to Figure 21-1, the ability to analyze the macro level is fairly simple. For example, go through the failure points from an externalization view first. This can be done, as shown in Figure 21-2, by performing a "what if" scenario on potential network outages. If the lease lines into the NAS servers go down, what applications go offline? Asking further questions qualifies the configuration for potential continuity insurance. For example, is the affected application or application service level compromised? If so, what is the recovery scenario?

In this manner, by working through the external scenarios, you can begin to develop a picture of potential fault points, their effect, and the basis for continuity insurance. In our example, with the leased lines being down, connecting any or all the remote offices would compromise their service level. Therefore, a level of recovery can be planned as insurance from this type of incident.

Participation

Planning and design of business continuity processes, resources, and environments require the participation of a diverse set of individuals. Although it's imperative to have the business users present, this may not always be the case. However, it should be the case that at the very least your colleagues in the data center participate, support, and even drive the plans and processes you develop. After all, the storage infrastructure is a key requirement for the continuation of automated business processes.

Without the participation and input from the business users you support, the plans you develop are considered "out-of-context." While that should not end your continuity planning, it puts the judgment of business application value and the assignment of recovery and redundant resources in making the storage infrastructure available totally within the IT organization. The out-of-context planning usually gets attention when the cost of business continuity is presented to the company.

The following includes additional detail and best practices when planning within your IT organization or within the user community:

- **Planning out of context**   This provides a level of difficulty in determining the financial and operational impact placed on application outages, which may be accomplished through effective planning sessions with application designers and development organizations. It's best, as stated previously, to provide a robust continuity plan that encompasses all the production processing and related data, and then present this to company management with the associated cost. This will quickly lead to participation of the end users who ultimately have to bear the burden of these costs.

- **Planning within context**   Planning continuity with the participation of the end users presents a much more realistic view of recovery and redundant requirements. Aside from a formalized project for business continuity, this should be integrated into existing capacity planning activities. Aside from formalized meetings, this offers a less intrusive method of gaining the information. This can be accomplished through activities such as worksheet-based surveys to end users that provide a macro view of the business impact and service level requirements.

- **Planning with our colleagues**   At a minimum, the participation of your colleagues within the data center is imperative. As pointed out in dealing with out-of-context planning, the involvement of application design and development management should be involved to provide additional analysis on the value of the data and application service levels.

The Role of Storage Networking in Business Continuity

Storage networking, in changing the reality of storage deployment and access, shifts the traditional views of business continuity planning. Data becomes centralized, consolidated, and maintained within its own infrastructure (for instance, SAN and NAS configurations), and as a result, it has also become more distributed within remote areas of the company. Fundamentally, the change in technology requires different tools or at least a modification of traditional tools such as backup/recovery software, data replication, and archival tools and products. Regardless of these changes, many of the fundamental storage planning activities should continue to be applied to storage networking configurations.

The following is an example of the types of information that should be gathered in evaluating the business continuity planning requirements.

- **Data ownership**   Data ownership continues to be more of a political question than a pragmatic one. However, finding the owner of the application data can provide the keys to the value, integrity, and necessity of it.

- **Application usage**   Finding what programs access the data can provide the means to uncovering data that may be overlooked in continuity implementations. For example, there is always that one file that only gets accessed once a month by the inventory control application—*if* it's online. Consequently, not including this file in the regular backups, disaster recovery copies, or archival process results in an unhappy recovery experience.

- **Data utilization**   This exercise provides a similar value to the application analysis. Not only does this uncover data that has not been accessed in months, quarters, or even years, it also provides a side benefit of increased storage utilization through the identification of unused data that can be archived to tape.

- **End users**   Relating the data to an end-user department, division, or customer will also put another important piece of the continuity puzzle into perspective. Although this may seem clerical and administratively oriented, the proper placement of data within the complex structure of a SAN or the remote environment of a NAS are important to physical determinations of continuity configurations.

- **Current infrastructure**   Understanding the current storage infrastructure, and applying the preceding bullets, provides a road map into what areas are most at risk. In terms of SAN and NAS, it will provide valuable insight into the placement of data from a NAS to a SAN and vice versa.

How Much Insurance Do You Need?

At some point, usually after you inventory what you have, estimate your requirements for continuity activities and resources. This exercise aids in assigning a value to the modifications in the current storage configuration installed, the additional redundant configurations you need, and other additional resources set for implementation in the event of trouble.

Level of Redundancy

How much of the production configuration needs to be replicated within what time period will be evident from your continuity analysis. In estimating the level of redundancy, it is necessary to understand the relationship to the minimum data capacity required, the number of users, and the level of access. For example, if you plan for full redundancy, then the data capacity, number of users, and access are simply duplicated in an adjacent configuration. However, this is rarely afforded given the cost, and therefore requires a level of adjustment that takes into account the type of outage, and the level of business operation required for a particular time period.

For example, for unscheduled outages, the level of operation must be maintained for deposit transactions, with the related data available. However, the other transactions may be down for a period of no more than 15 minutes for a single processing cycle.

Therefore, configurations have to reflect a level of redundancy to maintain the deposit suspense transactional data while the other transaction data, customer service, and portfolio services should have fault tolerant systems with a mean time to repair of 15 minutes per 12 hours.

Level of Requirements—How Much It Will Cost

In calculating these requirements, you must not only account for new configurations (there to meet necessary service levels), but also those modifications—reflected in existing production configurations—that accommodate redundant systems. In terms of NAS, this may be the addition of a redundant NAS device that mirrors the data. Within the more complex SAN configurations, requirements include: upgrades to switches to add expansion ports, E_Ports, software to enable interswitch linking, trunking, and redundant switch configuration and related devices.

Level of Associated Requirement— How Much It Will Really Cost

One of the most challenging activities within this exercise is the inclusion of additional hardware and software components you didn't think about initially in contemplating storage configurations. These expenses include additional software licenses, upgrades to existing software, and the cost of new devices such as adapters and redundant servers.

Storage Design and Implementation of the Business Continuity Plan

As you develop a new plan for the business continuity of storage networks, or modify an existing plan, there are key areas to consider that will enable the network to continue operating in a variety of circumstances. Among these are the integration of business continuity requirements into capacity planning disciplines, the effective tracking of storage system and device outages, and a realistic evaluation of sustained outage assessment.

On the technical side, the ability to effectively monitor performance and capacity of existing configurations, though challenging, is imperative (see Chapters 22 and 23). This includes an inventory and evaluation of the existing capabilities of storage functions (for example, RAID level support, environmental limitations, and remote settings).

SAN

The main design considerations for the SAN are the configuration of core switching and estimates regarding new redundant switches for recovery processing. Within this category are the number of expansion ports, the availability of dynamic ports and paths, and port utilization estimates. Secondary to the core switch is the storage strategy to facilitate replication of recovery data, the time and state requirements of replicated data, and the synchronous (or asynchronous) nature of this process. Thirdly, is the ability of the reconfigured infrastructure to handle the adjusted I/O workload.

It should be noted that many additional items are required to develop, design, test, and implement a full business continuity plan for SAN. These include server sizing, recovery site preparation, application portability, and required application software and subsystems, such as compatible file systems and database systems. Although outside the scope of this book, these items should be integrated into a well-designed plan and not overlooked.

NAS

NAS will be the most deceptive in preparing for business continuity planning. Given its ease of installation and maintenance, it's possible to overlook its potential problems. Design considerations should center on the requirements for data redundancy, and result in configuration to mirror production data either synchronously or asynchronously. This requires a NAS-to-NAS device configuration and should be driven by the requirements for complementary or compatible devices.

In addition, it will be necessary to provide redundant capacities and daily backup protections for respective devices. Over and above these are fundamental considerations to ensure that capacities are allocated so that as a failover scenario is implemented, the realities of the continuity plan workload can be handled.

Remote vs. Local

Redundant configurations that are local must adhere to cabling limitations. Remote configurations must maintain a strict level of monitoring to ensure the data maintains the prescribed level of consistency. Local redundancy costs can be much less than remote—however, full failover clustering systems can move costs well into the range of remote disaster recovery services.

Backup vs. Disaster

It is important to understand whether the configuration will support a local system or unit outage, or have to be part of an entire disaster recovery scenario. This simple characterization of the business continuity solution will result in a configuration direction focused on the appropriate support.

Expertise and Configuration Data

Trying to not overlook necessary components in assembling an alternative storage configuration to support a business continuity solution is a constant worry. However, the successful operation of disaster recovery storage configuration may never see production processing and hopefully never be used in a disaster scenario. Even so, these are configurations that certainly should be tested. A successfully tested configuration should provide the required information of configuration settings, files, and addressing schemes including storage arrays, switch ports, LUN assignments, and zonings used.

Many components of the backup storage infrastructure may have to be re-configured back into a production environment or used in an alternative configuration. If this is the case, or might be the case, be sure you document the configuration information for later access. It's best to rely on procedures and current information than ad hoc expertise to reinvent the backup configuration during each disaster recovery test.

Chapter 22

Managing Availability

Availability is driven by capacity and performance. Without consideration for matching the capacity of the storage size and configuration to the workload, availability becomes a guessing game. Consequently, there must be a sound basis for the existing storage capacities and configurations. However, taking reality into consideration, using the most overlooked work axiom—*do it right the first time*—the existence of a sound capacity plan for an initial configuration may not be the case. On the other hand, storage networking, SAN more than NAS, is a new solution and a learning curve always begins with mistakes. Therefore, this chapter begins with the assumption that mistakes have already happened, can easily happen, and in the best case, can be avoided.

The premise of availability for storage networks is the application of the five systems management disciplines in an iterative process. These will be discussed as they occur in a real-time continuum, but we'll also view them in a cyclic manner. The following illustration offers a peek into the activities that make up the cycle. As we can see, a capacity model and implementation may set the basis for the start of the cycle, but may not have much to do with the reality of daily data-center operations. Performance management is influenced by both configuration and change activities, and given its investigative characteristics, forms a logical beginning to availability.

The performance management activities are supported by external events that are tracked through problem and application management systems. All of these activities develop a synergistic relationship that cycles back to influence the capacity model. So you see, it is, and continues to be, an iterative process in providing available systems.

This chapter discusses these interrelationships as they are related to the SAN and NAS environments. By applying activities and concepts from systems and network management practices, the availability of storage networks characterizes their fundamental difference compared to existing direct-attached storage models. In addition, these discussions begin to demonstrate the immaturity and challenges still evident within this area of storage infrastructures. Focusing on both fundamentals of systems, and storage management, the scope of these discussions illuminate key issues and offer insight into providing availability in storage networking environments.

Availability Metrics

Providing a measurement of services within the storage network requires some type of metric. The most encompassing is the service level. Service levels exist on several levels. There are specific agreements with end users that define the level of service the IT department provides. There are internal service levels that are managed to provide a working measurement of systems and networking performance. Indeed, working with existing service levels for storage, if they exist, may be either too specific or fail to have sufficient depth to cover performance beyond pure capacity measurements. The key is the establishment of meaningful measurements for the SAN infrastructure that encompasses both storage systems and network specifications.

Establishing service levels for storage network configurations requires the integration of dependent system functions, related network activities, and specific storage elements as they come together to form the storage network infrastructure. First and foremost in the development of these metrics is the association of the workloads. A discussion of estimating workload I/Os can be found in Chapter 17. This is an important exercise because it forces discipline regarding establishing the user's side of the equation and assists in integrating storage configuration service levels into supported applications.

As discussed, two forms of service levels should be developed: an external articulation of services to the supporting business units and end users, and an internal service level that supports both the data center infrastructure and your application development colleagues (DBAs, other systems administrators, and business continuity teams). The external service to the business units is explained in the following section.

External Service Level for Storage Networks

The following can provide a data availability framework for working with external service levels.

Data Availability

This component defines which data is referred to with the service and when it will be available. In addition will be a understanding as to when the data will be unavailable. All data becomes unavailable at some point because of the need to back up files and volumes periodically, and because of the occasional system upgrade that makes all data unavailable while hardware, operating system, or application software is upgraded. These are typical of general service levels and should be included within those commitments. For storage service levels, however, the data center should note that particular availability requirements will be subject to additional or similar instances where the hardware, switch OS, or a management application will be upgraded. These may require the user data to be unavailable during those times.

Data availability is extremely important to the data center. The ability of meeting external service levels will center upon IT activities to define the service levels along with supporting the service levels.

- **Uptime** This metric is usually expressed as a percentage of the data availability period that the data center has committed to. This is driven by the need to keep data available for particular applications, user transactions, or general-purpose access (as with network file systems), and reflects the sensitivity of the business application to the company's operations. Examples are expressed in terms of 99.999, the five nines to distinguish that the data is committed to be available for that percentage of the overall time period it has been committed to. In other words, if an OLTP application requires a 99.999 uptime during the transaction period of 6 A.M. to 6 P.M. PST to support the operations of both coasts, then the percentage is applied to that 12-hour period. Therefore, in this example, the OLTP application requires the data be available 719.9928 minutes of that 12-hour (720 minutes) time period—effectively rendering this a 100-percent uptime for the data.

- **Scheduled Downtime** This metric defines the known time required to perform periodic maintenance to the data. Knowing this up front provides additional credibility to the storage infrastructure and reflects the time the data is unavailable to end users and applications. The important distinction is that the same data used in the transaction system very likely will be the same data that is accessed in batch mode later that night. Although transparent to the end users, this can be critically important to internal service levels.

Note *It's important to note the distinction between data availability uptime and response time. The main purpose of the storage infrastructure is to keep the data available for the required applications. Given that actual application response time is made up of a series of components that include the operating system, database, and network, the ability to provide metrics beyond the availability of users is beyond the storage infrastructure's scope. However, the commitment to I/O performance must be reflected in the internal service levels leveraged as a component of the overall response time.*

Data Services

This component of the service level defines the services that the storage administration offers.

Although the services listed next are traditionally accepted services of the data center, the storage infrastructure will accept increasing responsibility in meeting service levels surrounding these items.

- **Backup Service** Operations to copy specific sets or groups of data for recovery purposes due to data corruption or service interruptions.

- **Recovery Service**   The corresponding recovery operation that restores data compromised due to data corruption or service interruption.

- **Replication Services**   Services provided by the storage infrastructure that send copies of user data to other processing infrastructures throughout a company. Generally used to copy data to remote offices for local processing requirements.

- **Archival Services**   Services providing periodic copies of data for necessary legal, local policy, or governmental archival purposes. Used in conjunction with the backup service, they provide a duality of service.

Disaster Recovery Commitments

As part of the business continuity plan, these services and service levels offer data availability during the execution of the disaster plan.

Consider the key storage items listed next when developing service levels for business continuity and disaster recovery plans.

- **Data Recoverability Matrix**   It's unlikely that all data will be covered under a disaster site recovery plan. Therefore, a matrix, list, or report should be available regarding what data is available at any point in time prior to executing the disaster site recovery plan. The service levels and services here are to some degree a subset of services available during normal operations.

- **Data Uptime**   The same metric as the normal operating data uptime percentage and predefined processing time period.

- **Data Scheduled DownTime**   The same metric as the normal operating percentage, but using a predefined processing time period.

- **Restoration of Services**   A new level of service driven by the schedule for total restoration of services for a disaster site recovery plan.

User Non-Aggression Pact

It is always helpful to reach an agreement with a user community that accounts for the unexpected. This allows both parties to agree that unexpected circumstances do happen and should they occur, they should be resolved with mutual understanding and changes in the existing plan. This can be critical given the volatility of SAN installations and NAS data-volume requirements.

The following are a few of the unexpected circumstances that are worth discussing with end-user clients. These can form the basis for a non-aggression pact that will benefit both parties in managing to the agreed upon service levels.

- **Unexpected Requirements**   The most common set of unexpected circumstances is the unforeseen application that requires support but which hasn't been planned for. In terms of affecting the SAN installation, this can be costly as well as disruptive, given the scope of the new application storage requirements. Within the NAS environment, this is one of the strengths NAS brings to the data center. If the requirements can be handled through file access and NAS performance and capacities, then the NAS solution can be used effectively during these circumstances.

■ **Unforeseen Technology Enhancements** This is the most common circumstance when the initial SAN design proves insufficient to handle the workload. The requirement to retrofit the SAN configuration with enhanced components means additional cost and disruption. This can at least be addressed with the understanding that new technology installations are available.

■ **Mid-term Corrections** It is likely that any enterprise storage installation will experience either one or both of the preceding conditions. Consequently, it is extremely important to build into the user agreements an ability to provide mid-term corrections that are an evaluation of the current services and corrections.

Internal Service Levels for Storage Networks

Within the storage infrastructures, and especially the storage networking areas, the support is both to end users as well as other individuals in the data center. Therefore, there will be an internal set of service levels that support the other infrastructures within the data center. These at a macro level are the systems' organizations, of which storage may be a component, the support of systems administrators, and from which web masters, systems programmers, and system-level database administrators (DBAs) will be critical. On the applications side, storage remains an integral part of applications programmers, analysts, and maintenance programmers' requirements. Certainly, we can't forget the network administrators, help desk, and network maintenance people.

The following is a more detailed discussion on best practices for negotiating and determining service levels for internal IT co-workers and management.

■ **Storage Capacity** The most common requirement for the data center is the raw storage capacity necessary for applications, support processing, and database support, just to mention a few. A service level here will prove very productive in staying ahead of user requirements and system upgrades that require additional raw storage capacity. This is critical with SAN and NAS configurations, given that each has attributes that make upgrades more support-intensive. With the manipulation of switch configurations, zoning, and LUN management upgrades, storage capacity in the SAN environment is not a "snap on" activity. Although NAS provides a much easier way of increasing storage, the bundling of the storage device may provide more storage than required and external network performance effects may be more intense and challenging than they first appear.

■ **Data Availability** This service level is similar to the end-user service level, and in many ways forms the foundation for the application service level with the same end user. Over and above the commitments for production data, which should be addressed with the supporting applications personnel, is the need for data to be available for testing, quality assurance functions, and code development.

■ **Data Services** Again, similar to the end-user services specified in the external functions, are the services provided to assure backup/recovery and data archiving. These services include operating system copies, code archives, and backups for network configuration data to name a few. Relating these to the SAN infrastructure initiates an increase in the complexities of recovery operations. Given these installations are new and require additional procedural recovery operations to be developed, a learning curve is expected.

■ **Storage Reporting** Key to internal constituencies, this provides the basis for monitoring data usage and activity within the storage network configurations. It sets the stage for effective housekeeping activities by establishing either new or preexisting quotas, archival policies, and ownership tracking. In addition to these administrative tasks, it establishes a tracking mechanism to help fine-tune the storage configuration. This is key to the SAN environment where volume allocation, physical data placement, and systems/application access are controlled through the storage support personnel and your configuration.

Implementing the Plan

Now comes the fun part: the implementation of the storage network configuration. It's time to develop or redevelop the SAN or NAS configurations to suit your particular service levels. The configuration options, driven by service levels and both internal and external requirements, demand a particular level of availability. These are generally categorized as on-demand availability, highly available systems, or fault-tolerant systems. In the end, sensitivity to the end user is an external call and end users obviously have final say in determining their value. These categories are discussed next.

■ **On-Demand Availability** These systems support 80 to 95 percent availability for defined processing periods. They generally support transactional systems that do not significantly impact the daily operations of the company if they are down for a reasonable time. Most of these systems are data warehouse systems that are prone to outages given the level of data and their reliance on background processing. Others are those that provide purely informational services to internal users of a company, such as intranet systems, inventory, and educational systems. Figure 22-1 shows a typical cascading configuration supporting a data warehouse.

■ **Highly Available** These systems require 99.999 percent uptime, and given the right resources they can achieve this. They are characterized by applications that have a significant impact on the company's business if they are down. This includes systems such as OLTP financial and banking applications (for obvious reasons), retail and point-of-sale transactional systems, and customer relationship systems that allow customers to place orders, as illustrated in Figure 22-2.

- **Fault Tolerant** These systems cannot afford any downtime and must be available 24/7. This includes transportation systems such as those supporting air, emergency, mass transit, medical, and emergency 911 systems. For obvious reasons, these need to be supported by fully redundant systems that can provide full failover capability so operations remain uninterrupted. Figure 22-3 depicts a redundancy mesh SAN configuration supporting an emergency medical response application.

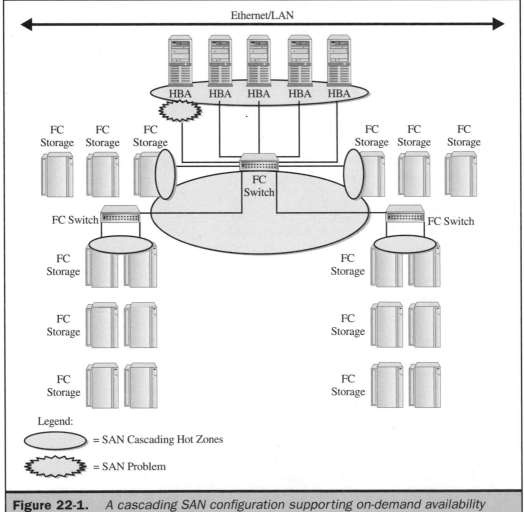

Figure 22-1. *A cascading SAN configuration supporting on-demand availability*

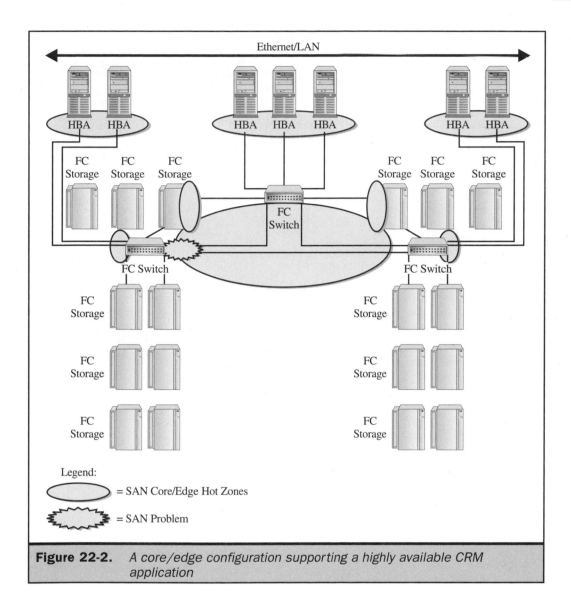

Figure 22-2. *A core/edge configuration supporting a highly available CRM application*

If we contrast these availability categories to SAN and NAS configurations, we find some simple guidelines can be applied to orient them toward appropriate configurations.

On-Demand Availability—NAS and SAN

NAS configurations for on-demand availability can be contained with entry- and workgroup-sized NAS devices. Availability levels in the 80 to 90 percent uptime range are generally acceptable in supporting shared files and network file services for PCs.

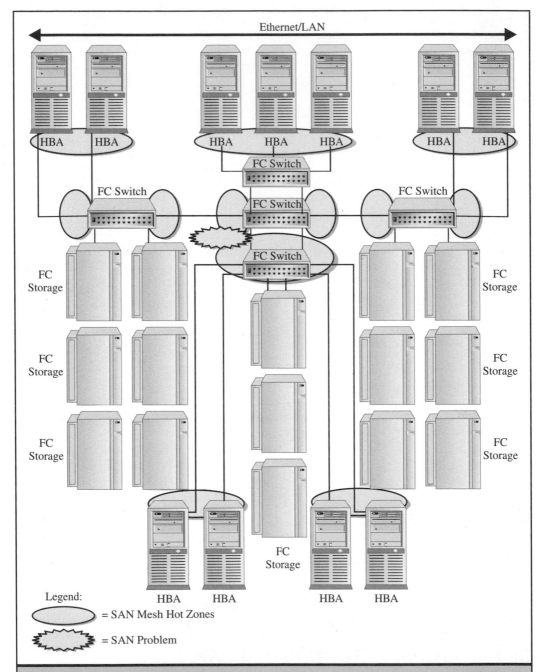

Figure 22-3. *A redundant mesh SAN configuration supporting a 24/7 application*

Given the reliability of the NAS devices performing this type of work, the storage availability will likely be close to the five 9s; however, the variable in keeping these service levels is the external effects of application servers and the local network. Given that scenario, if the external effects are managed within the internal service levels through agreements with your colleagues in the systems and network areas, and external agreements with end users (see Chapter 24) make these effects known, the NAS entry and workgroup devices will perform well.

SAN configurations supporting these areas can be simple or extended cascading configurations where the level of path redundancy is not required, and the performance factors are more oriented toward availability of the data. This will largely be a matter of the reliability of the FC storage devices rather than the switch configuration; however, with today's RAID array functions and their support of larger data segments, the reliability of these devices will be quite high. Because of this, data uptime can exceed 90 percent.

Highly Available Systems—SAN maybe NAS

For systems that require the five 9s, the more robust the underlying devices and the more flexible the configuration, the better the solution. As these systems will likely support the use of RDBMSs for data organizational models, the use of NAS becomes somewhat problematic. In terms of SANs, this means an entry point at which the robust nature of its storage devices and the flexibility of its switched fabric begins to show real value. However, the trade-off is increased complexity, as support for these availability models requires a core/edge configuration to ensure performance that includes consideration for interswitch duplicate paths that are necessary for redundancy. In some cases, the entire SAN configuration may need to be duplicated within a cluster operation, whereby a standby SAN configuration holds the failover system. In the end, this is very expensive and not recommended unless absolutely necessary.

Fault-Tolerant Systems—SAN only

Systems requiring full redundancy may either be highly proprietary systems that provide multiple levels of failover (such as 4- to 8-way clustering systems with OS extensions to synchronize the failover functions), or systems with a single failover used solely as a standby. Other systems may be fully fault tolerant in a tightly coupled system of MPP or high-end SMP architectures (see Chapters 7 and 8 for additional information on MPP and SMP configurations). Regardless of their configuration, these systems require storage. Many of these systems, being UNIX-based, can participate in SAN configurations leveraging the ability to access either shared storage at the hardware level, more sophisticated (and proprietary) shared data systems at the software level, or a combination of both. This brings the value of SAN configurations further into focus.

A word about NAS when used in fault-tolerant environments. It's not true that NAS solutions cannot be used in these environments; there are several caveats that must be considered. Among these are the uses of an RDBMS within the application, and subsequently in housing the database system and user data. If that's the case, NAS is more likely to be problematic given it has limited abilities with the relational data organizational model (see Chapters 9 and 11 on NAS architectures and NAS Software, respectively). In addition is the interconnection using a TCP/IP-based network with a speed fast enough to support failover operations providing a mirrored data environment. If this requires the installation of a short hop special 10Gbe switch and cabling, the cost may or may not be worth the effort. Lastly will be the flexibility affording the switch's network configurations. Each switch should have accommodations for redundant paths to handle additional as well as alternative paths for data communications.

Storage Availability—Considering RAID

RAID storage configurations are available for both SAN and NAS configurations. Certainly from an availability perspective, RAID has become a requirement for most data centers. Given its implementation, reliability, and cost, it has become a defacto standard for applications. Thus, the question becomes: what level of RAID to use for particular applications—or in terms of this book, what level to use for the I/O workload.

Here, RAID is used in basically two configurations: level 5 and level 1. Other RAID levels are used for specific application support like RAID level 10, also referred to as 0 +1, where files are duplicated with higher performance. However, this comes at the sacrifice of non-stop reliability given there is there is no parity information calculated or stored in this configuration. Other types, such as RAID level 4, are bundled into some NAS vendor solutions.

Considerations for RAID and its associated applications and availability include the following:

- **RAID Level 5** This level of RAID provides data striping on each device within the storage array. The parity information—the information the RAID software or firmware uses to reconstruct the data if a disk is lost—is also striped across the array. This configuration is generally used for high-transactional OLTP applications that require a high-availability service level. The caveat is the write-intensive nature of the application that will increase I/O latency given the increased write operations, as well as the storage array for the multiple writes necessary with the data and the parity information.

- **RAID Level 1** This level of RAID provides data mirroring with parity so the application can continue to run if one of the disk pairs is inoperative. This requires more storage capacity given it's a true duplication of the data, thus allowing a 2 to 1 ratio for data capacity (in other words, one byte of user data requires a duplicate or mirror). Consequently, a 100GB database table that uses RAID level 1 would require 200GB of storage on different disks. Additional data requirements for parity information are not significant and should not be taken into consideration. RAID level 1 is used for applications that require failover availability, or data-sensitive applications that require data to be available in case of corruption. This comes in handy with applications such as data warehousing, and some OLTP using failover configurations.

Finding the Holes

The most challenging aspect to managing storage networking availability is collecting, reporting, and analyzing the information, while the most important aspect of business application performance is accessing data. The data may be stored on disk, tape, optical, temporary cache, or other device. The location of the data becomes irrelevant; however, if the application cannot get to it, or the paths to the data are congested or critically impacted, the performance of the application will degrade, or worse, become unavailable.

The key to successfully monitoring and managing the performance of business applications is the consistent and proactive management of the critical paths to application data. Although software tools are becoming available, they provide a disparate, incompatible, and inconsistent view of storage information, not to mention storage networking configurations. No single tool provides consistent, proactive management functions that associate business applications with application data. IT management must choose from an assortment of tools that provide only discrete levels of empirical information, ranging from operating system metrics and database metrics, to I/O and disk metrics. IT users bear the burden of correlating these seemingly unrelated sets of information in an attempt to understand the effects of workloads on storage networking resources.

Where to Look

The deficiencies within storage software management tools are compounded by the requirements, costs, and expertise needed to support an increasing set of server platforms, operating systems, and major application subsystems such as relational database management, messaging, and transactional systems. The following points illustrate some of the challenges in managing storage network configurations, as well as the inefficiencies that contribute to business application availability.

- **Correlation Functions among Distributed Components**   Storage networks are distributed—meaning events happening on one node device or fabric switch can seriously degrade performance throughout the entire system. The ability to correlate important aspects of performance information as it effects the business application currently must be performed as a set of manual tasks.

- **Proactive Trending**   Today's IT managers are expected to effectively drive the bus while monitoring performance through the rearview mirror. Literally all reporting and trending is historical. The information which ultimately reaches the IT user is past tense and provides little value in determining real-time solutions to poorly performing business applications. Consequently, a response to an availability problem with a production configuration may require significantly more time to address.

■ **Identification of the "Root Cause" of a Problem**   The effects of the conditions stated previously means it is unlikely that the information discovered and reported to the IT user will provide any sort of root cause analysis. This makes the problem management aspect of availability problematic. The information provided to identify and correct the problem would likely address only the symptoms, leading to reoccurring results.

Finding, collecting, and reporting performance information as indicated in the preceding section will be difficult. As such, this should enter into the availability formulae when considering the appropriate configuration and resources. There are multiple sources that IT storage administrators can access to find this information. Given that it remains a manual effort to coalesce the data into something of value, the sources can provide a key to building a historical database of performance and availability information. Particular to the storage networks, these sources are the management information base or MIB (provided within the switch fabric operating system or the NAS RTOS), the hardware activity logs within the specific devices (such as the SCSI enclosures services (SES)), and the OS-dependent activity logs and files that are part of the operating systems attached to the SAN or NAS configurations.

This appears as a loose confederation of information, and it is. However, if one sets up a logical organization of sources, the ability to find, select, and utilize existing tools, and develop internal expertise in utilizing these resources will help a great deal in monitoring availability. The following are some guidelines for both NAS and SAN:

■ **NAS RTOS**   Essentially everything that is active within the NAS device is available through the NAS operating system. Although vendors have enhanced their offerings for manageability services for monitoring and reporting, they remain proprietary to the vendor and closed to user customization.

■ **NAS Configuration**   Looking at NAS devices as a total storage configuration requires that external sources of information be identified and accessed. These are multiple and can be defined through network and remote server logs. Again, these require the necessary manual activity to coalesce the data into meaningful information for availability purposes.

■ **Fabric Operating System Information**   Available within the switch MIBs. (Note that with multiple switches there will be multiple MIBs.) In addition, many switch vendors are enhancing their in-band management utilities and will provide more sophisticated services to access FC MIBs. The same can be said for storage management software vendors that are increasing their efforts to provide in-band software management services that communicate with external products running on the attached servers.

■ **HBA Information**   Available within the attached node server. However, it's important to note that HBA information coming from system log files must be integrated somehow into a single view. Although this may require additional IT activity, it can and should be accomplished with third-party storage management tools and system collection repositories such as the Common Information Model (CIM).

- **Storage Information**   Available within the attached node device through either MIBs, SES utilities, or activity log files generally operating within the RAID control units.

- **OS Information**   Available within the attached node server and dependent on the OS (for example, UNIX or Windows). There are multiple sources within UNIX environments to support, find, and select storage performance information. This also includes existing storage management products that support out-of-band management processing. Within Windows environments is a relatively new source: the Common Information Management database. This is an object database that provides activity information for all processes within the server and has become compatible with a large number of storage networking and system vendors.

- **Application Information**   Available within the attached servers are multiple sources of information depending on the type of application and its dependent software elements (for example, databases, log, and configuration files). Some of this information is being identified within the CIM database for Windows environments to augment third-party management software suites. For UNIX environments, there are third-party systems management software suites with CIM implementation just beginning. The inherent challenge of these approaches is the correlation of the application information to storage management activity and information.

Note   *The problem with any of these strategies, although well intentioned, is the increasing overhead these applications have on switch performance, cost, and flexibility. As pointed out in Chapters 11 and 15, the operating capacities within the NAS RTOS and SAN FC fabric operating systems are quite limited.*

Data Recovery

An advantage of SAN architecture is the leverage of node communications within the fabric to increase availability within the data maintenance processes. Within the data center are multiple maintenance and support applications necessary to maintain platform environments. Of these, none are more basic than backing up files and data for later recovery. The historical problem with these activities is the time lost to copy the data from online media to offline media, using tape media in most cases.

This integral data center practice can be broken into two major activities, each with their own problematic characteristics. First is the process of copying data from disk volumes and writing out the data to a tape volume. Given the disparity of the devices (see Chapter 6 for more on disk and tape devices), a performance problem is inevitable. However, it goes beyond device disparity and is exacerbated by the software architecture of the copy process that has been integrated into most backup and recovery software products. The problem is simple. The traditional, though arcane operation, requires data to be copied from the disk and buffered in memory within the initiating server. The server then issues a write operation for the data in the buffer and the subsequent I/O operation copies the data to the tape media mounted on the tape drive.

This double-write and staging process places a tremendous I/O load on the server executing the copy operation while reserving both the disk device and tape drive during the operation. Figure 22-4 shows how this impacts operations during a typical backup portion of the backup/recovery operation.

The second, and most important, part of this process is the recovery operation. As illustrated in Figure 22-4, the backup is the insurance premium to cover any disruptions and corruptions to the current online data, while the recovery operation is the claim payoff so to speak, when a problem has occurred and data needs to be recovered to both an uncorrupt condition and any previous state.

The recovery operation is different from the copy, even though it appears to be the reverse of the operation; it is far more selective regarding the data that needs to be written back to disks. This requires additional and specific parameters to recover data, such as the specific data to be recovered, from a specific time period, which should be restored to a specific state. The most complex of these operations begins when RDBMSs are involved. This is due to the state condition that needs to be restored during the recovery operation in order to bring the database table to a specific state through the processing of transactional log files.

Enter the Storage Area Network. Figure 22-5 demonstrates the capability of devices within the SAN configuration to communicate with each other, thereby allowing many of the server-based, data-centric maintenance/support applications to be optimized. The tremendous I/O load from typical backup operations can now be offloaded from the initiating server. This requires the data copy functions to be performed from storage network node device to storage network node device (in other words, disk-to-disk,

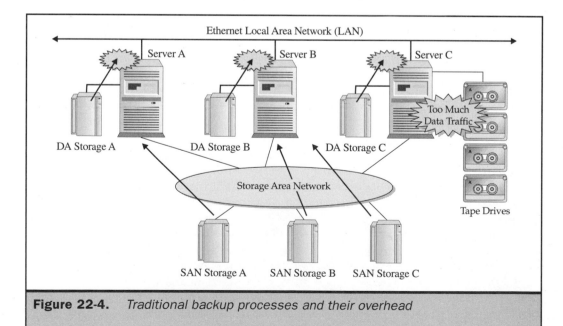

Figure 22-4.   *Traditional backup processes and their overhead*

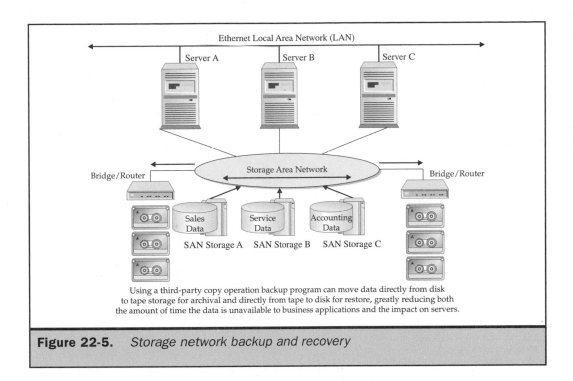

Using a third-party copy operation backup program can move data directly from disk to tape storage for archival and directly from tape to disk for restore, greatly reducing both the amount of time the data is unavailable to business applications and the impact on servers.

Figure 22-5.   *Storage network backup and recovery*

disk-to-optical, disk-to-tape, and so on). Given that the bulk of elapsed time during the traditional backup operation is the double writing of data to the server and then to the backup device, such as tape, this time is optimized through a direct copy operation under the control of the FC fabric working in conjunction with the backup/recovery software that still controls the overall process.

For example, if a typical copy operation used 100 I/O operations from the disk drive/ controller to the server path and a subsequent 200 I/O operations to the tape unit, that requires a net 300 I/O operations that the server must perform, not to mention the elapsed time in reserving the disk and tape units. By employing the SAN operation of the direct node communications using the extended copy operation of FC fabric operations, the server I/O can be reduced to a minimum of two to initiate the operation of the fabric in order to directly copy data from the disk to the tape units. The copy operation can thus be performed one time at the speed of FC hardware: 100MB/s with latency for tape bandwidth operations and buffers. Performance depends largely on the specifics of the data, as well as the switch and tape configurations, but suffice to say, the savings will be significant.

Keep in mind that the preceding example was only for the backup portion of the operations. We must also factor in the recovery part. Nevertheless, the savings will be similar to the copy operations—that is, copying the information from the tape to the disk. The operation executes the same way: by the backup/recovery software communicating with the SAN fabric, and the execution of the extended copy command through the fabric. The extenuating circumstances will be the destination of the recovery, the extent of the post processing of transaction logs, and the activity and location of the tape drives that must mount and process the log files.

The significant savings of copying data within a SAN should be taken into context regarding both backup and recovery, because the value in the backup and recovery operation to external service levels is the "R" part, or the recovery. In the end, the time it takes to restore data and application services is key.

Most business applications suffer during this maintenance process because data is unavailable during the time it is being copied. Although necessary for maintaining storage backup procedures and policies, this type of operation (that is, copying data directly from device-to-device) can greatly improve the availability of business applications by reducing the time in which data is unavailable.

Unfortunately, NAS differs in its server-based architecture (albeit a thin server) and its attachment to an Ethernet network. Backup and recovery operations are generally handled by a dedicated server within the subnetwork. NAS vendors have extended their solutions to include SCSI tape attachment. This allows for a self-contained NAS solution which includes its own backup/recovery system. Although it's important for NAS devices in remote locations to have an automated backup process, the capability of NAS to participate within the data center tape library solutions is likely to be a preferred solution for storage administrators.

NAS integration into enterprise-level applications is driving vendors to include data mirroring, snapshot capability, and self-contained backup/recovery operations. These functions have been extended into the NAS hardware and software solutions as well as their integration with FC storage. As this evolves, the ability to participate in device-to-device communication through an extended SAN fabric will make the extended copy operation possible.

Closing the Loop

As available service levels are negotiated, identifying the appropriate and specific information to ensure their availability commitments will become the main responsibility of performance management. Through effective monitoring and reporting of performance factors of the storage network, effective storage network configurations can build from the foundation of information and tools used in this process. With performance management in place, the next phase can be begin to evolve: the effective management of performance anomalies, or problems.

As problems start to be discovered, it will become necessary to ensure that these performance anomalies are accurately identified, tracked, and resolved. Thus begins the problem management phase that illuminates and justifies configuration changes, increases and decreases storage resources, and further modifies and enhances those resources necessary to ensure availability.

Chapter 23 will build on the activities, practices, and challenges illustrated and discussed in performance management and availability.

The Complete Reference

Storage Networks

Chapter 23

Maintaining Serviceability

The failure of a switch port, the inoperative disk drive, and the new fabric software all require service to the SAN. Upgrading the NAS storage array, the need to add Ethernet ports, and the installation of the new NAS device all require a change to the storage network configuration. Each of us is familiar with the call at 2:00 A.M. when the production application is down and problems point to the SAN or a suspected NAS device. These are definite problems and require an effective problem identification, tracking, and resolution system.

Servicing is defined by the activities necessary to maintain the hardware and software configurations of computer systems. Storage networks like other infrastructures require servicing. SANs, still being a relatively new technology, are more intensive than most for many reasons, not to mention the diversity of components that make up the configuration. NAS configurations, on the other hand, being somewhat more mature, require very little servicing, although this depends on their application and usage volatility. Regardless of either application of storage networking, each storage infrastructure benefits from a servicing system that provides significant configuration reliability and, subsequently, availability.

Servicing is often driven by problems that occur within the storage network configuration as well as by external problems that affect the performance of the storage network. Secondly, servicing is required for any changes to the configuration meant to fix problems and to enhance or upgrade configuration components. Considering another oft-used work axiom—*if it ain't broke don't fix it*—the necessity of using a variety of sometimes-compatible hardware and software components brings another dimension to this colloquialism.

From a systems management discipline, the next phase of activities are change management, problem management, and, as its cornerstone as indicated in the following illustration, configuration management. Each plays a pivotal role in the effective servicing of the storage network. Traditional storage management and elements of network management make up many of the elements that are necessary to service the storage network. This requires an integration of traditional configuration management and change management activities. Not to mention the effective development and integration of problem management into the data-center operations and help desk activities.

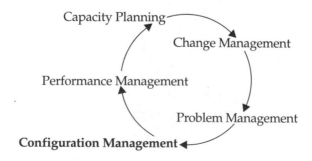

This chapter discusses the application of these management disciplines to the storage network environment. This includes the complexities of hardware/software compatibility issues that affect SAN configurations and the added value of keeping NAS release levels in sync with each other and the network software. Within the data center, one of the many technical issues to deal with is the integration into other system management disciplines that are already in place. Of these, problem management is one of the most challenging.

The activities to track changes within the storage network are beneficial in order to keep the devices compatible, correlate problem identification, and schedule maintenance activities. However, the benefits of effective change management within the storage network also provide value to external elements within the data-center environment. Integrating yet another level of change into the data center is a challenge. This chapter provides some insight into these potentially volatile situations and offers some guidelines to get things started.

Tracking the Configurations

Computer systems require the installation of multiple components that, when working together, form some type of system for producing effective results. Generally, those results are productive for the IT organization responsible for the system. The ability to manage the diversity of hardware and software components is referred to as configuration management. Configuration management establishes the inventory of a system, naming the components, their release and maintenance levels, and connectivity. Although configuration management is suited for both hardware and software, it is usually used in a segregated manner to track the hardware configuration and the software release levels, respectively.

Although the premise is that by keeping track of the components within the hardware or software configuration one can understand the economics in terms of tracking capital equipment, the alternative but oft-unused value of this discipline is the tracking of the inventory to understand what changes can be made, under what circumstances, in order to either correct a system deficiency or enhance the performance of the system to meet established service levels. Given that both hardware and software are likely to change over the effective life of a system, configuration management serves as both a driver to changes and a tool to identify problems.

Storage networking, being that it's a system, and a relatively new system at that, can benefit greatly from configuration management. Establishing an effective servicing practice for storage networking systems, and keeping track of the diversity of components that make up SAN or NAS infrastructures, can be extremely valuable.

What's different about SANs in configuration management is the number of separate components that make up the configuration. In addition to its diversity, the shared characteristics of both networking and storage technologies gives SANs a hybrid view to many people uninitiated in storage networking. At the same time, the SAN infrastructure is driven by the external effects of other compatible and collaborative systems, such as servers, networks, and software.

NAS poses a more chameleon-like problem. NAS configurations can be single or multiple in number, and while looking like storage, they are really a specialized server. This provides a configuration management discipline with some interesting problems in determining where to categorize this component and what elements make up the components. If it's a storage device, then it has no OS. However, NAS most definitely has an OS that needs upgrades, changes, and has the potential for problems. However, tracking as a storage device overlooks these critical elements. In addition, NAS configurations are driven externally by the network and remote servers or clients that contact it through remote communications.

The point is that storage networks, although computer systems in and of themselves, are different animals when it comes to categorizing them through traditional configuration management practices. Some thought must be given to these configurations as they are integrated into either existing configuration management tools or are used in establishing new practices that integrate both an inventory tracking for capital expense purposes and a foundation for tracking problems and change.

Physical Configuration Management for SANs

Configurations are likely viewed from a hardware and software perspective. Physical views of the SAN should provide the inventory of all equipment installed within the configuration. This requires all the typical information necessary for asset and capital inventory tracking, such as serial numbers, location, and ownership. In addition, there should be the same current information on firmware or micro-code releases and install dates. Many components in the SAN area come with some type of firmware, micro-code, and micro-kernel software that is release- and hardware-specific. It's important that this information is collected and stored, at a minimum, on a file, although a database is better for later access.

Thus, a decision will have to be made here in terms of categorization of software. Given that firmware and micro-code are hardware-specific, the micro-kernel that functions as the fabric OS must have a place here or in the software configuration tracking system. Consequently, the choice depends on the size of the configuration and what type of distinction there is between hardware and software support for servicing. In a large installation, this could be critical when it comes to avoiding confusion in tracking microkernel release levels in two places, or dodging confusion with other firmware and driver software that is specific to HBA and storage array controllers.

Figure 23-1 indicates the types of categories that may be considered in establishing the configuration management repository for SANs. Of course, this information can and should drive the digital rendering of the configuration for general reference and access.

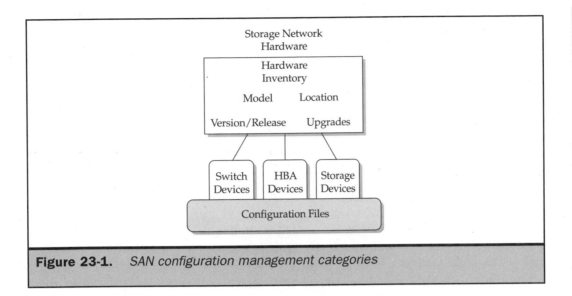

Figure 23-1.   *SAN configuration management categories*

Logical/Software Configuration Management for SANs

The logical configuration refers to the SAN software, but also should include the logical relationships that exist within the SAN configuration. These are the fabric zones, the LUN assignments at the server/HBA node, and the storage controller array nodes. In addition, there are additional elements within the fabric operating system that relate to the port IDs, fabric logins, worldwide naming services, and the management information base dictionary and layouts.

Configuration management for the logical and software functions is critical. Due to the diversity and complexity of the SAN software components, much time can be saved and downtime avoided through the effective documentation and monitoring of the fabric micro-kernel release and maintenance level, the HBA driver code release and maintenance level, and the storage array RAID driver and firmware release level. There should be an established configuration management for the attached servers. If not, the server OS release and maintenance levels will be mandatory.

Essentially, the software components of the SAN form a matrix of interdependent functions. A change in any has the potential to cascade problems throughout the SAN configuration. You can rely on interoperability labs of vendors, industry groups, and testing labs, to gather macro level compatibility information. However, the number of permutations far exceeds what these well-intentioned groups can provide. If that means providing a test bed for your applications within the configurations specific to your site, then it's well worth considering. In fact, it's no different than other test beds that you may require for application and system testing and should be integrated into testing facilities.

Figure 23-2 illustrates the configuration management categories and example specifications a data center may consider for SAN physical and logical components. The interrelationships and dependencies between components can quickly become overwhelming, which provides additional justification for building a repository of physical and logical components. However, one of the most difficult events to track are the dependencies from hardware to software components. Consequently, the ability to begin an integrated repository may save critical time as configuration changes can be tracked against the related hardware and software device dependencies.

Physical Configuration Management for NAS

Managing the physical configurations for NAS might seem like a simpler process than SAN, but it's not. The physical connections within the NAS configurations may be simple if they are installed in close proximity and operate within the confines of the data center. Even then, it can become confusing and a challenge because of the diversity of networks and network components. The network becomes the critical factor in establishing the configuration, and consequently, the NAS configurations pose a relatively difficult problem in regards to configuration management—that is, how to articulate and track individual components of the device and the external characteristics of the network hardware within the context of a system (in other words, the infrastructure).

Figure 23-3 illustrates the complexity of the external relationships between the network, the NAS device, and the attached servers. In a sense, it can be viewed as a loosely connected storage network, with dependencies associated with network topologies and protocols, server nodes, and file communications protocols. Unless the hardware and firmware release levels are inventoried and tracked in conjunction with the network, the NAS systems become unassociated storage servers unbound to the confines of the networks in which they operate. Bottom line, if there is a problem

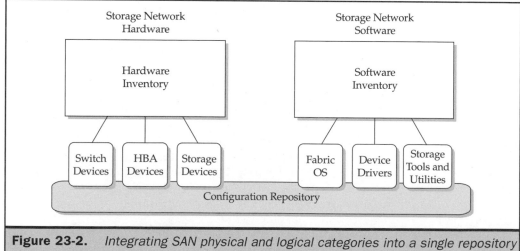

Figure 23-2. *Integrating SAN physical and logical categories into a single repository*

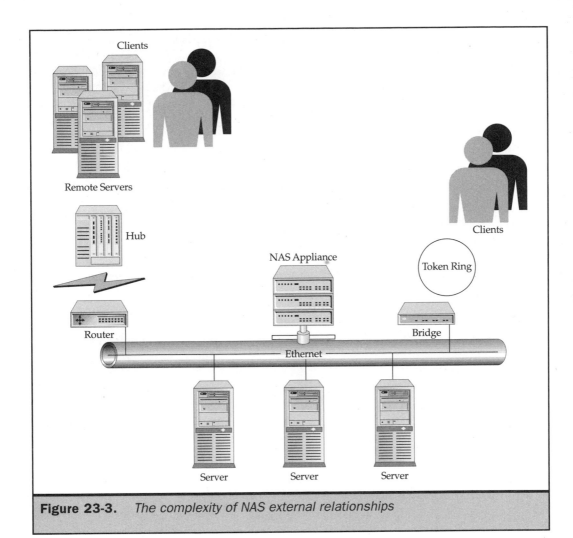

Figure 23-3.   *The complexity of NAS external relationships*

within the NAS device that's being perpetuated through the operations of a network device, the problem will be hard to diagnose and will likely repeat regardless of any changes within the offending NAS device.

Consequently, it's paramount that some type of relationship be established as the configuration management is instituted for the NAS configurations. This may require the NAS device being subsumed into the network configuration management disciplines, if they are established; however, this may not take into account the other relationship of the server component that is actually generating the I/O request. Given this third variable, the NAS configuration management must rely on two external factors for effective configuration management: the network and the server. Whether these are accounted for in the network disciplines or the system disciplines or a new storage network discipline, the benefits to problem investigation and upgrade analysis, as well as overall availability, are large.

Figure 23-4 indicates the types of categories that may be considered in establishing the physical configuration management matrix for NAS. Note that due to the complexities of the external relationships of the network devices, links into a network configuration repository enhance the value of the NAS physical configuration information. Of course, this information can, and should, drive the digital rendering of the configuration for general reference and access.

Logical/Software Configuration Management for NAS

Software for NAS becomes both simple and problematic. Simple in terms of the standardization of the NAS micro-kernel OS used, given that the configuration is a homogeneous vendor solution. Problematic in terms of how the NAS OS reacts to a network environment of heterogeneous components (for example, hubs, routers, and switches). Coupled with this is the reaction to a heterogeneous environment of server OSs that may cover both UNIX and Windows variants.

Given that the NAS micro-kernel forms a barrier to direct communications from remote clients to the storage arrays through file access, the storage arrays associated with the NAS solution are bundled and protected from extraneous and external access. The NAS storage upgrade path may be non-existent on entry-level devices and limited

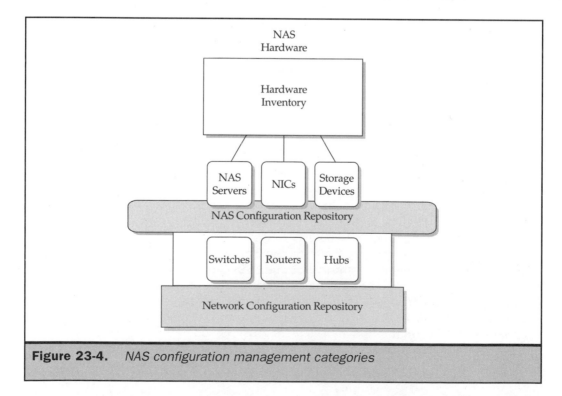

Figure 23-4. *NAS configuration management categories*

to specific vendor upgrades with larger enterprise-level devices. The RAID controller firmware will thus be important to problem investigation associated with vendor servicing.

Configuration management within the NAS infrastructure must encompass the NAS micro-kernel release and maintenance level, the storage RAID controller firmware release and maintenance level, and the network driver release and maintenance levels. These fundamental parts can be associated with network software, network components, and server OS release and maintenance levels to form an effective NAS configuration relationship matrix.

The logical constructs of NAS configuration can be valuable in micro views of the data storage strategies used in the NAS devices. In other words, these are the logical views of RAID deployment within the arrays with configurations like local mirroring and remote mirroring illustrating the synchronization methods used. Integrated with the logical storage information, the logical views of file system extensions supported by the NAS device should be documented.

Figure 23-5 indicates the types of categories that may be considered in establishing the software and logical configuration management matrix for NAS. The complexities of integrating both hardware and software should be taken in context with other configuration management files, repositories, and tracking mechanisms. Figure 23-5 suggests the linking of not only the network inventory but the systems inventory of application and database servers and related information. Of course, this information can, and should, drive the digital rendering of the configuration for general reference and access.

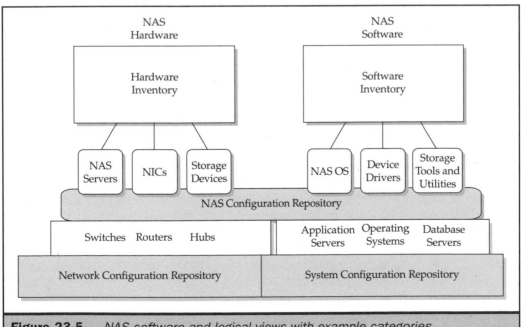

Figure 23-5.   *NAS software and logical views with example categories*

Investigating the Changes

What is change management and integrating SAN/NAS changes into an existing data center CM system?

When was the last time someone made a change to the configuration you were supporting? Don't know? Well, probably about five minutes ago, if you're operating in an unregulated environment. The chief creator problem is change. Something changed, and finding out what changed constitutes the bulk of problem analysis. Finding who changed what becomes more of a people management issue than technical. However, the discipline of change management within computer systems came about for just these reasons. Who changed what, when, and where is the mantra of change management.

If tracking and prioritizing changes is already an established discipline within the configurations you support, then you'll understand the value of integrating an unwieldy infrastructure like storage networking into the change management activities. The central value of managing change is that in the case of young technology solutions like SANs, almost 90 percent of the problems can be eliminated just by understanding the configurations and implementing reasonable changes.

The chameleon-like nature of NAS and the ease and attraction of Plug-and-Play provide a tremendous force in circumventing the change discipline. Well, you say, it's just some network storage and I can put it on the network in less than five minutes. Yes, you can, and you can also bring the network to its knees, lose all the data on the NAS, and corrupt the data on the redirected server. Wow, that's a lot of potential problems for Plug-and-Play. Regardless of whether we're accustomed to this type of service, it doesn't have to happen.

Forget the formalization of change committees and change windows for the SOHO environments. All you need is some common sense to discipline your changes. Developing a change management discipline can work just as well for small environments as for large environments. No one appreciates the use of the defragmentation process that runs during the peak of the server's day, especially when it crashes and all the sales transactions have to be reentered because the mirror on the NAS device didn't work. Consequently, even if you're not familiar with change management, starting with storage networks can be extremely beneficial, all in the name of availability.

Driving Change Through Configuration Management

An ongoing program of regular monitoring and analysis of the storage network configuration ultimately reveals changes that must be made to enhance performance or provide sufficient reliability to meet service levels. Whether this comes through changes in software or hardware activities, the ability to schedule, track, and implement these changes effectively, and in a non-disruptive manner, requires the disciplines of change management.

In many cases, however, there will be changes to the configuration that require a timely response. Consequently, there must be a prioritization within the change management system to handle these issues. In terms of SAN serviceability, the inoperative switch that impacts the service levels of a production application system must be analyzed given its relationships to the entire configuration and its effects on other components and systems being supported through the SAN configuration. This may require a quick response, but without sufficient and accurate knowledge of the existing configuration, the ability to identify and resolve the problem becomes difficult. Either the change is made without knowledge of its impact, or a lengthy analysis to document the configuration may elongate the outage or degrade the service.

Consequently, configuration management drives changes by documenting storage network "hot-spots" and quickly referencing the relationships within the configuration. In addition, an effective change management program can leverage the information within configuration management system diagrams to facilitate the problem resolution process in conjunction with change prioritization. Helping to facilitate the establishment of change prioritization is an added benefit of configuration management that drives change management in a positive direction.

How Problem Management/Resolution Becomes the Ying and Yang of Storage Networks

You can't fix a problem unless you change the configuration. You don't have problems unless there is a change to the system. This is the "yin and yang" of change management. Although we have yet to discuss problem management, we have described the effect of changes within the configuration being driven by problems that occur. Because storage networks are implemented using diverse components, they are exposed to a disparate set of external stimulus. They become the critical elements to production systems, however, and as such, they are the prime focus when diagnosing severity level one problems. In other words, storage is a key element to evaluate during system outages.

Consequently, managing change can drive the balance of change within the overall data center activities. After all, it's easy to blame everything on the new kid (say, storage network configuration), if they can't defend themselves. The need to enroll storage network configurations into change management activities allows many things, including the visibility of changes within the configuration, visibility to external changes that affect the configuration, and the ability to maintain a credible defense in problem identification activities.

The Effects of Capacity Upgrades on Change Management

One of the major factors that disrupt storage configurations are upgrades. Whether there're extending capacities or enhancing performance, these changes should affect existing service levels in a positive way; however, in many cases, capacity upgrades can provide unforeseen results and performance, generally in the wrong direction. These situations evolve from unscheduled or unmanaged change plans that do not account for adequate time to complete or consider the effects to related systems.

This is evident in the installation of additional storage capacity using NAS devices. Without sufficient consideration for the related network capacity and existing traffic, NAS devices can solve the storage capacity problem but create a network problem as a result. The other issue with NAS upgrades is the related file protocol services that need to be connected or reconnected after an installation. Installing or upgrading NAS device capacity may be quick in terms of configuring and identifying the network; reestablishing the drive mappings and device mounts for the new NAS devices are sometimes an overlooked detail.

SAN configurations provide a more complex activity for upgrades and capacity upgrades. Due largely to the diversity of components and their interrelationships, SAN upgrades and installations will require a significantly longer planning and analysis cycle than other storage configurations. For example, upgrading storage capacity has a ricochet effect within the configuration. Adding a significant amount of capacity is driven by increased access. The increased access may require additional node servers to be attached, and ultimately will place more traffic within the switch configurations.

If the extenuating situations as mentioned in the preceding example are not addressed, the SAN configuration can become compromised in the name of increasing service. Addressing these situations requires a discipline that is supported through a comprehensive change management system. The articulation of changes within the storage infrastructure drives the discipline to analyze the following: what's being changed, why, the desired result, and the plan for reestablishing service. Managing changes highlights the division of labor between software and hardware changes. It also highlights the division of responsibility in large configurations where the network part and the storage part are separated and supported by different groups, each having their own hardware and software expertise. Integrating change management into the storage configuration management process provides a forum to highlight all the required activities for servicing the SAN or NAS configurations.

Tracking Changes to Physical and Logical Configurations

Tracking of changes within a storage network is similar to the tracking of changes within the data center: a separation of hardware and software changes. Another view is to divide them into physical and logical categories. This mediates the traditional separation of hardware versus software, thereby integrating the component responsibility into combined or shared responsibilities. For example, the typical enhancement of storage capacity within a storage network is the installation of a new and larger storage array. This could be performed in an off-shift time period, or on a weekend, and no one would be the wiser.

However, it could also be scheduled within a change management system where the information regarding the upgrade, proposed activity, and scheduling are communicated to other areas that may be effected. This allows others to either consider the effects of the change and plan accordingly, postpone the change until issues are addressed, or, at a minimum, be aware that the possibility of problems could exist after the change date.

Because both NAS and SAN configurations are closely associated with hardware and software functions (see Parts III and IV for more details on the major components of these storage systems), the tracking of physical changes provides a method that encompasses both the physical aspect of the component as well as the bundled software configuration parameters that need to be addressed. For example, the recabling of a SAN switch to enable the installation of a new switch requires both physical changes and subsequent fabric changes. Viewing and administrating changes in this way forces the change process to encompass both hardware and software skills while ensuring the changes are analyzed in an integrated fashion.

The tracking of logical changes performs the same function within the change process, except that logical configurations are generally driven by changes to software components within the storage network. These may be enhancements to various features and functions, or maintenance of existing software elements such as the fabric OS, NAS micro-kernel, and storage and adapter drivers and firmware.

An example is the upgrade to the NAS micro-kernel software. This change, viewed from a logical perspective, should require an analysis of configuration management information regarding which relevant NAS devices are affected by an upgrade. The NAS target configurations would then be evaluated for subsequent firmware changes within the storage array controllers that may be required to support the new NAS kernel software. In addition, the micro-kernel change may have different levels of IP network support and will require the evaluation of the potential network components. Consequently, the change to the logical configuration brings in all of the NAS components, as well as the external elements that may be affected. This also forces the necessary storage and networking hardware skills to participate in the scheduling and implementation of the change.

Guidelines for Establishing Change Management in Storage Networking

The following guidelines can be used to provide the beginning of a change management program for storage networking. Even though a formal change management function may exist in your data center, the establishment and integration of storage networking as a valid change management entity is key to participation at a data-center level.

■ *Establish a link between storage configuration and change management.* This forces the evaluation of each change to be analyzed for the entire configuration, as well as other systems in the data center.

■ *Develop a relationship matrix between the key components among the storage network configurations.* For example, the relationship between the FC switch and the storage nodes is a fundamental and interdependent one. If the switch becomes inoperative, the storage is inaccessible and potentially magnified by several storage arrays supported by the switch. Using this example, it also provides a roadmap of Inter Switch Links (ISL) dependencies and other fabric nodes that are participating in the fabric.

■ *Establish an internal (within the storage network) change prioritization scheme and an external (outside the storage network) change effects scheme based on a storage network availability matrix.* The storage change prioritization scheme will define the levels of change based upon their potential effects on the storage configuration. The external change effects scheme will define the levels of how the storage configuration is affected by outside configurations of servers, networks, and other storage configurations.

■ *Establish a link between storage change management and problem management.* Additional discussion on problem management follows; however, it's important to mention the critical link between problems and change given their synergistic relationship. For example, if a storage configuration denotes a FC switch that is attached to five storage arrays and another two switches where information drives the relationship matrix that depicts its interdependencies. These component interdependencies drive the change prioritization scheme to reflect this component as a critical availability element within the configuration. The external changes affect change prioritization schemes that, in turn, reflect the risk to external systems supported by these components. Consequently, this will drive a level of change prioritization if and when a problem arises within this component.

Whose Problem Is It Anyway?

Storage problems within the data center can ricochet through production applications faster than any other component. Obviously, this is a reflection of their critical position within the diversity of components that support production processing. When problems occur, there generally is some type of trouble ticket system that logs problems for assignment and potential resolution. These systems provide an invaluable service when it comes to documenting and tracking problems, but does little to facilitate the entire aspect of problem management. Consequently, applying a trouble ticket system or help desk software to storage problems only addresses a small portion of problem management.

Problems, especially within the storage infrastructure, are resolved in a number of ways, depending on the data-center facility, administrator preferences, and management, or even the establishment of service levels. Regardless of data center–specific attributes and management styles, there are fundamental activities that reflect problem management disciplines as well as critical activities that must be performed to respond to storage problems effectively. The problem management disciplines are: problem prioritization, problem identification, and problem resolution. Overlaid with problem documentation and tracking, they form the fundamental parts of problem management. How these are implemented and integrated with storage networks is critical to the success and reliability of the storage infrastructure.

The Problem Prioritization Debate

There is no debate more dynamic within the data center than that surrounding problem prioritization. Someone must decide what constitutes a severity level one problem, as opposed to severity level two, three, and so on. This discussion becomes even more vigorous when dealing with storage, since storage contains the data, and ownership is an attribute of that data. If the data becomes unavailable, then the application that uses the data is unavailable and the level of impact is driven by the effect this situation has on the activities of the company. Consequently, end users drive the establishment of severity definitions with the data availability, vis-à-vis, storage availability. However, most are ill-equipped to handle or understand the level of complexity within the storage infrastructure to effectively provide this.

These discussions will become either a very complex issue or a very simple equation given the level of data ownership taken by the end user. If end users take data ownership seriously, then discussions regarding the definitions of data, usage, and management will become involved. However, if end users simply see the data center as the service supplying the data, the discussion can be reduced to a simple level of "on" or "off." In other words, either the data is available, or it isn't.

Regardless of these two perspectives, and their highly charged political engagement with end users, the data center must view problem prioritization in a more utilitarian fashion. Simply put, the complexities of providing data delivery and availability infrastructures must be managed within a matrix of interconnecting systems that are beyond the level of knowledge or interest of end users. Moving end users toward a utilitarian approach allows the data center to deal effectively with storage ownership and management of the infrastructure. Defining problems from an end-user perspective within this increasingly complex set of infrastructures allows data centers and underlying areas to define the prioritization required for the data utility. Key to establishing prioritization mechanics is storage networking.

The relationship between data availability and storage networking problem prioritization increases the complexity of this activity. Given the characteristics of data delivery and the evolution of decoupled storage infrastructures such as storage networks, the chances that problems will arise, given the level of interrelationships within the storage area, increases dramatically. This results in environments with increasingly complex storage problems while trying to maintain a simple utility data delivery system.

Problem Identification

Investigating and identifying problems within storage networking configurations is an ongoing activity—for three reasons. One, these technologies are still new and continue to be temperamental. Two, storage networks consist of multiple components that must interact both internally within themselves and externally with other components and systems within the data center. And three, the industry has not yet produced the level of tools necessary for effective operational problem evaluation and identification.

However, there are some key items to consider when looking at problem identification in these areas. Some activities don't require tools so much as basic problem-solving practices. Although this is beyond the scope of this book, the necessary activities should be mentioned in context with storage networks.

- **Accurate and Current Information**   Configuration management for installed storage networks should be accurate and readily available.

- **Diagnostic Services**   A minimum level of standard operational procedures should document the entry-level activities for problem investigation and resolution. This should include the dispatching of vendor service personnel in order to facilitate problem resolution.

- **Service Information**   Accurate and current information should be available to contact vendors and other external servicing personnel.

- **Tool Access**   Access to consoles and other logical tools should be made available to support and operations personnel. This includes current physical location, effective tool usage, diagnostic processes, and authorized access through hardware consoles and network-accessible tools.

In SAN environments, an effective guideline is to investigate from the outside in. Essentially, this requires the evaluation of problems that affect all devices versus problems that affect only specific devices within the storage network.

For problems that affect all devices, it's necessary to view components that are central to the network. Specific to SANs is access to the availability of the fabric operating services. The directly connected console is the most effective tool if network access is not available, while fabric configuration routines provide status information regarding port operations and assignments. There may be additional in-band management routines as well, which can be used for extra information.

For problems that affect only some of the devices, it becomes necessary to first view components that are common to the failing devices. If the total SAN configuration is not completely down, then out-of-band management routines can be accessed to provide a port analysis, port connections, and performance checks. In addition, the ability to telnet or peek into the attached node devices and node servers verifies the basic operations of the switch fabric.

Specific to the node devices are the mostly out-of-band tools which evaluate and verify the operation of storage devices, server HBA ports, and server operating systems. However, access through the fabric can also verify connectivity, logins, and assignments. Key to this area are the continued network drops from the fabric by node devices, a practice which can be traced more effectively through fabric access using configuration and diagnostic tools.

In NAS environments, the same approach can be used to identify failing components; however, NAS configurations are more accessible to typical performance tools. Therefore, the most effective approach is to view problems from the outside in by focusing on access points common to all NAS devices—for example, the network. This is followed by the investigation of individual NAS devices and related components that are failing.

The centralized approach can be used with existing network tools to monitor and respond to NAS network drops where access within a specific area may be the key to the problem (for instance, a network problem versus a NAS problem). This demonstrates how NAS devices require less overhead to identify problems because of their bundled self-contained status and their integration into existing networks as IP-addressable devices.

If problem identification focuses on an individual device, then the failing components may be simple to find given the bundled nature of the NAS solution and the available tools within the NAS microkernel operating system. All NAS vendors provide a layer of diagnostic tools that allow investigation of internal operations of the device. This becomes a matter of a failing server or storage components given the simple nature of the NAS device.

NAS devices are less expensive and easier to integrate into existing problem identification activities. Given their simple configuration and mode of operation as an IP addressable network component, they can be identified quickly through network tools. In addition, internal diagnostic vendor tools provide performance statistics and notification of failures.

Problem Tracking

Once a problem has been reported, the ability to document its particulars is critical to the identification process. Most data centers will have an existing problem documentation system associated with their help desks. Integration of these systems is important for setting the foundation for problem tracking within the storage network. This doesn't automatically mean that all problems will be documented through the help desk, however. Many storage network problems will come from internal sources where they're tracked and reported by data-center administrators, data base administrators, and network administrators, to name a few.

Even though these positions may report the bulk of problems, it does not guarantee those problems will be reported through the same trouble ticket system used by help desk and operations personnel. Thus, the foundation is laid for problem duplication and multiple reporting. This demonstrates just one of the challenges regarding implementation of the storage network into the problem tracking system. The same can be said for other key areas of the problem reporting process when it comes to critical and accurate reporting of problems.

Storage network problem documentation is made more effective by following a few general guidelines.

- **Consistent Reporting Process**   Ensure that problem reporting uses the same system for all external and internal users. This requires a certain level of internal discipline to get all administrators—both in systems and applications support— to utilize the same system. This is important because a problem reported externally may be linked to a problem reported internally, which will have more technical detail. An example is a network-shared drive that continues to be inaccessible, as reported by external users. An internal problem report indicates that the network HUB associated with that device has experienced intermittent failures and is schedule to be replaced. These two sets of information provide a quick level of diagnostic information that should lead the storage administrator to verify the NAS device internally and take steps toward a resolution that may require a different path to the storage.

■ **Historical Reporting and Trending**   One of the most valuable assets problem tracking systems provide is a database to view the history of a component or device, its past problems, and resolution. This can be extremely important as both SAN and NAS components are tracked and analyzed for consistent failures or weaknesses. For example, historical trends regarding complex switch configurations can be very helpful in identifying weaker components or trends toward failure as port counts become higher and higher and interswitch linking becomes more sophisticated. This proves a valuable tool in anticipating potential problems and thereby scheduling changes prior to a failure. This approach offers a proactive answer to problem management and subsequent downtime statistics.

■ **Experience and Expertise**   Tackling problems is one of the quickest ways to learn a system or technology. Using problem tracking information and configuration management information provides effective training for IT personnel new to storage networks.

Closing the Loop on Serviceability

Effective serviceability requires the establishment of both configuration management and problem management. Starting with a set of user requirements that result in the capacity plan, followed by the installation, the critical information contained with the physical and logical configuration documentation drives the effective response to problems.

Problem management establishes a method to effectively deal with problem servicing and the proactive servicing of the configuration. Key among problem management activities is the definition of prioritization. Although this can be a volatile activity, it's best kept as an internal data center activity where end-user data utility is a key goal. Problem identification is central to establishing credibility within the data center. Given SAN and NAS configurations, both can be analyzed from an outside-in problem identification perspective. Although SANs demonstrate a much higher level of complexity, they nevertheless lack the necessary tools to enhance the problem identification process. On the other hand, NAS configurations, given their operation as an existing network component, can take advantage of current network tools. NAS also has a level of maturity that offers internal diagnostic information, thus providing efficiencies in problem identification and resolution.

Without an effective practice for servicing the storage network, the complexities and potential confusion within configuration analysis and problem diagnostics will exacerbate system outages. Both configuration management and problem management are critical elements to the cycle of storage network management.

Chapter 24

Capacity Planning

lanning for storage capacity requires the analysis of future end-user demands and the effective management of existing storage resources, both of which support the ongoing processing demands of the business. Provisioning storage can be as simple as adding new storage devices to existing application servers, or as complex as the calculation of new storage demands for supporting a global Internet services application. Regardless of complexity or application, storage demands are end-user driven and reflective of the dynamics within the economics of application usage. For example, an upward trend in sales orders may generate an increase of 100GB of storage to the online application to handle the new business. New customers may almost always spark an increase in storage capacities as the systems expand to handle the customer and related files.

This expansion, and sometimes contraction, of user demands creates the necessity for planning the processing configurations necessary to meet these demands. This chapter brings our cycle of systems management disciplines to the starting point (see the following illustration): the beginnings, development, and/or evaluation of a capacity plan. Capacity planning for storage networks is a subset of overall storage planning, which supports a macro capacity plan for the enterprise, or at least the major components of the data center computer configurations. Consequently, our discussions within this chapter will reflect the support of the entire data-center infrastructure, while articulating the value of developing a capacity plan for storage network infrastructures.

Over time, data centers develop activities and practices necessary to keep up with computing capacities. This is generally referred to as the capacity plan. These practices and activities have matured and congealed into areas of specialization driven by the diversity that exists even in the most conservative IT organizations. These activities are generally divided along physical areas of responsibilities, as well as technological spheres of influence. Figure 24-1 indicates both the physical division of responsibilities within most data centers, as well as the expected technology segregation. This shows applications, systems, and networks as the dominant areas of responsibility. However, supporting the end-user community is generally an operational area that supports end-user computing and help desk functions, and which acts as a conduit of information driven by day-to-day operations of the major areas of specialization (for example, applications, networks, and systems).

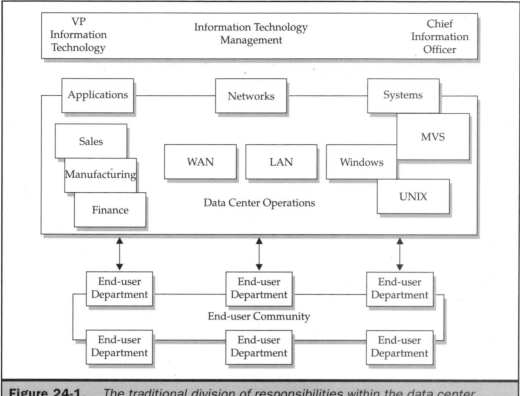

Figure 24-1.   *The traditional division of responsibilities within the data center*

Hidden within these organizational divisions are the sometimes invisible spheres of technology influence and expertise. These are characterized by the segregation of the application "elite" and the "back room" systems mechanics. This forms the major factions that deal with capacity planning activities. Given that capacity is driven by end-user demands, the application elite is called upon to use their system's analyst skills to communicate end-user future plans in terms that can be translated by the system's mechanics. Within this milieu of communications, the operational front liners form the ad hoc reality-based view of capacity requirements.

Consequently, one of the major segments of this chapter is the discussion of how user requirements can be interpreted properly and used as valid input into the storage planning process. As with any human communications endeavor, this requires a bit of diplomacy and tact to accomplish. Given that storage, and in particular storage networking, is often viewed as a third-level component within the enterprise capacity plan, care and understanding of the communications process provides a certain amount of value in accomplishing a successful storage networking capacity plan.

The importance of integrating storage into a larger plan cannot be overlooked. The need to articulate and justify complete resources (this includes hardware/software, facilities, and the human element) can make the initial enterprise capacity plan (that includes storage) a success. The reason is that storage has often been viewed as a commodity and is purchased in a manner similar to all processing commodities like memory, end-user software, and printers, by cost. However, the storage network changes that significantly, by offering a complete infrastructure that includes the support of multiple processing server configurations. Storage networks can hardly be seen as a commodity, regardless of what vendors want you to think. On the other hand, NAS, although easy to slip through the official capacity planning exercises, often has extenuating effects on other supporting infrastructures within the data center, such as the network.

Finally, the justification of a SAN or NAS configuration based solely on consolidation of storage, servers, or recovery purposes does not make a capacity plan. These can be characterized as internal user requirements that may or may not justify the use of either storage network solution. This is not to say that these are superfluous or self-indulgent requirements; however, they must relate to the business supported by the data center. Justification on a cost basis, which is usually the case for consolidation and recovery strategies, needs to be balanced by a long-term plan to allow the storage infrastructure to grow along with the storage demands of the business.

Also, the establishment of a plan does not dictate its success. The data center must manage the plan. This is especially important with technologies that are volatile, support dynamic growth, and which are critical to an application's success. This is what storage networks are, and that's why they need a storage networking capacity plan of their own. Once integrated into the enterprise plan, and having the confidence of data center management, the storage plan can play a vital and productive role in the long term.

Developing a Plan for Storage

Storage provisioning begins with a sound capacity plan to establish a reasonable configuration that supports the business applications and constituency of users—both end users and data-center users. Thus begins a chicken-and-egg scenario. It also provides the justification for things like beta installations prior to committing new technology platforms like SAN and NAS configurations to production environments.

To calculate and commit to availability metrics, the following guidelines should be considered in establishing a reasonable plan to support SAN or NAS configurations.

Analyzing End-User, Application, and Internal Systems Requirements

■ Develop a method of communications with end users, applications designers and developers, operations, and systems infrastructure colleagues.

■ Define a capacity storage metric and level of precision. This could be capacities in number of bytes with a precision to the nearest megabyte, or it could be a more esoteric work unit such as an application work unit calculated as 1 gigabyte per unit, or a relational database unit such as 1 megabyte per unit. Whatever you use, keep consistent with the metric and level of precision. Keep in mind that you should allow for incongruities in media, which may be reflected in disk and tape densities, sector sizes, and blocking architectures.

■ When collecting storage capacity requirements, remember to calculate both end-user aggregate data and the necessary overhead to support the data. For example, if end-user data for a database is 100GB, then the total data requirement will be 100GB plus the necessary overhead of database system, index, and temporary tables. Depending on the type of application, this could go as high as 50 percent of the aggregate user data storage requirement, rendering our example to 150GB required for current database physical storage. Other application systems such as e-mail, ERP, and CRM all have additional storage overhead requirements that are important to consider along with the aggregate user data.

Planning and Establishing Adequate Capacity Based Upon I/O Workload Estimates

■ An important consideration to storage capacity is the processing requirements that together with capacity requirements drive the configuration elements necessary to meet end-user demand. In order to accurately estimate these requirements, its necessary to translate user requirements into I/O workload estimates (see Chapter 17).

■ Using I/O workload identification recommendations (again, see Chapter 17) the application workload types begin to distinguish themselves. Consider size versus access as the applications demonstrate their workload characteristics such as OLTP, batch, messaging, and combinations of these. The size factor, as depicted in our discussion about capacity, must be considered along with the calculation of the I/O workload factors. This allows for the initial elements of the configuration to start to take shape.

■ Recovery factors also influence the configuration elements. My I/O workload guidelines provide a recovery factor for calculating the configuration elements (see Chapter 17). However, this calculation should reflect the necessary insurance required for particular data-center business continuity requirements (see Chapter 21).

■ Although a subset of recovery, the redundancy factor must not only be taken into account for recovery factors, but also for security and individual failover. Largely driven by system failover requirements, the redundancy in both NAS and SAN can be implemented within themselves, and thus can be a substantial factor in configuring redundant systems. Therefore, they should be considered as separate items even though they're related to recovery and business continuity at a macro level.

Establishing an External Capacity Driver Matrix

■ Application requirements drive most of the capacity requirements; however, they provide little if any insight into the storage configuration to support the business application. By developing an external capacity driver, you have identified the major influences that drive both capacity and performance.

■ System requirements drive the rest of the capacity requirements with overhead to OS, subsystems, and network requirements. However, these spheres of technology also exert influence on the configuration they feel are most appropriate to the processing of the business applications. By developing the external capacity driver, you have also identified the influences on the storage infrastructure.

Establishing a Reporting Mechanism

■ Once the end user, application, and systems requirements are translated and calculated into requirements for a storage configuration, develop a reporting mechanism on the activity of their storage usage. The system must be able to be as proactive as possible in order to show trends that are outside the requirements, and to compare them against the storage capacity plan.

Managing to Storage Capacity Plans and Established Service Levels

■ The establishment of the reporting mechanism begins the management of the plan. Given the translation of requirements to real storage resources, the users must be held accountable for their estimates. However, given the volatility of the technologies and the changes in business climates, things will change. Therefore, it's important to also establish an effective communication system track requirements to actual usage without retribution (see establishing a non-aggression pact).

- The User Non-Aggression Pact: It is always helpful to reach an agreement with a user community that accounts for the unexpected. This allows both parties to agree that the unexpected does happen, and should it occur, it should be resolved with both mutual understanding and changes to the existing plan. This can be critical given the volatility of SAN installations and NAS data volume requirements.

    - **Unexpected Requirements**   The most common set of unexpected circumstances is the unforeseen application that requires support but which has not been planned for. In terms of affecting the SAN installation, this can be costly as well as disruptive, given the scope of the new application storage requirements. Within the NAS environment, this is one of the strengths NAS brings to the data center. If the requirements can be handled through file access, NAS performance, and capacities, then the NAS solution can be used effectively during these circumstances.

    - **Unforeseen Technology Enhancements**   This is the most common circumstance when initial SAN design proves insufficient to handle the workload. The outcome of retrofitting the SAN configuration with enhanced components is additional cost and disruption.

    - **Mid-term Corrections**   It's likely that any enterprise storage installation will experience either one or both of the preceding conditions. Consequently, it's extremely important to build into the user agreements the ability to provide mid-term corrections that are an evaluation of the current services and corrections to requirements in order to continue to meet the committed services.

The Storage Analysis

Analysis of storage is divided into two distinct parts: new storage demands and existing storage allocations. Although these two different activities culminate in the same place, which are reasonable configurations that support end-user demands, the reason they are distinct is the following. The demands for new storage provide an opportunity to consider alternative methods to meeting the demands, rather than extending the current configuration. This is most appropriate in storage networking given the sometimes overlapping solutions that exist between NAS and SAN solutions. It is also appropriate when considering moving from direct-attached configurations where the storage demands are not closely tied to existing configurations.

Leveraging a Storage Upgrade

When considering a storage upgrade for capacity and performance, the analysis of a storage network should be part of the storage capacity planning activities. However, this does provide a challenge to the existing server infrastructure and installed storage components. Moving away from any of these requires additional hardware, software, and training. It also requires concurrence from the external drivers, such as applications and systems. Likely, each of these may be resistant to change and the ability to rely on information from the external driver matrix will assist in the justification of the "what's in it for me" scenario.

Analysis of existing storage can provide greater justification into storage networking solutions given the scalability limitations within the client/server direct-attached model (see Chapters 1 and 2). More often than not, the move to storage networking provides a longer term solution in supporting increased user demands. Using the previously described user requirements translations and I/O workload calculations, the justification can prepare the way for the necessary increase in expenditures as well as showing the short-term fix that adding storage to existing server configurations will have.

Establishing a New Storage Network

Analyzing new storage demands provides an opportunity to leverage a storage network— driven by user requirements and I/O workload analysis, the justification can be compelling. New storage capacity can be depicted in terms of scalability of capacity and performance, but also in its ability to consolidate some of the legacy storage into the storage network. This provides the first articulation and integration of internal consolidation factors that are so popular in justifying SANs. However, the same can be said for NAS devices if the storage and application characteristics are justified in this solution.

Working in conjunction with your systems colleagues, there can be real synergy in establishing a storage network strategy. First, is the consolidation of servers. That, in itself, is a large cost factor reduction in overall systems responsibility and administration. This will be augmented by added savings of OS and application license fees associated with multiple servers with direct-attached strategies. Finally, there is the added benefit of managing fewer server entities and the processing consolidation that occurs with the collapse of application processes into a single, albeit larger, server. These cost savings start to mediate the increased costs associated with a storage network solution.

A hidden benefit to systems administrators is the performance and problem management factors that come with storage networking. The consolidation of servers and the collapsing of the storage arrays translates to less network connectivity, minimum servers to manage, and consequently fewer things to go wrong. Establishing an agreed upon and reasonable metric for this allows a quantifiable benefit to be monitored when adopted. In other words, if putting in four NAS devices can collapse file servers on a 20:1 basis, then the quantifiable benefit will be losing 20 general-purpose servers for every single NAS device. If that were the case, then once the plan is implemented, the redeployment or retirement of the 80 servers, to use our example, would create excellent credibility for the plan and storage network.

Tools for Storage Analysis

Storage networking can be analyzed in two ways: the physical capacity and the performance of the configuration. Just as direct-attached storage configurations are monitored for storage allocation, usage, and access, storage networks need to provide the same information. The problem comes with both the lack of tools that account for multiple usages of networked storage arrays and the immaturity of system tracking databases that provide historical data. Performance monitoring in storage networks provides the same challenge regarding tool deficiencies and lack of historical data collectors.

There are several storage software choices when considering capacity and access monitoring tools. It is beyond the scope of this book to analyze or recommend any of these tools and should be a data-center specific choice dependent on the specific needs of the entire storage infrastructure. These tools fall into two categories related to a wide variety of tools known as storage resource management tools. Subcategories include the quota management and volume management tools.

Storage Resource Management

Quota management tools provide a mechanism to assign storage capacity quotas to end users or specific applications, or a combination of both. These provide a safety net in terms of storage usage and the potential of errant users or applications to utilize the majority of storage capacity in an unregulated environment. The quotas are generally set by administrators, either from a storage or systems perspective, and managed from a central location.

The majority of tools in these categories provide some level of reporting on storage utilization. The more sophisticated tools provide views from several perspectives: by end user, by application, by logical volume, or by logical device. These tools work well with file-oriented storage implementations; however, they become problematic when attempting to understand the storage usage of relational databases or applications employing an embedded database model.

It's important to note that in these cases, and given the installation of databases within the data centers (which is likely to be large), the monitoring of storage utilization and access needs to rely on the database monitoring and management tools. This provides another important element within the external capacity driver matrix (see establishing an external capacity matrix), which is the influence of database administrators, designers, and programmers. Given the transparent nature of the relational and embedded databases to the physical storage, the usage of these application subsystems needs to be managed in conjunction with the database expertise. However, it's also important to become familiar with these tools to understand the underlying physical activity within the storage infrastructure.

Volume Managers

Another category of tools that can provide storage analysis information are volume managers. These tools provide the ability to further manage storage by allocating the physical storage in virtual pools of capacity. This allows file systems and applications to access particular volumes that are predefined with specific storage capacity. This can be extremely valuable when allocating storage for particular applications that have specific requirements for storage needs and may become volatile if storage becomes constrained.

Like quota management tools, most volume managers have reporting mechanisms to track both usage and access. They also provide an important function and level of detail that enhances both performance analysis and problem determination. Volume managers work in conjunction with storage controller and adapter hardware to separate the logical unit (LUN) numbering schemes used by the hardware functions. As such, they provide a physical-to-logical translation that becomes critical in understanding the actual operation of a storage configuration. Given the complexities of SANs, these functions can be extremely important in problem determination and monitoring performance.

We have used volume manager examples in many of the figures within this book. As Figure 24-2 shows, they add relevance to naming storage devices within a configuration. As seen in this figure, a typical storage area network, prod01, prod02, and prod03 are disk volumes that contain the production databases for the configuration. The storage administrator through the services of the volume manager software assigns the specific volume a name. The volume manager, meanwhile, manages the storage pools, prod01, prod02, and prod03, transparently. Working in conjunction with storage controllers and adapters, the volume manager works to translate the LUN assignments within each of their storage arrays. In viewing the actual physical operation of the storage configurations, one must understand and look at the LUN assignments and activity within each storage configuration.

The quota and volume management tools provide a snapshot of storage usage and access. However, looking for a longer term historical usage becomes problematic. One of the continuing difficulties within the open systems operating environments is the lack of historical collection capabilities, although this situation continues for a number of reasons, such as disparate processing architectures, box mentality, and distributed computing challenges. Each of these provides a roadblock when systems personnel attempt to gather historical processing information.

Collecting Storage Information

Disparate operating systems provide the first problem, as the major contributor to the differences between vendors, but especially between UNIX and Windows operating environments. Historically, however, the centralized mainframe computing systems of IBM and others provided a unique architecture to gather processing data. Most examples

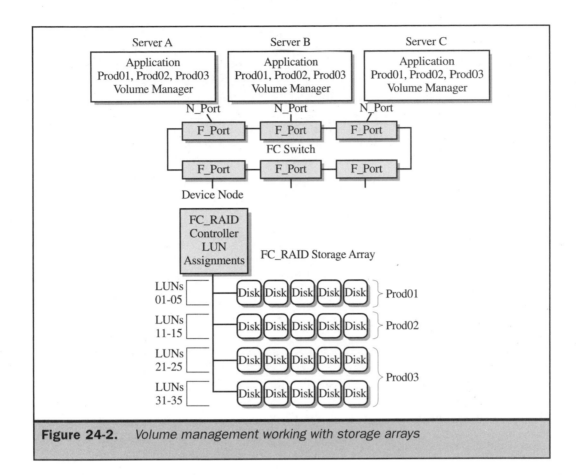

Figure 24-2. *Volume management working with storage arrays*

in this area point to the IBM System Management Facility (SMF) and Resource Management Facility (RMF) functions as models for what should be expected within the open systems area. Overall, this is not the case, and taken out of its centralized and proprietary context, the SMF and RMF models for historical information gathering do not fit well into the area of client/server and distributed computing.

The first area not covered by the IBM model is the collection and support of distributed computing configurations that have become commonplace within client/server installations. This is exacerbated by the open architectures of UNIX systems and lack of any standards in processing nomenclature. Consequently, there are multiple ways of viewing a process within the UNIX variants of the UNIX open systems model. This permeates into the storage space, as the nomenclature and operation of UNIX storage models are, by design, very flexible and open to vendor interpretation. So gathering data about a SUN configuration is a different exercise than gathering processing information about an AIX environment. If we throw in the increased open area of storage, vendor support for each of these environments makes the common historical database such as IBM's SMF and RMF impossible.

The second area that makes the centralized proprietary environment different is the distributed nature of processing. As servers became specialized, the ability to provide a historical record in context with the application became problematic at best. Consider a database transaction that executes partly on application servers, where application logic creates and submits a database query, which is executed on another server. The historical log of the application processing becomes difficult to track as it migrates from one server to another. With the distributed processing activity, the combined activity information transverses from one operating system to another with the related resource utilization. This example points out the problematic recording of database transactions within the context of the application.

We will integrate the complexities of a SAN into the collection discussion and provide yet another source of processing and resource information into the capacity planning equation. In terms of a SAN, this becomes the fabric and related micro-kernel operations in moving the data within the storage network. If we integrate the NAS environment, we integrate yet two more sources of processing: the NAS micro-kernel processing and the operating systems that run the network fabric. The collection of data for both SAN and NAS adds additional data collection points that are again distributed in nature.

The point is that the collection of data within the distributed environment continues to be problematic. Although there are some methods that attempt to deal with these issues, the need to develop an alternative to the historical collection of data becomes evident. Currently, only a limited number of software tools are effectively addressing this area using emerging standards that not all vendors have accepted. This exacerbates the situation for storage analysis within storage networks, given the difficulty in collecting valid storage activity information.

However, there are two basic initiatives to consider when collecting historical storage activity information. The first is the industry initiative of the common information model (CIM) that is an object-oriented database for collecting system processing details and device status. CIM is a Microsoft-initiated standard that has achieved some level of acceptance although its complexity continues to make it impractical for storage network usage. The other item is the usage of network-oriented tools which many storage-networking vendors include with their products: the management information base (MIB). These provide the quickest way of collecting information in-band for the SAN and within the NAS micro-kernel (although this isn't used as often in the NAS micro-kernel levels).

The Common Information Model and Storage Networks

The common information model (CIM) is an object specification that provides a uniform way of describing a computer and its components. The specification is used as a standard to write applications that access the objects as described within the model. The CIM initiative first started as a Microsoft object-oriented structure used mainly by the operating system to build a repository of general and specific information about the computer it was running on.

The objective of this functionality was to give hardware companies the ability to access their components within a network. Used for support and problem management, vendors quickly contributed to the Microsoft-led initiative with specifications for general computer components, concentrating chiefly on internal components for processors, adapter cards, and memory structures. However, it was also Microsoft's objective to evaluate a configuration in order to determine the requirements needed for particular operating system functions, applications packages, and licensing verification. Oddly enough, the initial releases of the CIM specification did not reflect any of the major peripheral and processing software components necessary to complete a computer configuration.

The Microsoft CIM initiative was soon passed to the Distributed Desktop Management Task Force, DMTF, a standards-based body that manages similar initiatives for distributed PCs. DMTF had already recognized the CIM initiative and included it as part of the initial releases of DMTF standards. The move to integrate CIM as a DMTF standard came about the time another consortium standard initiative was passed into the DMTF— this was WBEM, or web-based enterprise management.

The WBEM initiative began the development of particular standards for enterprise management of computers over the Web. As Microsoft was one of the original members of the WBEM consortium, one of the standards initiatives it began with was the CIM standard. So any vendor wishing to develop products that could be managed uniformly, regardless of vendor association, and managed over the Web, must meet the CIM and WBEM standards.

Consequently, specifications for general storage devices (say, IDE and SCSI drives) and offline media, such as tape and optical peripherals, were not added until later. The component descriptions for Storage Area Networks are very new and have only been added as of the writing of this book. However, given vendor acceptance and cooperation, CIM and WBEM do provide a uniform description for storage devices and storage network components. As these specifications are incorporated within vendor products, the data center begins to see a consistent view of the storage infrastructure.

The important points here are the eventual scope of the CIM specifications and the use of CIM as a standard. As a standard, that means sufficient vendors must integrate their product offerings into the CIM standard before the concept becomes relevant to the data center. As a meaningful solution, both vendors that develop management products as well as vendors that develop storage networking products must adhere to the CIM standard for this to be productive. In other words, it would be difficult if you have vendor A's disk products that conformed to the CIM standard, and vendor B's disk products that did not but conform to their own specifications of storage devices and activities. The same can be said for vendors who provide products for performance management and capacity planning—the standard must support all instances of CIM implementation at the storage hardware and software level. In addition, the CIM specification itself must have sufficient detail to provide value.

SNMP and MIBs

MIBs, on the other hand, have come through the standards process and been accepted as a valid solution for collecting and describing information about—get ready for this—networks. Yes, the MIB specification came from the network environment and continues to be used today as a fundamental element of network management activities.

Management information bases (MIBs) are very complex file-oriented databases that describe a network and its components and act as a repository for activity information that occurs within the network. The MIBs were the database for a distributed protocol that is used to access remote networks for management purposes. This protocol is known as the Simple Network Management Protocol, or SNMP. Anyone with networking experience should be quite familiar with this concept and protocol.

SNMP and their related MIBs create a way of collecting information for inclusion in performance, problem, and capacity management. However, SNMP and their related MIBs are complex systems that require specific programming to derive value. Many network management products base their functions on SNMP and MIB standards. This proximity of network technologies within the SAN environments prompted the inclusion of MIBs within the SAN switch software.

Leveraged by SAN vendors as an accepted network management tool, the SNMP and MIB combination for SAN management laid the groundwork for today's management repository for SANs. Although not as likely to be accessed or included within the micro-kernel applications, the NAS configurations can also be included in SNMP and MIB solutions. The caveat is the complexities of the solution and the long-term viability of the MIB. The data center must rely on third-party software products that integrate SNMP functions while allocating their own MIB files, or face writing their own SNMP scripts and defining the MIB files themselves. The latter is a complex, time-consuming task within the data center.

Modeling Performance and Capacity Requirements

One objective of the capacity planning activities is to estimate as accurately as possible the future needs of users. This generally can be accomplished from modeling the potential workloads and configurations for adequate fit. In general-purpose capacity planning terms, there are levels of modeling that can fit the needs of most data-center requirements. These solutions range from expensive and specialized software tools that model workloads and potential performance based upon hardware configurations, to vendor benchmarking that generally uses subsets of the actual data-center workloads, and the official performance councils that provide third-party benchmarks of vendor solutions.

The first set is the capacity planning modeling tools. Although these provide the greatest detail, their accuracy depends on the data applied to the model, and the expertise in analyzing the output of the benchmark results. Unfortunately, these tools have yet to be developed for storage networks, but through creative efforts could probably be modeled given sufficient time and money. Even then, the model would be an integrated simulation of workloads that share common storage arrays, or in the case of NAS workloads, that provide additional latencies as remote network drives.

The second set is the vendor benchmarks, although these by their very nature will be suspect given their inability to replicate the specifics of an individual data center. These simulations don't always have the disparate facilities that make up production data centers, and as a result, the benchmark may be skewed toward the vendor's solution. Wouldn't that be a surprise? However, vendor's benchmarks provide valuable insight into understanding the potential capacity and performance of an expensive storage infrastructure installation. The additional aspect is that many first-tier vendors have user benchmark centers where they test potential customer solutions as well as conduct their own interoperability testing.

The third set is the third-party benchmarks by non-profit corporations that sponsor testing and performance benchmarks of real-life configurations. These companies are likened to the insurance safety councils that perform crash tests. The performance councils take off-the-shelf equipment from vendors and build a real-life configuration in order to run a simulated workload based upon end-user applications, such as OLTP and data warehouse transactions. In other words, they test out the configuration in real-life scenarios so as to validate all the factors a data center would consider when purchasing the configuration. Two are relevant to the storage industry: the Transaction Processing Performance Council (TPC) and the Storage Performance Council (SPC).

The TPC provides benchmark testing of computer configurations using standard transactional sets. These benchmarks execute transactions that characterize database queries which simulate everything from simple queries to complex data warehouse queries that access multiple databases. The tests are run on vendor-supplied hardware and software configurations that range from homogenous hardware systems to heterogeneous software operating environments and database systems. The test results are generally published and available for purchase through the council. This allows data centers to monitor different levels of potential configurations at arm's length while obtaining information about potential cost-to-operating environment requirements. This provides an evaluation of storage from an integrated view, as storage configurations become part of the system's overall configuration.

The SPC is specific to storage and is the new kid on the block when it comes to evaluating vendor storage configurations. This is the most specific and productive modeling available to date for storage networking and capacity modeling. Their job is to be the insurance safety council for the storage industry and protect the data center from products that continue to be problematic in real-life implementations, while providing an effective feedback mechanism for vendors who strive for better goods.

The SPC-specific objectives are meant to provide both the data center and systems integrators with an accurate database of performance and price/performance results spanning manufacturers, configurations, and products. They also use these experiences to build tools that help data centers analyze and effectively configure storage networks.

They do this through a series of configuration requirements, performance metrics, and tests. The services can analyze small subsets of storage, from JBOD and RAID storage arrays to large-scale SAN configurations. However, all configurations must meet the following criteria prior to testing:

- **Data Persistence**   Storage used in an SPC test must demonstrate the ability to preserve data without corruption or loss. Equipment sponsors are required to complete audited tests that verify this capability.

- **Sustainability**   A benchmark configuration must easily demonstrate that results can be consistently maintained over long periods of time as would be expected in system environments with demanding long-term I/O request throughput requirements.

- **Equal Access to Host Systems**   All host systems used to impose benchmark-related I/O load on the tested storage configuration must have equal access to all storage resources.

- **Support for General Purpose Applications**   SPC benchmarks provide objective and verifiable performance data. Specifically prohibited are benchmark systems whose primary purpose is the performance optimization of the SPC benchmark results without corresponding applicability to real-world applications and environments.

Vendors who submit their products to these benchmarks must have their systems available to ship to customers within 60 days of reporting the SPC benchmark tests.

Probably the most valuable aspect of the SPC benchmarks is the actual test. The SPC has developed two environments that depict many of the workload demands we have previously discussed (see Chapter 17). The following describes two test scenarios that are run.

- **SPC1 IOPS (I/Os per Second) Metric**   An environment composed of application systems that have many users and simultaneous application transactions which can saturate the total I/O operations capacity of a storage subsystem. An OLTP application model makes up the benchmark where the success of the system rests on the ability of the storage system to process large numbers of I/O requests while maintaining acceptable response times to the end users.

- **SPC1-LRT (Least Response Time) Metric**   This environment depicts a batch type of operations where applications are dependent on elapsed time requirements to complete. These applications provide multiple I/O requests, which are often serial in nature—in other words, they must complete in a predefined order. The success of the storage system in these processing environments is dependent on its ability to minimize the response time for each I/O request and thereby limit the elapsed time necessary.

The SPC carefully audits and validates the results of benchmarks. Configurations and testing criteria is audited and validated either onsite or remotely through an audit protocol. This serves to provide the vendor with audit certification that the tests and configurations meet the SPC standards and testing criteria. A peer review is conducted upon the completion of benchmark results. Results are considered validated and become official upon the completion of the 60-day peer review process if no compliance challenges have been brought forward. Official results are available to SPC members on their web site and open to certain publication rights.

Implementing the Plan

Taking into account a comprehensive analysis of the existing or proposed storage infrastructure, implementation becomes the critical factor. A big factor in implementation is the acquisition of upgrade hardware and software or a completely new solution. Coupled with acquisition of the storage networking components is the scheduled installation, testing, and transfer of production storage data and workload I/O processing. This is followed by the initialization of the systems management cycle of activities.

Acquisition of storage capacity is an exercise in commodity purchases driven in most data centers by price. The best price per MB usually gets the business and drives storage vendors to differentiate their offerings in the firmware and software solutions that become part of the system. However, the storage networking business has turned this upside-down, with the necessity of new networking devices and the enhanced storage arrays and tape systems that must be FC-enabled. This has placed price in a more balanced perspective with other major purchase factors, such as reliability, service, and quality.

Consequently, the following guidelines can be used to assist in data-center acquisition strategies when purchasing storage networking solutions.

- **Competitive Bids**   It's important to gather at least three competitive bids for the configuration you are seeking. Ensure that the requirements for storage networking, be it SAN or multiple NAS solutions, are available to the vendors you have decided to work with. Be advised that "total solution" offerings that are provided through storage vendors and systems integrators allow them an additional revenue source.

- **OEM Knowledge**   Most storage networking vendors, especially larger system vendors, provide their solutions as a composite of external components supplied by the third-party companies. These companies provide their component, be it hardware or software, as an Original Equipment Manufacturer (OEM) supplier, and place their name on the device. This is commonplace in storage networking with most SAN solutions being made up of OEM suppliers. This is not a bad thing, but it's important to compare apples to apples when considering competitive bids. In other words, don't pay extra for the same FC equipment, such as switches, HBAs, or routers that is available through a competitive solution.

■ **Storage vs. the Network** Try to separate the storage part from the network part. This is especially helpful in SAN acquisition, given that the network portion is likely to expand at a different rate than the actual storage arrays. The storage capacity plan should provide for incremental upgrades through the planning cycle, generally a year in length. During this time, storage array acquisition can be part of the competitive bidding process, but should be negotiated with as little bid lock-in as possible. In other words, have the vendors consider bidding on the entire plan (for example, a complete year of requirements) to obtain a better price, service, and vendor commitment.

Design and Configuration

Many of the examples shown in the book depict storage networks supporting three common types of workloads: OLTP, Web Internet Based, and Data Warehouse. More details on these I/O workloads can be found throughout the book with additional guidelines on identification and estimating in Chapter 17. Typically, SAN configurations are comprised of combinations of 8-, 16-, and 32-port FC switches, with disk arrays commensurate with storage capacities that have been estimated with workloads. Within NAS installations, typical configurations can encompass both departmental solutions and support within the data center for more sophisticated applications. Another important point to consider is the external factors that influence the installation. These are Ethernet network modifications within NAS installations and should be considered prior to installation. SAN configurations are subject to the inclusion of intersystem-link ports (ISLs) and an integrated FC-SCSI bridge into a tape library.

Test Installation

It is important to define, configure, and install a permanent test installation environment. Putting a small configuration in place provides essential first-case experiences in the configuration and operation of both SAN and NAS installations. This also provides a test bed for testing future software and hardware upgrades while enabling an application testing facility.

Use the test installation to initiate a pseudo-management practice. Management becomes a very challenging activity, especially when operating the new devices and complexities in the SAN. It also is the most rapidly evolving practice, with constant change occurring in software tools and accepted practices. Additional discussion of storage network management topics can be found in Part VI.

Production Installation

Develop a production turnover activity where a formal change window is established. In many cases, this may need to be integrated into existing change management activity within the data center. Key among these is tracking the changes made to all components of the storage network (see Chapter 23). It becomes particularly troublesome if you formalize changes to the switch configurations and not to upgrades of critical components such as HBAs, routers, and attached storage devices.

An important aspect of product installation is establishing a backout practice. Because the storage network is an infrastructure in and of itself, the reliability can be problematic in the beginning, as with any new technology. However, being able to back out quickly and return the production environment to an existing state saves valuable time as you move into a storage networking environment.

Closing the Loop

Here, we come full circle. Back to the place we started in this part of the book—that is, a sound and well-thought-out capacity plan for storage networking. The benefits are evident in the increased availability, reliability, and success of the storage networking infrastructure. In addition to setting the basis for a manageable set of service levels, the capacity plan supports the external systems and applications departments in the data center. More important is the credibility it establishes for that support.

The rationale that storage networking is a new technology and does not lend itself to traditional or summary planning for capacity is incorrect. As we have demonstrated, the process of estimating resources and configurations can be done. However, it is an iterative process and one that becomes more accurate as mistakes and related information arise. As new information and tools become available, the accuracy and time required to plan for effective storage networking configurations will increase. Key among these will be the increased information collection methods and the ability to provide effective statistical predictions without the collection of months and months of detailed activity information.

This must be balanced against the fast-moving storage networking industry where new technologies become available almost every calendar quarter. The difficulties behind planning without the knowledge of technology advancements will move both the vendor community and the data center to reach some level of product planning communications that is beneficial to both parties. As discussed in Chapter 20, new innovations continue to affect the storage networking solution. Among these is the coalescing of SAN and NAS architectures and the advancement of traditional computer bus technologies into switched fabrics.

Storage networking has become the cornerstone of new applications within the data center and continues to deliver the scalable performance necessary for the future. However, these new storage functions must be applied in an organized and planned fashion. Capacity planning for storage networking infrastructures may form the foundation for the next level of storage management, culminating in a true paradigm shift within the data center.

Chapter 25

Security Considerations

As storage networks continue to grow and become more complicated, management processes and security procedures will play an integral role. While management is a key requirement in any type of storage infrastructure, security is the one component that could undermine the availability of both management and storage. This chapter provides an introduction to many of the existing and future security problems in storage networks and the correlating best practices that can be implemented today. Although this chapter will not cover every single storage security problem or provide in-depth coverage on each security exposure identified, it will discuss the architectural and tactical problems that most often plague storage networks and how to approach a solution for each of them.

While various trends have occurred in the digital marketplace over the past five decades, both storage and security have received more attention in the last decade (early 1990s to present) than the first four combined (excluding major governmental agencies' focus on security). Furthermore, with the growth of the Internet, security has been the focus of many conversations concerning network architecture, application design, and now storage technology.

The terms *storage technology* and *security architecture* would not have been mentioned in the same sentence a decade ago, or even five years ago. Today, however, with significant changes in the storage industry (the expansion of the storage network into the WAN and beyond the LAN) and due to education gained from the security mistakes in Internet Protocol (the numerous security problems with IP version 4), the relationship between storage technology and security architecture has become an important one. Today's storage industry has an opportunity to pursue and support a healthy security posture before storage security problems are widely identified and, more importantly, widely exploited.

It's important that you understand why storage and security must coexist so that you can anticipate an attack and understand an attacker's (hacker's) mindset. For example, consider a home with a front door, back door, and garage door as three legitimate entryways. The front door has three security devices: a door-handle lock, a dead-bolt lock, and a chain lock to prevent an intruder from entering. In addition, the homeowner has secured the back door with two security devices: a Master lock combination on the fence leading to the back door and a dead-bolt on the back door. The garage door is opened and closed only with a garage door opener, which is in the vehicle at all times. Additionally, the homeowner has purchased a security system to alarm the authorities in the event of a front or back door break-in (similar to an intrusion detection system, or IDS, in a network). This adds an extra obstacle for access to the front and back doors.

Note   *An IDS is a device that passively monitors networks to determine and report any type of malicious activity that is being conducted.*

Now consider the security of the house (or the computer network): The intruder must consider which is the best route, in terms of time and success, to enter the home (or network) and gather priceless goods. The front door contains three security devices. The door lock and dead-bolt can be picked, but this takes a significant amount of time and skill. Furthermore, even if the two locks were picked successfully, the chain lock would have to be cut with an industrial sized chain-cutter, requiring more skill and time. And then there's the alarm to consider. As a result, the front door sounds like a tough option.

For the back door, the fence Master lock combination will also take a significant amount of time because an infinite amount of combinations would need to be attempted. Even after the combination is finally "brute-forced," the back door dead-bolt would have to be picked, also taking time and skill. Even if this door were opened, the alarm would sound. This option also seems pretty unpromising.

The garage door is secured with the garage door opener. However, most garage door openers do not use an overly complicated infrared architecture to open the garage door. In fact, a local hardware store usually carries a device that spans several channels that might connect on the correct channel and open any garage door. In addition, most hand-held devices, such as Palm and PocketPC, can have applications that capture the infrared signals of a garage door opener to open it exclusively with the hand-held device. The purchase of this device, and the fact that the homeowner will probably be opening/closing her garage at the same time every morning, can result in an intruder using a hand-held device to capture the infrared signal and eventually open the garage. Once inside the garage, the only thing stopping the intruder is the house garage door—but many homeowners do not lock that door because of the assumption that an intruder would not be able to enter the locked garage.

This home example relates to the digital storage network and the mindset of a digital attacker. Although the storage network is not the traditional access point for most attacks, a savvy hacker can avoid the hassle of subverting multiple firewalls, switches, router Access Control Lists (ACLs), Virtual Private Network (VPN) devices, and IDS sensors to gain access to data via the less-protected storage network that has direct access to all of the important data.

Note *Router ACLs are used to allow or deny access to networks based on IP addresses. VPN devices allow for remote networks or individual users to connect to internal networks in a safe and secure manner. A VPN allows multiple networks in different geographic locations to exist as a large virtual network.*

Attackers are not interested in gaining administrator rights or even root access to a given host; rather, they are interested in access to data. The fact that the storage network contains sensitive data and is not adequately protected (similar to the house garage doors) leaves the perfect opportunity for an attacker. Furthermore, many of the storage protocols in place today, such as Fibre Channel and iSCSI, are bandwidth and throughput-focused protocols with security usually absent (similar to the poor infrared channels on many garage door openers). This scenario leaves the "door" wide open for attackers to subvert storage protocols and get direct access to data, without compromising one firewall or encryption device.

Even though the storage network is often not protected thoroughly, it has access to the company's critical data and intellectual property. The myth that the storage network cannot be reached by attackers is easily subverted with a variety of techniques that are usually easier than going through traditional networks with multiple firewalls, switches, router ACLs, VPN devices, and IDS sensors. This fact makes the decision easy for the attackers on which route they should take to access data quickly and easily.

This chapter introduces the concept of security in storage networks and discusses basic principles and best practices to consider. The following topics are discussed:

- Overview of computer security
- Security methods
- Storage security technology
- Storage security challenges
- Fibre Channel SAN security
- NAS security
- Best practices

Overview of Information Security

While security threats used to mean hackers defacing web sites and short-term embarrassment for an organization, new security threats are more serious matters—corrupting or deleting intellectual property, which results in the loss of revenue. The old model of viewing information security as an end result, such as a product, was not successful because it did not support the core principles of a strong security posture. In today's model, security is viewed as a process of good policies and procedures and is more successful and realistic. Security is not a product for an auditor to check off as he or she reviews a list of items. A strong security process in an organization provides a strong foundation to build upon and supports a stable security platform.

To support a good security process, basic security elements should be addressed. These elements can be applied to different aspects of storage networks, such as devices, applications, protocols, appliances, and so on. The following are typical security elements that must be addressed by any secure solution:

- Authentication
- Authorization
- Auditing
- Integrity
- Encryption
- Availability

Authentication

Authentication is the process by which an entity is verified. The entity can be a packet, a frame, a login request, or another entity. In all cases, the entity is identified and then authorized or unauthorized. Authentication and authorization are heavily dependent on each other, because one can be subverted easily in the absence of the other.

Authorization

Authorization is the process of determining which privileges are granted to which authenticated entity. Note that authorization is not the same as authentication. Authorization simply allows or denies actions based on a set of assumed authenticated credentials. Whether the authenticated credentials are valid is not possible to verify with authorization. Authorization views a set of authenticated entities and allocates *rights* to those entities.

Auditing

Auditing is the ability to capture and retain events that occur within the network or specific devices or applications. While auditing is considered a *passive* security element, it can make a network aware of a security incidence, which is often half the battle. In the absence of a pure security technology in the storage network, such as a firewall, it is imperative that auditing on storage devices and applications be increased and enabled to the fullest extent. An unsuccessful attack left unnoticed can leave an organization crippled in security.

Integrity

Integrity is the assurance that unauthorized parties have not modified an entity. Furthermore, integrity confirms that the data has not been altered in transit from the source to the destination. It allows a network to depend on other security elements, such as authentication and authorization.

Encryption

Encryption is the process of protecting information from unauthorized access or modification by converting it into *cipher-text* that can be accessed only through appropriate credentials or keys. Encryption also allows an untrusted entity, such as a network, to be used without additional security elements for support. For example, using encryption with a VPN device allows remote users to use the untrusted Internet as a medium for business operations. Similarly, the use of encrypted protocols, such as Secure Shell (SSH), allows users to use in-band data networks for management functions.

Availability

Availability means ensuring that resources are on hand for legitimate users, applications, or network devices when requested. Security enables availability by ensuring that unauthorized user access or denial-of-service attacks will be unsuccessful in a given storage object. If an attacker's goal is simply to affect a loss of revenue for a given organization, stealing the organization's data is not the only method that can be used to accomplish this; simply making part of the storage network unavailable would result in loss of business operations, which equates to the loss of revenue.

Overall, an organization's storage environment must address these security elements in some form to support a strong storage security posture. The solution must also enable a process to grow and maintain the storage security posture over an undefined period of time. A strong presence in security at one point in time does not necessarily equate to a strong security presence in the future. A successful security plan will foster growth and provide stability to the storage network over a period of time.

Security Methods

Critical for security is a layered security model, also known as *defense in depth*. In the defense-in-depth model, layers of security are built in conjunction with one another in a complementary fashion. Many networks are built with the "M&M model,"—that is, hard on the outside and soft on the inside. This model crumbles after a single penetration of the outer perimeter. A defense-in-depth model would not crumble if any devices were subverted, such as the outer perimeter, because it would contain security layers behind each device.

An example of the defense-in-depth model in the storage network is an ACL on a storage node, such as an EMC or Network Appliance NAS head, that restricts or permits access according to IP address or subnet. These ACLs complement the required authentication and authorization procedures by the storage appliances and/or operating systems. With this model, if one or both of the security elements were subverted, the attackers would still be denied access if they were not sending the request from the correct IP address. Figure 25-1 illustrates the defense-in-depth model.

The defense-in-depth model allows organizations to protect their critical and sensitive storage data by eliminating any single point of failure. As shown in Figure 25-1, the model can be as simple as enabling security features on operating systems, storage switches, NAS heads, and even back-end disk arrays. Additionally, security controls can be placed on host-bus adapters (HBAs), network interface cards (NICs), client workstations, storage nodes, and storage applications. Because the storage industry has not yet come up with any pure security device, such as a firewall, security features need to be enabled and explored at other devices to support a defense-in-depth architecture to the fullest extent.

A single layer of security does not adequately protect an organization's storage network, proprietary data, or intellectual property. In addition, identified security weaknesses in one area, such as a storage application, can actually nullify strong security measures in other areas, such as a storage switch. A layered security model, in which security is emphasized at key segments throughout the storage network rather than one or two segments, supports a strong storage security posture.

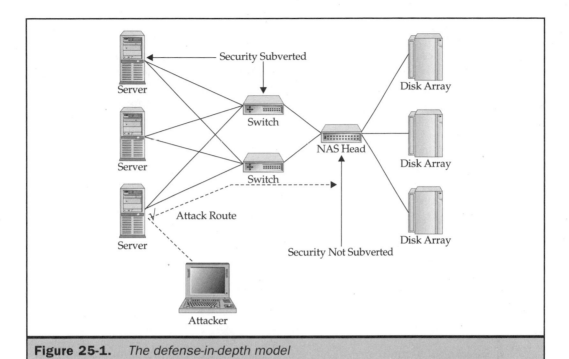

Figure 25-1. *The defense-in-depth model*

Storage Security Technology

The storage security technology industry is currently in the development phase, and in this process more questions than answers have been uncovered. However, emerging storage security organizations are designing solutions to help secure storage networks from both unauthorized users and accidental configuration mistakes. Existing storage vendors are also extending their product features to include security solutions. The following sections discuss the following storage security technologies that are under development as well as those that have already been deployed:

- Inline encryption
- Encryption at rest
- Key-based authentication
- Two-factor application authentication

Inline Encryption

Currently, the T11 committee is working on an initiative to incorporate IP Security (IPSec) technology established in the IP industry into the storage industry with iSCSI and Fibre Channel Security (FCSec). T11 has established a framework that will use ESP (Encapsulating Security Payload) in Fibre Channel layer 2 to protect frame data. ESP within the Fibre Channel frame will be able to provide confidentiality between two end nodes, such as a switch and an HBA.

Additionally, ESP will be able to enhance frame security by providing authentication, integrity, and anti-replay protection for each frame. This will prevent common attacks at the frame/packet layer, such as session hijacking, spoofing, and Man-In-The-Middle (MITM) attacks (described later in the chapter). The adoption of FCSec technology into the storage community will allow for greater flexibility for a storage network. Specifically, the key goals for the FCSec architecture are as follows:

- Node-to-node authentication
- Node-to-switch authentication
- Switch-to-switch authentication
- Frame-level encryption

Node-to-node authentication will allow each entity to authenticate frames transmitted between two nodes. This allows for the integrity of each frame between the two nodes and ensures against spoofing or replay attacks in the fabric.

Node-to-switch authentication will be similar to node-to-node authentication in that it ensures integrity in each frame. Additionally, node-to-switch authentication will allow switch management tools to contain added strength in their allocation mechanisms (for example, zone allocation).

Switch-to-switch authentication will allow each switch to ensure the integrity of data and management, such as Simple Name Server (SNS) information, to be protected against transport layer attacks. In addition, switch-to-switch authentication will reduce the possibility of a rogue switch gaining instant control of the entire fabric.

In addition to the authentication capabilities of FCSec at the frame level, confidentiality can be provided by using encryption of each frame as it exchanges data between two entities, including both node and switch entities.

Encryption at Rest

The encryption of data at rest uses a different approach than inline encryption. Standards committees are developing technologies such as FCSec to protect data and authentication for inline encryption. Encryption of data at rest is being addressed by new storage vendors and new storage products.

Data at rest is one of the most commonly overlooked risk areas in storage security. While most security efforts focus on protocols and architecture, the security of data at rest tends to be incorrectly assumed as secure. Data on disk is often considered secure because it is kept deep inside the storage network, with multiple storage devices restricting access. However, these types of security assumptions expose the data both to accidental actions and unauthorized activity.

Several new organizations are designing products to encrypt the data before it reaches the disk. At that level of encryption, if the storage node is compromised, the attacker will not have readable access to any of the data residing on the disk. In the event of a configuration error, the data on the disk may not be fully exposed due to the encrypted format of the data.

Various storage devices protect the data at rest in different ways, but all of them try to accomplish the same goal of protection. The encryption solutions that encrypt data on disk protect against possible configuration errors or mistakes commonly found in storage networks. Configuration errors are the most common problems identified in storage networks today. If controls are not in place to mitigate possible configuration issues, the ability to compromise data in the storage network might be larger than expected. Additionally, since storage networks are complicated by nature, the likelihood of a configuration error incorrectly exposing the SAN (Storage Area Network) is higher than for many other types of networks.

Figures 25-2 and 25-3 demonstrate two scenarios of configuration errors that might lead to the compromise of data. Figure 25-2 shows how configuration errors can occur at the storage switch. Figure 25-3 shows how an encryption device can protect against storage configuration errors.

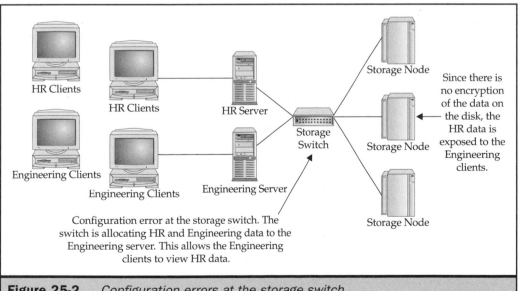

Figure 25-2.   *Configuration errors at the storage switch*

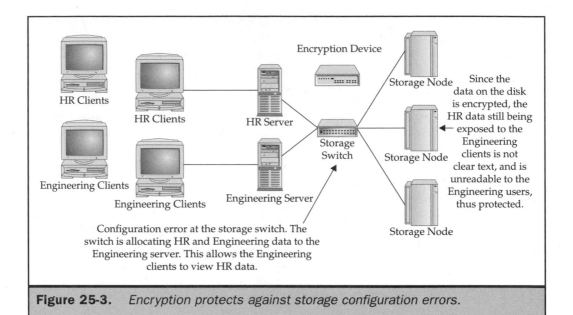

Since the data on the disk is encrypted, the HR data still being exposed to the Engineering clients is not clear text, and is unreadable to the Engineering users, thus protected.

Configuration error at the storage switch. The switch is allocating HR and Engineering data to the Engineering server. This allows the Engineering clients to view HR data.

Figure 25-3.   *Encryption protects against storage configuration errors.*

Key-Based Authentication

Fibre Channel-Generic Services-3 (FC-GS-3) is another technology that T11 standards organizations have developed. Key server technology is discussed in FC-GS-3 to enable key-based authentication, which supports the best practice of two-factor authentication in storage devices, such as switches, appliances, and clients. Unlike the FCSec project, the FC-GS-3 project is not solely a project about security. FC-GS-3 includes specifications dealing with management, directory service, time service, alias service, and other services. However, we will be referring to FC-GS-3 only in terms of the key server technology that it addresses.

The Key Distribution Service discussed in FC-GS-3 will provide a method for secure distribution of public and private keys in a storage network used for authentication, similar to a KDC (Kerberos Distribution Center) in IP networks. The security "key server" in the storage network would use a level of encryption to protect the keys and underlying protocols for verification purposes. By using a key server, data would be signed, providing a secure means of authenticating the original node as well as verifying the data was not modified during transit. This method of using a key server is often referred to as *CT* (*Common Transport*) *authentication.*

CT authentication is the process of authenticating requests between a client and a server. The CT authentication mechanism creates a hash based on an algorithm and secret key to represent the message signature associated with the sender. The hash is transferred as an extended preamble to the receiver. Upon receiving the hash, the receiver computes the hash before authenticating it, using the same algorithm and secret key, to make sure the hashes match.

The key server in the storage network would contain a copy of each node's unique distribution key. The key server would then authorize the security connections between two nodes and would generate a key to use for authentication. This authentication key is then used by one node to authenticate to the other node. The single point of failure in the specification is the key server. If the key server does not contain the proper amount of security, the authentication model that the key server supports cannot be considered secure. Figure 25-4 shows an example of an authentication procedure using FC-GS-3.

A practical example of FC-GS-3 would be the authentication of a World Wide Name (WWN) of an HBA in a storage network. In the "Fibre Channel SAN Security" section of this chapter, the security problems of WWN are discussed. It would not be best practice to use a WWN as the sole entity for authentication. The process of using FS-GS-3 to identify HBAs uniquely would allow the use of WWN without concerns of spoofing or replay attacks being performed successfully. Since WWNs are not reliable as a secure means of host identification, using a key server will minimize the risk of spoofing or session hijacking and allow the use of WWN with an acceptable level of integrity in the authentication process.

Currently, many switch vendors, such as Brocade and McData, are using a hybrid of the FC-GS-3 specification by using switch-to-switch key authentication. In this approach, each switch contains a unique key to authenticate to another switch. Instead of using a third key server device, the two nodes are directly authenticated to each other using their own keys. While this approach may not be as secure as having a key server, it does prevent a variety of attacks, primarily the ability for a rogue switch to take control of a given fabric, its simple name server, and its zoning architecture.

Two-Factor Application Authentication

Two-factor authentication for key applications, such as storage management applications, is becoming a significant requirement for protecting storage networks. The fact that storage management applications can subvert the majority of other security controls within the storage environment makes the management applications a significant target for most attackers.

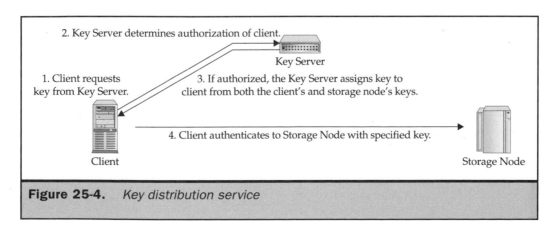

Figure 25-4. *Key distribution service*

Currently, many management applications rely on a username/password combination for authentication. As best practice, a single username and password should not be the only security entity protecting a storage network. For example, an unauthorized user should not be able to plug into a network with his favorite backup program and successfully manage storage agents because he was able to guess the username/password combination or spoof an IP address.

Requiring more than a username and password or an IP address for authentication is possible. To address this issue, certain vendors have included a second level of authentication within the management application itself. These management applications use public and private keys for authentication with authenticated Secure Sockets Layer (SSL) or Kerberos technology to mitigate some of the exposures described so far. Therefore, if an unauthorized user has plugged into the network and successfully guessed a password or spoofed a management IP address, the attacker's rogue backup software would not be able to gain access to the storage agents since a second level of authentication is required. The second level of authentication required from a client application to the server application and/or agents could use tokens, digital certificates, Kerberos tickets, public keys, or other forms of security. This type of application design may utilize usernames/passwords and IP addresses, but it also utilizes credentials implicit in the client application to authenticate to the server and/or storage agents.

Note *Tokens, digital certificates, Kerberos tickets, and public keys can be used for authentication. All these security entities can be delivered digitally to authenticate a sending node to a receiving node, such as storage management software, in place of or in addition to username/ password authentication.*

Storage Security Challenges

As the storage industry grows, with both SAN and NAS architectures, the requirements for storage security will also grow. Storage security will need to accomplish a number of milestones and challenges to become mainstream in storage networks.

Unfortunately, a typical "milestone" that uncovers the need for security in a particular industry is often some type of successful and well-publicized attack. For example, wireless security technology, specifically 802.11b, would not have been viewed as such a severe security issue if hackers were not easily able to break Wireless Equivalency Protocol (WEP) encryption. Despite the weakness of 802.11b, many organizations did not invest in wireless security until well after the fact of the discovery of the security problem.

While a break-in might have encouraged organizations to invest in wireless security, to approach security after a breach costs an organization significantly more time, money, and resources. Unlike the wireless industry, the storage industry has more to protect than a possible credit card number going over the wireless network in semi-clear-text. The storage system has an entire organization's intellectual property, sensitive data, and possibly customer information to protect and maintain. Therefore, a successful storage security attack would be more severe than a typical network attack.

Another major challenge in storage security is industry acceptance. Many storage administrators and experts believe security issues in Fibre Channel, storage devices, and storage architectures are not important issues, for a variety of reasons. However, because storage security has significantly more to protect than other types of networks, the storage industry should be more aggressive in fixing and solving security issues.

For example, consider the security problems encountered in Cisco routers and switches in the early 1990s. These routing and switching devices were developed based on availability and functionality. However, due to the security weakness of IPv4 combined with IP device weaknesses, the devices were easy to subvert and/or compromise. The same argument can be made for storage products that focus on bandwidth or speed and not necessarily security. The weakness of IPv4 and Fibre Channel, combined with potential storage device weaknesses, may well lead to the same results that the IP industry faced.

Industry must face the following key storage security challenges:

- Products and solutions
- Encryption
- Security standards and specifications
- Bandwidth/functionality tradeoffs

Products and Solutions

The first and major storage security challenge is the lack of security product solutions and storage security features in current products. As described earlier, no pure security products are currently available for storage networks to permit or deny access to certain storage nodes. Furthermore, a firewall or similar device would have to support 2 Gbps throughput to hold any type of acceptance and success in the storage industry. Currently, only certain firewalls can support near gigabit throughput, and these are available only for IP networks. There is no such thing as a Fibre Channel firewall.

An additional storage security challenge is the lack of security features in storage products today and the quality of security features that are included in existing products. A good example to demonstrate this problem is the zoning and Logical Unit Number (LUN) masking capabilities in Fibre Channel networks. The zoning capabilities in Fibre Channel switches and LUN masking capabilities in storage nodes were originally developed for segmentation, not security. While the segmentation tools are good for secondary security, they are not adequate to use as primary security tools. In addition, using zoning and LUN masking as the only security tools does not support a best practice storage architecture. In fact, using zoning and LUN masking as security tools is similar to using virtual LANs (VLANs) as the only security tools in an IP network— which would exclude the use of better security devices, such as firewalls, router ACLs, and VPN devices to protect the network. Cisco has stated many times that VLANs should not be viewed as security tools, but rather as segmentation tools. VLAN's *hopping* ability (the ability to jump across one VLAN to another) has been demonstrated by security professionals in a variety of tests.

In addition, most storage products provide only Telnet and web (HTTP) capabilities for a management, both of which are clear-text protocols that can easily be sniffed. The use of encrypted management protocols, such as Secure Shell (SSH) or encrypted web (HTTPS), is still in the process of being adopted.

Encryption

Encryption technology is another major challenge in the storage industry. Inline encryption in both IP and Fibre Channel mediums is difficult to implement without significant bandwidth penalties. IP networks that have bandwidth capabilities of Gbps are reduced to Mbps transfers once encryption technology is in place. Similarly, Fibre Channel networks with 1.0 to 2.0 Gbps capacities would also be reduced to probably less than half that amount. Considering the fact that Fibre Channel is often deployed specifically because of bandwidth capacities, the fact that encryption would directly negate those capabilities is a significant security problem for storage security engineers.

As mentioned, encryption of data at rest is another security challenge. The major challenge of data at rest is interoperability with different types of storage devices. In addition, interoperability of all types of storage appliances should be a requirement supported by standards bodies; unfortunately, competing vendors may not share this perspective.

Security Standards and Specifications

Lack of security standards and specifications is also a significant problem in the storage security industry. A good example is zoning definitions in Fibre Channel switches. The term *hard zoning* is defined one way for certain Fibre Channel switch organizations and another way for other organizations. Some switch vendors refer to *hard zoning* as the act of locking physical port numbers to a particular zone on a Fibre Channel switch. Other switch vendors refer to *hard zoning* as a routing tool in which routes will not be broadcasted to non-participants of the zone. This disparity between definitions is a standards problem. The lack of storage security standards, from encryption specifications to zone definitions, leads to technologies that do not coexist easily across various storage vendors. In addition, the lack of security standards and specifications will lead to competing vendors developing technology that will most likely not interoperate with one another's products. This will make an end user's storage security architecture a frustrating process to design and implement.

Standards in storage security need to define terms and protocol specifications before storage vendors grow impatient. For storage security features, tools, and products to be successfully adopted by end users, a clear classification of any type of architecture needs to be in place. Standards need to be developed in the following areas:

- Encryption standards
- In-line and at-rest standards
- Standardization of storage security terminology and definitions
- Authentication standards

Bandwidth/Functionality Tradeoffs

Bandwidth and functionality tradeoffs are key challenges in creating storage security. Any type of functionality or bandwidth loss incurred to gain added security will not likely be successful in the storage industry, especially since many storage networks are deployed for the mere purpose of bandwidth and functionality offerings. Any type of solution must have a minimal affect on storage functionally while demonstrating clear interoperability with existing storage features.

Fibre Channel SAN Security

Fibre Channel SAN security deals with a variety of issues ranging from Fibre Channel frame authentication to Fibre Channel switches. Fibre Channel SAN is an emerging technology that still has many items under development, such as management, virtualization and interoperability. Furthermore, although some progress has been made regarding security in Fibre Channel networks, several opportunities exist for growth.

In this section, we discuss some of the security problems in Fibre Channel SANs, at both the frame and device levels. We continue to address some solutions to these security problems and best practices. The following items will be discussed:

- Zoning
- WWN spoofing
- Fibre Channel (FC) frame weaknesses
- Sequence ID and control number
- Disruption of flow control
- MITM attacks (SNS pollution)
- E_port replication
- LUN masking

Zoning

Zones are to Fibre Channel switches as VLANs are to IP switches. Zones are used to segment the fabric into groups, in which certain nodes are a part of a zone and have access to other nodes in the same zone. Storage nodes could be a part of multiple zones or part of a single zone.

Two types of zoning are used, soft zoning and hard zoning. In soft zoning, the SNS in a switch uses an HBA's WWN for zoning. An SNS is a table located in each switch and shared among switches in the same fabric, which separates WWN into the correct zones. Figure 25-5 shows an example of soft zoning. In the figure, WWN 9382108xxxx, 3859658xxxx, and 3582968xxxx have full access to each other. However, if any of these WWNs try to access zone B members, such as 0038283xxxx, access would be denied.

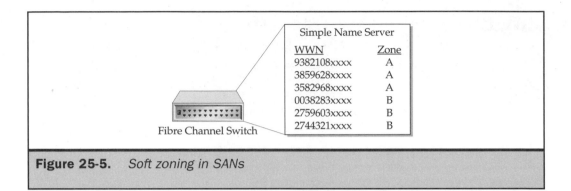

Figure 25-5.   *Soft zoning in SANs*

Hard zoning is not only different from soft zoning but is another term that has multiple definitions. One definition for hard zoning is "the act of locking physical ports to certain zones." For example, physical ports 1 through 4 would be zone A, physical ports 5 through 8 would be zone B, and so on. If a WWN was connected to port 2 and tried to access port 6 in zone B, it would be denied access. Figure 25-6 shows an example of this definition of hard zoning.

Another definition of hard zoning is a routing procedure. If route-based zoning is implemented, certain routes will be publicized for certain storage nodes. For example, if node 1 were allowed to access node A, node 1 would be notified about the route to node A. If node 1 were not allowed to access node A, node 1 would not be notified about node A. However, if node 1 knew the existence and route to node A, hard zoning, according to this definition, would not prevent node 1 from this access. Hard zoning, in this reference, is not a restrictive tool; rather, it's an information tool.

World Wide Name Spoofing

WWN is used to identify an HBA in a storage area network. WWN is used for authorization of data from one particular zone to another. Additionally, WWNs are used in soft zoning procedures on storage switches to separate certain servers and data. Soft zoning separates WWNs into different zones. Because a switch contains an SNS table that matches up each WWN to a particular zone, a particular WWN would be granted or denied access to another storage node based on the results of the SNS zone table.

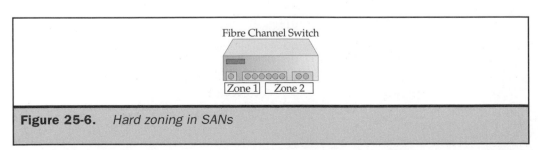

Figure 25-6.   *Hard zoning in SANs*

WWN spoofing is a high-risk problem in storage area networks because WWNs are often used as the only tool for granting authorization. WWN spoofing is as simple as loading up the device drivers included with the HBA and changing the WWN. An attacker can then spoof a WWN and gain access to data. The switches that contain the zone information would grant access to this spoofed WWN because it authorizes the WWN and does not authenticate it. Figure 25-7 illustrates this type of attack.

As best practice, hard-zoning procedures can be used to deter spoofing problems. The physical definition of hard zoning would not use WWN for authorization, but rather the physical port numbers. If an attacker spoofs another WWN, the hard-zoning switch would still not grant it access since the physical port on the switch is trying to gain access to another port to which it does not have authorization, regardless of what WWN it claims to be. However, using the route-based definition of hard zoning, WWN spoofing would not be a good alternative. Because the route-based definition is not a restricted tool, but rather a tool used to deliver routing methods, a hard-zoning switch could still be subverted if the attacker knew the address and the route to its target. Therefore, if a WWN were spoofed with route-based hard zoning, access would be permitted.

Frame Weaknesses

Fibre Channel architecture contains five different layers, numbered 0 to 4. Despite the differences between IP and Fibre Channel, Fibre Channel frames contain weaknesses that are similar to current weaknesses in IPv4 packets. These IPv4 weaknesses have been turned into vulnerabilities and exploited at a variety of levels. The weaknesses in Fibre Channel frames are specifically in Fibre Channel layer 2, known as the framing

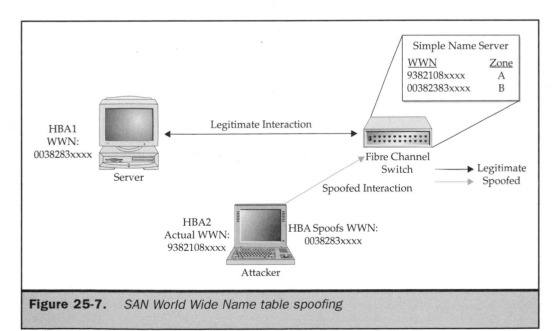

Figure 25-7.   *SAN World Wide Name table spoofing*

protocol/flow control layer. Fibre Channel layer 2 is where most security issues have been identified. Fibre Channel layer 2 contains the frame header, which contains the 24-bit source address of the frame, the 24-bit destination address of the frame, the sequence control number (Seq_Cnt), sequence ID (Seq_ID), and the exchange information (Exchange_ID).

As shown as Figure 25-8, layer 2 contains the sequence control number and the sequence ID. A *sequence* is a series of one or more related frames transmitted unidirectionally from one port to another. The sequence series is responsible for keeping the connection alive between two nodes. A given frame must be a part of some sequence between two end nodes. Frames within the same sequence have the same sequence ID (Seq_ID) in the frame header, which is kept to identify frames that belong in the same transmission process between two nodes.

In addition, as each frame is transmitted in a sequence, the sequence count number (SEQ_CNT) is incremented by one. Therefore, that transmission can remain initiated and frames can remain ordered by the incrementing process. However, the fact that the sequence ID is a constant value, thus predictable, and the sequence control number is incremented by a predictable number, which is one, makes the sequence series a predictable value. Because the sequence series is responsible for maintaining the session between two nodes, an attacker would be able to launch a session-hijacking attack and take control of the session.

This attack was made popular with IPv4 packets with similar problems of predictability in Initial Sequences Numbers (ISNs). In ISNs, the hijacking packet would simply need to guess the predictable sequence, similar to the Fibre Channel frame, and take control of a management or data session. Figure 25-9 illustrates this attack at a high level.

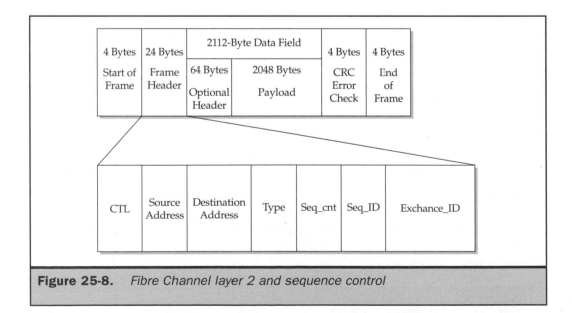

Figure 25-8.   *Fibre Channel layer 2 and sequence control*

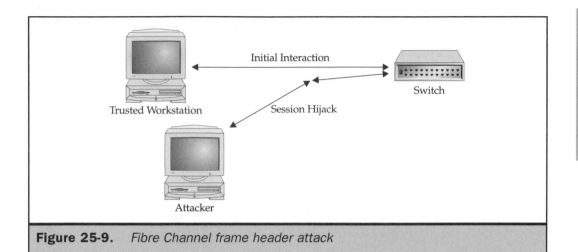

Figure 25-9.   *Fibre Channel frame header attack*

The use of predictable session information leaves Fibre Channel frames vulnerable. Additionally, in-band management protocols, such as SCSI Enclosure Services (SES), can allow management sessions to be hijacked and exposed to unauthorized users. As in-band management methods and applications grow, the weaknesses of the session information in Fibre Channel frames could amplify and result in loss of data.

The solutions for predictable sequence numbers in Fibre Channel frames needs to be similar to the solutions for IPv4 vulnerability. Operating system settings and encryption technology enabled IPv4 weaknesses to reduce the likelihood of successful hijacking attacks. Similarly, Fibre Channel frames need to make session information unpredictable. This change can come from the HBA drivers that are installed on the operating systems or within the fabric itself. Either solution should be able to address the static nature of sequence IDs and the predictably of sequence control numbers.

While encryption may be a solution for an IPv4 network, using encryption as a solution for Fibre Channel frames is not as easy, since encryption involves extra overhead and bandwidth costs that may not be acceptable in SANs. As a mitigating solution to encryption, separate out-of-band management networks should be deployed to eliminate the possibility of an attacker hijacking management frames to access storage devices and their data.

Disruption of Flow Control

Flow control is responsible for message flow between two Fibre Channel nodes. In Fibre Channel networks, devices transmit frames only when each device is ready and able to accept them. Before these devices can send and receive frames, they must be logged in to each other and must have established a *credit level* to send and receive the correct amount of frames. The establishment of credit from one storage node to the other is conducted at the Exchange_ID level of the frame header. This *credit* refers to the number of frames a device can receive at a time. This value is exchanged with another device during login, so each node knows how many frames the other node may receive.

The problem with flow control is that Fibre Channel frames are unauthenticated. An attacker can therefore send out incorrect Exchange_ID information to a variety of addresses, thus creating a temporary denial-of-service between two nodes. For example, because frames are unauthenticated, an attacker could replace valid frames with incorrect frames that contain a higher Exchange_ID number between two nodes. Because one node will now be sending more frames than can be received, the receiving node will be unable to accept the frames properly and will not be able to respond appropriately. Similarly, instead of creating a higher Exchange_ID number, an attacker could lower the number for the Exchange_ID information, thus leaving one node waiting for more frames to process. This would result in the frames being passed slower from one node to the other, delaying the process of data communication.

The solution for the disruption of flow control is authenticated frames. Because the process of exchanging ID information requires logging in to the other node, authentication of the node should also be addressed at this point. However, while this attack is successful for the disruption of flow control, the disruption is actually quite minimal and the fabric has the ability to correct itself quickly.

Man-in-the-Middle Attacks

MITM attacks have plagued IPv4 networks for some time. The problem in IPv4 is the use of Address Resolution Protocol (ARP) packets. ARP is a protocol that matches a machine's NIC address—known as the *Media Access Control (MAC) address* of the machine—to an IP address. However, both the IP address on a network and the MAC address can be easily spoofed. Because no authentication of ARP packets is required in IPv4, a spoofed IP address to another MAC address can redirect information to unauthorized users. The attacker could send out ARP packets that match their MAC addresses to a target's IP address. Therefore, when data is sent to the target, the data will be sent to the attacker since the target's IP address matches the attacker's MAC address.

This attack can be partially replicated in Fibre Channel networks. Fibre Channel switches include a table, referred to as the Simple Name Server. The SNS matches up WWN (similar to a MAC address) to the 24-bit address of the storage node. Since Fibre Channel frames are also unauthenticated, an attacker can use any traffic analyzer program to generate frames in the fabric with a target's 24-bit address and the attacker's WWN, thus changing the SNS information. The SNS would have an updated entry for the 24-bit address with a new WWN. When traffic is being sent to the target's 24-bit address, it would go to the attacker's machine since it matches up to the attacker's WWN.

As shown in Figure 25-10, an attacker sends out a modified frame to xFFFFFE to log in to the fabric (FLOGI). The modified frame has a source address of another trusted entity on the fabric, such as another trusted switch, and the WWN of the attacker. The fabric assumes that the attacker is now the legitimate host since the switch's 24-bit address is matched to the attacker's WWN. All frames destined for the real node are passed to the attacker and then to the legitimate node.

An MITM attack is simply *polluting* the SNS table with switches. Polluting the SNS could also be conducted when joining the fabric. An N_Port would send a FLOGI (fabric login) to the well-known address of xFFFFFE (similar to a broadcast in the IPv4). The switch receives the frame at xFFFFFE and returns an accept frame (ACC).

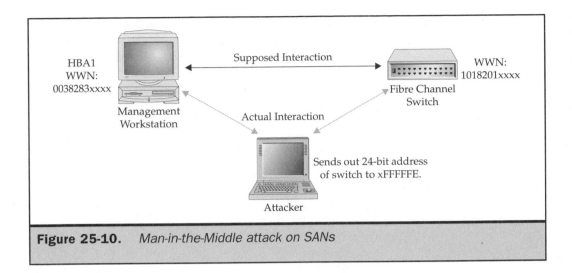

Figure 25-10. *Man-in-the-Middle attack on SANs*

The service information would then be exchanged. Because no validation is required to receive an accept frame, an attacker could send a modified 24-bit address to xFFFFFE to attempt to corrupt the SNS table in the switch. As soon as the attacker receives the accept frame, the attacker knows that the SNS table has been modified.

LUN Masking

A *Logical Unit Number* (LUN) is a unique identifier that is used to differentiate between devices, including physical or virtual disks volumes. LUN masking allows nodes to be aware only of other files or data blocks that they are authorized to access. This is implemented by masking off LUNs that may be available. Similar to zoning, LUN masking is a segmentation tool that has been used for security. LUN masking can be implemented at three levels: at the HBA, at the storage controller itself, and using a third-party device in the storage network.

HBA-based LUN masking uses driver utilities that map WWN to LUNs. The HBA drivers contain masking features that allow the WWN to view only a certain set of authorized hosts. Masking at the HBA level offers easy implementation since a third-party device would not be required in the SAN; however, it does require additional system administration resources since each HBA in a storage network would have to be individually configured. This solution may work well for small storage environments, but it is virtually unmanageable in large SANs. In addition, since LUN masking occurs at the HBA level, if the operating system were compromised, an attacker could change the masking information without any other security controls preventing this. This would allow an attacker to load up device drivers and change the allocation to include as many LUNs as desired, thereby negating any security gained by the masking rules.

Conducting LUN masking at the storage controller is another way of implementing LUN security. The storage controller would map access privileges from each HBA's WWN to the authorized LUN. LUN masking at the storage controller level is probably the best alternative for most SANs, since it has the ability to scale in large storage networks and does not require an extra storage device to add undue overhead. In this scenario, however, LUN masking is dispersed across many storage devices instead of being centrally managed at one device.

The third method of implementing LUN security is using a third-party storage device for allocation. The third-party device would be placed between the client nodes and the storage nodes. The device would handle requests for LUNs before they proceeded to the storage controller. Once the requests have been made, the device would grant or deny access. If the request is granted, it is forwarded to the storage devices. This solution scales appropriately to enterprise-sized storage networks and provides a central resource for LUN management. However, it places yet another storage device in the storage network. Furthermore, it adds another layer of overhead from the client node to the storage controller.

Table 25-1 compares and contrasts each type of LUN masking technique and the pros and cons of each.

LUN Masking Type	Pros	Cons
Storage controller	Scaleable to large SANs. No undue overhead with another storage device. Security cannot be subverted by an operating system compromise.	Management of LUN allocation is dispersed throughout the SAN instead of being centrally managed.
Third-party device	Scaleable to large SANs. Centralized management of LUN allocation. Security cannot be subverted by an operating system compromise.	Added overhead by placing another storage device in the SAN.
HBA level	No undue overhead with another storage device.	Only possible in small SANs (not scaleable). Management of LUN allocation is dispersed throughout the SAN instead of being centrally managed. Security can be subverted by an operating system compromise.

Table 25-1.   *LUN Masking Techniques Compared*

E_Port Replication

E_port (FC extenstion ports) replication is a feature in many Fibre Channel switches. Each port on a switch has a particular function (refer to Chapters 14 and 15 for additional information on FC ports). Each type of port holds a different function, whether it connects two client nodes together or connects two switches together. An E_port, for example, connects two switches together, enabling the connected switches to exchange routing and zoning information.

Because no authentication is required, E_port replication security is not guaranteed. If a storage server provider (SSP) were extending its fabric to a client using unauthenticated E_port replication, the simple act of plugging in the storage provider's E_port to the client E_port would exchange routing and zoning information for the entire fabric, not just for a specific zone. This would allow an unauthorized switch to access information.

To prevent accidental E_port replication, port-type locking and key-based authentication between switches can be used. Products from major switch vendors, including Brocade, McData, and Qlogic, can lock port types rather easily. For example, if physical ports 1–11 connect only client nodes to storage nodes, the port type can be locked to n-type. Similarly, if only port 12 is used as an E_port, it can be locked using port-type locking. This would prevent an attacker from replacing a client node with a switch and have an E_port exchange information from the two switches automatically.

Key-based authentication between the switches is also a best practice to prevent unauthorized E_port replication. Key-based authentication would require each switch to authenticate before being added to the fabric. This would disable any type of communication to and from the switch until validation keys or certificates have been exchanged from the joining switch to the existing switches.

NAS Security

Network attached storage (NAS) security addresses security at a device level. Traditionally, NAS devices, such as filters, are marketed as pure storage devices. Even though many are also deployed as storage devices, most, if not all, have built-in operating systems, usually based on some sort of UNIX flavor, that include services and protocols that need to be secured in a way similar to any other type of device on a network. Additionally, NAS devices are usually based on IP technology, using Ethernet or gigabit Ethernet, which is threatened by the IPv4 exposures. The two most common implementations of the NAS are Common Internet File System (CIFS) and Network File System (NFS). The following section focuses on security concerns of CIFS and NFS NAS devices.

Common Internet File System

CIFS is a standard protocol that is used for data sharing on remote storage devices on IP networks. CIFS security focuses on two security elements: authentication and authorization. Two types of access rights can be used for CIFS, each with its strengths and weaknesses: these are share-level authentication and user-level authentication.

Share-level authentication is based on share points and passwords. Because share points can be made available to multiple users with required authentication of each user, no accountability or authentication is required on a user-by-user basis.

Following are its specific vulnerabilities:

- User accountability or authentication is not required by individual users (no record of the access).

- A single password, which is shared by design, is responsible for the entire share point.

- Passwords must be changed every time an employee is terminated or resigns.

- Passwords are transmitted in clear-text (however, all Windows 2000/XP machines and NT 4.0 service pack 3 machines support non-plaintext password authentication).

Per-user password authentication for a NAS appliance is best practice in terms of security. Some key options are required to attain a desired level of security. Both LAN Manager and NT LAN Manager (NTLM) have associated severe security weakness, making them capable of being reversed engineered and reduced to the equivalent of a clear-text protocol. A good solution is to use Windows support of NTLM v2.

In addition to NTLM v2 for username/password protection, Server Message Block (SMB) signing should be used for CIFS SMB communication. SMB signing places a digital security signature into each SMB packet, which is then verified by both the client and the server. Without SMB signing, the server authenticates the client, but the client never truly authenticates the server, so mutual authentication is not completed. As best practice, mutual authentication should be enabled, especially in an IP network, to eliminate the possibility of IPv4 attacks.

Network File System

NFS is also a standard protocol used for data sharing on remote storage devices on an IP network. NFS is basically the equivalent of CIFS, but in the UNIX environment. NFS is used to allow a computer to mount (share) files over a network. NFS began as a User Datagram Protocol (UDP), but many Transmission Control Protocol (TCP) implementations exist today.

Like CIFS, most NFS implementations have security weaknesses:

- NFS communication is not encrypted (all traffic is in clear-text).

- NFS clients (hosts) have a limited level of authentication.

- NFS users are not easily authenticated.

As best practice, NFS storage devices should not solely grant or deny access to NFS mounts based on the host name of the client. IPv4 attacks allow host name and IP spoofing to be accomplished quite easily, possibly exposing the entire storage appliance to unauthorized users. Furthermore, this type of NFS mounting does not require passwords for authentication, exposing the data significantly.

Furthermore, per-user password authentication for an NFS appliance is best practice in terms of security. However, some key options need to be enabled to secure this method properly. Obviously, clear-text communication should not be used from an NFS client to NFS appliance. Certain NFS appliance vendors do support RSA/DES encryption with NFS communication. This will eliminate the transfer of sensitive information, such as usernames, passwords, NFS mounts, file handles, and contents of data.

Note   *RSA (Rivest, Shamir, Adleman) and DES (Data Encryption Standard) are algorithms used for encryption and authentication systems.*

In addition, Kerberos (v5) is supported by many appliance vendors, which significantly reduces the risk of username and password credentials being compromised or replayed. Here are some specific solutions:

- Encrypt NFS communication with either RSA/DES algorithm (supported by most vendors).
- Do not authenticate based solely on host name.
- Enforce Kerberos (v5) for username/password authentication.

Best Practices

As mentioned, a defense-in-depth architecture protects a storage network's critical data. However, a layered security model can be subverted if simple best practices are not followed when designing storage security. For example, consider the home security example. The homeowner had spent several thousand dollars buying locks and security systems for her home. However, a simple best practice, such as not locking the house garage door, could negate all the other strong security measures that she had placed in the home.

Simple best practices in storage security can help prevent many of the common security attacks that unauthorized users will attempt. Adhering to the majority of these best practices can leave an attacker frustrated or bored and motivate him to move to another target or stop the attack altogether.

Following are some basic best practices to follow:

- Strong passwords
- Configuration
- Strong management
- Clear-text management
- Remote connectivity
- Operating system security
- Storage appliance services

Passwords

Using strong passwords and changing default passwords on storage devices is good security practice. Whether it is an EMC Cellera, a Network Appliance filter, or a Brocade switch, basic and simple passwords can be easily obtained and guessed. In addition, because most storage appliances have some sort of web management capability that is enabled by default, accessing the storage appliance and guessing passwords is not difficult for an accomplished attacker. Several tools exist to brute-force web-based authentication forms that can attempt more than 100 passwords in only a few minutes.

Weak passwords lead to a bigger problem, subscribing to the myth that storage networks are isolated and cannot be accessed from regular corporate networks. Many storage administrators believe that the storage network is not easily accessible. However, one of the primary purposes of a storage network is to connect devices on the network to back up data. Therefore, since these connections are permitted, storage networks *are* accessible, either indirectly or directly.

Using weak passwords can also significantly cripple storage security. While many organizations change weak passwords from *prom* or *password* to *admin* or *manage*, both *admin* and *manage* are common passwords that are contained in most tools that attackers use to crack accounts.

Following is a list of some common passwords. If these passwords are used in your storage network, consider changing your password policy for storage devices:

password	monitor	*<switch vendor>*	Config
admin	temp	*<company name>*	Test
manage	root	Letmein	secret
prom	backup	Secureme	keepout
filer	KuSuM	abcd1234	Test123
netcache	momanddad	Money	green

Configuration

Good configuration practices can build a solid security foundation in a storage environment. Furthermore, poor configuration practices, an abundance of configuration errors, or the lack of configuration options can significantly decrease the security posture in a storage network.

Most often, an attacker will complete a successful attack not because of some elite security problem that she has discovered on the spot, but rather because of poor configuration decisions and/or configuration errors that lead to wide open and unprotected devices. For example, a minor configuration error, such as a storage administrator allocating the incorrect LUN to a given WWN, can expose data that is not authorized. A major configuration error, such as a storage appliance backing up an entire file system with world-readable access permissions, can also expose all data to unauthorized users. Both have a significant impact on the security posture of the storage network, despite one being major and one being minor.

The lack of understanding of security options and/or features in existing storage products may also lead to poor configuration decisions. For example, many end users are not aware of several security options that are readily available on their storage appliances and/or storage switches today. Not only are these security features not well advertised by vendors, but end users do understand how to use them. This combination often leads to end users making configuration decisions that don't work for security and not considering configuration decisions that are secure.

Management

Management is a critical component to storage security architecture. Since functional storage networks rely heavily on storage management practices, it is imperative that a strong management environment exist. Because storage network management contains a significant amount of control, a compromise of any management entity would give an attacker a considerable amount of privileges.

Protecting management interfaces for a storage network is a significant best practice. It is possible to attack many storage solutions through the Web, Telnet, or SNMP management interfaces. In many cases, gaining access to management interfaces is as simple a wire sniffing, session hijacking, and replay attacks. In other cases, it is as simple as loading an appropriate management program and logging in to the management application.

Many storage devices and applications rely on unsafe and clear-text protocols (such as Telnet, SNMP, FTP, CIFS, or NFS) to communicate both data and management commands to and from storage devices. Support for encrypted data channels, such as SSH, have not been adopted universally. Issues also exist with the networking devices that are used to support the storage environment. These devices are subject to attack and may be managed in unsafe ways.

In addition to using unsecure protocols, many organizations make a common mistake by plugging their management interfaces on storage devices, such as switches and storage appliances, into the internal corporate network. Connecting the management interface of a storage appliance into the internal LAN potentially gives any internal employee, external VPN user, third-party business partner, or external onsite contractor/ consultant the ability to connect to the device and attempt to log in. In addition, if the management methods use clear-text technology, such as Telnet or web browsers (HTTP), the exposure is amplified. Table 25-2 lists a set of best practices for storage security.

Risk	Solution
Insecure channels for management	Use encrypted management protocols such as SSH and SSL. SSH with port forwarding can be used with many storage applications. HTTPS (SSL) is available on some storage devices that offer web management. Also, HTTPS provides the ability to wrap clear-text web management, such as HTTP, around an SSL tunnel.
Hard coded (a user name/password that does not change) or weak username and passwords	Enforce two-factor authentication for all management to reduce the likelihood of compromise due to a username and password being lost.
Shared channels for management	Do not plug management connections to normal, internal networks. Segment the management network by isolating it from any other network in the organization, especially the internal LAN.
Shared accounts	When possible, limit authenticated users to perform functions within the job responsibility (e.g., backup administrators versus storage administrators). Avoid complete authorization of all management functions to every authenticated user.
Share applications	When possible, use filtering to restrict management of storage devices to a limited number of management clients. Filtering can occur at the operating system or application level, limiting the accessibility of any users loading a management application and managing the storage network.

Table 25-2.   *Best practices for storage security*

Remote Connectivity

Remote connectivity, such as dial-in lines, modems, and call-home capabilities of storage devices, are often overlooked when considering security issues in storage networks. Many storage network engineers have not explored the remote side of dial-in lines, modems, or call-home devices to ensure that the security of the remote network is not undermining the security of the storage network. Remote connectivity can leave a well-secured storage network vulnerable to an attack.

It is important to know and understand which storage devices can perform what network actions without any user interaction. The following questions should be asked when using any kind of device that uses remote connectivity:

- Are the storage devices using secure protocols?
- Do the remote connections require two-factor authentication?
- What kinds of controls are placed on the remote connections (other than username and password)?
- Are any IP address limitations or requirements necessary to attempt a valid connection?

Operating System Security

Operating system security is a best practice that is often ignored in storage networks. An operating system can act as a gateway into the storage network since it is connected to the internal LAN and to the back-end SAN. However, little concentration of security is placed on these systems—it's similar to having a firewall that connects the outside, untrusted Internet with the internal corporate network with a rule that allows any IP address to access any IP address.

In a storage network, operating systems are often the only "firewalls" that protect access to data. A compromised operating system can enable an unauthorized user to attack storage devices, such as switches and storage appliances, directly, and to attempt sniffing techniques. This makes the operating system an easy attack target. For example, consider a Fibre Channel SAN that has an HBA in an operating system for backup purposes. In addition to the HBA, the operating system also has a NIC that is plugged into the internal LAN. If proper operating system security has not been placed on the server that has both a connection to the storage network and a connection to any other network, the operating system may be responsible for partial or even complete unauthorized access to the SAN.

Many storage networks consist of unsecured and default installations of several types of operating systems, from all flavors of UNIX to all versions of Windows. Many environments do not contain a host hardening or a secure build process for operating systems that exist in storage networks. This gives an attacker an opportunity to compromise a system in such a way that he can be placed directly inside the storage network, making further attacks easier. Figure 25-11 is a graphical representation of the importance of operating system security.

Storage Appliance Services

Storage devices such as Network Appliance (NetApp) and EMC devices contain a significant amount of system services that are not all storage related. For example, most storage vendors support storage protocols such as CIFS and NFS. However, in addition to running CIFS or NFS services, it would not be unusual to see FTP (File Transfer

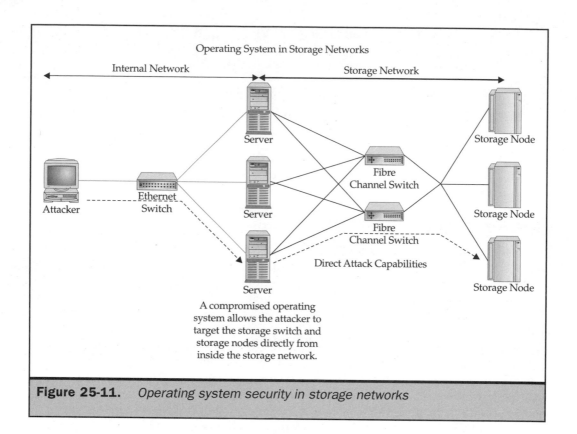

Figure 25-11.   *Operating system security in storage networks*

Protocol), Telnet, Simple Network Management Protocol (SNMP), mount, portmapper, Domain Name System (DNS), HTTP, NetBIOS, RSH, syslog, and others running on these storage devices.

Similar to an operating system with default installations, storage devices can be unsecure in the default state. As a best practice, storage devices, such as filers, data movers, and NAS heads, should be deployed with a minimal amount of services and with unnecessary default modules disabled. This process not only secures the storage device, but it also allows the core service of the system, such as the storage protocol, to run as the sole module. A minimalist approach to storage devices leaves less room for error and less possibility of security exposure. An accidentally enabled SNMP daemon could leave the storage appliance vulnerable to information disclosure. Even a general SNMP vulnerability, which would affect all SNMP devices, would leave the storage node vulnerable to direct compromise from this single service enabled. In general, it is best practice to disable all storage device services except the required storage protocols and management protocols.

The Complete Reference

Storage Networks

Part VII

Appendixes

Appendix A

NAS Case Study: The International Image Processing Company

The International Image Processing Company, or IIP, provides a proprietary digital imaging service to academic, educational, and government institutions throughout the United States. Its computer imaging services provide clients with the ability to transfer physical documents, such as historical books, documents, and newspapers, as well as photographic images, such as historical photos, video images, and medical images, into digital media. The company's clients range from major universities to some of the largest archival government institutions.

Despite the scope of its clients, IIP is a small business with less than $5 million in revenues, with plans to grow threefold in five years if it can increase its capacities to bring on more clients. IIP has a small but distributed business organization with headquarters in Texas and major client work sites in New York City, Washington, D.C., and San Francisco. Due to the nature of IIP's work, its IT staff is integrated into the specialized work force that the company employs—given the digital scanning software and processes that are integral to their work. The company also employs two dedicated IT technicians—one for hardware and another responsible for infrastructure software. Additional IT-related activities are handled through the imaging software support and configuration personnel.

The company was challenged by its dependencies on storage, created through its software scanning processes that were increasingly exacerbated by new clients. Daily operations could quickly utilize a terabyte of data storage. Because the imaging scanning product was archived to clients using both optical and tape storage devices, if operations ran short on available storage, the imaging processes would slow and eventually stop until sufficient space was freed up for operations. This slowed billing and eventually cash flow.

The storage situation reached critical levels that started to impact the company's ability to handle new clients and subsequently impacted its planned business growth.

IIP was in the classic predicament of needing a high-performance solution, while being restricted by a minimum budget and a limited IT staff. The evaluation of potential storage solutions ranged from storage area networks (SANs) to IDE RAID solutions. While a network attached storage (NAS) solution would satisfy the size requirement, NAS remained a problematic solution because it also had to be managed remotely at the New York, Washington, D.C., and San Francisco sites.

IIP chose a general-purpose solution, even though its processes were largely proprietary, which was a matter of thoughtful strategy on IIP's part to utilize standard hardware and OS platforms. The NAS solution was chosen for its ability to integrate easily into a small IP environment, while being able to deploy remotely with some level of remote management.

This case study will discuss the IIP storage and related processing problems and challenges in detail. These drove the activities involved in identifying the company's workload and analyzing potential storage solutions. Finally, we discuss how IIP concluded with the decision to implement NAS and the subsequent transition to the new storage model.

The Situation Analysis

IIP developed its storage solution from years of experience in scanning and duplicating photographic images, ranging from military applications to historical documents. The challenges had always been the time required to scan an image, versus the quality required for large clients. This had given way to the amount of space required for each image, given that the IIP client base dealt with millions of images.

The type of work IIP performed was not directed toward the market of flatbed scanners nor even larger scanners in terms of quality and production process requirements. Instead, IIP developed a process and proprietary software that used specialized digital cameras to scan images of various dimensions, physical states, and types—various papers, photographic techniques and types, and so on. The process, coupled with the scanning stations, provided a production-oriented environment where imaging could take place 24/7, if required. The process and software included a fully complete life cycle of imaging capture, correction, and quality assurance before it was placed on a CD or tape for shipment to the client.

Clients of IIP had requirements to digitize documents and photographs to provide a wider distribution and availability of these items through the Internet. Consequently, these clients had become part of the growing movement within both the academic community and public sector to save historical documents. For the most part, these markets are just emerging, given the tremendous amount of material that remains to be scanned and digitized.

IIP's client requirements could run into the 500,000-plus number of images for a single project. That type of work drove the production-oriented environment introduced by IIP in the late 1990s.

IIP Systems Infrastructure

IIP maintained a distributed infrastructure with its headquarters in Texas and field locations in New York, Washington, D.C., and San Francisco. Figure A-1 illustrates the configurations at the headquarters' locations. Here you see the integration of capture stations, process servers, correction/quality assurance workstations, database servers, and archive servers. Each field location is set up in an identical fashion. Each is linked to the headquarters' network and web server through a virtual private network (VPN). E-mail and FTP services are handled in this manner. Architecturally, this setup was designed for future development of remote scan processing and diagnostic imaging services.

The imaging process will describe the storage utilization scenarios and why the process is so data-centric. Figure A-2 depicts the process from start to finish.

1. *Physical images are entered into a database.* The database drives and tracks the processing of images from capture to output on media. In IIP's case, the database is a relational database that tracks the location and status of the scanned image

so that at any one time the image can be located and accessed for specific purposes. The initial step in the process is to have the image scanned into the system. An important note regarding the database: Because of certain restriction and challenges with unstructured data and relation technology, the scanned images are actually stored as files within the system. Therefore, the database is actually quite small, as its main job is tracking the locations and characteristics of the scanned image.

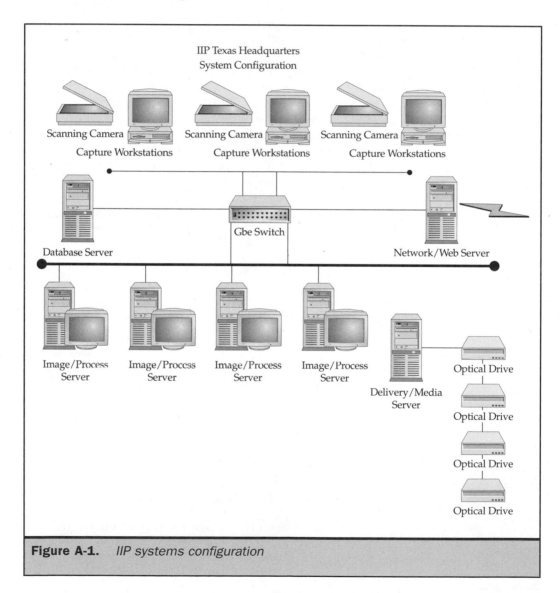

Figure A-1.   *IIP systems configuration*

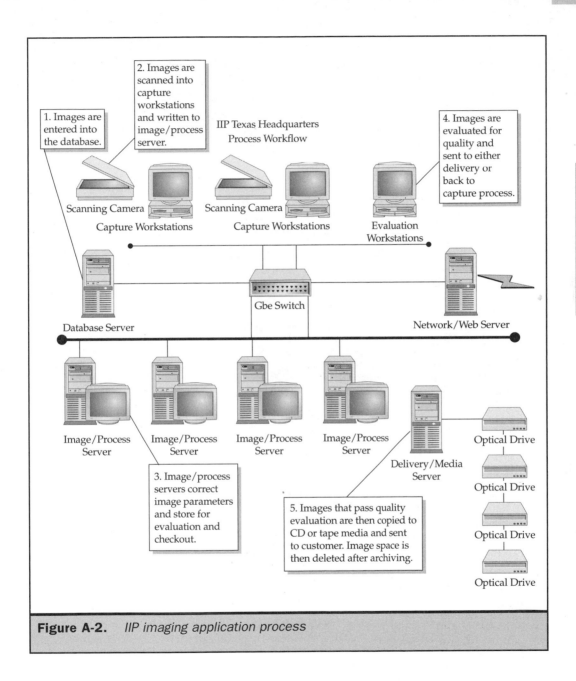

Figure A-2.   *IIP imaging application process*

2. *At the capture station, the images are scanned into the system.* Capture stations are high-end workstations that communicate with the specialized digital cameras. A camera scans the image into the capture station; then the capture software,

running on Windows 2000 Professional, writes the scanned image to a network drive on an available process server over the network and moves to the next image. Average images range from 300 to 500MB per raw image.

3. *The process server automatically corrects the image for perspective and positioning and updates the database.* The process creates another set of files for the corrected image. This set of files is smaller because it contains only the changes made to the image. The image is then ready to be evaluated and checked out.

4. *The image evaluators view each image for correct quality of preset parameters, as discussed with clients.* If the images meet the quality criteria, they are sent to checkout for delivery to media servers. However, they may need manual correction, which is performed at the evaluation workstations or sent back for rescanning, as required. This is all tracked by the database.

5. *The delivery point is the media servers where the completed images are batched together and written to optical media, CDs, or tape, per the requirements of the client.* At this point, a final verification is performed, and if passed, the storage becomes available for more scanned images on the process servers.

Problem Detail

What IIP had not foreseen were the systems infrastructure requirements for this type of production work. This required the calculation of both processing cycles and, most of all, the amount of storage space that would be needed on a daily operational basis. Because IIP is a small business, it had resisted a formal capacity plan and had relied on its ability to respond quickly when additional capacities were needed. That meant the additional servers were purchased on an "as-needed" basis, with most of the hardware being "do-it-yourself" built chassis and motherboard configurations.

With this orientation to developing and maintaining the hardware portion of the systems infrastructure, the storage challenges were met with larger and higher speed internal IDE disks. This gave rise to additional server installations that were needed to handle the post scan image processing (see Figure A-2, Steps 2 through 4). This then prompted the acquisition of dedicated media servers to write out the client images using CD or tape media. This is the archival system on the backside of the process (see Figure A-2, Step 5—the delivery process). This meant that a faster network was necessary to speed the transmission of scanned raw files to the process servers, and ultimately it placed the problem back at the storage infrastructure once again as the image scans overtook the capacities on the servers.

A stopgap effort was a move to IDE RAID to provide adequate storage for the process servers. This was largely driven by the "do-it-yourself" mode of the hardware and severe limitations of budgets constraints. Although the IDE RAID facilitated a quick fix, IIP's flexibility in providing reliability and backup protection was problematic. In many cases, the volatility of the data movement over the period of one week could easily surpass more than five terabytes running through a single process server. As the tremendous write activities continued, the IDE drives generally failed twice a month, with minimal success running data protection with RAID level 1. However, the space it provided offered a brief interlude to the space problems that shut down the process entirely.

Given that additional business was coming in with more restrictive time constraints for completion, IIP concluded that a longer term solution had to be found.

The Search and Evaluation

The IIP hardware and software IT personnel researched the solution along with assistance and input from the imaging software specialist. They found that a SAN was a valid consideration, since it appeared to be the choice of others working with unstructured data such as video and audio projects. However, they found that the imaging system, although proprietary by its methodology, used open and commodity levels of hardware and operating environments and was further open to additional solutions that integrated well into the small business environment. Another alternative was to move to larger process servers with external SCSI drive arrays, to scale up in both process and storage power. Yet another alternative was the consideration of a NAS solution, which would integrate easily with the existing network, would use file systems, and would have the capacity they needed.

Estimating the Workload

The IT personnel, working with an outside consultant, used the guidelines mentioned in Chapter 17 in identifying the company workloads. They further moved to understand the types of configuration needed for all three possible alternatives. First looking at the SAN configuration, followed by the larger server with external RAID, and finally the potential NAS configuration. The results are summarized in the following sections.

Workload Identification   Looking at a year's history of scanning images, the IIP team concluded that the workload was complex and data-centric, and it fit somewhere between online transaction processing (OLTP) and data warehousing. The workload encompassed OLTP characteristics when scanning the image and then transmitting the write transaction to the process server. Although developed as a synchronous process, it was recently changed to an asynchronous process to facilitate greater throughput at the capture station. However, this still required a sequential write process at the process server as each image was scanned.

On average, the image scans were 300MB in size. The calculation of 300 images per shift × three capture stations working two shifts provided the necessary throughput. It was determined that at least 540GB of free space was needed to accommodate the daily scanning process. This required that the overall storage infrastructure be able to accommodate a 566MB per second throughput rate.

Workload Estimates for SAN   Using the guidelines described in Chapter 19, we can quickly calculate that the required components for a SAN could be handled by one, 16-port switch, given that a single point of failure is acceptable for the installation; or it could be handled by two, 8-port switches for some level of redundancy. Three HBA adapters with 2 ports each for redundancy and performance would be required for the process servers. However, not to be overlooked, this configuration will require additional Fibre Channel storage arrays to accommodate and be compatible with the new Fibre Channel storage network. Given that the total capacity of 540GB needs to be available every 24 hours, we can estimate that two storage arrays of 500GB each would provide the necessary capacity with sufficient free space to handle peak utilization as images are processed through the system.

Workload Estimates for Direct Attached   Aligning the requirements to new servers, we find that all the process servers would have to be upgraded. This would also require that the storage capacities be carefully aligned with each process server. Even with this alignment, specific workload affinity would have to be observed to utilize the storage effectively. On the other hand, the process server could more easily share storage across the network but would have to reflect some level of duplication for storage requirements to accommodate the total capacity, essentially doubling the entire storage requirement.

This would require, in addition to new servers installed, OS software upgrades, with appropriate maintenance and all the necessary activities of a major system installation. It would result in a normal disruption of service and reliability characterized by new system installations. However, the new servers would have to be configured to handle the I/O throughput of an aggregate of 566MB per second. This would require each server to handle 188MB per second if the workload is evenly distributed, which in most cases will not be the case; however, we will use this for estimating purposes. That relates to a minimum of six Ultra-wide SCSI-3 adapters necessary to handle the sustained rate of 188MB per second. This requires the total storage to be divided among the servers, and subsequently the adapters, and places a limitation of approximately 120GB per LUN. Thus, a more complex management problem in terms of flexibility of reconfiguration based on required storage would be necessary, given that one capture station could generate 180GB of images every 24 hours.

Workload Estimates for NAS   Using the worksheet and guidelines in Chapter 19, we can calculate that our workload requirements are definitely within the mid-range NAS device configuration and probably just under the enterprise NAS solutions. Our calculations indicate that the workload requires the following minimum requirements:

- Two network paths
- Eleven data paths

- An additional path for redundancy (calculated using 10 percent special applications category)
- 13.2 total logical paths
- Comparing total logical paths to data paths = 83 percent

Using the quick estimate NAS Sizing Factor Table in Chapter 19, we select mid-range even though our sizing factor is within the enterprise range. This is based on the special application circumstances and because the aggregate data is below a terabyte and would be physically segmented within the aggregate data capacity estimate. In addition, we considered the workload being further characterized by limited users working with an almost dedicated Gbe network.

The NAS solutions also offer the flexibility of storage incremental selection—for example, installing two large NAS servers and one small server, or one large and two medium-sized servers. These solutions also provide the flexibility of RAID processing, network compatibility, and non-disruption to the existing server configurations. In addition, these solutions can be easily configurable to support the scanning projects and mapped as network drives with the same flexibility. They will also provide a closed, yet remotely accessible, solution for the remote network configurations.

One last word on our estimating process: We recognize the characteristics of the small integrated IT staff and the company's lack of any formal capacity planning activities. The process of workload identification and estimates provides this company a level of direction and planning. The result of this exercise has identified that the mid-range NAS devices can meet the company's workload now and within a limited planning period. However, it also provides an insight into future challenges IIP will encounter, as its staff has become aware that it borders on moving into enterprise solutions of either the NAS type or probably a SAN if the budget for infrastructure can support either.

IIP Storage Solutions

IIP chose to acquire a NAS solution for headquarters and each of its remote work sites. The evaluation proved that the requirements for capacity, access, and budget were well suited to the NAS solution.

Given the growth and support required for IIP for the next 12 months, the ability for the organization to absorb a new technology such as Fibre Channel would have been beyond the current budget limitations. In addition, the learning curve mistakes with the SAN could not be afforded with a small company such as IIP, where there is no time, space, or budget for test or beta machines. The IIP IT evaluators determined that SANs would probably be in the company's future as bandwidth catches up to the current network capacity and the need to provide capture stations with at least 100MB-per-second speeds just to keep up with the increased scanning capture operations.

IIP Storage Evaluation Results

The requirements and evaluation are further depicted in Table A-1. The evaluation is based on a score of 1 through 10, with 10 being the highest, or best, score. Vendor selection is specific to the customer and the competitive nature of an acquisition, although it is recommended that a minimum of three bids be requested once workload estimates have been concluded.

We have estimated pricing only as a general reference point. Included in these pricing estimates are total components for system operation, additional software required, and storage array costs. Training for the SAN solution is an add-on, however it's a highly recommended item.

IIP Storage Acquisition and Implementation

Along with the storage requirements, IIP provided a list of service requirements it had developed in conjunction with an outside consultant. These requirements, along with the capacity, access, and management parameters, drove the decision to go with NAS. Although cost was a factor, the costs of the proposals were all within 10 percent of each other.

Implementation of the NAS devices provided additional activities. Although minimal, these still provided additional time before the devices were used in production. The

Criteria	SAN	Direct Attached	NAS
Meets I/O workload performance and capacity specs	9	5	8
Ease of installation and maintenance	3	4	7
Scalability of storage capacity	7	2	7
Compatibility with existing storage infrastructure	5	6	8
Composite score	24	17	30
System price	$150,000 ($175,000 w/training)	$235,000	$75,000

Table A-1.   *Storage Solution Evaluations for IIP*

items are summarized in the following list. Note that any of these are reflective of the operating environment and maintenance status of both operating systems and the network.

- **Network Directories Not Recognized on Network**   Required additional upgrade to network for compatibility with NAS server network software.
- **Network Directories Being Dropped**   Required additional upgrade to Windows 2000 Server software to reflect NAS devices.
- **NAS RAID Not Working**   RAID configured improperly, and reconfigured to reflect recovery parameters.
- **NAS Integrated Backup**   Used as archival to tape media, however, requires update to database to reflect new delivery device.
- **NAS Slower Performance from Capture Stations**   NAS set up to use NFS file protocol, overhead to write much higher than before. Investigating solutions or optimization.

The IIP NAS Solution

The final configuration provides increased storage capacity and enhanced performance. The IIP scanning process is now being upscaled with new customers and imaging projects. In addition, the space is being utilized on an automated basis from new project initiation to deletion after delivery. Figure A-3 illustrates the NAS configurations that support the revised IIP systems infrastructure.

Figure A-3's NAS configuration illustrates the increased capacity for storage of images, but it also provides the foundation for image access through the Internet. This was designed into the system to allow the remote work sites that have identical installations to upgrade to NAS devices. Over and above the increased capacity at all sites will be the potential ability to access images across the IIP storage network infrastructure. In other words, images scanned in New York could be evaluated in Texas, Washington, D.C., San Francisco, or other remote offices as they begin operation. This is an added business efficiency that takes advantage of the imaging expertise across the company without regard to location. It also allows clients eventually to be provided test and quality images through the Internet to further facilitate the delivery and client acceptance process.

In summary, the NAS solution turned out to be a good fit for IIP. Even though its application appeared to have many proprietary processes and software processes, NAS operated within the bounds of leveraging commodity infrastructures for networks, systems, and storage. With the exception of the database server, all the servers within the IIP infrastructure now share the available storage in the NAS devices. The acknowledgment of this value further expands the use of the NAS solution as the company began to configure its web and imaging software code development on the NAS devices.

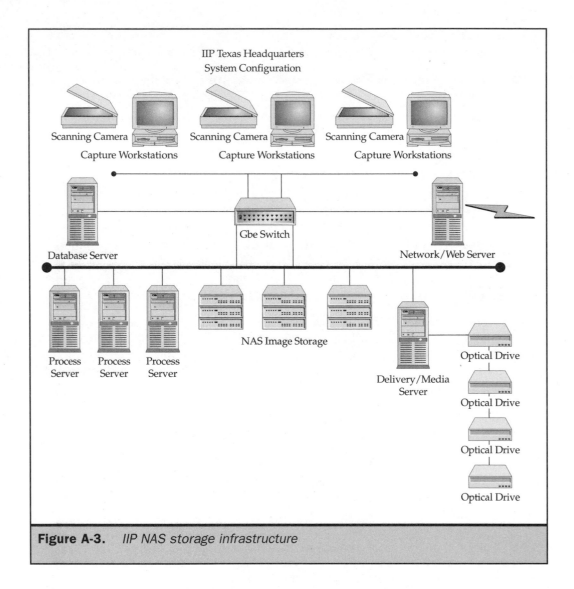

Figure A-3. *IIP NAS storage infrastructure*

The NAS solution for IIP provided a cost-effective solution for a small company, but it also provided the company with the necessary storage resources for expanding its business, which had grown dependent on a storage-centric product. The company's storage infrastructure is now poised to grow into the future with either more sophisticated products such as a SAN, or to continue to scale economically with further uses of NAS devices. Either way, IIP now has the business flexibility to meet the growing dynamics of the imaging business.

Appendix B

SAN Case Study: The Import Auto Industry

T he import auto industry provides distribution services for automobiles manufactured in both Europe and Asia. Most successful international automakers have expanded to provide an extensive presence in North America, as most have populated manufacturing plants in the United States, Canada, and Mexico.

The activities that surround the distribution of products within the U.S. have provided a rich datacentric set of activities that has prompted leading-edge data centers in the U.S. Because the automakers' IT organizations' data centers have had to address data-processing activities on an international level, they have consistently been ahead of many other U.S.-based companies in their abilities to handle data on an international basis as well as becoming involved with leading computer technologies. In addition, government regulations exacerbated the amount of the data these companies must collect, analyze, and address.

Although the international aspect of these companies requires that specific additional data center issues be addressed, they must also deal with the basic systems of business in terms of reporting, tracking, and analyzing data. What makes the auto industry unique in many respects is the various sources of revenue that it derives from its products, much of this transparent to the consumer. Key among these activities is the sale of parts products, service contracts, and the increasing amount of technical support provided to dealerships. Many of these are reflective of the increased technological advances within the automobiles themselves. In addition, warranty products and services must be tracked and accounted for. For example, each time a warranty claim is presented and processed within a dealership, the manufacturer pays for the service, parts, and support. Although these activities are not restricted to just the auto industry, it does set the foundation for a set of required information that means that an extremely large amount of receivables be managed by the U.S. distribution companies. This necessitates a synchronized transaction between dealer, distributor, and manufacturer to resolve.

The results of all these operations and interactions make this industry an extremely datacentric and data-sensitive enterprise. The composite collection of IT organizations within the U.S. that represents these companies has become the key user and consumer of high-end computer systems and technologies. However, in many cases these organizations must work in tandem with headquarters data centers in both Europe and Asia. This requires the U.S. data centers to implement or become compatible with a strategy that has been developed outside the United States. Working with the levels of autonomy, each of the U.S. data centers has laid the foundation for the tactical types of technology trends they can justify and implement. This issue has both advanced and stifled some of the most productive trends within these data centers.

This case study discusses the activities surrounding the analysis, justification, and implementation of a storage area network (SAN) to support a major restructuring of key application systems within a major international auto distributor in the United States. The company was advanced in its installation of state-of-the-art mainframes and distributed systems. These systems supported the U.S. headquarters, parts distribution centers, and its extensive network of dealerships. However, the major applications supporting these areas lagged the rest of IT, with largely centralized systems without the necessary distribution of data from the mainframes to enhance or synchronize the data that existed on the distributed systems. Consequently, a consistent and timely analysis of the key areas of the enterprise remained problematic.

This evolved as the company executives mandated more data to analyze portions of the business—key among these are parts, service/warranty, and sales lines of business. They placed hard requirements to the IT executives to facilitate the development of and restructuring of current data warehouse applications into a more responsive set of data marts as well as a corporate data warehouse that provides relationships to the key revenue indicators of the company.

The industry's IT area had been restricted by a static budget for the last two years as the auto business has tried to stabilize its operations and financial positions. IT employs 350 personnel, with an additional 50 to 60 contractors employed at any one time. Within this organization, the technical support area has 35 personnel, with enterprise storage administration being supported by one full-time and one part-time systems programmer. This small contingent works to administrate and support storage operations in conjunction with the assigned mainframe systems programmers and UNIX and Windows systems administrators.

The Situation Analysis

The current application model consists of all critical application systems being run on the mainframes. These are generally OLTP-type applications that provide support to all business functions within the headquarters and distribution centers. These online applications are supported by a heavy batch cycle of processing within a very restricted online and batch-processing model. The dealership network is a separate entity with restricted access to limited sets of inventory and sales data. The applications targeted for redesign and redeployment are some of the few that are operated from the UNIX open systems area. These are the current data warehouses for sales, warranty, service, and parts. They are currently loaded from the operational databases on the mainframe during a nightly batch cycle.

The new application requirements are to restructure each data warehouse and distribute its data into a smaller data mart supporting each of the individual lines of business (LOB). The demands require that the warranty and service data warehouses be consolidated into a larger integrated data warehouse, along with a smaller but integrated data mart for each LOB. In addition, the larger, but longer term requirements are to build a corporate data warehouse to provide key executives with real-time analysis on sales and issues affecting sales. Although this requirement is beyond the scope of this study, the impact will be affected by the storage infrastructure that is ultimately selected by the storage administration team.

Figure B-1 depicts the current systems configuration overview and data capacities as provided by the storage administrator.

The challenge is to develop an infrastructure that will house the information and provide online access to the predefined analysis that will be run against the data. A common set of service levels has been agreed to in the requirements meetings with end users. However, these were approved by the application and database designers

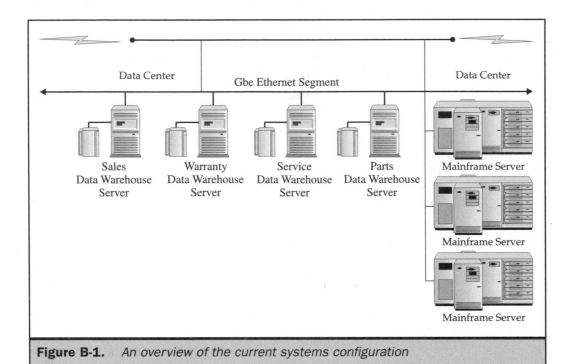

Figure B-1. *An overview of the current systems configuration*

without the concurrence or involvement of the storage admin team, much less the technical support group. Consequently, the storage team's job is to develop the infrastructure that will support the predefined capacities, processing requirements, and online service levels. These are summarized in Figure B-2 and Table B-1.

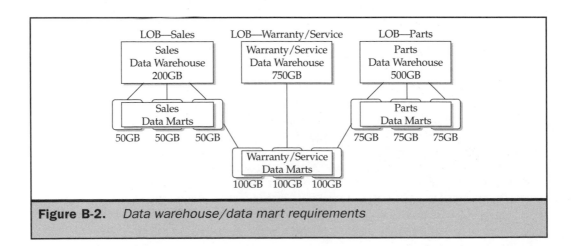

Figure B-2. *Data warehouse/data mart requirements*

Processing Req.	Sales DW/DM	War/Service DW/DM	Parts DW/DM
Age of Data < 24 hours	✓	✓	
Age of Data > 24 hours			✓
Batch Loads	Mon–Fri: nightly	Mon–Fri: nightly	Mon–Sat: nightly
Response Time	< 3 seconds	< 10 seconds	< 10 seconds
Availability	Mon–Fri: 6 A.M.–7 P.M. Sat–Sun: 8 A.M.–5 P.M.	Mon–Sat: 24x7 Sun: as available	Mon–Sat: 6–7 P.M. Sun: as available

Table B-1. *Processing and Service-Level Requirements for Data Warehouse and Data Marts*

Armed with the following information, the storage team had the task of supporting the IT applications area in developing these business systems. Working with the application designers, the timeline was approximately six months, in which the last three were given over to development and beta testing of the new data warehouse configurations.

The Search and Evaluation

The storage team concluded that any solution had to scale to the multi-terabyte level. This was deduced by a quick but careful analysis of current utilization, historical trending of growth, and current estimates. Current utilization of the data warehouse applications was around 750 to 800GB of aggregate data, combining both user and database overhead. This was accommodated through the current installation of 1 terabyte of external SCSI-based storage capacity installed over three UNIX servers (summarized in Figure B-1).

The other quick conclusion was scalability of access given the large amounts of storage; end user access and capability to load and update the databases would be key to the feasibility of any solution that would meet the processing requirements and service levels. The new requirements, as provided by the application design team, called for an additional capacity of 1.125 terabytes, moving the total requirement for the data warehouse and data mart applications to well over 2 terabytes. The team had calculated that the data warehouse storage utilization was growing at 40 percent per year, with no indication that it would decrease.

The storage team had to validate key pieces of information before embarking on its search for solutions. First, it was asked, was the validity of current estimates it received from the application designers for aggregate user data, or did it include overhead estimates for database overhead from the DBAs? Second, were these estimates for day-one installation or have some growth factors been built in? The answers turned out to be good news and bad news, and some new news, which called for even new challenges.

The good news was that the estimates included the overhead as estimated by the DBAs. Consequently, the aggregate data sizing could be used as is. The bad news was that these were day-one estimates. In other words, this was the capacity needed when production started and reflected the actual storage required for the sourcing of the data from the mainframe databases. The new news was that the consolidation of warranty and service data warehouses would continue to use two different database products; therefore, the consolidation would not occur immediately and the two data warehouses would run in tandem until they would be consolidated later in the year. Consequently, the storage team needed to add an additional factor for two databases; doubling the current capacity estimate accomplished this.

Available Alternatives

Considering all the available estimates, and validating the capacities, processing requirements, and services levels, the new data warehouse infrastructure would need to support a 3-terabyte capacity. Further investigation indicated that the user community—although comparatively small, with less than 250 end users—would require an I/O workload of multiple gigabytes per transaction. This also carried over into I/O workload for loading and updating the database, creating an additional multiple-gigabyte workload per transaction. In summary, calculations indicated a total I/O workload of 29,300GB for a 24-hour period. This was reduced to 1200GB per hour and subsequently an aggregate of 20GB per second.

Using an external direct attached storage strategy that would simply enhance the current configurations would require additional servers and additional SCSI storage arrays. A quick estimate revealed a requirement of approximately 50 new servers with the maximum of SCSI adapters for each server to meet the aggregate I/O workload of 20GB per second. An alternative to this scenario would be to replace existing servers with a much larger server machine, such as a UNIX mainframe server, where the machine could be partitioned to run the individual data warehouses with dedicated resources. However, this solution also would require the new storage arrays, although the existing arrays could possibly be used in conjunction with these.

By utilizing the guidelines for estimating SAN capacity (see Chapter 18), it turns out that a SAN configuration will require a total of 240 ports, including calculations for recovery and redundancy factors. Given the type of workload—datacentric (high I/O content), transactional with batch updates, and less than 250 end users—the configuration could be handled by 15, 16-port switches, or 4, 64-port director class switches. However, this solution also requires that new storage arrays be purchased for compatibility and performance within the storage network. This strategy does provide the possibility of utilizing the existing servers.

The storage team, in conjunction with technical support management, chose to evaluate the UNIX mainframe alternative compared with the SAN configuration. This evaluation took place as a mini-capacity planning exercise, since this requirement was addressed from an existing capacity plan that was in place. Consequently, the IT executives, to provide the flexibility to evaluate solutions outside the context of existing budget plans, invoked the end-user non-aggression pact. (Refer to Chapter 23 regarding storage network capacity planning and Chapter 22 for end-user non-aggression pacts.) This exercise revealed an interesting comparison.

Storage Evaluation Results

The UNIX mainframe was a high-end SMP machine that was capable of being partitioned into 2 to 16 logical processing partitions. The SAN configuration was analyzed as 4, 64-port director class switches, with 12 HBAs installed across the existing data warehouse UNIX servers—for example, 4 HBAs each. The storage arrays were configured with 3 terabytes of capacity with specific configurations for each solution—for example, one set for the SCSI-based UNIX mainframe and a different set of arrays for the Fibre Channel–based SAN.

The requirements and evaluation is further depicted in Table B-2. Our evaluation is based on a score of 1 through 10, with 10 being the highest, or best, score. Vendor selection is specific to the customer and the competitive nature of an acquisition. It is recommended that a minimum of three bids be requested once workload estimates have been concluded.

Note   *We have estimated pricing only as a general reference point. Included in these pricing estimates are total components for system operation, additional software required, and storage array costs.*

Requirement	SAN	Direct Attached
Meets I/O workload performance and capacity specs	9	8
Ease of installation and maintenance	3	4
Scalability of storage capacity	7	4
Compatibility with existing storage infrastructure	5	8
Composite score	24	24
System price	$700,000	$1,850,000

Table B-2.   *Storage Solution Evaluation Table for Data Warehouse/Data Mart Applications*

Solution Acquisition and Implementation

The storage admin team recommended the SAN solution with subsequent approval from IT executives and reluctant concurrence from the application design team. Because this would be the first installation of the storage networking technology for the data center and because of the visibility of the applications, the design team's reluctance was understandable. However, an integrated plan was developed to provide beta support for the application testing of new data warehouse and data mart prototypes.

The decision was based upon both price and performance. Given the increased throughput with the Fibre Channel–based storage arrays, the SAN solution appeared to be one of the most adaptable solutions for this type of high-end throughput application—that is, an aggregate 20GB per second of data. Specifically, the ability to source the data warehouses from the mainframes into the UNIX servers for subsequent preprocessing, loading, and updating was appealing. Moreover, the shadow of the impending corporate data warehouse project provided the pivotal requirement that pushed the decision toward the SAN. The decision makers realized that if the UNIX mainframe strategy was chosen, another would be required to handle the additional load of the corporate data warehouse. Finally, the ability of scaling the SAN or adding another SAN would be more cost-effective, but it would also be more responsive to the application needs in the short and long term.

The installation of the SAN provided additional internal requirements and surprises, but none that were unmanageable or extremely cost intensive. These centered on the new operational characteristics of the SAN, the additional software tools required, and the responsibility for maintaining the SAN software and hardware (from an IT organizational view). Each of these issues was handled within the beta period of installation and subsequent prototype testing of the applications. These issues are summarized in the following section.

SAN Operational Issues

The new SAN required a learning curve and subsequent integration into the existing data center hardware and software processes. The storage admin team and select members of the systems administration team took vendor classes, which provided an overview specific to the vendor product selection and additional guidelines on installation and preinstallation planning.

The installation was somewhat more problematic because of the problems any new infrastructure has in moving into the data center. The issues were centered on three areas: facilities and location; fundamental management processes, such as meeting the existing data center operations rules; and integration into existing server, network, and storage wiring mechanisms.

■ **Facilities and Location**   This was handled by accommodating more space within the existing server and storage areas. However, given the less restrictive lengths, the storage was initially planned for installation in the mainframe storage area on a different floor. This was scratched because local proximity (for example, server to switch to storage) was better during the initial production cut-over period. However, the flexibility of subsequently moving the storage to another area, given the increased length capability of Fibre Channels, turned out to be an additional plus for the data center facilities planners.

- **Management Processes**   Perhaps the most troublesome issue was the operational integration into the data center. Because of the fundamental processes of each SAN director, this required that additional data center operational policies and processes be developed, followed by training and orientation of key operational staff members. The ability to provide configuration information and real-time performance information continues to hamper this aspect of the operation; however, this is becoming more adaptable as the operations of SAN become familiar to both operations and systems/storage admin staff.

- **Integration into Data Center**   One of the most difficult activities surrounding the installation and subsequent expansion of the SAN is the integration of wiring complexities and integration into the existing complexities of server and network wiring and switching structures. The ability to implement, manage, and track this process remains quite difficult as more than 200 ports are routed to appropriate points of contact. Although not unlike their Ethernet counterparts, and comparatively small next to the LAN/WAN wiring closets, the critical sensitivity to a lost, unconnected, or inoperative port can affect the highly visible application such as the company's data warehouses. Existing plans call for the SAN infrastructure to be separated from the existing LAN/WAN configurations.

New SAN Software Tools

Once prototype testing was in place, it became apparent that new tools were necessary for managing the storage across the SAN. The requirements specifically came from the need to manage the storage centrally across the supported servers. This required some level of both centralization and drill-down capability for specific array and individual devices access. This was accomplished through the acquisition of new volume management tools and vendor-specific management tools for the storage arrays, both having specific functionality for Fibre Channel–based SANs.

The next level of tool that proved to be more problematic was the backup/recovery tool. Due to the nature of the application, data warehouses generally don't require the stringent restore functions that an OLTP application would need. Therefore, the ability to perform standard backups would impact the nightly update function or prove to have little value to an analysis that uses a 24-month rolling summary of data. Consequently, rebuilding or reloading the data warehouse can be done on a basis that is less time sensitive—for example, performing a rolling backup once a week and probably on the day when the least processing occurs. Given the large amount of data, the specific challenge to relational databases, a snapshot function is being pursued for those database tables that are the most volatile and time consuming to rebuild and reload. In the case of a complete volume or array outage, the snapshot would allow the DBAs to go back to a specific time period and reload and update the database within a minimum amount of time.

IT Organizational Integration

The responsibility to evaluate and justify the SAN initially was given to the storage administration team. The installation and support of the SAN beta testing was accomplished through a team approach, using the expertise of systems admins, application designers, and DBAs, with leadership from the storage admin team. As the SAN became a production entity, the team dissolved into its daily responsibilities and the nebulous nature of some of the SAN components began to affect the total mean time to recovery (MTTR) for any problem scenario.

Consequently, IT management is faced with an interesting dilemma of providing shared responsibility for the SAN or developing a new infrastructure group focused on storage. There are pros and cons for either direction. This study indicates the somewhat conservative nature of the industry to continue to share responsibility across the SAN components. The network, the systems, and the storage staff are all responsible for the SAN or various components of the SAN. This unfortunately results in the increase of the MTTR, since this type of arrangement creates the "it's not my problem" scenario. (Refer to Appendix C for details on how this manifests itself in a storage networking management business case.)

The SAN Solution

The final configuration provides the increased storage capacity and enhanced performance that was expected of the solution. The data warehouse/data mart project was accomplished on time and has proved to be responsive to the I/O workload. Because the estimates were accurate and allowances were built into the configuration for expansion, the storage capacity and access performance is ahead of the I/O workload estimates and business requirements, making both of these execute within service levels.

The current configurations are moving into the planning for the next highly visibly project, the corporate data warehouse. However, this time it has complete concurrence from the application design teams, the DBAs, and system administrators. Further planning is being considered to consolidate additional storage and servers within the data centers. The two outstanding caveats remain the organizational fluidity of responsibility and the continued organizational challenges to effective wiring management. The first continues to elongate any problem associated with the SAN configuration, and the second continues to facilitate the singular failure of port mismanagement, exacerbating the first issue.

The configuration shown in Figure B-3 illustrates a summarization of the data warehouse/data mart application systems. The ability to portray a 200-plus port configuration is beyond the scope of this study. However, it's important to point out the results that the SAN solution provided this company with the ability to manage its business more effectively through the use of multiple technologies. The functionality of the relational database to facilitate the analysis and relationships among business functions has provided a 40 percent increase in the amount of parts sold and a 25 percent cost containment in the area of technical support. More importantly, the applications have been used to reduce the warranty receivables significantly, and that results in an important improvement to the company bottom line.

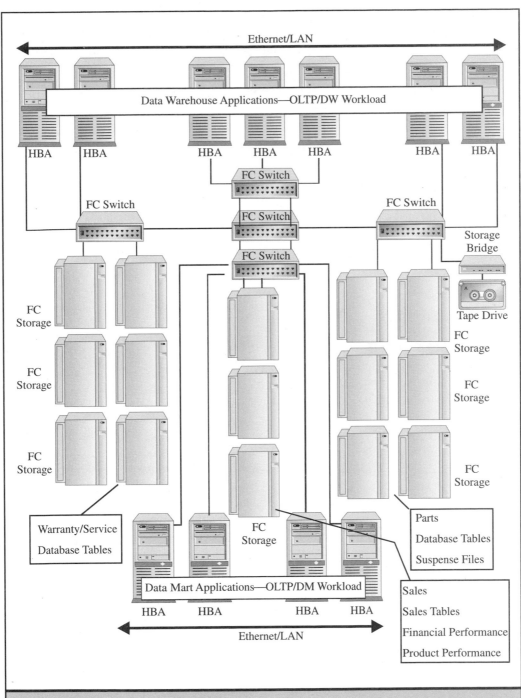

Figure B-3.   *SAN storage infrastructure*

The SAN solution provided the infrastructure for these applications. The ability to move and access data at the increased levels of Fibre Channel SAN configurations has provided this company with a significant competitive edge. This case study illustrates the success that storage networking can have with an adequate and reasonable application and I/O workload planning set of activities.

Appendix C

SAN/NAS Management Case Study: The Southwestern CD Company

The most important aspect of business application performance is the ability to access data. Data stored on disk, tape, optical media, or temporary cache, using the traditional direct attach storage models will be less susceptible to performance and operational anomalies than data stored through the network model. Although the location of the data should be irrelevant, if the application cannot get to it or the paths to the data are congested or critically impacted, the performance of the application will degrade—or worse, become unavailable. The ability of an IT staff to locate, identify the cause, and correct these anomalies becomes more problematic as storage configurations move into SAN and NAS configurations.

The key to successfully monitoring and managing the performance of any application starts with the consistent and proactive management of the critical paths to application data. In most cases, this is done with an assortment of vendor- and user-developed tools that support management of storage configurations. In Part VI of this book, we discussed many of the accepted management disciplines that become the foundation for a well-run IT organization, none of which will be more important in this case study than performance management. Having said that, performance management is tied to the necessary yet mundane activities of configuration management and the need for an orderly problem management system of processes and procedures.

In this study you will discover that in the storage networking area, the availability of tools and coordinated systems will be lacking greatly. As a general industry trend, management tools lack the implementation of successful technologies by three to five years. This situation is becoming even more significant and problematic as the integration of infrastructures needs to be taken into account in both small and large configurations. As the chapters on connectivity options for both SAN and NAS point out, the effects and counter-effects of storage networks are experienced on an enterprise-wide basis.

Unfortunately, as this case study will demonstrate, today's storage management industry remains in an often misguided and confused startup mode with point products and integrated storage management architectures and standards useful only to those companies selling industry controversies. However, storage management has become an effective catch-up mechanism for large vendors, especially those in the software management sector, who have more integration challenges than the small startups.

Nevertheless, regardless of vendor size, the current assortments of products are characterized by the following deficiencies, to name only the major ones:

- No correlation of functions among distributed components
- No collection of statistically useful data
- No proactive performance, configuration, or capacity trending
- No identification of "root cause" to problems

All this makes for a challenge when you are faced with installing, managing, and maintaining a storage area network and network attached storage solutions, in addition to the challenge the SAN and NAS vendors have in compensating for these inadequacies. This study will illustrate many of the problems and potential solutions when the Southwestern CD Company deals with its initial SAN experiences.

The Deferred Responsibility Scenario— or Who's Doing What to Which Data?

The Southwestern CD Company distributes all types of entertainment CDs to both wholesalers and retail outlets large and small across North America. From its headquarters in Scottsdale, Arizona, the company ships on average 250,000 CDs a week. By purchasing directly from several manufacturers at optimal prices, the company has achieved revenues of approximately $51 million per annum. Its profit margin is based upon moving product effectively to its retailers to leverage the current entertainment fashion for both music and movies. Because it competes with other, larger distributors, Southwestern must offer better services and a more competitive price structure.

The CD distribution industry is based upon time to market and can rely heavily on technology to facilitate and provide a competitive advantage to the ordering process. CD products are purchased from manufacturers with a return policy that allows the retailers and, subsequently, the distributor to return unsold products. These market dynamics are reflected in the price, generally at the retail level, although the competitive positioning based on availability and amounts can be experienced at the distributor level.

An IT department of 15 people supports the company. Ten permanent personnel and five contract programmers staff the department. They do not have specific storage expertise, but they rely on their systems administrators to handle the operating system infrastructures that include the storage configurations. Their configuration is Microsoft-based with the exception of the database servers, which are UNIX machines running a popular relational database system. They have recently implemented a SAN to consolidate their databases and provide more responsive order-entry and sales-entry applications.

In conjunction with order-entry and sales-entry applications, the company runs an accounting application, a sales analysis application, and corporate e-mail, all from within its Metro Data Area (see Chapter 2). The recent implementation of the SAN has consolidated data from all of these applications within the available storage resources. All applications are now centrally accessible through the SAN.

The company's configuration, business applications, and client network is depicted in Figure C-1.

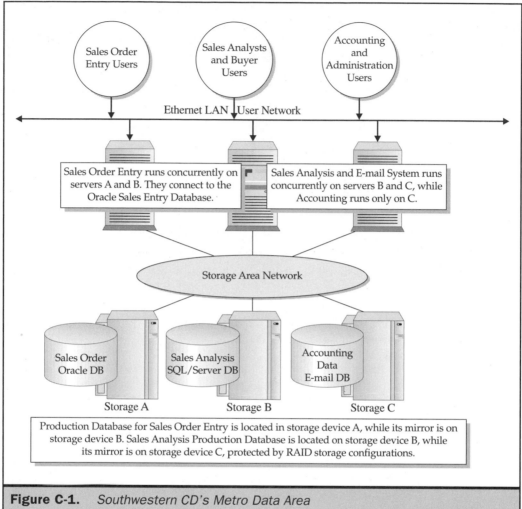

Figure C-1.   *Southwestern CD's Metro Data Area*

The Problem

The company's new sales-entry application has experienced periodic slowdowns in its performance. In certain instances, the database has had to be restarted and reorganized to resume operation. Although the rationale behind this has yet to be analyzed or understood, restarting appears to restore performance for a time—all of which takes time away from the sales department, which cannot enter sales data while the system is down. Today's scenario, however, is further complicated. It's the end of the month and the day begins with a handful of frustrated phone calls from sales personnel, who either can't log in to the application or are suffering because the application is running extremely slowly.

Business Situation

At the end of the month, the sales department really needs to hit its numbers so that the orders can be booked for this quarter. Order quotas come from the Southwestern executives, are part of the quarterly goals, and are the basis for the financial incentives for the sales management staff. They rely heavily on the system to be up and performing optimally to enter as many orders as possible. Over and above is the new pricing structure on the hot new CD products they can sell to their largest retailers, to which they are still trying to sell.

Technical Scenario

The IT department is short staffed, because the database programmer recently quit to take a job at a bank. The application database administrator (DBA) now has new and additional responsibility for the systems aspects of the production databases. The periodic slowdowns happened before the SAN installation; however, they were never completely debugged and root causes were never identified. The problems appear to have gotten worse as the SAN went into production. All of the user table data has been transferred to the SAN disk arrays, which was the last activity the recently departed database programmer accomplished.

Problem Dialogue

The following is a summarization of the IT department's events and activities in determining the cause and solution to the problem.

9:45 a.m.—After numerous calls to the Help Desk over the past hour, the IT operations manager fills out a "trouble ticket" and assigns it to the DBA.

10:45 a.m.—Busy implementing the next release of the database while parsing additional database design changes, the DBA, having worked through most of the night, arrives to work late. The DBA initiates the database management program, which provides performance metrics on the database, leading to the following conclusions: the sales-entry database is up and running, and a number of deferred writes are filling up the temporary storage. The DBA decides the problem is an operating system anomaly and reassigns the "trouble ticket" to the Windows administrator.

11:00 a.m.—The Windows administrator, who is also the LAN administrator, is busy implementing a new LAN segment to facilitate the expansion of the accounting department. Consequently, he must be paged when there is no response to the "trouble ticket" within the allotted time.

11:15 a.m.—The Windows/LAN administrator logs in to the sales servers and initiates the OS management software, which provides performance metrics on each of these systems. Two anomalies become apparent: client transactions are being queued at an increasing rate, and this is putting stress on the system as memory and temporary space within the database becomes saturated. System-level paging has increased to an alarming rate. (See Figure C-2.)

11:30 a.m.—After a brief discussion with the DBA, the Windows/LAN administrator and DBA concur that a reboot of the sales system and reinitialization of the databases will clear up the problem. By this time, the entire sales-entry system is down. A message is broadcast via e-mail and voice-mail stating that the sales-entry system will be rebooted during lunch. The VP of sales estimates $500,000 in sales has not been entered. He is not pleased.

12:30 p.m.—The DBA and the Windows/LAN administrator discover that although the servers are rebooting, the database is extremely slow coming up. The Windows Performance Monitor tool now indicates that few I/Os are being serviced from the sales servers. After further discussion, the two hit upon the possibility that some external application is impacting the reboot of the databases.

12:45 p.m.—Inquiries are made and the two discover a large archive job has been running since 8:00 A.M. Initiated by the Sales Analysis department, the job was to dump two years' of sales history from the SQL Server database running on the ADMIN server. Not surprisingly, the sales history database is stored within the same storage subsystem as the sales-entry database. The DBA and the Windows/LAN Administrator (who've ordered in lunch by this point), attempt to contact Sales Analysis management to get permission to stop the archive job and restart it later that night or over the weekend. The entire Sales Analysis management team is out to lunch, of course.

2:00 p.m.—The DBA finally contacts a Sales Analysis manager and negotiates a stop to the archive job, which will restart later that night—but with the mandate that he (the DBA) have the data archived and reorganized for his department by 9 A.M. the next morning. The DBA is not pleased.

3:00 p.m.—The Windows/LAN administrator and DBA terminate the archive job and restart the sales servers and sales-entry databases, all of which come up running at optimum levels. The second message is broadcast via e-mail and voice mail: "System's up. All's well that ends well."

3:30 p.m.—Sales personnel are finally back online and able to enter sales data into the system.

Epilogue

The analyses surrounding activities of problem identification, determination, and correction are indicative of the state of management within storage networking environments. The following epilogue, or post analysis, can provide some insight into the hidden problems that can develop as storage configurations move into a networked setting.

Root Cause

In this case, unexpected I/O activity from a single server impacted the capacity of the I/O subsystem and storage network to the degree that it severely limited the operation of the sales-entry application and access to their data sharing the same network.

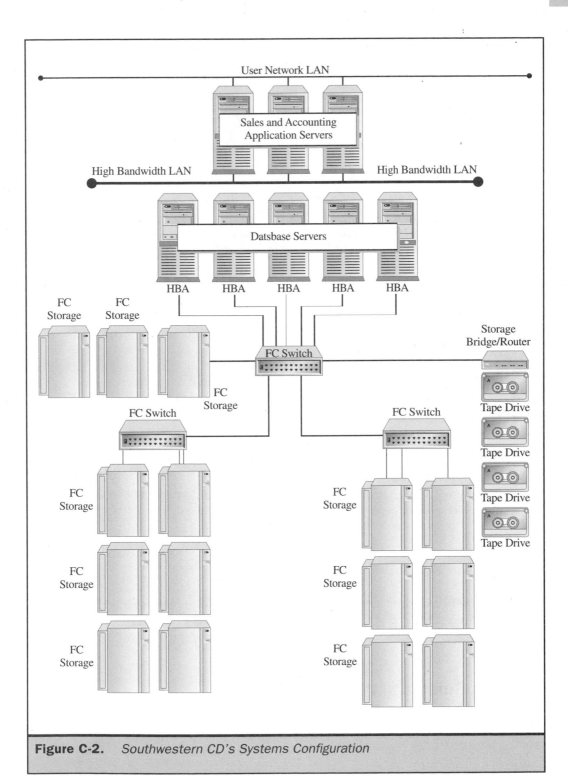

Figure C-2.   *Southwestern CD's Systems Configuration*

Solutions

Unscheduled archive jobs were terminated and rescheduled, sales servers were rebooted, sales-entry databases were reinitialized, and recovery programs were run.

Downtime

In effect, the sales-entry application was down from 8:30 A.M. to 3:30 P.M., a total of 7 hours. Due to the sales-history database not being archived and reorganized, it was unavailable for a longer term, some 12 hours.

Effect on Business

As a result, sales was unable to log all of the day's orders, subsequently losing an estimated $1 million in backlog business. Downtime of the sales-entry database also adversely affected other departments, including purchasing, whose buyers were unable to meet order deadlines to record manufacturers, which will increase costs by approximately $2 million for the next month.

Effect on IT

IT management reviews the steps taken to resolve this problem and concludes the following:

- More correlation of information across the systems is needed.
- Greater attention should be given to the "root cause" of a problem.
- No integrated tools are available to coordinate the actions of the Windows/LAN administrator and the Oracle DBA.
- The Windows administrator and the DBA must work toward proactive trending in estimating storage resource requirements.
- Additional storage restrictions must be put in place to prohibit processing intrusion into the Sales production environment.

Evaluation

This scenario can be evaluated in three ways:

- Business rules and policies
- The processing configuration limits and choke points
- What available tools and practices are currently available that are relevant and appropriate to this scenario

Business Rules and Policies

The Southwestern CD Company, like many companies, lacked a complete evaluation and definition of the business applications it was supporting. Prioritizing sales entry, sales analysis, and other workloads would have provided metrics for dealing with many of the timing issues. Defining these rules and policies is the responsibility of the business user and the IT department and should be performed up front, if only on a macro-level (that is, sales-entry must have highest availability of all applications).

Knowledge of Processing Configurations

Not knowing the processing configuration, especially the storage network configuration, was especially harmful in this case. More importantly, knowing and understanding the limitations of the storage network in context to the supported servers masked the root cause of the problem. Finally, and most importantly, was the lack of association between the storage network and related devices to the business application. Had this association been made, the problem would have been identified within 15 minutes and resolved within 30.

Available Tools and Practices

Unfortunately, in this case, any available tools are probably of little use in identifying root causes. The following points provide a quick summary of the value of the major tools currently available:

- **Storage resource management (SRM)**   Defensive, reactionary information received after the fact. SRM tools are resource-focused, operate without business policy, and provide no correlation of information across distributed servers; in addition, they have no relationship to the business application.

- **Backup/recovery**   Adding new and/or bolstering existing backup/recovery software to the storage network. This is complementary, at best, to resolving the problem. The benefit of faster recovery time is not part of the root cause of the outage. Although necessary, backup/recovery bears no relation to the business application.

Although more software tools are becoming available, they continue to provide disparate, incompatible, and inconsistent levels of information on the storage infrastructure. No single tool provides consistent, proactive management functions that associate business applications with application data. IT management must choose from an assortment of tools that provide only discrete levels of empirical information, ranging from operating system metrics, to database metrics, to I/O and disk metrics. IT users bear the burden of correlating these seemingly unrelated sets of information in an attempt to understand the effects of resources on business applications.

The deficiencies within these tools are compounded by the requirements, costs, and expertise needed to support an increasing set of server platforms, operating systems, and major application subsystems such as relational database management, messaging, and transactional systems.

The following points illustrate only a few of the major deficiencies challenging today's management tools, as well as the inefficiencies surrounding business application availability:

- *No correlation functions among distributed components.* Today's business applications are distributed, which means that events happening on one server can seriously degrade performance throughout the entire system. The ability to correlate important aspects of performance information as it effects the business application is currently unavailable.

- *No proactive trending.* Today's IT managers are expected to drive the bus effectively while monitoring performance through the rearview mirror. Literally all reporting and trending is historical. The information that ultimately reaches the IT user is about incidents that have already occurred and provides little value in determining real-time solutions to business applications that perform poorly.

- *No identification of root cause to problems.* The effects of the conditions stated previously means it is unlikely that the information supplied to the IT user will provide any sort of root cause as to why a business application is down, not to mention any information intended to identify and correct the problem. Most activities address only the symptoms, leading to reoccurring results.

As far as practices go, this case study illustrates a competent and responsive IT department with processes in place for problem notification and assignments. However, the specific expertise and focus of the individuals contributed to the time it took to pinpoint the problem—that is, the database was up but was not processing any transactions.

The following points present alternatives to consider when providing a long-term solution:

- **Reconfiguration/isolation**   Adding hardware (servers, switches, and so on)—also known as "throwing money at it." Although a possible long-term solution, this can essentially convolute the problem and put storage isolation as part of the IT solution matrix, thus limiting the inherent benefits of storage networking. Also, reconfiguration/isolation provides no direct association or long-term benefit to the applications.

- **Increased manpower**   Hiring more people to monitor and manage the storage infrastructure by business application—also known as "throwing money *and* people at it." This could be a solution, but a highly improbable one, given the monitoring requirements, expertise required, and associated costs. This solution does in fact relate to the business application, but only at a prohibitive cost.

Final Analysis

More powerful servers and storage subsystems are quickly evolving into Metro Data Areas characterized by high data traffic, inevitable congestion, and complex problems relating to data availability. The Internet is also driving the Metro Data Area theory by increasing exponentially the number of data highways leading in and out of these already congested areas.

Business applications are distinguished from other applications through their direct association to the business, their size, and their mission-critical requirements. They are supported within storage systems by practices and products that manage various aspects of maintaining the storage devices and data. Business applications can be enhanced with storage networking technology, although a host of problems remains that will cause difficulties relating to data availability. Currently, no tools directly relate the business application to the storage network.

Through a composite IT scenario, the realities behind operating with a storage networked environment were illustrated in this case, as well as the challenges in problem identification, isolation, and solution within these configurations. Although a SAN configuration was used, a NAS configuration could just as easily be substituted for the same effect. Evaluation of the scenario indicated that best practices and current tools would not minimize or stop these types of availability problems.

Steps to Better Storage Networking Management

As demonstrated in this case study, the association of business applications to computing resources remains for the most part at macro-levels, at best, and not at all within new technologies, such as storage networks. Storage networks, given their disparate components and critical interrelationships, have evolved into an infrastructure category within the data center. As such, they have become a tremendous challenge to manage as a complete entity, much less integrated into the logical set of applications and supported systems. The following provides additional information on what's required for new tools. This is further augmented by best practices for managing storage networks.

The Need for Next-Generation Performance Management Tools

The most critical element of performance for a business application is its availability to its own data. Consequently, a level of performance tools is needed that closely associates the business application with storage networking resources. These tools should provide a level of functionality to perform the following:

- Correlate business application performance information across servers and storage networks
- Provide metrics and monitoring for proactive trending of performance and take appropriate action based upon previously established business rules
- Identify root cause areas, if not components, to IT support personnel and make appropriate recommendations based upon previously established business rules

Such a set of tools would enhance IT management's ability to manage business applications within increasingly complex application and storage networked configurations. These tools would move IT professionals closer to the critical elements of business application performance.

Storage networking best practices to observe include the following.

- *Eliminate unnecessary downtime.* Decrease the negative business impact of storage networking and enhance the inherent abilities of storage networking technologies.

- *Automate performance management tasks.* Decrease the cost to IT management and staff, and maintain specialization in storage networking as implementation and production use increases.

- *Learn/associate business to infrastructure.* Root cause analysis, proactive processing, and management can provide solutions before outages occur.

The following guidelines can provide some visibility into dealing with the Southwestern CD company scenario:

- *Focus maintenance efforts on critical resources—before they go inoperable.* Identify the critical resources through effective configuration management activities and processes. These can help in focusing efforts on current configuration and processing scenarios.

- *Proactively manage growth and change within the storage networked configuration.* As the storage network moves into production, be proactive through an effective problem management and ongoing capacity plan. This will allow the identification of problems and changes to capacity. Further accommodations can be helpful through an effective change management program that will identify and focus on processing anomalies and activities.

- *Gather value oriented performance data.* This will probably be the most intrusive and time-consuming task, given the lack of availability and the programming necessary to gather information from disparate sources such as MIBS, Common Information Model, and vendor statistical collections. This can also provide valuable input to vendors and industry during problem-resolution scenarios and activities.

The Complete
Reference

Appendix D

Glossary

489

ALU A component of the computer's central processing unit where mathematical calculations are assembled and executed. CPU-intensive devices and applications rely on the ALU heavily, which in turn utilizes temporary storage in locations of CPU registers and system-level cache.

application development life cycle Activities that surround the design, development, and implementation of computer applications. These are generally characterized by logical phases of work that progress in a contiguous fashion. Business justification, external and internal design, coding, testing, and deployment characterize these activities.

archival The activities of moving data from an online storage device to an offline or removable storage device for long-term storage. Archiving data generally results from data that has not been accessed in a specific time period, consequently taking up valuable online disk space. It is distinguished from backup and recovery by being available for reloading into an online system for later access.

backup/recovery Copying data from an online storage device to an offline device for protection against possible data corruption, storage outage, or site disaster. These functions differ from archival activities and functions by making a copy of the data and their time requirements in order to provide a specific data state and other information for recovery purposes.

bandwidth A set of frequencies that designate the band of electronic wavelengths used to transmit signals within a computer system and reflect the transmission capacity of the link. This is measured by the address of the data that can be transmitted and the speed of the signals through various cycle times measured in MHz (megahertz).

blade computing A method of loosely connecting discrete computer systems through a common bus. Blade computing is made up of small, powerful, fully functional, general-purpose computers that are optimized with only CPU, memory, and I/O bus components. Server blades, as they are known, are used in conjunction with an I/O backplane that supports connectivity to a common set of I/O devices, including various storage devices, network devices, and control functions.

block   A unit of data used with storage devices and systems that requires a contiguous block of data accessed with each I/O instruction of the system. Block sizes are dependent on both operating system and storage device types, but have direct relationships to the efficiency of the system's I/O operations.

bus   A system that provides the interconnection between various devices within computer systems. Generally characterized by a singular and priority-driven operation between two devices within the bus—one transmitting instructions and data, the other receiving them. Various bus mechanisms are used within a computer system such as the PCI bus to interconnect CPU, memory, and I/O adapters, with storage buses such as SCSI providing interconnections to multiple storage devices.

business application   A set of computer programs that automates the functions or operations of a business. This is different from utility or management applications that are computer programs which automate or enhance the management of the computer systems. Examples include systems such as backup/recovery and disk defragmentation systems.

capacity plan   Activities that identify business elements and translate these into workload requirements. These include the projection and configuration of systems that effectively process the workload requirements. Historically, capacity planning has included processor, memory, and storage capacity as a holistic system. However, storage networking separates the I/O workload from the computer systems and demands a new set of activities that estimate I/O workload but which are integrated back into the supported processor complex.

CD-ROM   Storage type that utilizes a polymer material for encoding information which is then subsequently read using a laser light source. CD-ROM has yet to be fully integrated into FC SAN; however, it can be used in some configurations with a SCSI bridge/router. CD-ROM drives are available as NAS devices and can be configured as network storage devices, with certain limitations.

cluster   In terms of computing, it's a collection of interconnected CPU resources that provide shared efficiencies, such as workload balancing, reliability, availability, and serviceability to the supporting infrastructure. In terms of storage, it's the smallest addressable unit on a disk drive as used by Windows operating

APPENDIXES

systems. Cluster sizes are dependent on the total storage capacity of the disk—therefore, the larger the disk, the larger the cluster. This has a direct relationship to the efficiency of the system's I/O. Writing a single file to a large cluster uses the entire cluster. Consequently, writing a 1k file to a 32k cluster utilizes the entire space.

Common Internet File System (CIFS) A distributed file system used with Windows operating environments that allows files to participate within networked file systems and network attached storage. CIFS has become an ad hoc standard in enabling Windows clients to participate and share files within networked environments.

controller A device which controls and manages multiple devices that communicate with a computer system. Storage systems utilize controllers extensively to control and manage multiple storage devices that communicate within a bus system.

CPU The central processing unit (CPU) is the mechanism that processes instructions which invoke all other actions within the computer and ultimately produce the results of the end-user application. The CPU is dependent on its basic architecture in how it operates and processes instructions. Two popular architectures are the Reduced Instruction Set (RISC) and Complex Instruction Set (CISC). Each processes instructions differently; however, both utilize temporary locations, such as registers and system-level cache, and initiate I/O operations.

cylinder A measurement of disk geometry, where the association of tracks is measured vertically within the multiple platters of a disk drive. Cylinder allocations can have significant performance benefits for applications that access large amounts of information on a read-only basis.

data mart Related to the data warehouse type of application, the data mart is generally designed around a single subject. Consequently, the scope of the information is reduced, along with its relationships, within a greater set of information. For example, a data warehouse application that supports customer financial accounts will have all customers, their accounts, and their related attributes. However, a data mart providing secondary support may only have information that relates to a subset of this information such as customers in a particular region, or a set of financial products and their status. These subset applications are datacentric, and although they utilize a smaller set of data, they remain challenging given their distributed requirements and use of relational databases.

data warehouse   A type of application that allows end users to analyze historical information on a set of related subjects. For example, a data warehouse for a financial application may have information for the past three years on all customers, their accounts, and any related attributes. Therefore, using relation data base technology, an end user can query all customers in a particular set of states that have moved within the last year and have brokerage accounts. These applications are datacentric and can be the largest users of both storage and processing capacity within a data center.

Digital Linear Tape (DLT)   A format for magnetic tape that has become an ad hoc standard for open systems. The architecture is based on the DLZ1, a special compression algorithm where data is written on the tape in dozens of straight-line (linear) tracks, usually 128 or 208. Capacities are vendor-dependent but range to >50GB of data when compression is used. A variant of DLT technology, Super DLT, provides capacities to move beyond the 100GB on a single cartridge.

Direct Access File System (DAFs)   A file system used specifically with NAS devices, where file access bypasses the normal file location services through the OS and storage controllers and utilizes a new service called virtual interface (VI). This allows files to be transferred through direct-memory transfers, which circumvent the overhead of TCP processing for file access. This, however, requires that a number of new components be implemented, including a new type of network card which enables the VI protocols and NAS devices that process direct memory addressing.

director   A class of storage switching devices that are generally defined as having the attributes of >64 ports, additional hardware functions that enable redundancy within the switch, and related software that configures recovery and redundancy features.

disk compression   Operations that allow data on a disk to be compressed for efficiency of space utilization. Compression algorithms usually find all spaces and duplicate characters and remove these from the storage data source. These are then replaced when the data is accessed.

disk defragmentation Disks read and write information in a random manner, which is part of their value in accessing data. However, as write operations occur over time, the disk becomes fragmented as the drive writes related data blocks out to available blocks, clusters, or sectors, depending on the type of disk device and operating environment. This fragmentation of the disk, with related data spaced all over the geometry of the drive, begins to cause performance problems since it takes the disk head longer to read the segments of the file, or find available space within a fragmented disk. Defragmentation, sometimes referred to as defragging, moves all the scattered blocks, clusters, or sectors into a contiguous space on the drive, essentially reorganizing the drive so it can operate more efficiently.

embedded database Many computer applications come with a database integrated with each function. Other applications are unattended and utilize databases to collect or store data for its operations, such as an automobile, HVA systems, and aeronautical systems. Each database included in these applications integrates an embedded database. The embedded database is tightly integrated with the application programs and cannot be used for other general-purpose applications. These applications, and moreover their embedded database elements, can be challenging to storage given they have limited performance and allocation parameters. Therefore, their inherent limitations have to be compensated for by the processing infrastructure.

F_Port A FC switch port designated to connect participating nodes, known as N_Ports, to the FC network. These nodes can be devices such as storage arrays and servers.

fabric A Fibre Channel switch, or multiple Fibre Channel switches, that are interconnected in a networked topology to facilitate the physical transmission of FC frames between any two N_Ports. This includes the software operating within the control of a microkernel that facilitates the operation of a FC switch. The software functioning within the control of a microkernel operating system provides the base level services that form the switch fabric network. The fabrics are vendor-dependent and although compliant with FC standards, they have levels of differences in how they implement many of the FC operations.

Fibre Channel (FC) Fibre Channel is a network connectivity standard for a serial I/O bus, with the capability of transmitting data between two N_Ports at 100 MBps. Principally, the X3T11 committee of ANSI governs this standard.

file allocation table Disks have tables of contents so they can access the data stored in a responsive manner. Most operating environments support some type of file allocation table that resides on the disk and stores information regarding the files and physical locations of the data on that disk.

file system File systems are the operating system functions that manage the stored data within the computer. Most file systems allow users to organize their data into a defined naming and hierarchical structure. File systems function in networked environments by permitting other computers to access their data by providing access to segments of the file system. File systems maintain various levels of data integrity by monitoring and managing the processes that allocate and write data to the files. This becomes problematic with storage network environments as multiple systems with their own file systems attempt to manage the files they own—a particularly difficult problem in a SAN where multiple servers may access the same storage array, device, and subsequent file. NAS devices have less of a problem with this since they provide remote file services and offer centralized ownership of files that reside on NAS storage devices.

frame A component of the Fibre Channel standard that describes the method and specifications of the basic transmission packet that encapsulates the user data.

G_Port A port on a FC switch designed to function as an F_Port or an E_Port that connects both nodes. This can be external to FC switches through interswitch links (ISLs), and SCSI-to-FC bridges/routers. This type of universal port is becoming increasingly popular in developing simpler port utilization structures. These ports are vendor-dependent on implementation.

Head and Disk Assembly (HDA) The mechanical assembly that houses the read and write heads for a magnetic disk. The assembly moves mechanically over the spinning platters of the media as it performs its operations. Additional functionality has been moved into the HAD to facilitate greater read/write performance.

InfiniBand An I/O standard that provides a switched fabric network replacing the traditional bus networks of computers. The InfiniBand standard requires that all I/O be connected through an InfiniBand switch with the added benefit that connecting computers together makes clustering a more scalable and efficient process.

iSCSI A new I/O standard that provides for the execution of a SCSI-based I/O operation over a TCP/IP network. This allows a server to execute a block I/O operation to a remote storage device. The new standard provides additional specifications for encapsulating SCSI-based commands into TCP communications and transferring them through an IP packet to corresponding SCSI-based storage devices that are IP addressable and have compatible TCP processing capabilities. Initial implementations have required new NIC cards to support these functions at both the server and storage device level.

JBOD Defined as "just a bunch of disks," this term defines a storage array in which all devices within the array are addressable independent units. These provide additional capacity but do not offer any fault resiliency in the event of an inoperable drive. Partitioning data throughout the disks and providing a layer of virtualization services is generally part of the I/O management of the operating system. These functions are also available through third-party software applications.

Linear Tape Open (LTO) A format for magnetic tape that competes with digital linear tape. LTO uses a linear multichannel bidirectional format but adds an enhanced timing-based servo (a device that automates a process of error correction for a mechanism), hardware data compression, and efficient error correction. Initially developed by a consortium of IBM, HP, and Seagate, it now has two different formats— one for fast data access and another for greater storage capacity. The Accelis format uses 8mm tape on a two-reel cartridge that loads at the mid-point to provide fast data access, specifically for read-intensive applications. The other is the Ultrium format that uses a single reel of half-inch tape to maximize storage capacity, specifically for write-intensive applications, such as archival and backup functions. Ultrium-based products offer a >100GB capacity, while some vendors are approaching the 1TB capacities.

LUN A term used with addressing SCSI devices within a SCSI bus system. A logical unit number (LUN) is defined at the controller level to access, control, and manage the devices within the connected bus. LUNs provide a level of virtualization when communicating with the operating system, and subsequently the application, by shielding the application from the complexities of knowing physical addressing and access information for disk or tape I/O operations.

LUN management The activities, functions, and capabilities that make up the manipulation, control, and assignments of LUNs within SCSI bus systems. These generally take the form of configuration parameters for controller initialization through microcode, but can assume higher levels of functionality, especially when managing multiple SCSI bus systems.

LUN masking Part of LUN management where certain servers access specific SCSI devices within the shared SCSI bus environment, while other servers are blocked from accessing specific LUNs.

micro-kernel A special type of operating system that can be optimized for a particular application. Both SAN and NAS devices use micro-kernels to provide base level operating system services to the SAN switch and NAS server, respectively.

MPP A term used to describe a massive parallel-processing configuration. These configurations are made up of multiple processors (often numbering in the hundreds), sharing no system resources except a high-speed interconnect. They are currently used to address complex scientific, academic, or business analytical processing such as measuring earthquakes, nuclear explosions, and very high-end data warehouse applications, by breaking the application tasks into activities that can be processed in parallel. The processing nodes within MPP systems often have their own storage arrays; however, in some cases, some nodes have a common I/O configuration.

N_Port The FC port that is designated for participating nodes, such as servers and storage arrays. These ports are configured through a Host Bus Adapter (HBA) and used to connect to the FC switch F_Ports.

NVRAM A type of shared memory that is used by multiple system processors. Non-volatile random access memory is a portion of memory that ensures data integrity with the data that is written to the disk as multiple processor I/O operations take place across the same data.

APPENDIXES

PCI Bus   A bus system to connect peripheral devices, which has become a standard within the industry. PCI buses provide the interconnections to the internal and external storage devices through adapter connectivity points, but also provide the interconnections between the CPUs, RAM, and caching systems.

Relational Database Management System (RDBMS)   A database system that allows for the organization and access of data using relational operations. RDBMS architectures are developed from tables where entities are defined with each table and attributes are defined as columns or fields within the table. These databases have become the preferred method of storing information for both transactional and analytical systems. RDBMS architectures provide their own file systems and special I/O operations given they are table-driven and have different data access and storage characteristics than file systems.

SCSI   A standard term for a type of bus storage architecture used with block-level devices such as disks and tape. The Small Computer Systems Interface (SCSI) defined the standards used with connecting storage through parallel bus architectures. Forming the largest install base of storage devices today, the SCSI command structure has superseded its bus application and is used with both FC protocols and the newly defined iSCSI standard.

service levels   Service levels exist on several levels. There are specific agreements with end users that define the level of service the IT department provides. Internal service levels are managed to provide a working measurement of systems and networking performance. Service levels for storage, if they exist, are often integrated into the internal system service levels and are comprised only of capacity measurements for end users. The establishment of meaningful measurements for the storage-networking infrastructure that encompasses storage, systems, and network specifications have yet to be developed.

SMP   Symmetrical multiprocessing defines a configuration that provides multiple computing nodes supported by both shared memory and shared I/O configurations. These are generally characterized by multiple CPUs within the same cabinet. The scalability restrictions have long centered on the limitations of the shared I/O structure and related performance problems with storage scalability. SMP configurations are greatly enhanced by the inclusion of storage networks, especially SANs that provide additional bandwidth and speed to the I/O storage subsystem.

snapshot A term used for copying online data at a synchronized time and providing a copy of a data volume, file system, or database for later access. Used in response to user data requiring 24/7 access, snapshot configurations generally require a duplicate volume to be operating so that the actual copy is made from the duplicate volume. This allows uninterrupted backup operations, and provides a consistent snapshot of the data at the time it was executed. Once the snapshot (backup) is taken, the duplicate volume then resynchronizes itself with the primary online volume and continues processing.

T11.3 standard The ANSI Fibre Channel standard specifications. All vendors whose products support Fibre Channel work through this set of specifications. The ANSI Fibre Channel X3T11 Committee governs these.

tape compression A setup of functions and operations that allows data on a tape to be compressed for space efficiency purposes. Compression algorithms usually find all spaces and duplicate characters, and remove these from the storage data source. These are then replaced when the data is accessed.

temporary storage These consist of various locations within a computer system where data is stored temporarily until it can be used by the CPU or written on a storage device. These locations are considered internal when described as system cache, CPU registers, and memory buffers in RAM. They are external when considered as part of a peripheral such as a block device.

track A fundamental measurement of a disk's geometry that spans the circle made by the disk head as it makes a single rotation of the media platter. Track sizes, therefore, are relative to the size and density of the media platter. Tracks are formatted for use with an operating environment by way of the operating system dividing the tracks into clusters or sectors. Tracks aligned vertically with multiple platters make up another measurement called a cylinder.

zones Functions within a FC switch that allow the ports to be segmented into individual areas for node access. Authorized access lists for each port provides login services to the switched fabric defined zones. Zoning can further be determined regarding the attributes of the ports, node login addresses, and login attributes. This allows the SAN to define access to authorized devices such as servers to attached storage devices such as disk and tape arrays.

Index

T

INTERNATIONAL CONTACT INFORMATION

AUSTRALIA
McGraw-Hill Book Company Australia Pty. Ltd.
TEL +61-2-9900-1800
FAX +61-2-9878-8881
http://www.mcgraw-hill.com.au
books-it_sydney@mcgraw-hill.com

CANADA
McGraw-Hill Ryerson Ltd.
TEL +905-430-5000
FAX +905-430-5020
http://www.mcgraw-hill.ca

GREECE, MIDDLE EAST, & AFRICA
(Excluding South Africa)
McGraw-Hill Hellas
TEL +30-210-6560-990
TEL +30-210-6560-993
TEL +30-210-6560-994
FAX +30-210-6545-525

MEXICO (Also serving Latin America)
McGraw-Hill Interamericana Editores S.A. de C.V.
TEL +525-117-1583
FAX +525-117-1589
http://www.mcgraw-hill.com.mx
fernando_castellanos@mcgraw-hill.com

SINGAPORE (Serving Asia)
McGraw-Hill Book Company
TEL +65-863-1580
FAX +65-862-3354
http://www.mcgraw-hill.com.sg
mghasia@mcgraw-hill.com

SOUTH AFRICA
McGraw-Hill South Africa
TEL +27-11-622-7512
FAX +27-11-622-9045
robyn_swanepoel@mcgraw-hill.com

SPAIN
McGraw-Hill/Interamericana de España, S.A.U.
TEL +34-91-180-3000
FAX +34-91-372-8513
http://www.mcgraw-hill.es
professional@mcgraw-hill.es

UNITED KINGDOM, NORTHERN, EASTERN, & CENTRAL EUROPE
McGraw-Hill Education Europe
TEL +44-1-628-502500
FAX +44-1-628-770224
http://www.mcgraw-hill.co.uk
computing_europe@mcgraw-hill.com

ALL OTHER INQUIRIES Contact:
Osborne/McGraw-Hill
TEL +1-510-549-6600
FAX +1-510-883-7600
http://www.osborne.com
omg_international@mcgraw-hill.com

META Group is a leading research and consulting firm, focusing on information technology and business transformation strategies. Delivering objective, consistent, and actionable guidance, META Group enables organizations to innovate more rapidly and effectively. Our unique collaborative models help clients succeed by building speed, agility, and value into their IT and business systems and processes. For details, connect with metagroup.com.

Simply put, META Group helps companies transform their business through technology. Since 1989, we've provided consistent information technology (IT) research, analysis, and consulting so that our clients can accelerate the delivery of technology solutions—saving time and enhancing profitability.

Publicly traded (Nasdaq: METG) since December 1995, META Group offers proven models to ensure that organizations are fully prepared to seize market opportunities, counter competitive threats, and avoid expensive mistakes. Serving as each clients' personal radar screen, META Group monitors the IT/business world to deliver an accurate, unbiased view of what works (and what doesn't) to speed innovation and keep pace with the new economy.

Our dialog with thousands of IT users and vendors—ranging from global giants and government organizations to midsize companies and small, bleeding-edge technology vendors—provides us with the necessary perspective to offer comprehensive best practices. And because this dialog is ongoing, we're able to continually hone our vision and provide timely, targeted "best methods" for our clients' diverse challenges.

Every day, in more than 35 countries around the globe, META Group addresses thousands of complex issues for a growing client base. Our world-class, industry-leading analysts and seasoned consultants—the mindspring behind our quality research—provide the fresh thinking our clients need to surpass their performance goals.

Using a straightforward approach, we also provide the clear direction our clients need to transform their businesses. META Group is the only organization in the industry to deliver structured methodologies and innovative programs that speed the business transformation of our clients—ensuring continued effective performance as they change.

META Group, Inc.
208 Harbor Dr.
Stamford, CT 06912
203.973.6700 phone
203.359.8066 fax
metagroup.com